# FELLOW ROMANTICS

KV-197-431

Edinb

P

University of Edinburgh

30150     025316230

# Fellow Romantics
## Male and Female British Writers, 1790–1835

Edited by

BETH LAU
*California State University, Long Beach, USA*

EDINBURGH UNIVERSITY LIBRARY
WITHDRAWN
ASHGATE

© Beth Lau 2009

All rights reserved. No part of this publication may be reproduced, stored in a retrieval system or transmitted in any form or by any means, electronic, mechanical, photocopying, recording or otherwise without the prior permission of the publisher.

Beth Lau has asserted her moral right under the Copyright, Designs and Patents Act, 1988, to be identified as the editor of this work.

Published by
Ashgate Publishing Limited
Wey Court East
Union Road
Farnham
Surrey, GU9 7PT
England

Ashgate Publishing Company
Suite 420
101 Cherry Street
Burlington
VT 05401-4405
USA

www.ashgate.com

**British Library Cataloguing in Publication Data**
Fellow Romantics : male and female British writers, 1790–1835. – (The nineteenth century series)
   1. English literature – 19th century – History and criticism 2. Authorship – History – 19th century 3. Romanticism – Great Britain
   I. Lau, Beth, 1951–
   820.9'145

**Library of Congress Cataloging-in-Publication Data**
Fellow romantics : male and female British writers, 1790–1835 / edited by Beth Lau.
   p. cm. — (The nineteenth century series)
   Includes bibliographical references and index.
   ISBN 978-0-7546-6353-9 (alk. paper)
   1. Romanticism—Great Britain. 2. English literature—Women authors—History and criticism. 3. English literature—Male authors—History and criticism. 4. English literature—19th century—History and criticism. 5. English literature—18th century—History and criticism. 6. Women and literature—Great Britain—History—19th century. 7. Women and literature—Great Britain—History—18th century. 8. Men and literature—Great Britain—History—19th century. 9. Men and literature—Great Britain—History—18th century. I. Lau, Beth, 1951–

PR457.F36 2009
820.9'145—dc22

2008044428

ISBN: 978-0-7546-6353-9

**Mixed Sources**
Product group from well-managed forests and other controlled sources
www.fsc.org Cert no. SA-COC-1565
© 1996 Forest Stewardship Council
FSC

Printed and bound in Great Britain by
MPG Books Ltd, Bodmin, Cornwall.

# Table of Contents

*General Editors' Preface*     *vii*
*Notes on Contributors*     *viii*
*Acknowledgments*     *x*

Introduction     1
    *Beth Lau*

1   Revisiting the Egotistical Sublime: Smith, Wordsworth, and the
    Romantic Dramatic Monologue     17
    *Jacqueline M. Labbe*

2   Coleridge and Robinson: Harping on Lyrical Exchange     39
    *Ashley Cross*

3   Romantic Ambivalence in *Frankenstein* and *The Rime of the Ancient
    Mariner*     71
    *Beth Lau*

4   "Something must be done": Shelley, Hemans, and the Flash of
    Revolutionary Female Violence     99
    *Susan J. Wolfson*

5   Spiritual Converse: Hemans's *A Spirit's Return* in Dialogue with
    Byron and Shelley     123
    *Alan Richardson*

6   William Wordsworth and Felicia Hemans     139
    *Julie Melnyk*

7   "Does not it make you think of Cowper?": Rural Sport in Jane Austen
    and Her Contemporaries     159
    *Barbara K. Seeber*

8   The Uses and Abuses of Imagination in Jane Austen and the
    Romantic Poets     179
    *Beth Lau*

9   "Beautiful but Ideal": Intertextual Relations between Letitia Elizabeth
      Landon and Percy Bysshe Shelley                                        211
      *Michael O'Neill*

10  Romantic and Victorian Conversations: Elizabeth Barrett and Robert
      Browning in Dialogue with Byron and Shelley                            231
      *Jane Stabler*

    *Index*                                                                  *255*

# The Nineteenth Century Series
## General Editors' Preface

The aim of the series is to reflect, develop and extend the great burgeoning of interest in the nineteenth century that has been an inevitable feature of recent years, as that former epoch has come more sharply into focus as a locus for our understanding not only of the past but of the contours of our modernity. It centres primarily upon major authors and subjects within Romantic and Victorian literature. It also includes studies of other British writers and issues, where these are matters of current debate: for example, biography and autobiography, journalism, periodical literature, travel writing, book production, gender, non-canonical writing. We are dedicated principally to publishing original monographs and symposia; our policy is to embrace a broad scope in chronology, approach and range of concern, and both to recognize and cut innovatively across such parameters as those suggested by the designations 'Romantic' and 'Victorian'. We welcome new ideas and theories, while valuing traditional scholarship. It is hoped that the world which predates yet so forcibly predicts and engages our own will emerge in parts, in the wider sweep, and in the lively streams of disputation and change that are so manifest an aspect of its intellectual, artistic and social landscape.

Vincent Newey
Joanne Shattock
University of Leicester

# Notes on Contributors

**Ashley Cross** is an Associate Professor of English at Manhattan College. Her articles on the Shelleys and on Mary Robinson have appeared in *Women's Studies*, *ELH*, *Women's Writing*, and *Studies in Romanticism*. She is currently working on a book on Mary Robinson.

**Jacqueline M. Labbe** is Professor of English and Comparative Literary Studies at the University of Warwick. She is the author of *Charlotte Smith: Romanticism, Poetry and the Culture of Gender* (Manchester University Press, 2003), *The Romantic Paradox: Love, Violence and the Uses of Romance, 1760–1830* (Macmillan, 2000); and the editor of Volume 14: *Poems*, of *The Works of Charlotte Smith* (Pickering and Chatto, 2007) and *Charlotte Smith in British Romanticism* (Pickering and Chatto, 2008). She is currently working on a study of Smith, Wordsworth, and Romanticism.

**Beth Lau** is Professor of English at California State University, Long Beach. She is the author of *Keats's Reading of the Romantic Poets* (University of Michigan Press, 1991) and *Keats's* Paradise Lost (University Press of Florida, 1998). She also edited the New Riversides edition of Jane Austen's *Sense and Sensibility* (Houghton Mifflin, 2001) and co-edited (with Diane Hoeveler) *Approaches to Teaching Bronte's* Jane Eyre (MLA, 1993). Her recent work includes several articles on Jane Austen's affinities with the male Romantic poets.

**Julie Melnyk** is Associate Director of the Honors College and Coordinator of the interdisciplinary Humanities Sequence at the University of Missouri. She is the author of *Victorian Religion: Faith and Life in Britain* (Praeger, 2008) and editor of two collections of original scholarly essays: *Women's Theology in 19th-Century Britain* (Garland, 1998) and, with Nanora Sweet, *Felicia Hemans: Reimagining Poetry in the 19th Century* (Palgrave, 2001). She is currently working on a book titled *Christianity, Community, and Subjectivity in Victorian Women's Religious Literature*.

**Michael O'Neill** is Professor of English at Durham University and a Director of Durham's Institute of Advanced Study. He has published widely on Romantic, Victorian, and twentieth-century poetry, especially on Shelley. His most recent books are *The All-Sustaining Air: Romantic Legacies and Renewals in British, American, and Irish Poetry Since 1900* (Oxford University Press, 2007) and (co-edited with Charles Mahoney) *Romantic Poetry: An Annotated Anthology*

(Blackwell, 2007). With David Bindman and Stephen Hebron, he also co-authored the exhibition catalogue *Dante Rediscovered* (Wordsworth Trust, 2007).

**Alan Richardson** is Professor of English at Boston College. He is the author of *British Romanticism and the Science of the Mind* (Cambridge University Press, 2001), *Literature, Education, and Romanticism: Reading as Social Practice, 1780–1832* (Cambridge University Press, 1994), and *A Mental Theatre: Poetic Drama and Consciousness in the Romantic Age* (Pennsylvania State University Press, 1988).

**Barbara K. Seeber** is Associate Professor of English at Brock University in St. Catharines, Ontario. She is author of *General Consent in Jane Austen: A Study of Dialogism* (McGill-Queen's, 2000) and articles on Austen in *LIT: Literature Interpretation Theory, Eighteenth-Century Fiction, Persuasions On-Line*, and *Lumen*. Her current research interests include adaptations of Austen and Animal Studies.

**Jane Stabler** is a Reader in Romanticism at the School of English, University of St. Andrews, Scotland. Her interests include poetic form and intertextuality in the Romantic period. She is currently researching a study of the ways in which the writings of the Byron-Shelley circle influenced the next generation of English poetic exiles in Italy. Her publications include *Byron, Poetics and History* (Cambridge University Press, 2002), which was awarded the British Academy's Rose Mary Crawshay Prize in 2003.

**Susan J. Wolfson** is Professor of English at Princeton University and the author of *The Questioning Presence: Wordsworth, Keats, and the Interrogative Modes of Romantic Poetry* (1986); *Formal Charges: The Shaping of British Romantic Poetry* (1997); and *Borderlines: The Shiftings of Gender in British Romanticism* (2006). She is co-editor, with Peter Manning, of *Selected Poems of Lord Byron, Selected Poems of Hood, Praed, and Beddoes*, and *The Romantics and Their Contemporaries* (vol. 2a of *The Longman Anthology of British Literature*); and with Marshall Brown, of *Reading for Form* (2006). On her own she has produced innovative editions of Felicia Hemans (2000), John Keats (2007), and Mary Shelley's *Frankenstein* (2002, 2006).

# Acknowledgments

First and foremost, I should like to thank all of the contributors to the volume, who not only have produced perceptive, learned essays but who have been cooperative, punctual, and a pleasure to work with throughout the long process of bringing this book to completion. They have made my job as editor as smooth and painless as it is possible for such a task to be.

Several of the contributors lent their aid in special ways. Ashley Cross's session on "Coleridge and the Gendering of Creative Expression" at the Modern Language Association Convention in 2002, where both she and I presented papers that in revised form are now included in the present volume, provided an initial airing of some of *Fellow Romantics'* main ideas and premises. Ashley was one of the first authors to commit an essay to the collection and maintained her belief in the book's importance over many years. Alan Richardson also was an early supporter of the topic of this volume. In 2003 he, along with Jim McKusick and Marilyn Gaull, invited me to co-chair two sessions on "Male and Female Romantic Writers in Dialogue," sponsored by the Wordsworth-Coleridge Association, at that year's Modern Language Association Convention, an experience that advanced my thinking about the topic in important ways. Susan Wolfson provided extremely helpful professional advice at a crucial stage in the book's development.

Others besides the contributors have aided the book's conception and evolution. The idea for this volume was conceived in conversation with Pamela Clemit, who subsequently has continued to provide helpful perspective and advice in person and via email. Anya Taylor has been an enthusiastic supporter of the project even when I had doubts about its viability. Vickie Myers on numerous occasions has been a sympathetic listener and useful sounding board for ideas. Others who played a role in the book's development include Fiona Price, Brad Sullivan, Bridget Keegan, and Ben Robertson.

Several Scholarly and Creative Activities grants from California State University, Long Beach, gave one course released time from teaching that allowed me to make progress on the book during semesters when I otherwise would have had little opportunity for research. I am extremely grateful for the gift of time these grants afforded.

Heart-felt thanks go to all of the staff at Ashgate but in particular to Ann Donahue, the commissioning editor, for her belief in and understanding of the project, her prompt responses to all of my questions, and the reasonableness of her expectations and advice. Her goal always seemed to be for the book to realize its full and best potential, and she accommodated deviations from official guidelines or made perceptive suggestions for improvement in that spirit. The anonymous reader's report helpfully recommended revisions that made the book better in numerous ways.

All of the essays in *Fellow Romantics* are published here for the first time, with the exception of my "Romantic Ambivalence in *Frankenstein* and *The Rime of the Ancient Mariner*," an earlier version of which appeared as "*The Rime of the Ancient Mariner* and *Frankenstein*" in *Samuel Taylor Coleridge and the Sciences of Life*, ed. Nicholas Roe (Oxford: Oxford University Press, 2001). It was this essay that first sparked my interest in exploring affinities between male and female Romantic writers, and I therefore wanted it to have a place in the present collection. I thank Oxford University Press for permission to reproduce the essay, which has been substantially revised and updated.

Last but not least, Roger Young has not read a word of this book, but he witnessed most of its life span and provided beneficial distraction as well as emotional and technical support. Thank you, Roger, for your patience and companionship.

# Introduction

## Beth Lau

The essays in this collection explore similar interests, modes, methods, and practices among male and female writers of the British Romantic period. The premise of the volume is that men and women of the late eighteenth and early nineteenth centuries participated in many of the same literary traditions and experiments, and that they influenced and interacted with one another in dynamic and fruitful ways. *Fellow Romantics* studies male and female writers together, emphasizing common ground and creative dialogue among them.

The recovery and analysis of long-neglected women writers has been one of the most important and stimulating recent developments in the field of Romanticism. Initial studies of Romantic women writers have tended to emphasize their differences from the six major male poets of the mid-twentieth-century canon: William Blake, William Wordsworth, Samuel Taylor Coleridge, Lord Byron, Percy Bysshe Shelley, and John Keats. Women poets, novelists, essayists, and playwrights have been characterized as participants in a female literary tradition with its own values and concerns apart from and often critical of the work of contemporary male writers. Harriet Kramer Linkin and Stephen Behrendt, for example, state that women poets previously were ignored because their works do not fit "paradigms associated ... with a small group of canonical male poets"; instead, a distinctly different "literary, cultural, social, intellectual, and aesthetic dynamic ... informs their writing." Romanticism itself has been described as a fundamentally "masculine phenomenon," in Marlon Ross's words, which oppressed and excluded women. Invoking A. O. Lovejoy's classic essay "On the Discrimination of Romanticisms," many critics claim that women's writing renders invalid traditional understandings of the period and call for a redefinition of Romanticism as a collection of disparate schools and voices with few shared attributes.[1] Some even argue for dispensing with the term Romanticism altogether,

---

[1]    Harriet Kramer Linkin and Stephen Behrendt, eds., *Romanticism and Women Poets: Opening the Doors of Reception* (Lexington: University Press of Kentucky, 1999), 1; Marlon B. Ross, *The Contours of Masculine Desire: Romanticism and the Rise of Women's Poetry* (New York: Oxford University Press), 3. Critics who cite A. O. Lovejoy's "On the Discrimination of Romanticisms" (*PMLA* 39 [1924]: 229–53) to support the idea that women writers constitute a strain of Romanticism separate from that of the canonical male poets include Paula Feldman and Theresa M. Kelley, eds., *Romantic Women Writers: Voices and Countervoices* (Hanover: University Press of New England, 1995), 10, and

on the grounds that it is not applicable to many writers, especially women writers, of the age.[2]

Besides those already cited, other books that develop these perspectives and helped to establish their predominance include Margaret Homans's *Women Writers and Poetic Identity*, Susan Levin's *Dorothy Wordsworth and Romanticism*, Meena Alexander's *Women and Romanticism*, and Anne Mellor's collection of essays *Romanticism and Feminism*.[3] Two major studies of Romantic women writers that have been especially influential are Marlon Ross's *The Contours of Masculine Desire* and Anne Mellor's *Romanticism and Gender*.[4] Ross claims that Romantic ideology developed largely as a defensive reaction against the proliferation of women poets in the late eighteenth and early nineteenth centuries and sought to exclude women by defining poetry as an inherently masculine enterprise. Mellor's book argues that, so different are the outlooks and literary practices of men and women of the period, we should speak of two separate Romanticisms, a masculine and a feminine version.

The essays in the present volume reorient our attention toward common points of engagement among Romantic writers of both genders. Instead of segregating literary men and women of the period into separate traditions, this collection proposes that we view them as "Fellow Romantics" who inhabited the same or overlapping literary and cultural milieus and whose works employ similar motifs and express many shared aspirations, convictions, anxieties, and conflicts. The essays link William Wordsworth and Charlotte Smith; Mary Robinson and Samuel Taylor Coleridge; Felicia Hemans and Wordsworth, Lord Byron, and Percy Bysshe Shelley; Mary Shelley and Coleridge; Letitia Landon and Percy Shelley; Jane Austen and various male Romantic poets; and the young Barrett Browning, Byron, and Shelley. In the process, these essays suggest that Romanticism may be considered, not a monolithic phenomenon, yet a more unified and coherent movement and period than many recent scholars have claimed.

Even as he helped launch the study of Romantic women poets in his 1989 book, Marlon Ross warned that "As we recover [women writers'] place in history,

---

Carol Shiner Wilson and Joel Haefner, eds., *Re-Visioning Romanticism: British Women Writers, 1776–1837* (Philadelphia: University of Pennsylvania Press, 1994), 7.

[2]     For example, Anne K. Mellor and Richard Matlak title their anthology of Romantic-era literature simply *British Literature 1780–1830* (Ft. Worth: Harcourt Brace, 1996). In the Preface and Introduction to the anthology, the editors explain their reasons for dispensing with the term "Romantic" to characterize the period.

[3]     Margaret Homans, *Women Writers and Poetic Identity: Dorothy Wordsworth, Emily Brontë, and Emily Dickinson* (Princeton: Princeton University Press, 1980); Susan Levin, *Dorothy Wordsworth and Romanticism* (New Brunswick: Rutgers University Press, 1987); Meena Alexander, *Women in Romanticism: Mary Wollstonecraft, Dorothy Wordsworth, and Mary Shelley* (Basingstoke: Macmillan, 1989); Anne K. Mellor, ed., *Romanticism and Feminism* (Bloomington: Indiana University Press, 1988).

[4]     Anne K. Mellor, *Romanticism and Gender* (New York: Routledge, 1993).

we must be sure not to examine them in isolation. Too wary of wedding them erroneously to the romantic movement, we may stray too far in the other direction and forget their complex interactions with romantic discourse."[5] For the most part, however, this has been the trend in Romantic studies; the pendulum has swung predominantly in the direction of viewing women writers separately from the men and emphasizing differences and antagonisms between the sexes. In 1995, Isobel Armstrong advocated what she admitted was a "one-sided" approach to examining women's poetry "in isolation from male poetry." "The next step," she explained, "will be to look at the interaction of the two—but let us postpone this until women's work is known better."[6] The time, I believe, is ripe for moving to this next level and studying interrelations between literary men and women. *@ body level*

*Paphian*

To be sure, other works besides the present volume have challenged the gender complementary model of Romanticism and examined women writers in relation to male contemporaries. Betty Bennett consistently emphasizes Mary Shelley's indebtedness to and compatibility of outlook with her father William Godwin, husband Percy Shelley, and other male associates such as Lord Byron. Susan Morgan in the Introduction to *Sisters in Time* insists that works by nineteenth-century men and women "are deeply and positively intertwined" and that any study that ignores these connections is "dangerously inaccurate." In both this book and in her *In the Meantime: Character and Perception in Jane Austen's Fiction*, Morgan frequently draws parallels between the works of Austen and other nineteenth-century women writers and those of their male contemporaries. Three other books have appeared recently—by Clara Tuite, William Galperin, and William Deresiewicz—that situate Jane Austen in relation to the Romantic movement and male Romantic poets. Another work that directly compares male and female Romantic writers is Joanne Wilkes's book-length study of Lord Byron and Mme. De Staël. In addition, Marjorie Stone and Judith Thompson's *Literary Couplings* contains two essays that treat literary collaboration between men and women in non-adversarial terms (Anne D. Wallace's "Home at Grasmere Again: Revising the Family in Dove Cottage" on Dorothy Wordsworth and William Wordsworth, and Alison Hickey's "'The Body of My Father's Writing': Sara Coleridge's Genial Labor" on Sara Coleridge and Samuel Taylor Coleridge).[7]

---

5    Ross, 6.

6    Isobel Armstrong, "The Gush of the Feminine: How Can We Read Women's Poetry of the Romantic Period ?" in Feldman and Kelley, 32.

7    For Betty Bennett's views, see especially *Mary Wollstonecraft Shelley: An Introduction* (Baltimore: The Johns Hopkins University Press, 1998); Susan Morgan, *Sisters in Time: Imagining Gender in Nineteenth-Century British Fiction* (New York: Oxford University Press, 1989), 8; Susan Morgan, *In the Meantime: Character and Perception in Jane Austen's Fiction* (Chicago: University of Chicago Press, 1980); Clara Tuite, *Romantic Austen: Sexual Politics and the Literary Canon* (Cambridge: Cambridge University Press, 2002); William Galperin, *The Historical Austen* (Philadelphia: University of Pennsylvania Press, 2003); William Deresiewicz, *Jane Austen and the Romantic Poets* (New York:

Others who have challenged the concept of separate male and female literary traditions include Laura Claridge and Elizabeth Langland, who argue against narrowly conceived gender typologies and binary thinking in the introduction to their *Out of Bounds: Male Writers and Gender[ed] Criticism*, a collection of essays that examines ways in which English and American male writers resisted and subverted patriarchal constructions of gender; the collection includes three essays on male Romantic poets. Tim Fulford in *Romanticism and Masculinity* argues for a more nuanced understanding of its subject than has prevailed in previous studies that oppose male to female Romantic writers. According to Fulford, although male Romantic writers at times uphold traditional notions of masculinity and femininity, in other ways their works destabilize these categories and call "women's subordination to masculine power into question." Others who challenge readings of the male poets as inhabiting and upholding traditional gender roles include Teddi Chichester Bonca, who explores conventionally feminine qualities in Percy Bysshe Shelley's character and writing, and Anya Taylor, who demonstrates Samuel Taylor Coleridge's many positive relationships with women and interest in women's issues.[8]

Among works that focus on women writers, Adriana Craciun's *Fatal Women of Romanticism* resists the idea that "women writers in [the Romantic] era experienced and articulated a distinct, gender complementary Romanticism in reaction to the canonical Romanticisms of male writers." Her book studies female Romantic writers' depictions of violent or "fatal" women, a subject formerly regarded as the domain solely of male authors. Kari Lokke also rejects "gender-complementary models of Romanticism" and challenges the view that women did not participate in the transcendent strain in Romanticism.[9] All of the works listed in this and the

---

Columbia University Press, 2004); Joanne Wilkes, *Lord Byron and Madame de Staël: Born for Opposition* (Aldershot: Ashgate, 1999); Anne D. Wallace, "Home at Grasmere Again: Revising the Family in Dove Cottage," in Marjorie Stone and Judith Thompson, eds., *Literary Couplings: Writing Couples, Collaborators, and the Construction of Authorship* (Madison: University of Wisconsin Press, 2006), 100–23; Alison Hickey, "'The Body of My Father's Writing': Sara Coleridge's Genial Labor," in Stone and Thompson, 124–47.

    [8]    Laura Claridge and Elizabeth Langland, eds., *Out of Bounds: Male Writers and Gender[ed] Criticism* (Amherst: University of Massachusetts Press, 1990); Tim Fulford, *Romanticism and Masculinity: Gender, Politics, and Poetics in the Writings of Burke, Coleridge, Cobbett, Wordsworth, De Quincy and Hazlitt* (Cambridge: Cambridge University Press, 1999), 18; Teddi Chichester Bonca, *Shelley's Mirrors of Love: Narcissism, Sacrifice, and Sorority* (Albany: SUNY Press, 1999); Anya Taylor, *Erotic Coleridge: Women, Love, and the Law Against Divorce* (New York: Palgrave Macmillan, 2005).

    [9]    Adriana Craciun, *Fatal Women of Romanticism* (Cambridge: Cambridge University Press, 2003), 1; Kari E. Lokke, *Tracing Women's Romanticism: Gender, History, and Transcendence* (London: Routledge, 2004), 2. Although Lokke states that her book resists the idea that "Romantic philosophy and art were inherently inimical to women's values and interests," she does claim that the women novelists she studies created "feminine and (proto-) feminist visions of spiritual and artistic transcendence that constitute a critique of

previous paragraph concentrate on either male or female writers, however. None is devoted to exploring parallels and interrelations among a representative selection of literary men and women of the period.

An important contribution to the study of gender issues in the Romantic period is Susan J. Wolfson's recent *Borderlines: The Shiftings of Gender in British Romanticism.* Wolfson's study seeks to move beyond the "schematic binaries" of the first wave of Romantic feminist criticism, which divided the field into "the 'masculine' canon and the 'feminine' of (excluded) women's writing." Wolfson instead explores "borderlines" between masculine and feminine spheres, or zones where "men and women face each other and continually negotiate, and across which occur more than a few strange shifts and transactions." In her analyses of the works and critical receptions of Felicia Hemans, Maria Jane Jewsbury, Lord Byron, and John Keats, Wolfson identifies ambiguities, instabilities, contradictions, and combinations in the way gender is portrayed.[10] Although she frequently compares male and female writers, however, Wolfson too divides her chapters into those on women and those on men; she does not directly juxtapose the writers she studies in her exploration of ways in which they resisted or complicated traditional definitions of masculine and feminine (as she does in her essay on Felicia Hemans and Percy Shelley in the present volume).

The 2007 collection *Romantic Women Poets: Genre and Genre*, edited by Lilla Maria Crisafulli and Cecilia Pietropoli, contains a section entitled "Romantic Female and Male Poets: Dialogue and Revision," but of the three essays in this section one concentrates solely on women writers (Cecilia Pietropoli's "Women Romance Writers: Mary Tighe and Mary Hays") and another treats texts by male writers as important influences on those by women but, as the title indicates, argues that the women critique and revise their male models (Gioia Angelleti's "Women Re-Writing Men: The Examples of Anna Seward and Lady Caroline Lamb"). The third essay in this section, Richard Cronin's "Felicia Hemans, Letitia Landon, and 'Lady's Rule,'" is the only one that does not present literary relations between male and female writers in oppositional terms, as he claims that Alfred Tennyson's first two volumes were heavily indebted to the works of Hemans and Landon,

---

Romanticism from within" (2). She therefore still distinguishes female from male Romantic writers and portrays them in oppositional relationships.

[10]   Susan J. Wolfson, *Borderlines: The Shiftings of Gender in British Romanticism* (Stanford: Stanford University Press, 2006). Passages quoted are from pp. xvi, 3, xviii. Wolfson also has published a number of influential essays exploring complex gender identities in the male poets as well as literary relations between female and male Romantic writers, several of which are incorporated in *Borderlines*. See, for example, "'Their She Condition': Cross-Dressing and the Politics of Gender in *Don Juan*," *ELH* 54 (1987): 586–617; "Feminizing Keats," in *Critical Essays on John Keats*, ed. Hermione de Almeida (Boston: G. K. Hall, 1990), 317–56; "Hemans and the Romance of Byron," in *Felicia Hemans: Reimagining Poetry in the Nineteenth Century*, ed. Nanora Sweet and Julie Melnyk (Basingstoke: Palgrave, 2001), 155–80; and "Teaching Hemans with Byron," *European Romantic Review* 17 (2006): 93–9.

but this point takes up only two and a half pages in the thirty-one-page piece. Another essay in this collection, Diego Saglia's "Ending the Romance: Women Poets and the Romantic Verse Tale," notes common elements in verse narratives by male and female Romantic writers but follows the usual paradigm in insisting on differences between men's and women's treatment of the genre, highlighting "areas of contention between male and female writing."[11]

Some of the works closest in conception to *Fellow Romantics* treat American and seventeenth- or eighteenth-century British writers. Karen Kilcup's *Soft Canons* consists of essays that explore nineteenth-century American "male and female writers together … their mutual influences, their alliances and alienations, and their constructions of the terms of literature." Another collection of essays on American writers, titled *No More Separate Spheres!* and edited by Cathy N. Davidson and Jessamyn Hatcher, is devoted to challenging the binary thinking inherent in the concept of separate male and female literary traditions. In this collection, the essays do not necessarily compare male or female writers, but when texts by men and women are examined separately the emphasis is on how they break down or complicate conventional gender categories. Ann Messenger's *His and Hers: Essays in Restoration and Eighteenth-Century Literature* consists of eight chapters, each of which compares two or more male and female British authors from the Restoration and eighteenth century. Her introduction, like those in the Kilcup and Davidson and Hatcher volumes, makes a case for the value and timeliness of studying literature by men and women together rather than within separate and adversarial traditions.[12]

Finally, Kathryn R. King's essay "Cowley Among the Women: or, Poetry in the Contact Zone" challenges the usefulness of approaches that study women writers within "separate female lineages and networks" and treat "[t]heir engagements with male literary tradition … as debilitating encounters with an order assumed to be masculinist, hostile, oppressive, sealed-off, and, except as something to be resisted or subverted, more or less unusable." Such approaches, King argues, "restrict the register of tones we are prepared to hear in women's texts" and "remove women writers from their own historical contexts" by detaching them from "the philosophical debates, political propagandizing, and various literary conversations occurring during their time." King explores the example of Abraham Cowley, who many early modern women writers regarded as "a model, a stimulus, even a kindred spirit." In particular, she examines Jane Barker's poem *The Necessity*

---

[11]    See Lilla Maria Crisafulli and Cecilia Pietropoli, eds., *Romantic Women Poets: Genre and Gender* (Amsterdam: Rodopi, 2007). Pietropoli's essay is on 197–208, Angeletti's 241–58, Cronin's 209–39, and Saglia's 153–67; the quotation from Saglia is on 156.

[12]    Karen Kilcup, ed., *Soft Canons: American Women Writers and Masculine Tradition* (Iowa City: University of Iowa Press, 1999), 6; Cathy N. Davidson and Jessamyn Hatcher, eds., *No More Separate Spheres! A Next Wave American Studies Reader* (Durham, NC: Duke University Press, 2002); Ann Messenger, *His and Hers: Essays in Restoration and Eighteenth-Century Literature* (Lexington: University Press of Kentucky, 1986).

*of Fate* alongside Cowley's *Destinie* and finds many parallels between the two works. She also points out ways in which Barker's poem expresses differences between the woman writer's situation and that of her male contemporary. King nonetheless concludes that, as the case of Jane Barker illustrates, "writing by men" can be enabling for women, "affording [them] an opportunity to adapt significant parts of their literary inheritance to their own ends."[13]

*Fellow Romantics* builds on the work of all those who have questioned binary approaches in the study of male and female writers.[14] The volume proposes that much can be gained from exploring common ground and interrelations among literary men and women of the Romantic period instead of examining them chiefly in terms of their ideological differences and separate cultural spheres. By demonstrating women's participation in literary movements and modes formerly associated with the major male Romantic poets, new aspects of the women's writing are brought to light and conventional gender categories complicated and disrupted. At the same time, directly comparing writings by men and women allows us to see new characteristics of the male writers as well.

For example, Julie Melnyk's essay on Wordsworth and Felicia Hemans and mine on Jane Austen and the Romantic poets draw attention to aspects of the male writers' works not usually considered: Wordsworth's later, Christian poems and various of the male poets' distrust of the imagination, respectively. Michael O'Neill's essay on Letitia Landon and Percy Shelley also explores Shelley's doubts about the imagination and disillusionment with Romantic ideals, at the same time as it demonstrates Landon's "sympathy with the Romantic project." Jacqueline Labbe argues that many of both Charlotte Smith's and William Wordsworth's supposedly personal lyrics are actually dramatic monologues, expressing the thoughts and feelings of literary personae rather than of the authors themselves, a point of view that disrupts the common reading of male poets (especially Wordsworth) as egotistical and woman poets as self-effacing. Both Ashley Cross's essay on Coleridge and Robinson as well as mine on Coleridge and Mary Shelley reveal anxieties about literary authority in male as well as female writers. In addition, my essay notes the importance of relationships and community for both Coleridge and Mary Shelley, thereby challenging the common practice of contrasting women's celebration of human bonds to men's embrace of individualism and solitude (at the same time, the essay argues that *Frankenstein* shares with *The Rime of the Ancient Mariner* a covert sympathy

---

[13]   Kathryn R. King, "Cowley Among the Women: or, Poetry in the Contact Zone," in *Women and Literary History: "For There She Was,"* ed. Katherine Binhammer and Jeanne Woods (Newark: University of Delaware Press, 2003), 43–5, 56.

[14]   My survey of scholarship in this introduction outlines major trends and cites many significant and representative works, especially books, but it necessarily omits numerous articles and monographs. Other scholars who have argued both for and against separate male and female literary traditions are cited by contributors to this volume in their essays on particular writers.

with ambitious, anti-social impulses and hostility toward family members). Alan Richardson's comparison of "Spirit" poems by Hemans, Byron, Percy Shelley, and Wordsworth reveals that the male poets were less committed to a transcendent state than was their female contemporary, contradicting the view that men were more drawn to the sublime and women to the earthly and quotidian. The image of Hemans as a champion of domestic values is also challenged by Julie Melnyk's analysis of the later Hemans's attraction to the figure of the vatic poet-prophet and by Susan Wolfson's attention to Hemans's fascination with war and retributive female violence. Barbara K. Seeber demonstrates Jane Austen's participation in contemporary debates on animal and human rights, and my essay on Austen argues that she ought to be included in studies of the Romantic imagination, as her treatment of imagination is similar to that of the male poets. Jane Stabler's study of Elizabeth Barrett's and Robert Browning's literary relationships with Byron and Shelley complicates traditional gender categories in a number of ways. For example, at a time when Byron was considered a quintessentially masculine and Shelley a feminine poet, Barrett Browning preferred the former and Browning the latter (though each learned to value the other's favorite Romantic poet).

Instead of changing our understanding of Romanticism by adding a new set of writers who are studied separately from the more traditional figures, the latter of whom retain their customary characteristics, this volume proposes that Romanticism can be more meaningfully and fundamentally reconceived by exploring interactions and conversations among literary men and women, all of whom shed light on one another's works. Thus Romanticism may be expanded and complicated but the term retained to designate a rich, diverse literary period in which a set of shared attributes may nonetheless be discerned.

These shared attributes often involve conflicts—between self and community, reason and passion, tradition and innovation, violence and forbearance, earthly and spiritual, idealism and realism, imagination and judgment—with which both men and women struggled. Rather than assign one set of beliefs and values to male writers and an opposing set to women, it is often more accurate to recognize the mutual ambivalences in Romantic writers of both genders. Essays in this collection that highlight tensions and conflicts in the works of male and female writers include Susan Wolfson's "'Something must be done': Shelley, Hemans, and the Flash of Revolutionary Female Violence," which explores both Hemans's and Shelley's ambivalent portraits of women who commit violent acts in resistance to patriarchal authority; Michael O'Neill's "'Beautiful but Ideal': Intertextual Relations between Letitia Elizabeth Landon and Percy Bysshe Shelley," which argues for a mix of hope and despair, belief and skepticism, emotion and stoicism, in the work of both poets; and my two essays, "Romantic Ambivalence in *Frankenstein* and *The Rime of the Ancient Mariner*" and "The Uses and Abuses of Imagination in Jane Austen and the Romantic Poets," which examine Mary Shelley's and Coleridge's celebration and undermining of intimate relationships, and Austen and the male poets' simultaneous distrust and celebration of the imagination, respectively.

Treating male and female writers as fellow Romantics need not involve ignoring legitimate differences among them. Without question, women and men were subjected to disparate roles and life experiences in the late eighteenth and early nineteenth centuries and these inevitably affect and find expression in their works. As Kathryn King notes in her study of Cowley and early modern women, however, such differences can be exaggerated and obscure areas of contact between male and female writers. Moreover, it is worth keeping in mind that no two individuals are ever exactly alike, and comparisons of any writers, even those with a great deal in common, will inevitably turn up differences that bespeak the unique preoccupations and talents of each. The major male Romantic poets are hardly uniform in their styles, themes, and emphases, nor were they unconflicted in their attitudes toward one another. Blake regarded Wordsworth's poetry as antithetical to his own beliefs and values, as he made clear in the harsh comments he wrote in the margins of Wordsworth's *Poems* (1815) and *The Excursion*.[15] Wordsworth's and Coleridge's literary and personal relations were notoriously complex, both enabling and disabling to each poet. Byron, Shelley, and Keats all resisted aspects of the older Romantic generation's poetry and also experienced rivalries among themselves, with Shelley at times defining himself in contrast to Byron and Keats in contrast to both Shelley and Byron.[16] When women writers at times deviate from the model of male writers—as we see in essays by Alan Richardson, Julie Melnyk, Susan Wolfson, Michael O'Neill, and Jane Stabler in this collection—they may be defining their own literary identities in response to important predecessors and rivals just as the male poets did themselves. As Harold Bloom argues, challenging and departing from aspects of another "strong poet's" work is an essential step in any major writer's development.[17] Women

---

[15]     See *The Complete Poetry and Prose of William Blake*, ed. David V. Erdman, commentary by Harold Bloom, rev. ed. (Berkeley: University of California Press, 1982), 665–7.

[16]     Some of the many works that analyze the complex, love-hate relations among the male Romantic poets include Lucy Newlyn, *Coleridge, Wordsworth, and the Language of Allusion* (Oxford: Clarendon Press, 1986); Paul Magnuson, *Coleridge and Wordsworth: A Lyrical Dialogue* (Princeton: Princeton University Press, 1988); and Gene W. Ruoff, *Wordsworth and Coleridge: The Making of the Major Lyrics* (New Brunswick: Rutgers University Press, 1989) on Wordsworth and Coleridge; Charles E. Robinson, *Shelley and Byron: The Snake and Eagle Wreathed in Flight* (Baltimore: The Johns Hopkins University Press, 1976) on Shelley and Byron; G. Kim Blank, *Wordsworth's Influence on Shelley: A Study of Poetic Authority* (New York: St. Martin's Press, 1988) on Shelley and Wordsworth; and my Keats's *Reading of the Romantic Poets* (Ann Arbor: University of Michigan Press, 1991) on Keats and Wordsworth, Coleridge, Byron, and Shelley.

[17]     See Bloom's *The Anxiety of Influence: A Theory of Poetry* (New York: Oxford University Press, 1973) and *A Map of Misreading* (New York: Oxford University Press, 1975). Bloom applies his model of writers' relationships to their strong predecessors only to men. I argue that many of its essential features also apply to women. This claim challenges Sandra M. Gilbert and Susan Gubar's assertion that nineteenth-century women writers did

Romantic writers, like the male poets, engaged in creative dialogues with their most important contemporaries, formulating their own styles and points of view through a combination of emulation and resistance.

A major goal of previous work on Romantic women writers has been to secure their place in a canon from which they were largely excluded for the past hundred or so years. As Karen Kilcup notes, it is common and "may be necessary" initially to study a disadvantaged group like women writers in isolation from "the 'mainstream'" in order to achieve for them "an acknowledged presence in literary history." "We need to ask, however," Kilcup continues, "how long such a separate identity is useful." Kilcup proposes that "it may be more beneficial … to inquire into the conversations between, and the meshing of, 'traditions' … while continuing to value the particularity of each."[18] I would argue that the place of women writers in the Romantic canon will be more, not less, secure if their works are integrated with those of men. Discovering ways in which women participated in many of the same movements and engaged in dialogue with their male contemporaries will knit them into our understanding of the period in ways that will make it more difficult to extricate them in future. After all, the practice of studying women writers separately from men was common in the nineteenth century, when anthologies and reviews grouped women together as "poetesses," "songstresses," or "lady fictionists," signifying that women could not be considered equally alongside men because of their radically different interests, styles, and, by implication, level of achievement.[19] Crisafulli and Petropoli in the Introduction to *Romantic Women Poets* note that the disappearance of women from the Romantic canon was aided by the tendency in the nineteenth century to marginalize women's poetry in "a sort of literary ghetto," and they quote approvingly Frederic Rowton's lament that his 1848 anthology *The Female Poets of Great Britain* is the first of its kind.[20] They fail to consider, however, that anthologies like Rowton's contributed to the ghettoizing of women's poetry. By the same token, current scholarship that

---

not suffer from a Bloomian anxiety of influence but rather from an anxiety of authorship (*The Madwoman in the Attic: The Woman Writer and the Nineteenth-Century Literary Imagination* [New Haven: Yale University Press, 1979], 45–51). Jane Stabler's essay in this volume on Elizabeth Barrett's and Robert Browning's literary relationships with Byron and Percy Shelley challenges Bloom's theory that poetic influence is linear and vertical, corresponding to a parent/child model, and instead argues that it often involves lateral "sibling" responses to actual or near contemporaries.

[18]    Kilcup, 2–3. King also acknowledges the value of initially studying women writers in isolation from men but then questions the usefulness of this approach as a persistent or exclusive mode of inquiry (43–4). See also Wolfson, *Borderlines*, xvi–xvii, 3.

[19]    For examples of such anthologies and critical studies see Elaine Showalter, *A Literature of Their Own: British Women Novelists from Brontë to Lessing* (Princeton: Princeton University Press, 1977), 74, and Joanne Shattock, ed., *Women and Literature in Britain, 1800–1900* (Cambridge: Cambridge University Press, 2001), 2.

[20]    Crisafulli and Pietropoli, 2.

segregates women from men risks perpetuating the marginalization of women writers.

The major reason to consider common ground and dialogue among male and female Romantic writers, however, is that by doing so we gain a more accurate understanding of the period than we gain by studying them in isolation. The fact is that men and women in the late eighteenth and early nineteenth centuries did read one another's works, inhabited many of the same coteries, influenced one another, and associated in a variety of ways. As Kilcup notes, it has been chiefly critics and reviewers who have insisted on segregating male and female writers; the writers themselves "often seemed to interact briskly and profitably." King insists that viewing women solely within female traditions "wrench[es them] out of their own cultural and historical contexts," since they did inhabit spheres--personal, intellectual, and artistic--that included men.[21]

The ten essays in *Fellow Romantics* follow an alternate paradigm, exploring zones of contact (see King, 44) or borderlines (in Wolfson's terms) in the encounters and exchanges between literary men and women of the Romantic period. Each essay treats one or more male and female writers and examines affinities in their works. Some of the essays explore cases in which the writers clearly were familiar with and directly allude to the others' writing: Ashley Cross's study of poems by Mary Robinson and Samuel Taylor Coleridge; Julie Melnyk's essay on William Wordsworth and Felicia Hemans; Alan Richardson's on "Spirit poems" by Hemans, Byron, and Shelley; Michael O'Neill's on Letitia Landon and Percy Shelley; my essay on Mary Shelley's *Frankenstein* and Coleridge's *The Rime of the Ancient Mariner*; and Jane Stabler's on Barrett Browning, Browning, Byron, and Percy Shelley. Such studies document the networks of influence and dialogue among male and female writers of the Romantic period (and in the case of Stabler's essay, the period of transition or overlap between Romantic and early Victorian eras).

Other essays explore common attitudes and literary practices not necessarily the result of direct contact but reflecting shared temperaments and outlooks among male and female Romantic writers as well as mutual participation in the spirit of the age. Such essays include those by Jacqueline Labbe on Charlotte Smith's and William Wordsworth's "Romantic dramatic monologues"; Susan Wolfson's analysis of Percy Shelley's and Felicia Hemans's ambivalent portrayals of female violence; Barbara K. Seeber's exploration of parallels in Jane Austen's, William Cowper's, and various male Romantic poets' treatment of male rural sports, in which animal rights are linked to issues of human rights; and my essay comparing the male poets' and Austen's similar attitudes toward the imagination. (Many of the essays treat both instances of direct influence among writers as well as cases of shared attitudes and motifs not attributable to specific borrowings. Indeed, it is not always possible to distinguish direct allusion from similarities in ideas or style that each writer may have developed independently of the other. In addition, it can be argued that writers are disposed to be most influenced by other writers with whom

---

[21]    Kilcup, 3; King, 57.

they identify and whose views they find congenial to their own.[22] Thus shared outlook and direct influence are related rather than distinct phenomena.)

In keeping with the prominence of poetry for the period, the majority of writers featured in the volume are poets (Cowper, Wordsworth, Coleridge, Byron, Percy Shelley, and Keats among the men, and Smith, Robinson, Hemans, Landon, and Barrett Browning among the women). Novelists are represented by the important figures of Mary Shelley and Jane Austen. Felicia Hemans's significance as arguably the most important woman poet of the Romantic period—given the size and variety of her corpus, its popularity and influence in the nineteenth century, and the richness and complexity of many of her poems—is reflected in the three essays devoted to her work.[23] These essays together demonstrate without question how extensively Hemans's work employs Romantic motifs and engages with the poetry of her major male contemporaries—how she is, as Michael O'Neill likewise characterizes Landon, a "fellow traveler" in "the visionary company of High Romantics" who can be fully integrated in the Romantic canon rather than (or in addition to being) segregated in a separate female tradition.

No collection of essays can exhaustively cover its subject but instead will explore a selection of writers and topics reflecting its contributors' special interests and areas of expertise. This collection is no exception; it does not pretend to treat all of the relevant figures, genres, networks, and affinities among literary men and women from 1790–1835. Many other female and male writers could and should be studied as "Fellow Romantics." It is hoped that this collection will provide examples of how such studies may be conducted and stimulate further work in this vein, as a means of achieving both diversity and continuity, expansion and consolidation, in the Romantic canon. As the anonymous reader at Ashgate was kind enough to suggest, the essays in *Fellow Romantics* "[open] up a host of new literary relationships yet to be charted."

## Works Cited

Alexander, Meena. *Women in Romanticism: Mary Wollstonecraft, Dorothy Wordsworth, and Mary Shelley*. Basingstoke: Macmillan, 1989.

Angeletti, Gioia. "Women Re-writing Men: The Examples of Anna Seward and Lady Caroline Lamb." In Crisafulli and Pietropoli. 241–58.

Armstrong, Isobel. "The Gush of the Feminine: How Can We Read Women's Poetry of the Romantic Period?" In *Romantic Women Writers: Voices and*

---

[22]    On the significance for literary influence of one writer's identification with another see Leon Waldoff, "Keats's Identification with Wordsworth: Selective Affinities," *Keats-Shelley Journal* 38 (1989): 47–65.

[23]    On Hemans's importance in the Romantic period see Cronin, 209–10. As Cronin notes, Hemans's status as the major poet of the literary scene from 1825–1835 was long obscured in twentieth-century scholarship and has only begun to be re-established.

*Countervoices*. Ed. Paula R. Feldman and Theresa M. Kelley. Hanover: University Press of New England, 1995. 13–52.

Bennett, Betty. *Mary Wollstonecraft Shelley: An Introduction*. Baltimore: The Johns Hopkins University Press, 1998.

Blake, William. *The Complete Poetry and Prose of William Blake*. Ed. David V. Erdman. Commentary by Harold Bloom. Rev. ed. Berkeley: University of California Press, 1982.

Blank, G. Kim. *Wordsworth's Influence on Shelley: A Study of Poetic Authority*. New York: St. Martin's Press, 1988.

Bloom, Harold. *The Anxiety of Influence: A Theory of Poetry*. New York: Oxford University Press, 1973.

—. *A Map of Misreading*. New York: Oxford University Press, 1975.

Bonca, Teddi Chichester. *Shelley's Mirrors of Love: Narcissism, Sacrifice, and Sorority*. Albany: SUNY Press, 1999.

Claridge, Laura, and Elizabeth Langland, eds. *Out of Bounds: Male Writers and Gender[ed] Cricitism*. Amherst: University of Massachusetts Press, 1990.

Craciun, Adriana. *Fatal Women of Romanticism*. Cambridge: Cambridge University Press, 2003.

Crisafulli, Lilla Maria, and Cecilia Pietropoli, eds. *Romantic Women Poets: Genre and Gender*. Amsterdam: Rodopi, 2007.

Cronin, Richard. "Felicia Hemans, Letitia Landon, and 'Lady's Rule'." In Crisafulli and Pietropoli. 208–39.

Davidson, Cathy N., and Jessamyn Hatcher, eds. *No More Separate Spheres! A Next Wave American Studies Reader*. Durham: Duke University Press, 2002.

Deresiewicz, William. *Jane Austen and the Romantic Poets*. New York: Columbia University Press, 2004.

Feldman, Paula R., and Theresa M. Kelley, eds. *Romantic Women Writers: Voices and Countervoices*. Hanover: University Press of New England, 1995.

Fulford, Tim. *Romanticism and Masculinity: Gender, Politics, and Poetics in the Writings of Burke, Coleridge, Cobbett, Wordsworth, De Quincey and Hazlitt*. Cambridge: Cambridge University Press, 1999.

Galperin, William. *The Historical Austen*. Philadelphia: University of Pennsylvania Press, 2003.

Gilbert, Sandra M., and Susan Gubar. *The Madwoman in the Attic: The Woman Writer and the Nineteenth-Century Literary Imagination*. New Haven: Yale University Press, 1979.

Hickey, Alison. "'The Body of My Father's Writing': Sara Coleridge's Genial Labor." In *Literary Couplings: Writing Couples, Collaborators, and the Construction of Authorship*. Ed. Marjorie Stone and Judith Thompson. Madison: University of Wisconsin Press, 2006. 124–47.

Homans, Margaret. *Women Writers and Poetic Identity: Dorothy Wordsworth, Emily Brontë, and Emily Dickinson*. Princeton: Princeton University Press, 1980.

Kilcup, Karen, ed. *Soft Canons: American Women Writers and Masculine Tradition*. Iowa City: University of Iowa Press, 1999.

King, Kathryn R. "Cowley Among the Women: or, Poetry in the Contact Zone." In *Women and Literary History: "For There She Was."* Ed. Katherine Binhammer and Jeanne Woods. Newark: University of Delaware Press, 2003. 43–63.

Lau, Beth. *Keats's Reading of the Romantic Poets*. Ann Arbor: University of Michigan Press, 1991.

Levin, Susan. *Dorothy Wordsworth and Romanticism*. New Brunswick: Rutgers University Press, 1987.

Linkin, Harriet Kramer, and Stephen C. Behrendt, eds. *Romanticism and Women Poets: Opening the Doors of Reception*. Lexington: University Press of Kentucky, 1999.

Lokke, Kari E. *Tracing Women's Romanticism: Gender, History, and Transcendence*. London: Routledge, 2004.

Lovejoy, A. O. "On the Discrimination of Romanticisms." *PMLA* 39 (1924): 229–53.

Magnuson, Paul. *Coleridge and Wordsworth: A Lyrical Dialogue*. Princeton: Princeton University Press, 1988.

Mellor, Anne K. *Romanticism and Gender*. New York: Routledge, 1993.

Mellor, Anne K., and Richard Matlak, eds. *British Literature 1780–1830*. Ft. Worth: Harcourt Brace, 1996.

Messenger, Ann. *His and Hers: Essays in Restoration and Eighteenth-Century Literature*. Lexington: University Press of Kentucky, 1986.

Morgan, Susan. *In the Meantime: Character and Perception in Jane Austen's Fiction*. Chicago: University of Chicago Press, 1980.

—. *Sisters in Time: Imagining Gender in Nineteenth-Century British Fiction*. New York: Oxford University Press, 1989.

Newlyn, Lucy. *Coleridge, Wordsworth, and the Language of Allusion*. Oxford: Clarendon Press, 1986.

Pietropoli, Cecilia. "Women Romance Writers: Mary Tighe and Mary Hays." In Crisafulli and Pietropoli. 197–208.

Robinson, Charles E. *Shelley and Byron: The Snake and Eagle Wreathed in Flight*. Baltimore: The Johns Hopkins University Press, 1976.

Ross, Marlon B. *The Contours of Masculine Desire: Romanticism and the Rise of Women's Poetry*. New York: Oxford University Press, 1989.

Ruoff, Gene W. *Wordsworth and Coleridge: The Making of the Major Lyrics*. New Brunswick: Rutgers University Press, 1989.

Saglia, Diego. "Ending the Romance: Women Poets and the Romantic Verse Tale." In Crisafulli and Pietropoli. 153–67.

Shattock, Joanne, ed. *Women and Literature in Britain, 1800–1900*. Cambridge: Cambridge University Press, 2001.

Showalter, Elaine. *A Literature of Their Own: British Women Novelists from Brontë to Lessing*. Princeton: Princeton University Press, 1977.

Taylor, Anya. *Erotic Coleridge: Women, Love, and the Law Against Divorce*. New York: Palgrave Macmillan, 2005.

Tuite, Clara. *Romantic Austen: Sexual Politics and the Literary Canon*. Cambridge: Cambridge University Press, 2002.

Waldoff, Leon. "Keats's Identification with Wordsworth: Selective Affinities." *Keats-Shelley Journal* 38 (1989): 47–65.

Wallace, Anne D. "Home at Grasmere Again: Revising the Family in Dove Cottage." In *Literary Couplings: Writing Couples, Collaborators, and the Construction of Authorship*. Ed. Marjorie Stone and Judith Thompson. Madison: University of Wisconsin Press, 2006. 100–123.

Wilkes, Joanne. *Lord Byron and Madame de Staël: Born for Opposition*. Aldershot: Ashgate, 1999.

Wilson, Carol Shiner, and Joel Haefner, eds. *Re-Visioning Romanticism: British Women Writers, 1776–1837*. Philadelphia: University of Pennsylvania Press, 1994.

Wolfson, Susan J. *Borderlines: The Shiftings of Gender in British Romanticism*. Stanford: Stanford University Press, 2006.

—. "Feminizing Keats." In *Critical Essays on John Keats*. Ed. Hermione de Almeida. Boston: G. K. Hall, 1990. 317–56.

—. "Hemans and the Romance of Byron." In *Felicia Hemans: Reimagining Poetry in the Nineteenth Century*. Ed. Nanora Sweet and Julie Melnyk. Basingstoke: Palgrave, 2001. 155–80.

—. "Teaching Hemans with Byron." *European Romantic Review* 17 (2006): 93–9.

—. "'Their She Condition': Cross-Dressing and the Politics of Gender in *Don Juan*." *ELH* 54 (1987): 586–617.

# Chapter 1
# Revisiting the Egotistical Sublime: Smith, Wordsworth, and the Romantic Dramatic Monologue

Jacqueline M. Labbe

This essay questions the period-bound nature of the dramatic monologue to suggest that the egoistic personae developed by William Wordsworth and Charlotte Smith function as its Romantic version.[1] Moreover, it questions the gendered binaries developed by critics proposing that male writers concern themselves with the Self while female writers pursue a feminine ethic of care for the Other. Instead, I will argue that both Smith and Wordsworth concentrate on establishing the parameters of the Poet, filtered through an exploration of the artfully-constructed Self. Looking in particular at *Elegiac Sonnets* and *Lyrical Ballads*, I will investigate how the "theatrical," to use Judith Pascoe's term, underpins and indeed creates the personalized narrators of the poems.[2] Instead of seeing the poems as thinly-disguised autobiographies, I read their presentations of sincerity and authenticity as dramatized, and the position of Poet as itself a role, a function made possibly by Smith's and Wordsworth's abilities to write Selves that are simultaneously Self and Other. The egotistical sublime, then, instead of functioning as an unconscious revelation of solipsism, becomes a tool by which the poets can act out fantasies of unified subjectivity. For the late eighteenth century, fascinated with an emerging culture of celebrity and individuality, Smith's and Wordsworth's poetry helped to form an expectation that the poetical was personal. It also undermined such expectations and created a space within poetry that critiqued these narrow parameters. For Smith and Wordsworth, the investigation of what constitutes *a*

18thc
legacy

---

[1]    It is as well to state at the outset that I am not attempting to recategorize all of Smith's and Wordsworth's personae as the subjects of dramatic monologues; see also note 23. Nor am I suggesting that just because a poem is voiced by a speaker it is a dramatic monologue. Rather, I am interested in the ways that certain of Smith's seemingly "personal" sonnets and certain of Wordsworth's seemingly self-based lyrics display subjective personae that the poems themselves eventually discredit. This is a key aspect of the dramatic monologue as formalized by Tennyson, Barrett Browning, and Browning. While their Victorian heirs developed and named the form, this essay contends that it was not beyond the scope of the two masters of Romantic subjectivity, Smith and Wordsworth.

[2]    See *Romantic Theatricality: Gender, Poetry and Spectatorship* (Ithaca: Cornell University Press, 1997).

Poet is less gender-inflected than their explorations of *themselves* as poets. Each seems to critique a kind of ur-Poet, a Romantic construct characterized by the very ego that Keats associated with Wordsworth himself.

Keats is so very matter-of-fact in his identification of the "wordsworthian or egotistical sublime" and its contradistinction from his own version of the "poetical Character" as chameleonic and without identity that his definition goes by and large unchallenged.[3] With its lowercase "w," "wordworthian" becomes an adjective, detached from the person Wordsworth although derived from how Keats read him: as overwhelmingly inhabiting his poetry, and as a Self defined by an excessive writing of the Self. It's not difficult to see that for Keats, Smith's poetry would occupy the same space: writing wherein the "nature" and "identity" of the poet, far from being "annihilated," take center stage and claim full readerly attention (279, 280). Smith, of course, encourages this response with her increasingly detailed and personalized Prefaces and Dedications; Wordsworth may be more retiring but the force of the poetry remains the same.[4] However, to describe the autobiographical—perhaps more accurately called the meta-autobiographical—poetry of the two as dramatic or dramatized allows us to interrogate the certainty of Keats's formulation. As far back as 1957, Stephen Maxfield Parrish described *The Thorn* as Wordsworth's dramatic monologue; seeking to move the development of the genre back a poetic generation is not in itself new.[5] Even for Parrish, however, *The Thorn* was proto-Victorian in its enactment of the monologue: Wordsworth wrote a poem not about a mother or a tree, but about a speaker whose nature was revealed through his own first-person narrative (101 *passim*). Turning to the meta-autobiographical poems of both Smith and Wordsworth allows for a more specifically Romantic version of the dramatic monologue to emerge: one in which the egotistical sublime is the pose rather than the drawback, and in which the writing of the Self is achieved through deliberately literary inscription and blissfully unaware elocution.

Interestingly, most critics who explore the autobiographically sincere and authentic in Romantic poetry focus on Wordsworth, and most acknowledge, at least in passing, the constructed nature of Wordsworthian sincerity, despite its self-conscious appearance as unmediated. Robert Langbaum, writing in 1957, notes that "whether the romanticist projects himself into the past, nature, or another person, he never forgets that he is playing a role," and that sincerity is an "effect" to be

---

[3]    Letter to Richard Woodhouse (27 October 1818), in *Selected Poems and Letters by John Keats*, ed. Douglas Bush (Boston: Houghton Mifflin, 1959), 279.

[4]    For a detailed discussion of Smith's strategies in her Prefaces, see my *Charlotte Smith: Romanticism, Poetry and the Culture of Gender* (Manchester: Manchester University Press, 2003), chapter 1. Judith Pascoe also notes that Smith "narrow[s] the distance between author and narrator of her poems" in the increasing detail of the Prefaces (17).

[5]    Parrish included this essay in chapter 3 of *The Art of the Lyrical Ballads* (Cambridge: Harvard University Press, 1973).

"achieved."[6] David Perkins refers to "the drama of sincerity" and "the impression of spontaneity," arguing that poetic form "compromises the ideal of sincerity."[7] Even Lionel Trilling calls poetic sincerity "a congruence between avowal and actual feeling."[8] But critics agree in presenting Wordsworth as somehow innocent, a kind of dupe of sincerity's propensity to expose its own falsity in representation. He is a poet who strives for authenticity: "he writes as though he were talking to close friends or to domestic companions"; he "wr[ites] of a self in whose authenticity he utterly believed."[9] Leon Guilhamet probably takes this position furthest when he writes that, for Wordsworth, "the language of sincerity, drawing sustenance from truth, leads men to understand truth."[10] None of these critics, writing between 1957 and 1974, would have admitted Smith to the same plateau on which they placed Wordsworth, but her tone is equally intimate, whether crying out for succor in the *Sonnets* or recounting conversations with friends in the Prefaces. When she calls herself "an early worshipper at Nature's shrine"[11] she offers the same "autobiographical illusion" and follows the same strategy of giving "facts from within" that Langbaum finds in Wordsworth (52, 78). For both poets, sincerity and authenticity animate much of the poetry; the question is not whether this is true, but whether the two poets are at the mercy of sincerity's inherent insincerity, or whether they play with this tension and consequently with the picture of the Poet as authentic, emotionally open, transparently Selfed.

The concept of the sincere Wordsworth is informed by a critical investment in the idea of Romantic writers as moving against the mainstream of their culture, derived from understandings of their poetry as by definition experimental, innovative, and anti-cultural, coupled with an understanding of authenticity as a poetic goal, even if a compromised one. However, even as the Romantic poetry written by Wordsworth builds on its literary past, representing continuity as well as innovation, so too the poetic Self written into his and Smith's poetry develops in a culture highly interested in public displays of personality and subjectivity. Studies of Wordsworth subsequent to Guilhamet's began to note a more conscious

*[handwritten margin note: B's secret self / body — @ this is what he wanted to portray, reaction to spectacle]*

---

[6]  Langbaum, *The Poetry of Experience: The Dramatic Monologue in Modern Literary Experience* (London: Chatto and Windus, 1957), 25, 33.

[7]  Perkins, *Wordsworth and the Poetry of Sincerity* (Cambridge: The Belknap Press of Harvard University Press, 1964), 2, 210, 84.

[8]  Trilling, *Sincerity and Authenticity* (London: Oxford University Press, 1972), 2.

[9]  Perkins, 143; William Galperin, *Revision and Authority in Wordsworth: The Interpretation of a Career* (Philadelphia: University of Pennsylvania Press, 1989), 66.

[10]  Guilhamet, *The Sincere Ideal: Studies on Sincerity in Eighteenth Century English Literature* (Montreal: McGill-Queen's University Press, 1974), 276.

[11]  *Beachy Head*, 346, in *The Poems of Charlotte* Smith, ed. Stuart Curran (Oxford: Oxford University Press, 1993). All quotations of Smith's poetry are from this edition, but see also *Poems*, ed. Jacqueline Labbe (London: Pickering and Chatto, 2007), vol. 14 of *The Works of Charlotte Smith*, gen. ed. Stuart Curran (London: Pickering and Chatto, 2005–2007).

and self-aware poetic stance: Frances Ferguson, in 1977, countered the isolationist egotistical sublime image of the poet by simply, and vitally, noting the "various provisions for an audience" even in Wordsworth's seemingly most private poetry, which immediately introduces the idea of performance, even though Ferguson did not name this as such.[12] William Galperin extends Ferguson's insight so that the audience becomes the guarantor of Wordsworth's sincerity: the Authentic Self "was written as, and was the product of, an interchange with a hypothetical reader"[13]: the poet is compelled to create poetry in which his sincerity is maintained and verified. If the Romantic poet—Wordsworth or Smith—writes poetry that implies its own audience, however, then a performance has begun and authenticity itself is replaced by its dramatized understudy. Therefore, according to Sheila Kearns, writing about the self "involves … the performance of a reading of the self in and through the construction of the autobiographical text"; for Elizabeth Fay "romantic sincerity is also an aestheticization of the self.… [A]cting and being (acting the role of the self) are the same"; for Pascoe, "Wordsworth was drawn to dramatic realizations of the self" (219).[14] Even Deborah Forbes, who attempts intriguingly to fuse the sincere with the performative, says that Wordsworth "is a sincere poet *because* he makes his sincerity questionable": in other words, he now controls that of which he was previously understood to lack awareness.[15]

Curiously, even as they formulate a new critical understanding of Wordsworth as decidedly performative, and of the autobiographical poem as more dramatic than authentic, none of these critics explores the place of the dramatic monologue in Romantic autobiographical poetry—or rather, as I called it above, the meta-autobiographical. Indeed, Forbes rejects the idea fully, explaining that while a poem like *Tintern Abbey* could be a dramatic monologue, the readerly need to believe in a "speaker-poet" overrides this possibility; otherwise the speaker's "imprecision" and "mysticism" becomes "laughable": "it is truer to the poem, and to everything we know of Wordsworth, to believe that we are supposed to share the speaker-poet's sense of awe in the face of things he cannot explain."[16] This reading, of course, re-engages with the sincere, since what seems to underlie Forbes's comments is a desire to read the poem as truthful in the Guilhamet sense. Without "truth," without a speaker-poet whose ego creates the sublimity of the incomprehensible, the poem fails. Forbes's stance is very close to Langbaum's, who

---

[12]    Ferguson, *Wordsworth: Language as Counter-Spirit* (New Haven: Yale University Press, 1977), xiv.

[13]    Galperin, 66.

[14]    Kearns, *Coleridge, Wordsworth, and Romantic Autobiography: Reading Strategies of Self-Representation* (Madison: Fairleigh Dickinson University Press, 1995), 25; Fay, *Becoming Wordsworthian: A Performative Aesthetics* (Amherst: University of Massachusetts Press, 1995), 2, 16.

[15]    Forbes, *Sincerity's Shadow: Self-Consciousness in British Romantic and Mid-Twentieth-Century American Poetry* (Cambridge: Harvard University Press, 2004), 34.

[16]    Forbes, 85.

judges that "Wordsworth never consciously discovered the dramatic monologue, though he is always hovering on the edge of the form," writing instead dialogic "dramatic lyrics" where the subject is the Self rather than the exploration of another created Self.[17] This frequent critical return to an evocation of Wordsworth's Self suggests more the constancy of Keats than of Wordsworth; it seems precisely the discomfort Wordsworth's technique arouses—the suspicion that his persona is not nearly as coherent as it pretends to be—that prompts so many readers to realign Speaker and Poet. As Fay points out, "Wordsworthian scholars do not like to regard William Wordsworth as invested in roles beyond that of seer and sage because the concept of role playing seems deliberately at odds with Wordsworth's insistent sincerity."[18] For the purposes of my argument, it is exactly this insistence that allows the coherence of Wordsworth's speaker to be questioned. Similarly, Smith's insistence on sorrow and personal need, and its primacy for her readers both then and now, hints at its own artifice. For both poets, the poetry of the Self coupled with the exploitation of an expectation of sincerity—an expectation that each encourages—results in the Romantic dramatic monologue, a mode allowing each poet to engage with and simultaneously undermine the attractions of a self-focused subjectivity.

Once we begin to question not only a stressed sincerity but also an emphasized autobiography, then the key elements of the Victorian dramatic monologue are easily transposable.[19] The dramatic monologue is spoken by a "first-person … speaker [who] is indicated not to be the poet" in the presence of a "silent auditor" with a "high degree of naturalistic presentation"; "the poet must convince us of the actuality of the character in order to secure a full emotional engagement."[20] Of course, if the speaker is the Duke of Ferrara or a murderous madman then his difference from the poet is easy to maintain. The Romantic dramatic monologue explores exactly the figure of the Poet, dwelling on his/her tendency towards self-aggrandizement, intense introspection, self-conscious literariness. Critics have tended to read these poetic attributes as derived from the autobiographical self presented in the poetry, the unconscious self-exposure of the egotist. But in a culture saturated with spectacle—theatrical, political, journalistic, even poetic (think the Della Cruscans, for instance)—and increasingly fascinated by celebrity, then attempts by a poet to ascertain "What is a Poet?" are at least hinting towards

---

[17]  Langbaum, 53.

[18]  Fay, 18. Fay's excellent book is second only to Pascoe's in opening news ways to read Wordsworth. Where our arguments differ is in her emphasis on Dorothy as an equal partner in the creation of "Wordsworth"; for her, "Wordsworth" hides a double, William/Dorothy identity. By contrast, I see a multiple Wordsworth/"Wordsworth"/Wordsworth-as-"Wordworth" aesthetic informing his meta-autobiography.

[19]  This transposition, of course, works both ways if we accept the existence of the Romantic dramatic monologue.

[20]  Alan Sinfield, *The Dramatic Monologue* (London: Methuen, 1977), 42, 1, 42, 45. Sinfield refers to the "simple sincerity of the Romantic poetic 'I'" (60).

a drama of self-representation, especially when the answer is that "He is a man speaking to men": a man declaiming, performing, delivering a monologue.[21] Or, in the case of Smith, a woman whose private sorrows are publicly pronounced: "toujours des Chansons tristes" (Preface to the Sixth Edition of the *Elegiac Sonnets*, 6). In other words, the Author writes a Self (Persona) who, within the poetry, enacts a sincere and authentic selfhood. In so doing, the Persona inadvertently exposes his/her limitations as a self-obsessed Subject through a self-reflexive poetics, all in the presence of an auditor: a Friend, a Sister, a reader who is implicitly (sometimes explicitly) invoked. Poetry, then, is the vehicle by which the exemplary Romantic poet, Wordsworth or Smith, writes the Romantic ego into being, and calls its value into question.[22] As auditors, we are simultaneously seduced and repulsed by the display of selfhood. Do we rescue Smith or dismiss her as a pest? Do we admire Wordsworth or accuse him of solipsism?

Viewing the meta-autobiographical as a dramatic feint, to use Sinfield's term, means reviewing the egotistical sublime as Keats's misreading. By the time he makes his judgment, in 1818, the figure of the Romantic poet is well-established, in many ways derived from the personae explored by Smith and Wordsworth. The general applicability of Keats's pronouncement to a certain style of writing probably accounts for his lower-case "w," while the fall from favor Smith's poetry had already undergone, combined with the young poet's unease with identifying a female poet's influence as central, justifies "wordsworthian" over "smithian." For both older poets, poetry affords a space wherein experimentation with different forms of subjectivity is possible, and to insist on the reliability, the *authenticity*, of the autobiographical misses, I think, the fundamental innovation of both poets: seeing that poetry itself creates subjectivity, that sincere expression is always mediated in some way by the artistic process, and that even the most autobiographical verse flirts, at the least, with artifice. Reading the autobiographical

---

[21]    Scholars are currently reassessing the extent to which the Romantic period was dominated by spectacle and celebrity. See Pascoe; Gillen D'Arcy Wood, *The Shock of the Real* (New York: Palgrave, 2001); Adriana Craciun, *Fatal Women of Romanticism* (Cambridge: Cambridge University Press, 2003); Tim Fulford, "The Electrifying Mrs. Robinson," *Women's Writing* 9 (2002): 23–36; Claire Brock, "'Then Smile and Know Thyself Supremely Great': Mary Robinson and the 'Splendour of a Name'," *Women's Writing* 9 (2002): 107–26; John Barrell, *Imagining the King's Death* (Oxford: Oxford University Press, 2000). Pascoe views the peripatetic Wordsworth as spectacle and links his impromptu rural performances with those of strolling players and minstrels (196 and *passim*).

[22]    In a related remark, E. R. Harty states that "even in those cases where the poet *intends* to speak in his own voice, to express his own thoughts and feelings, by employing a poetic genre he automatically abdicates his right to be so construed." Harty's view, that poetry as a genre is inherently artificial, is one that I am sympathetic to, although I think that both Smith and Wordsworth exploit the dramatic potential of poetry rather than being subject to it. See "Voice and Enunciation in the Dramatic Monologue and the Lyric," *Unisa English Studies* 28 (1990): 14–21 (quoted passage on 14).

as meta-autobiographical, then, means that we can interpret some of the "I"s of the *Elegiac Sonnets* and the *Lyrical Ballads* as a characterization of selfhood by Smith and Wordsworth, their attempts at understanding the nature and character of the Poet, and their identifications of the encompassing Poet's drawbacks.[23]

## The *Elegiac Sonnets* and the Depths of a Poet's Sorrow

It has already become a critical commonplace that Smith uses her *Sonnets* to explore—some would say indulge—her sorrows, ranging from her unhappy marriage to her unsettled lawsuit and poverty to her worries and grief over her children. As the recent edition of her *Letters* has shown, however, Smith could suit her tone to her genre; while the letters are frequently angry and distressed, they are seldom woeful or self-pitying.[24] The problems that led to her unhappiness are well documented by Smith in an almost legalistic way: she frequently backs up her complaints with facts, figures, and papers to prove her point. The straightforward determination evinced by the letters functions as a competing form of autobiography to that written into the *Sonnets*, which themselves offer a variety of Selves from which to seek the "real" Charlotte Smith.[25] And readers duly seek; as Pascoe notes, the *Sonnets* created a "cult of the beleaguered and self-dramatizing female, a poetic identity that brought Smith considerable success" as her readers responded with a sympathetic consumerism to the need expressed in the poetry.[26]

---

[23]  I would not want to argue that *all* of the two poets' autobiographical work is dramatized; for Wordsworth, there is fully documented investment in the personal nature of his writing, while Smith's Augusta sonnets clearly express her personal bereavement, even if not always from the point of view of a mother (see *Charlotte Smith*, chapter 2). But to explore the ways in which their poetry undercuts even as it creates the highly personalized Romantic Poet allows for a deeper critical understanding of the interplay between the "real" and the imagined in the period. See, for instance, Gillen D'Arcy Wood, *The Shock of the Real*, for an exploration of the varieties of spectacle and trompe l'oeil available for consumption.

[24]  See *The Collected Letters of Charlotte Smith*, ed. Judith Stanton (Bloomington: Indiana University Press, 2003). Smith was a copious letter-writer, as were many accomplished women of her time, and great caches of her letters have survived, with new ones continuing to turn up since the publication of Stanton's magisterial edition. See, for instance, my "Gentility in Distress: A New Letter by Charlotte Smith (1749–1806)," *The Wordsworth Circle* 35 (2004): 91–3. In addition, a new group of ninety-threee letters to Smith's publisher Cadell have recently been unearthed in the library of the Brighton Royal Pavilion, now lodged in the East Sussex Public Record Office.

[25]  I discussed some of these personae in *Charlotte Smith*, which is mainly concerned with the gendering of the Selves Smith concocts. See also Labbe, "The Seductions of Form in the Poetry of Cristall and Smith," in *Romantic Form*, ed. Alan Rawes (Basingstoke: Palgrave Macmillan, 2007), 154–70.

[26]  Pascoe, 16.

As Pascoe's use of the term "self-dramatizing" suggests, however, the sincerity of the *Sonnets* is compromised by what Pascoe defines as the "performative" but which I see as *performance*: not Smith acting out her sorrows for an appreciative audience, but Smith composing a speaker who is determined by the expression of sorrow. Further, true to the dramatic monologue, the speaker exposes her personal limitations inadvertently, through the act of composition itself; the poet critiques a speaker who laments ceaselessly but who does nothing to improve her situation.[27]

Because of the intensity of the Prefaces to her *Sonnets*, in which Smith the author constructs a Poet at the mercy of "'the Honourable Men'" who control the lawsuit over her father-in-law's will, the sonnets, whether transplanted from her novels, translated from Goethe or Petrarch, or transparently spoken by an autobiographical Charlotte Smith, appear as the collective woes of the author.[28] But Smith is as diligent in undercutting this appearance once in the body of the work as she is in cementing it in the paratexts. Smith's speakers take up a variety of sorrowing stances, and she varies her endorsements of their styles. The speakers of Sonnets XII, XLIV, and LXXX, for instance, do little more than sit and lament their fates. In each, Smith vocalizes a passive victim, one who longs for the release of death but who does nothing to forward it. The speaker of Sonnet XII, "Written on the Sea Shore.— October, 1794," is not specifically gendered in the poem, but the accompanying plate, showing a female figure, suggests a female speaker—not, however, Smith, given the youth and physical vulnerability of the woman.[29] The speaker occupies, then, a space associated with the woes of Charlotte Smith, but is dissociated from her via the plate. Further, the "mournful temper" of the speaker's "soul" is linked by pathetic fallacy with the "wild gloomy scene" (8, 7), while the poem's tone is overdetermined by the storm-tossed imagery; in other words, this speaker writes a poem whose very compositional seamlessness invites investigation of its sincerity. As Daniel Robinson has persuasively argued, Smith's use of the term "essays" in the title of the first editions of the *Sonnets* (*Elegiac Sonnets and Other Essays*) points to the inherent experimentation of the collection: "the 'elegiac sonnet' is for Smith very much an experiment, an 'essay,' that is, an attempt," and the *Sonnets* as a whole

---

[27]    As my discussion will show, only certain of Smith's sonnets conform to this pattern. Although many, if not most, of the sonnets fit the parameters of the "complaint," a familiar lyric stance especially suited to the abandoned woman persona, it is my argument that Smith creates distinctions at the level of structure and form rather than plot or tone. In this way, some complaints are more valid than others. My thanks to the anonymous reader whose astute observations helped clarify this point.

[28]    *The Poems of Charlotte Smith*, ed. Stuart Curran (New York: Oxford University Press, 1993), 5. Pascoe also makes this point: Smith "narrows the distance between author and narrator of her poems" through her paratexts (17).

[29]    As I argue in *Charlotte Smith*, the pains Smith takes in her paratexts to situate herself as aged and scarred by her troubles disallows any easy identification of herself with the attractive ingénues portrayed in the plates. See chapter 1 of my book for further discussion.

engage in "the deliberate yoking of seemingly disparate forms."[30] Given this fact, it is significant that Sonnet XII, the first to feature the passive speaker, is written so very correctly. The imagery is unimpeachable, the tone wholly consistent, and the rhyme scheme unadventurous, even if also "illegitimate": *abba cddc effe gg*.[31] Smith's rhyme schemes often furnish clues to the meaning of her sonnets, and here the very regularity of the rhyme suggests that for Smith, this speaker is lacking a fundamental spark.

Sonnet LXIV, "Written in the church-yard in Middleton in Sussex," also demonstrates a poetic perfection that regularizes its macabre content. Often discussed as an example of Smith's "striking" morbidity (Robinson, 193), it features the passive speaker whose strength of imagery is not matched by strength of character. The speaker subsumes herself to the scene she witnesses: invisible in the poem until line 13, even her sex is unclear, intimated only by the poem's similarity of scene to Sonnet XII. Again, a speaker watches an external tumult and wishes for, but does not seek, the "gloomy rest" of the dead (14). The poem updates the graveyard school, its details of decomposed bodies more conventional than is usually acknowledged.[32] Its macabre imagery in this context is less innovative than thoroughly poetical, and its rhyme scheme is again regular although, significantly, it deviates from the Shakespearean pattern in the third quatrain: *abba cddc ecce ff*. The slight disruption to the full regularity of Sonnet XII suggests the critical intervention of the poet in the construction of the sonnet's self-regarding speaker. As if impressed by the potency of her imagery, the speaker suffers a lapse in the rigor of her rhymes. The speaker-as-poet, defined by her sorrows, paralyzed by their evocation, grasps for rhyme but can only repeat herself. Smith shows the effect on poetry of an overriding concern, a monomania the expression of which requires compositional convention but which also corrupts this convention from within.[33]

Sonnet LXXX, "To the invisible moon," sees the speaker attempt a more vigorous style, only to fall back into a dramatized passivity. The sonnet opens by invoking Sonnet IV, "To the Moon," in such a way as to differentiate this speaker

---

[30]    "*Elegiac Sonnets*: Charlotte Smith's Formal Paradoxy," *Papers on Language and Literature* 39 (2003): 200, 185.

[31]    Smith uses the term in the Preface to the First Edition of the *Sonnets*, and Robinson notes that "in the eighteenth century, the kind of sonnet that Smith writes—three quatrains and a couplet, like Shakespeare's--was a bastardized form" (186n.1).

[32]    This poem's actual generic continuity has not been remarked. As Robinson explains, most critics discuss this poem in terms of its suggestive content as developed by a woman writer. See Robinson, 193n.11.

[33]    In this context it is interesting that one of Smith's contemporary readers, John Thelwall, singled out Sonnet LXIV for its generic completeness: "Perhaps it is not saying too much to declare, that in the narrow compass of these fourteen lines, are included all the requisites of good poetry: vivid painting, numerous harmony, sublimity of thought and expression, and pathos of sentiment" (qtd. in Robinson, 193n.11).

from that of the earlier sonnet. Where the "I" in Sonnet IV "delight[s] to stray" "by [the moon's] pale beam" (2, 1), this speaker emphatically negates the comfort the "soft Evening's Queen" offers to those who feel merely "mild Sorrow, such as Hope has not forsook" (1, 5). Once again passive and still, the speaker states that "*I* prefer from some steep rock to look / On the obscure and fluctuating main" (7–8). Like the speaker of Sonnet XII, this Poet prefers the "troubled deep" (10) to the "mild and placid light" of the moon (Sonnet IV, 5). And like that speaker, this one does little more than compose herself. Constructing a parallel series of fiery images ("the martial star with lurid glare," "the red comet shakes his blazing hair," "the fire-ting'd waves," 9, 11, 12) and the by-now familiar regular Shakespearian rhyme scheme (*abab cdcd efef gg*), the speaker takes refuge in poetic correctness. However, even as this correctness was undercut by repetition in Sonnet LXIV, here Smith utilizes near-rhyme to link lines and thereby suggest her speaker's incapacity: Queen/serene and reign/main (1, 3, 6, 8). Suffused by a generalized woe, compelled to write and rewrite her sorrow, the passive speaker takes refuge in poetic perfection, displaying for her readers her ability to compose, to be an expressive Poet. But the more she writes, the more her expression is overcome by its own constructedness: correctness increasingly gives way to mere convention. This is the poet who wears out her welcome; what Fay calls Smith's "'naturally' melancholic pose" characterizes a Poet who cannot see beyond her own sorrow, and cannot write anything else.[34]

The dramatizing of the passive speaker allows Smith to explore the ways in which poetry enables subjectivity. By writing a speaker whose personality she on the one hand seems to claim and on the other simply declaims, Smith demonstrates what E. Warwick Slinn views as the unique performativity of poetry: poetry is "a cultural event which participates in cultural reality, reconstituting or reshaping that reality in the very act of reiterating its norms; and its capacity for referential aberration, pointing in both directions, both inside and outside itself, draws attention to the double action."[35] As dramatic monologues, these sonnets enact sorrow and also undermine its influence. It is because not all the sonnets feature a passive speaker whose grief is unspeakable that we can query the reality shaped by these, following the hints that Smith embeds in the composition of such seamless poetry. Unimpressed with poetic posturing, Smith allows her passive speaker to expose her own limitations as a poet and as a persona through the very medium that lends her a kind of reality. But these poems do not plumb the depths of the poet's sorrow; Smith gives more credence to the speaker of the sonnets

---

[34]   Fay, 22.

[35]   "Poetry and Culture: Performativity and Critique," *New Literary History* 30 (1999): 66, 57–74. While Slinn, Pascoe and Fay all talk about "performativity," Pascoe and Fay emphasize performativity *in* poetry where Slinn theorizes about the performativity *of* poetry. My argument effectively synthesizes these two positions: Smith, in writing dramatic monologues, shows the performance of the persona to be performance, but she also demonstrates the essential suitability of poetry to the creation of performance.

she transplants from her various novels, whose sorrows are less generalized but whose compositional pedigree is more complex. This effect is achieved in two main ways: she creates clear links between the novel-sonnets' tropes and those of other more ostensibly autobiographical sonnets, and she allows the speakers of the novel-sonnets to compose more innovative poetry. This is especially clear in the five sonnets she includes from her novel *Celestina*, all spoken originally by Celestina and thus doubly feminized in the *Sonnets*. Moreover, since most editions of the *Sonnets* signal the novel as source in the sonnets' titles, readers approach them as they do the Werther sonnets, aware of an existing backstory. Indeed, just as the five Werther sonnets enact a kind of playlet, so too the five Celestina sonnets can be seen as five acts in a drama. The dramatic element of the Celestina sonnets is thus both more and less obvious: more because the knowing reader recognizes the "I" as someone other than Smith, less because the connections Smith forges between the sentiments uttered by Celestina are also those of the autobiographical Smith-poet.

As the sequence opens, Smith hints at the constructed nature of the poems by using "supposed" in the title: "Supposed to have been written in a church-yard, over the grave of a young woman of nineteen" (Sonnet XLIX). Robinson notes that this is one of the few sonnets to mourn a specific death,[36] but he does not elaborate on the double feint the poem offers: the specific death is here only "supposed," and the mourning figure is both "From the novel of Celestina" and the general *Sonnets* speaker.[37] Although she eventually banishes the poems' novelistic origin to the notes, Smith does not eliminate the information altogether; the poems' speaker, therefore, becomes indeterminate: is she Smith, Celestina, or some hybrid of the two? Sonnet XLIX, featuring the speaker lamenting "over the grave of a young woman," reverses expectations by congratulating the dead "virgin" on her escape from "human ills" and her achievement of the constancy of the love of her "youth": "still for him shall faithful Memory save / Thy form and virtues from the silent grave" (9, 5, 11, 13–14). Whereas in the novel, Celestina composes this poem to mark her "despondency over having lost, as she thinks, the love of George Willoughby" (*Poems*, 45, n. to Sonnet 49), in the *Sonnets* this poem resonates most clearly with Sonnet XXIV, "By the same [Werter]," in which Werter imagines the effect his death will have on Lotte/Charlotte: "Yes—CHARLOTTE o'er the mournful spot shall weep, / Where her poor WERTER—and his sorrows sleep!" (13–14). The speaker of Sonnet XLIX substitutes an existing corpse for her own projected one, but the scenario is the same: the bereft lover lingers over the grave of the deceased, remembering. The auditor in this poem, the dead woman, is enlivened by the aware reader, who knows *Sonnets*-style despair when she/he reads it. The familiarity of the scene begins to undercut its pathos—this is, after all, Sonnet

---

36    Robinson, 190.

37    From the first to the eighth edition, this sonnet, and the four following, are entitled "From the novel of Celestina" and "From the same." From the ninth edition on, Smith switches to the titles noted in my discussion of the poems.

XLIX, but little has changed since Sonnet XXIV. The stagnation in sentiment is slightly relieved by a more adventurous poetic structure than that managed by the passive speaker discussed above—*abab baab bcbc dd*—which goes beyond simple repetition to suggest an inwardness and self-obsession expressed through rhyme. The structure is also provocative, simultaneously arranged in three quatrains and a couplet by rhyme, and in two quatrains and a sestet by punctuation, as if the speaker-poet is using poetry to explore competing articulations of selfhood.

In fact, all the Celestina sonnets exhibit structural innovations except Sonnet LIII: "The Laplander." Sonnet L, with its sorrowful "Farewel, ye lawns!—by fond remembrance blest,/ As witnesses of gay unclouded hours" (1–2), reflects the nostalgia of many of Smith's more clearly autobiographical sonnets to the river Arun and the South Downs, where she contrasts the happy "dear days" "when thoughtless joy, and infant hope were mine" with the "sense of pain" and "breaking heart" she now feels (Sonnet XXXI, 13; Sonnet XLV, 3; Sonnet V, 7, 8). Sonnet L's speaker, too, sets her past happiness in a specific landscape (glossed as "Alvestone, Willoughby's country seat" by Curran, 46, note) and uses her departure to signal her emotional loss. Her rhyme scheme, *abab bcbc dede ff*, falls back on the repetition of the passive speaker, but her structure utilizes the combination practiced in the previous sonnet. Sonnet LI: "Supposed to have been written in the Hebrides," recalls Smith's sonnets of longing addressed to or about her dead daughter Augusta: "I could with *thee* for months and years be blest; / And of thy tenderness and love possest, / Find all *my* world in this wild solitude."[38] Its rhyme scheme reflects the speaker's increasing torment—*abba caac dede ff*— and its structure innovates on that of the previous two sonnets by substituting an octave/sestet for the quatrain/quatrain/sestet arrangement.

The speaker thus continues to perform her anguish poetically, while Smith continues to exploit what Slinn calls poetry's "referential aberration" and its ability to "foreground constitutive language through intensive poetic devices."[39] Smith's deployment of rhyme and structure in the Celestina sonnets provides the key whereby we can interpret the drama the speaker performs. The speaker, having begun by declaiming over a grave and then moving through scenes of farewell and longing, now initiates a subjective split, imagining an "unhappy Pilgrim ... divided far from all he fondly loves, / [Who] Journeys alone, along the giddy height / Of these steep cliffs" (1, 3–5). The Pilgrim's situation anticipates that of the speakers of two later sonnets, an exception to the backward looking of the other sonnets but one which demonstrates Smith's interest in creating contrasting speakers who perform similar emotional states. Sonnet LII presents a figure imagined by the speaker who wanders alone through a December night and whose situation prompts the speaker to call herself "unblest" (11; a motif revisited in Sonnet LXII: "Written in passing by moonlight through a village, while the ground was covered with

---

[38]   As I discuss in *Charlotte Smith*, most of Smith's Augusta sonnets have a romantic, rather than a maternal tone. See chapter 2, "*Elegiac Sonnets* I: The Good Mother" (64–90).

[39]   Slinn, 66, 69.

snow," whose speaker is also "unblest" [1]).[40] The figure, on the "giddy height," "hears, with ear appall'd, the impetuous surge / Beneath him thunder!" (4, 8–9), even as the lunatic of the much-studied Sonnet LXX: "On being cautioned against walking on an headland overlooking the sea, because it was frequented by a lunatic" "views with wild and hollow eyes / Its distance from the waves that chide below" while the speaker positions herself "on the giddy brink" (3–4, 9). Although the rhyme scheme of Sonnet LII is fairly regular, it veers off towards the end (*abab cdcd efefef*). More importantly, in this poem the speaker-poet loses control over structure. The sonnet is one long sentence, divided by clauses into a 9-line segment, a 4-line segment, and a 2-line segment; line 9 ends and begins a segment. Further, lines 1, 8, 11, and 14 contain 12, 12, 11, and 12 syllables respectively. This moves beyond poetic innovation, which Smith supports, to poetic breakdown. Order is only restored, in Sonnet LIII: "The Laplander," through a complete loss of the speaker's subjectivity. Describing the Laplander, the poem recalls both Sonnet XLIII, "The unhappy exile" and Sonnet LIV, "The sleeping woodman. Written in April 1790,"[41] but unlike them it subsumes the speaker entirely to the figure: the "I" does not appear. Written *abab cdcd efef gg* in an octave/quatrain/couplet structure, the poem is mechanical, "perfect" like those of the passive speaker, but here Smith seems to be allowing the speaker to perform absence rather than presence. The speaker-poet thus dramatizes the ultimate despair, a complete loss of self, in a kind of poetic suicide. Smith does not forgo the "I" very often, and to do so here indicates her compositional distance from the poem's speaker, and the speaker's culpability.

## The Lyrical Ballads: Curious William

Where Smith creates speakers whose passive indulgence in their own sorrows she critiques through structure, Wordsworth often focuses on his personae's limitations as revealed through their overweening fascination with their own imaginative development. In turning to Wordsworth, one turns as well to layers of readerly assumptions and conclusions, such as that he is a poet who speaks truth, by which I mean both an emotional veracity and an historical one.[42] Once the "I" is introduced, it is an autobiographical "I," and although certain aspects of his personal past may

---

[40]   Sonnet LXII also originates in a novel, *The Old Manor House*, published two years after *Celestina*.

[41]   Since *Celestina* was published in 1791, this date seems almost pointedly to emphasize the continuity between Sonnets LIII and LIV.

[42]   See, for instance, Leon Guilhamet as quoted above; as he elaborates, for Wordsworth, poetry connects readers to "truth": the "real language of men" equates with the "real feelings of men" and "poetry, as communicator of feeling, is the humanizing quality in truth" (271–2, 274). It is important to re-emphasize that I am not arguing that Wordsworth never writes autobiographically; however, he destabilizes the "real" in the

be exaggerated, revisited, or otherwise retold, readers have mainly felt that to read, say, *Tintern Abbey* or *Nutting* was to gain insight into the true nature of the poet. If we approach these poems as dramatic monologues, however, which is strikingly easy to do—they have identifiable first-person speakers, they have an auditor, they have compromised speakers—then a new layer emerges, one of implicit critique and discomfort. We see this in the way that the speakers of *Tintern Abbey*, *Nutting*, and *Lines left upon a seat in a Yew-Tree* are odd, peculiar, and strange.

In his highly personalized poems *Yew-Tree*, *Nutting*, and *Tintern Abbey*, the meta-autobiographical illustrates the pitfalls of a concentration on Self and its development. Clearly, Wordsworth was exercised by the idea of poetic evolution, but as *Yew-Tree* shows, he was also cautious about the pitfalls associated with such a concentration on Self. In these poems Wordsworth develops a persona whose self-interest overrides the poetry to the point of estrangement from sense, clarity, and, especially, the reader, who is both appealed to and sealed off from the poetry. The "stranger" addressed by the speaker is less alien to the poem than the putatively autobiographical speaker. As Wordsworth noted when speaking of Robert Burns, the poet may "avail himself of his own character and situation in society, to construct out of them a poetic self—introduced as a dramatic personage—for the purpose of inspiriting his incidents, diversifying his pictures … and giving point to his sentiments."[43] To read these poems, then, as "meditation[s] upon the live tissue of the poet's own, genuine experience" is to miss that composing moments wherein a poet "gives birth to his sublime ego, his self as a poet" is as much a pose, a feint, in Sinfield's terms, as it is a "fact."[44] Wordsworth uses the familiarity of the voice, its resemblance to his own, to explore what it means to be self-conscious to the point of absurdity, where landscape, friends, poetry itself become merely outshoots of the poetic imagination.

Wordsworth tries out his persona of the self-obsessed speaker in *Lines left upon a Seat in a Yew-Tree*. Here, he distances his speaker from the poem's subject, but as many critics have pointed out, the poem pushes the idea of a resemblance between subject and speaker: "the speaker becomes that subject of whom he speaks.… The speaker and his subject are one divided self."[45] This is the secret as

---

poems I discuss when he allows his very "Wordsworthian" speakers to trip themselves up, unwittingly, through their sympathetic shortcomings.

[43]    *The Prose Works of William Wordsworth*, ed. W. J. B. Owen and Jane Worthington Smyser, 3 vols. (Oxford: Clarendon, 1974): 2:125. Quoted in Brooke Hopkins, "Wordsworth's Voices: Ideology and Self-Critique in *The Prelude*," *Studies in Romanticism* 33 (1994): 279n.2.

[44]    Jean Deurbergue, "Time, Space, and the Egotistical Sublime: The Unity of 'Tintern Abbey,'" *Bulletin de la Faculté des Lettres de Strasbourg* 47 (1969): 216. Although Deurbergue's stance may strike readers as outdated, it is worth comparing to Deborah Forbes's, quoted above.

[45]    Galperin, 76, 79. See also David Perkins, who views the poem as a self-parody: "One might say that he had composed his verse in distaste of the public and found further

recognized by the reader and as exposed inadvertently by the speaker. Reinstating the autobiographical, such approaches find meaning by projecting Wordsworth into his portrait of collapsed subjectivity. However, Wordsworth uses a displacement of subjectivity to achieve a combination of the subjective and the objective in this poem. The slippage that encourages the identification of speaker with subject allows him to dramatize estrangement; the repeated appeals to a "Stranger" further this effect, since the Stranger is both an auditor (the reader's stand-in) and an aspect of the speaker himself, an internalized audience of one witnessing the speaker's attempt to overcome his own attraction to isolation. Galperin sees this technique as part of Wordsworth's mythic self-creation: "the creation of a 'Poet' by creation of an Other in whose image the poetical self ... is simultaneously fashioned."[46] The poetical self in *Yew-Tree* is less than ideal, though certainly mythic. In true dramatic monologue fashion, the poem begins in mid-speech: "—Nay, Traveller! Rest" (1).[47] The auditor, compelled to stop, finds that his curiosity is assumed by the speaker, whose tale of "one who owned / No common soul" (12–13) anticipates Smith's picture of the clearly Wordsworthian figure in *Beachy Head*.[48] As he unfolds the story of the solipsist whose "unfruitful life" (29) is spent in resentment of an unappreciative world, he also composes a natural setting redolent of a Wordsworthian ethos: "he would gaze / On the more distant scene; how lovely 'tis / Thou seest, and he would gaze till it became / Far lovelier, and his heart could not sustain / The beauty still more beauteous" (30–34). Images like these recur, more forcefully, in both *Tintern Abbey* and *Nutting*, and it is in the confluence of the poems that its self-referentiality emerges. This speaker rehearses obsessions that Wordsworth then assigns to a personalized speaker in the other two poems: the recluse has special gifts "by genius nursed" (13); he intends to benefit the world with their dissemination, but meeting "jealousy and hate" (16) he turns inward, retreats to nature, and ends his days looking only and "ever on himself" (52).

On its own this poem is simply narrative, a moral tale cautioning against solipsism. Read in the context of the other two, however, its status as a tonic against the self-obsessions of *Tintern Abbey* and *Nutting* become apparent. When the speaker in *Tintern Abbey* recalls "evil tongues, / Rash judgments ... the

---

reason for distaste in the reception he encountered" (151). Mary Jacobus also sees the poem as self-projection in *Tradition and Experiment in Wordsworth's* Lyrical Ballads (Oxford: Clarendon, 1976).

[46]   Galperin, 67.

[47]   *Lyrical Ballads*, ed. R. L. Brett and A. R. Jones, 2nd ed. (London: Routledge, 1991). All quotations of Wordsworth's poems are from this edition. The resonances with "Nay, we'll go / Together down, sir" (*My Last Duchess*, 53–4) are telling; Browning, at least, seems to have picked up on the poem's inherent drama as well as its darkness.

[48]   Smith's portrait of the hermit who excites the curiosity of "tir'd hind[s]" and "peasant girls" reads like an elaboration on the story sketched by Wordsworth in *Lines* (see *Beachy Head*, 506–671). Smith's response to Wordsworth's mythmaking points to the self-reflexive nature of the poem, but it also demonstrates its dramatic tone.

sneers of selfish men, / ... greetings where no kindness is, [and] all / The dreary intercourse of daily life" (129–32), we are back in the world of *Yew-Tree*: "the taint/ Of dissolute tongues ... jealousy, and hate, / And scorn. . . . / [And] neglect" (15–18). Although more expansive and detailed, the nature that attracted and nurtured *Tintern*'s speaker is the same as that which nourishes and compensates *Yew-Tree*'s. Indeed, the poetic sensibility that the speaker unfolds in *Yew-Tree* *is* "Wordsworthian," barring the "rash disdain" (19) that the more securely Wordsworthian speaker carefully avoids indulging in. *Yew-Tree* acts as a kind of "note to Self," where the Self addressed is the dramatized Poet whose obsessions with recognition and appreciation overcome his more attractive traits of skilled natural observation and sharp poetic style. As with Smith, this is partly revealed at the level of compositional structure; when the speaker writes "what if here / No sparkling rivulet spread the verdant herb" (2–3) we are reminded of all the waters that "murmur" elsewhere in Wordsworth's poetry, and when he ponders "What if these barren boughs the bee not loves" (4) we balk at the awkward phrasing of the line. By displacing his potential for total isolation onto the recluse in *Yew Tree*, but simultaneously revealing his sympathy for and identification with his doppelgänger, the speaker inadvertently dramatizes his alliance with, rather than difference from, the recluse. The reproach of the poem's last stanza as self-directed is clarified if we turn briefly to *Lines written in early spring*, where the speaker's refrain "Have I not reason to lament / What man has made of man?" (23–4) and the poem's overall tone of despairing contempt suggest that the speaker of this *Lines* and the recluse of *Yew-Tree* are the same—and hence the speaker of *Yew-Tree* is also one with them.

The self-estrangement of *Yew-Tree*, and its picture of the Poet as a curiosity to be observed, reverberates in *Tintern Abbey*. Here, the coherence and conviction of the Poet's self-representation mask what is, in effect, an enactment of the estrangement infecting *Yew-Tree*. Despite the many and varied ways in which the poem has been associated with Wordsworth's own personal and poetical development, it nonetheless figures as one of the most perfectly formed of Wordsworth's dramatic monologues, especially if one reads something like *Yew-Tree* as an entr'acte. Forbes's need to discount *Tintern* as a dramatic monologue and reinstate the sincere in order to avoid reducing the poem to the "laughable"[49] ironically enough points to the deep significance of the poem's dramatizing of poetic sensibility. Similarly, Richard J. Onorato's insistence that, "despite the seemingly dramatic utterance of [*Tintern Abbey*], the poet [plainly] does not pretend to know more than his 'character' says" illustrates the strength of the character inhabiting the poem.[50] Whereas the speaker in a Victorian dramatic monologue is, mainly, separate from and unlike the author (*In Memoriam* would serve as a notable exception), Wordsworth's version constructs a speaker who is, vitally, both Self and Other: an

---

[49] Forbes, 85.

[50] See *The Character of the Poet: Wordsworth in* The Prelude (Princeton: Princeton University Press, 1971), 29.

Other dependent on aspects of the Self who writes the poem, but who is estranged from the sincere and authentic. In *Tintern*, the Romantic dramatic monologue is uttered by a speaker who functions as a dramatized Self: who is, therefore, not Wordsworth but the Poet, pulled back from the despair of *Yew-Tree* by the presence of a distinct auditor, the Sister.

Wordsworth's contention that he composed the poem extempore during a walking tour and that "not a line of it was altered, and not any part written down til I reached Bristol" is frequently quoted as evidence of the poem's authenticity; Gill's response is typical: this account is "clearly essentially correct."[51] However, Wordsworth's statement of the poem's composition history is no more than that, an assertion. Setting the desire to read the poem autobiographically aside, its use of autobiography to underpin the drama infuses the poem with performative import. As the poem opens, the scene is set in the first twenty-three lines: the famous "steep and lofty cliffs," the spreading prospect, the deliberately pastoral vista. As the second verse-paragraph opens, the speaker shifts to the drama of the Self: his visceral connection to scenes of natural beauty, his reliance on "feelings ... / Of unremembered pleasure" and "that serene and blessed mood" in which he "become[s] a living soul" (31–2, 46). By the third verse-paragraph, the speaker begins to declaim, voicing a soliloquy derived from "the picture of the mind" (62): a theatrical phrase by which Wordsworth indicates the speaker's pose. The conversational tone of "I cannot paint / What then I was" (76–7) and the self-delusion that allows the speaker to convince himself that "other gifts / Have followed" the loss of "aching joys" and "dizzy raptures" (87–8, 85, 86) further contribute to the poem's presentation of a dramatized speaker. The poet who here constructs a world in which the present is always better than the past, and for whom obscurity—both in phrasing and in his own self-conception—is always preferable to plain speaking, is as peculiar as the recluse in *Yew-Tree*.[52] Further, his auditor is completely subsumed to the picture the speaker paints of himself as idealized poet. This speaker-poet cannot see beyond his own conception of the world of psychological growth, and therefore his auditor becomes merely a representation of his former self. Self-obsession means that the poet sees only himself, and by locating, in the final verse-paragraph, his disturbed past and possible unpleasant future in his sister, he is able to recast what had been "hours of weariness" (28) as "[un]disturb[ed] ... chearful faith" (133–4).

---

[51]    Stephen Gill, *William Wordsworth, A Life* (Oxford: Clarendon Press, 1989), 692. Gill situates *Tintern Abbey* as one of "Wordsworth's greatest autobiographical poems," which "seizes imperiously on the 'facts,' to forge a poetic fiction with which to convey essential truth" (152).

[52]    Forbes argues, following Galperin, that doubt is the element that threatens to disable the poem, but that Wordsworth abandons this, thus showing the sincerity of doubt. However, by composing a dramatic monologue, Wordsworth avoids the awkwardness of introducing, only to abandon, a key trope; instead, the uncertainty regarding doubt functions as another way in which his obsessed speaker exposes his own limitations.

The "impression of spontaneity" the poem creates, and that Wordsworth encourages in the Fenwick note, is not borne out by the "abstract, polysyllabic, orotund, and, in short, successfully dignified and emphatic" diction Perkins also notes.[53] Dignified and emphatic as it is, the diction of the poem, its deliberately obscure and mysterious phrases, its uncertain tone, and its unaware theatricalisms are the product of a speaker whose need to be poetic by being a Poet overwhelms his ability to "speak to men" using their language. Instead, we get a picture of the Romantic Poet as peculiarly self-obsessed, the subject of the strolling minstrel described by Pascoe (196 *passim*). Where *Yew-Tree*'s speaker enacts despair, *Tintern*'s exults, having been supplied with an auditor whose vulnerability supplies what *Yew-Tree* lacks: a sympathetic audience. And where *Tintern Abbey* provides the drama of the self-obsessed Poet, *Nutting* supplies his backstory. By installing both a present and a past "Self" in *Nutting*, Wordsworth emphasizes the speaker's concentration on his own needs and desires. *Nutting* uses memory to suggest that the self-obsessed speaker feels curiosity only about his own poetic development; the philosophy of the last few lines shows, not insight, but blindness. The theatricality of the poem almost disguises its import as a dramatic monologue; Wordsworth grants the speaker a kind of self-awareness but disables it almost immediately in the pride and complacency with which the speaker reviews his past: "a Figure quaint," "my frugal Dame," "more ragged than need was," "I forc'd my way" (7, 10, 13, 14). The sensual scene that excites the man lost in memory, his "voluptuous" enjoyment of its luxuries, and the inevitable violence of his destruction of the bower contribute to the making of a Poet for whom everything, especially pliant Nature, exists to forward his own poetic project. Wordsworth embeds in the poem allusions to his other key dramatic monologues: the "temper known to those, who, after long / And weary expectation, have been bless'd / With sudden happiness beyond all hope" (26–8) which reverses the gloom of the recluse in *Yew-Tree*; "the violets of five seasons" and "fairy water-breaks [that] do murmur" (30, 32), which recall the opening lines of *Tintern Abbey*; the conflation of "my present feelings with the past," the "sense of pain," and the "Spirit in the woods," which also invoke *Tintern*.

The poems are linked via allusion, the speaker revealed to be the same, and the concerns identical: how does the Poet justify his ways to men? Ferguson describes "the perceptions and the language which repeatedly construct narrative roles for Wordsworth," and calls *Nutting* a "drama, a rewritten romance" with a "script" that Wordsworth "self-consciously follow[s] … until experience no longer matches" (75). But this seems to be exactly what needs to happen; the speaker must follow a script until thrown off-guard, and then must expose his inability to submit to his experience, and instead must attempt to conquer it. To suggest that *Wordsworth* both writes the poem and is unable to master its deviations from a "script" is to say that he is at the mercy of his poetry, that *it* writes *him*. Rather, the speaker of this dramatic monologue fails to appreciate the ramifications

---

[53]    Perkins, 210, 206.

of his concentration on Self, and so his closing turn to the hitherto invisible auditor resonates with self-absorption and shallow mystification: "Then, dearest Maiden! move along these shades / In gentleness of heart; with gentle hand / Touch,— for there is a Spirit in the woods" (53–5). Unwilling to sustain this turn away from the Self, the speaker unsurprisingly puts a halt to the Maiden's progress and abruptly concludes the poem. As with *Yew Tree* and *Tintern*, Wordsworth writes *Nutting* obscurely, using a diction reliant on metaphor and repetition, and while such a style is effective individually—that is, critics can make much of "a sense sublime / Of something far more deeply interfused" (*Tintern*, 96–7) or "a sense of pain" (*Nutting*, 51) or "his heart could not sustain / The beauty still more beauteous" (*Yew-Tree*, 34–5)—when read as a group the images begin to lose their potency. They begin to sound like the images a poet would use who is trying to display his poetical talents, who is asserting, through diction, his artistic depth. They transform the individually autobiographical to the meta-autobiographical, and they suggest that for Wordsworth, as for Smith, poetry is performative because it is poetry that allows for the construction, and consequent undermining, of inadequate types of poetic subjectivity.

## What is a Poet?

Brooke Hopkins has said that the opening lines of *The Prelude* offer "a perfect version of Keats's 'egotistical sublime,' except that … the passage tends to expose rather than indulge in it."[54] This is a key distinction. Keats, a perceptive reader of poetry, recognizes that Wordsworth is doing something out of the ordinary in his poetry of the Self, but perhaps because the Poet-figure that Wordsworth creates is so coherent; or perhaps because, even by 1818, Keats as a reader has an expectation of what constitutes the "wordsworthian"; whatever the reason, the plausibility of the self-obsessed Poet overtakes the hints at his constructedness. Smith, too, is a victim of her own success; the personalities of the *Sonnets* became subsumed into the one figure most visible to her readers: Smith herself. The performative technique that each poet develops relies on an active readership, rather than a passive one: a readership that reads to learn through analysis and thought. As Slinn puts it:

> Poetry . . . depends upon a form of double utterance, by both poet and reader.... [And] if it is to function as critique by foregrounding its verbal activity, it requires a reader actively to realize that, not just by registering its eloquence or illocutionary effect, but by (re)enacting its full discursive process--the whole complex of the poetic act. This [is a] readerly act … of analysis and understanding

---

[54]     Hopkins, "Wordsworth's Voices: Ideology and Self-Critique in *The Prelude*," *Studies in Romanticism* 33 (1994): 297.

as well as enunciation.... [and] requires close analysis of formalist as well as thematic features.[55]

Reading Smith's and Wordsworth "autobiographical" poetry closely loosens the tie between author and speaker until the autobiographical becomes the feint on which the poet can base her or his dramatic monologue. And having untied the biographical knot, both poets can explore the possibilities poetry offers for a knowing exploration of dramatized selfhoods.

Smith and Wordsworth use poetry to establish the subjective nature of the speaking "I" because both recognize that poetry only pretends to be natural; both, in other words, comprehend the inherent insincerity of sincere writing, the basic artifice of the authentic. Exploiting the artificial nature of poetry, they respond to as well as contribute to the late eighteenth-century desire for public displays of subjectivity: Smith takes the sonnet forward from the pathos introduced by Gray, for instance, and Wordsworth tells tales in *Lyrical Ballads*: an anticipation of Mary Robinson's more overt style in her 1800 *Lyrical Tales*. Their shorter poems, then, act as tasters, as previews to the more complex interweaving of subjectivities they later pursue. *Beachy Head* and *The Prelude* will refine the dramatic monologue, developing a more nuanced interplay between artifice and subjectivity. Self-exposure, in the Romantic dramatic monologue, is not about exposing the Self through autobiography (Forbes's "uniquely authentic self-expression"), nor does it provide "an example in living, an engagement of the whole being of the poet—his imagination, but also his conscience and his intellect—in the whole of his experience."[56] Smith and Wordsworth are both more complex than this. Striving for authenticity, or using poetry to develop a philosophy of life—these, they show, are the concerns of self-conscious, self-identified "Poets," whose egos provide the most fertile ground for growing poetry, whose spontaneous overflows are caught and preserved but not cultivated. Instead, Smith and Wordsworth are engaged in exploring the ramifications of self-exposure; they use poetry exactly because its form allows for experimentation. As they innovate at the level of structure, they demonstrate the vital link between formal concerns and the creation of the voice of the poet. Theirs are experiments with Selfhood as well as with structure. To call the subjectivities on view in their dramatic monologues mere examples of the egotistical sublime, then, is to misread one of the most vital contributions of Smith and Wordsworth to the development of Romanticism: their understanding that poetry, written well, performs Selfhood rather than reflecting Self.

---

[55]   Slinn, 71.

[56]   Forbes, 10; Perkins, 111.

## Works Cited

Barrell, John. *Imagining the King's Death: Figurative Treason, Fantasies of Regicide*, 1793–1796. Oxford: Oxford University Press, 2000.

Brock, Claire. "'Then Smile and Know Thyself Supremely Great': Mary Robinson and the 'Splendour of a Name.'" *Women's Writing* 9 (2002): 107–24.

*The Collected Letters of Charlotte Smith*. Ed. Judith Phillips Stanton. Bloomington: Indiana University Press, 2003.

Craciun, Adriana. *Fatal Women of Romanticism*. Cambridge: Cambridge University Press, 2003.

Deurbergue, Jean. "Time, Space, and the Egotistical Sublime: The Unity of 'Tintern Abbey.'" *Bulletin de la Faculté des Lettres de Strasbourg* 47 (1969): 203–16.

Fay, Elizabeth. *Becoming Wordsworthian: A Performative Aesthetics*. Amherst: University of Massachusetts Press, 1995.

Ferguson, Frances. *Wordsworth: Language as Counter-Spirit*. New Haven: Yale University Press, 1977.

Forbes, Deborah. *Sincerity's Shadow: Self-Consciousness in British Romantic and Mid-Twentieth-Century American Poetry*. Cambridge: Harvard University Press, 2004.

Fulford, Tim. "The Electrifying Mrs. Robinson." *Women's Writing* 9 (2002): 23–35.

Galperin, William. *Revision and Authority in Wordsworth: The Interpretation of a Career*. Philadelphia: University of Pennsylvania Press, 1989.

Gill, Stephen. *William Wordsworth, A Life*. Oxford: Clarendon Press, 1989.

Guilhamet, Leon. The *Sincere Ideal: Studies on Sincerity in Eighteenth Century English Literature*. Montreal: McGill-Queen's University Press, 1974.

Harty, E. R. "Voice and Enunciation in the Dramatic Monologue and the Lyric." *Unisa English Studies* 28 (1990): 279–99.

Hopkins, Brooke. "Wordsworth's Voices: Ideology and Self-Critique in The Prelude." *Studies in Romanticism* 33 (1994): 279–99.

Jacobus, Mary. *Tradition and Experiment in Wordsworth's Lyrical Ballads*. Oxford: Clarendon, 1976.

Kearns, Sheila. *Coleridge, Wordsworth, and Romantic Autobiography: Reading Strategies of Self-Representation*. Madison: Fairleigh Dickinson University Press, 1995.

Labbe, Jacqueline. "The Seductions of Form in the Poetry of Ann Batten Cristall and Charlotte Smith." In *Romanticism and Form*. Ed. Alan Rawes. Basingstoke: Palgrave Macmillan, 2007. 154–70.

—. "Gentility in Distress: A New Letter by Charlotte Smith (1749–1806)." *The Wordsworth Circle* 35 (2004): 91–3.

—. Charlotte Smith. *Romanticism, Poetry and the Culture of Gender*. Manchester: Manchester University Press, 2003.

Langbaum, Robert. *The Poetry of Experience: The Dramatic Monologue in Modern Literary Experience*. London: Chatto and Windus, 1957.

*Lyrical Ballads*. Ed. R. L. Brett and A. R. Jones. 2nd ed. London: Routledge, 1991.

Onorato, Richard. J. *The Character of the Poet: Wordsworth in The Prelude*. Princeton: Princeton University Press, 1971.

Parrish, Stephen. *The Art of the Lyrical Ballads*. Cambridge: Harvard University Press, 1973.

Pascoe, Judith. *Romantic Theatricality: Gender, Poetry and Spectatorship*. Ithaca: Cornell University Press, 1997.

Perkins, David. *Wordsworth and the Poetry of Sincerity*. Cambridge: The Belknap Press of Harvard University Press, 1964.

*The Poems of Charlotte Smith*. Ed. Stuart Curran. Oxford: Oxford University Press, 1993.

*The Prose Works of William Wordsworth*. Ed. W. J. B. Owen and Jane Worthington Smyser. 3 vols. Oxford: Clarendon, 1974.

Robinson, Daniel. "Elegiac Sonnets: Charlotte Smith's Formal Paradoxy." *Papers on Language and Literature* 39 (2003): 185–220.

*Selected Poems and Letters by John Keats*. Ed. Douglas Bush. Boston: Houghton Mifflin, 1959.

Sinfield, Alan. *The Dramatic Monologue*. London: Methuen, 1977.

Slinn, E. Warwick. "Poetry and Culture: Performativity and Critique." *New Literary History* 30 (1999): 57–74.

Trilling, Lionel. *Sincerity and Authenticity*. London: Oxford University Press, 1972.

Wood, Gillen D'Arcy. *The Shock of the Real: Romanticism and Visual Culture, 1760–1860*. New York: Palgrave, 2001.

## Chapter 2
# Coleridge and Robinson:
# Harping on Lyrical Exchange

Ashley Cross

In an early part of her *Memoirs*, Mary Robinson bemoans her state as she reflects on her ability to commune with nature: "Unquestionably the Creator formed me with a strong propensity to adore the sublime and beautiful of his works! But it has never been my lot to meet with an associating mind, a congenial spirit, who could (as it were abstracted from the world) find an universe in the sacred intercourse of the soul, the sublime union of sensibility."[1] Robinson had begun her *Memoirs* in 1798, already in ailing health, as one of the many efforts she made in the last years of the 1790s to solidify a reputation for herself as a Romantic writer. Though she never completed these *Memoirs* before her death (she only got as far as her affair with the Prince of Wales; her daughter finished them), they reveal a writer intent on creating sympathy for herself as a victim of a "too acute sensibility" who turned to "literary labor" at first as a means of survival.[2] Her claim never to have found "an associating mind" appears a bit disingenuous, however—another one of Robinson's gestures at representing herself, as other poets were increasingly doing, as an original and tormented Genius; for as early as 1797, Robinson had begun an exchange with another figure who functioned in many ways as the sort of "congenial spirit" she sought: Samuel Taylor Coleridge.[3] Their individual

---

[1]    Mary Robinson, *Memoirs of the Late Mrs. Robinson, Written by Herself*, ed. Maria E. Robinson (London: R. Phillips, 1801), 1:142.

[2]    Ibid., 1:12, 1:184.

[3]    In her recent and otherwise excellent biography, Paula Byrne suggests that Coleridge and Robinson met as early as 1796 at a dinner at Godwin's (*Perdita: The Literary, Theatrical, Scandalous Life of Mary Robinson* [New York: Random House, 2004], 321). Byrne bases her argument on two entries, dated 25 February and 4 March 1796, in William Godwin's unpublished diaries. It has since been pointed out by Adam Sisman and Pamela Clemit that a meeting between Coleridge and Robinson at this time is an impossibility. Clemit identifies the C, in Godwin's entry, "Sup at Mrs. Robinson's with C," not as Coleridge but as Thomas Abthorpe Cooper. Coleridge and Godwin met first at Thomas Holcroft's on 21 December 1794, but not again until 30 November 1799. The pair had tea with Robinson on 15 January 1800 for the first time (Clemit). See Adam Sisman, "Coleridge, Mary (Perdita) Robinson, and 'Kubla Khan,'" *The Friends of Coleridge* (*TLS*—Letters, 2 December 2004), <http://www.friendsofcoleridge.com/Kubla Khan.htm> (accessed 24 September 2005), and Pamela Clemit, "Coleridge, Godwin and Mary Robinson: The Identity of 'C,'" *The*

poems and poems to each other were being regularly published in *The Morning Post*. And on 15 January 1800, when Robinson was poetry editor of *The Morning Post*, Robinson and Coleridge finally met. During that year, Robinson's last, they exchanged several poems and letters and shared an interest in opium-induced reverie, parenting, and a desire for poetic reputation (and perhaps even a mixed admiration, envy, and competitiveness with William Wordsworth).[4] Coleridge went on to be one of Robinson's biggest supporters after her death.[5]

Much has been said in recent criticism about Coleridge's and Robinson's explicit poetic exchanges written during their time at *The Morning Post*, especially Robinson's response to Coleridge's *Kubla Khan* in her poem *To the Poet Coleridge* and Coleridge's *A Stranger Minstrel*, written to Robinson just before her death at the end of 1800.[6] Much less has been said about the poems written to each other at the end of 1797 and earlier ones (especially from 1796) that reflect their similar perspectives. In this article, I will focus on several of these earlier poems in order to reveal Coleridge's and Robinson's intricate relations of exchange and debt at the beginning of their relationship and perhaps even before, in the initial stages

---

*Friends of Coleridge* (*TLS*—Letters, 18 February 2005), <http://www.friendsofcoleridge. com/TLS2.htm> (accessed 24 September 2005).

[4]    See Daniel Robinson, "From 'Mingled Measure' to 'Ecstatic Measures': Mary Robinson's Poetic Reading of 'Kubla Khan,'" *The Wordsworth Circle* 26.1 (Winter 1995): 4–7. Robinson's and Coleridge's explicit poetic exchange includes Coleridge's *Apotheosis* in response to Robinson's *Ode to the Snow-drop*; Robinson's *To the Poet Coleridge* in response to *Kubla Khan*; Coleridge's *A Stranger Minstrel*, *Alcaeus to Sappho*, and *The Mad Monk*; Robinson's *Ode Inscribed to the Infant Son of S. T. Coleridge* and *Jasper*; Robinson's *The Haunted Beach* in response to Coleridge's *Rime of the Ancient Mariner.*

[5]    See Coleridge's letter to Southey about including Robinson's work in the *Annual Anthology* (25 January 1800, *The Collected Letters of Samuel Taylor Coleridge*, ed. Earl Leslie Griggs, 6 vols. [Oxford: Clarendon Press, 1956], 1:562–4) and his letter to Robinson's daughter, Maria (27 December 1802, *Collected Letters*, 2:903–6).

[6]    See especially Betsy Bolton, "Romancing the Stone: 'Perdita' Robinson in Wordsworth's London," *ELH* 64 (1997): 727–59; Stuart Curran, "Mary Robinson's *Lyrical Tales* in Context," *Re-Visioning Romanticism: British Women Writers, 1776–1837*, ed. Carol Shiner Wilson and Joel Haefner (Philadelphia: University of Pennsylvania Press, 1994), 17–35; Tim Fulford, "Mary Robinson and the Abyssinian Maid: Coleridge's Muses and Feminist Criticism." *Romanticism on the Net* 13 (February 1999), <http://users.ox.ac. uk/~scat0385/kublarobinson.html> (accessed 25 August 1999) and *Romanticism and Masculinity: Gender, Politics, and Poetics in the Writing of Burke, Coleridge, Cobbett, Wordsworth, DeQuincey, and Hazlitt* (New York: Palgrave, 1999), 66–128, especially 112–24; Susan Luther, "A Stranger Minstrel: Coleridge's Mrs. Robinson," *Studies in Romanticism* 33 (1994): 391–409; Kathryn Ledbetter, "A Woman of Undoubted Genius: Mary Robinson and S. T. Coleridge," *Postscript* 11.1 (1994): 43–9; Judith Pascoe, "Mary Robinson and the Literary Marketplace," in *Romantic Women Writers: Voices and Countervoices*, ed. Paula R. Feldman and Theresa M. Kelley (Hanover: University Press of New England, 1995), 252–68; Daniel Robinson; and Lisa Vargo, "The Claims of 'real life and manners': Coleridge and Mary Robinson," *The Wordsworth Circle* 26 (Summer 1995): 134–7.

of their awareness of each other as important poets. As I have argued elsewhere, these complicated relations of debt permeate their whole relationship.[7] Here, I will closely analyze the explicit poetic exchange—the conversation—between Robinson and Coleridge in their snowdrop poems (Robinson's *Ode to the Snow-drop* and Coleridge's *The Apotheosis; or, The Snow-drop*) and trace the imagery of these reciprocal works to a group of their thematically-linked poems from the 1790s that suggest an implicit earlier exchange as well as a parallel poetic development. The overt dialogue of the snowdrop poems thus becomes the means for opening up these less-noticed earlier poems so that their conventional imagery—flower, Chatterton (who came to symbolize misunderstood genius for the Romantic poets), the eolian harp, and nightingale—resonates more deeply as a dialogue about poetic authority. These images appealed to Robinson and Coleridge as poets trying to establish their reputations. On the one hand, using such traditional imagery situates them clearly within the dominant literary tradition, stretching back to the Greeks. On the other hand, these particular images are especially enabling for Robinson, who was trying to overcome her earlier reputation as the Prince of Wales's mistress, and Coleridge, who was just beginning his career. Whereas the flower and Chatterton images privilege the weak and socially marginalized with whom Robinson and Coleridge identified, the eolian harp and nightingale images suggest that poetry derives from an unconscious, external but natural source that especially sensitive individuals could access by surrendering themselves. In analyzing their parallel imagery comparatively in these earlier poems, in particular those of 1796, I hope to show that Robinson and Coleridge share a similar anxiety about their poetic authority and are more invested in each other's poetry, at an earlier point in time, than has thus far been argued.

Building on recent criticism that foregrounds their mutual responsiveness to one another, I contend that Robinson's and Coleridge's exchange of poetry and ideas reveals two poets working in tandem to bolster their own and each other's reputation. These goals are mutually inclusive, not exclusive of one another. While they did enjoy a "newspaper flirtation," as David Erdman has called it, that grew into a serious poetic relationship at the end of Robinson's life, they were also highly aware of each other as increasingly prominent poets, even before they worked together at *The Morning Post*. Their relationship was certainly ambivalent throughout but especially in its earlier stages as each was asserting his/her poetic authority in the wake of the Della Cruscan literary phenomenon but before *Lyrical Ballads* appeared as the defining Romantic text. Moreover, neither writer responds to the other's work outside of his or her own poetic self-interest. Nonetheless, Coleridge and Robinson saw each other as poets worthy of attention because of their similar poetic and political sensibilities. They shared, at least momentarily, what Robinson calls "the sacred intercourse of the soul, the sublime union of sensibility" in their poetic exchanges. In its bridging of traditionally gendered

---

7    Ashley Cross, "From *Lyrical Ballads* to *Lyrical Tales*: Mary Robinson's Reputation and the Problem of Literary Debt," *Studies in Romanticism* 40 (2001): 547–70.

Burkean aesthetic categories, that "sublime union of sensibility" might also be called, in Coleridge's words, a form of the "androgynous mind."[8] In the poems I examine below, the eolian harp, and its associations with a series of other poetic figures (the flower, the misunderstood poetic genius, and the nightingale), becomes the figure for this lyrical exchange. For both Robinson and Coleridge, poetry is inspired by strong emotion that develops when one surrenders oneself to the powerful forces within and outside oneself, a submission to the other either in the form of nature or another person of similar sensibility that, paradoxically, authorizes the poet.

Recent criticism has begun to articulate the complexity of Robinson's and Coleridge's relationship and to stress the mutuality of their interactions. While Coleridge may have made the first overt move in this exchange, hoping for a Jacobin ally to enhance his public voice (Vargo) and a less threatening colleague than Wordsworth had become (Fulford), he was soon confronted by the intensity of Robinson's responses. Robinson was an adept player of the literary reputation game, making gestures that appear worshipful at the same time as they foreground her own poetic authority.[9] As Susan Luther points out, on first glance the congratulatory nature of many of these poems makes Coleridge appear as Robinson's gallant, while Robinson seems to act as a heroine of sensibility. But a deeper reading of the poems reveals a more complex situation behind their mutual congratulation, a relationship that involves both nurture and self-interest, both other-investment and self-authorizing. Though Robinson and Coleridge appear to play out traditional gender roles in the snowdrop poems, in fact Robinson's and Coleridge's complex dynamic reveals a lyrical exchange that is enhanced by gender difference, rather than inhibited by it, as close perhaps as it was possible to come to intellectual equality across gender at that time.[10]

Reading Robinson's and Coleridge's relationship as a mutually enhancing exploration of gender categories and poetic reputation depends on recognizing an important shift in the critical understanding of Coleridge's relationship to

---

[8]     1 September 1832, *Specimens of the Table Talk of S. T. Coleridge*, ed. Henry N. Coleridge (London: J. Murray, 1835), 146 (Project Gutenberg), Ebook #8489, <ftp://ibiblio. org/pub/docs/books/gutenberg/etext05/8tabc10.txt> (accessed July 2005).

[9]     See, for example, Robinson's metrical and content revisions of "Kubla Khan" and *Lyrical Ballads*.

[10]    Both Luther and Tim Fulford persuasively argue that Robinson and Coleridge are working out their own specifically gendered anxieties about writing. Their arguments suggest that Robinson and Coleridge used each other to redefine their gendered poetic roles—for Robinson, this meant escaping the role of beautiful object and valorizing her lyric voice apart from her personal history (Luther, 396–7); for Coleridge, this meant figuring out how to negotiate those feminine elements that challenged the traditional Burkean concept of masculinity as raw power (Luther, 408; Fulford, "Mary Robinson and the Abyssinian Maid"). My focus here is on their mutual interest in reconfiguring conventional poetic figures to create an image of the poet figure whose receptivity combines sensibility and sublimity.

women generally, and to women writers in particular, a shift that corresponds to a movement in Romantic studies away from the idea of separate, gendered Romanticisms. While earlier critics emphasized Coleridge's failure to find a female equivalent despite his admiration of women (Jackson), his trivializing of the feminine (Ellison), or his usurpation of female procreative power (Mellor), more recently critics have stressed Coleridge's engagement with women intellectuals, like Mary Wollstonecraft, Mary Shelley, and others, as well as his ability to listen to them (Taylor) and to consider the alternatives they might offer to traditional models of masculinity (Fulford).[11] As Fulford argues in "Mary Robinson and the Abyssinian Maid: Coleridge's Muses and Feminist Criticism" and in *Romanticism and Masculinity*, though Coleridge is finally unable to sustain an alternative to the gendered roles of chivalry and sensibility, he "opens gender roles and gendered poetics to question."[12] Given Coleridge's investment in "dialogue as an arena for recognizing the Other," as Anya Taylor has shown, it seems worth considering how his specific dialogue with Robinson, a woman writer whose plight evokes his sympathy and whose profession attracts his praise, might offer an alternative model of literary relations between male and female Romantic writers.[13]

This reading also requires thinking about Robinson's position differently as well. It means recognizing her prior authority and fame, but also her insecurity about the basis for that fame because of her theatrical and sexual history. Though she often underscores her feminine difference in poems written in exchange with Coleridge, Robinson, already a well-known writer in the late 1790s, writes with an authority that disrupts the traditional gender pattern of female writers trying to make their way in a male-dominated market. She sees her femaleness as giving her special status in that feminine experience provides the basis for sensibility, but she also is a staunch Wollestonecraftian, who believes in male and female equality. The trajectory of her career does not fit the model of feminine and masculine Romanticism that Anne Mellor posits in *Romanticism and Gender*. Nor does she fit the model of the poetess. Though she began as a Della Cruscan, she ended her career as a Romantic poet who saw herself as able to help the careers of the young Wordsworth and Coleridge. Her interactions with Coleridge are thus

---

[11]    H. J. Jackson, "Coleridge's Women, or Girls, Girls, Girls Are Made to Love," *Studies in Romanticism* 32 (1993): 577–600; Julie Ellison, *Delicate Subjects: Romanticism, Gender, and the Ethics of Understanding* (Ithaca: Cornell University Press, 1990); Anne K. Mellor, *Romanticism and Gender* (New York: Routledge, 1993); Anya Taylor, "Coleridge on Persons in Dialogue," *Modern Language Quarterly* 50 (1989): 357–74, "Coleridge, Wollstonecraft, and the Rights of Woman," in *Coleridge's Visionary Languages: Essays in Honour of J. B. Beer*, ed. Tim Fulford and Morton D. Paley (Cambridge: D. S. Brewer, 1993), 83–98, and *Erotic Coleridge* (New York: Palgrave Macmillan, 2005); and Fulford, *Romanticism and Masculinity.*

[12]    Fulford, "Mary Robinson and the Abyssinian Maid: Coleridge's Muses and Feminist Criticism."

[13]    Taylor, "Coleridge on Persons in Dialogue," 366–7.

aggressively confident, self-promoting, and respectful, an assertion of both her gender difference and her equality.

One of Coleridge's and Robinson's earliest explicit poetic exchanges occurs in their snowdrop poems, which employ the conventional poetic image of the flower for its associations with the victimized female and with poetry.[14] This double association made the flower an especially evocative image for articulating anxiety about poetic authority. As a figure of the weak, oppressed, and socially marginalized, this image not only evokes the empathy for the other that both Robinson and Coleridge saw as essential to their poetry; it also embodies their awareness of poetic reputation's fragility. Both poets saw a means of asserting their poetic authority through an emotional identification with the victim. Coleridge's *The Apotheosis; or the Snow-drop* (3 January 1798, *Morning Post*) directly takes up Robinson's *Ode to the Snow-drop* (26 December 1797, *Morning Post*), a fairly simple poem that ends with Robinson's somewhat maudlin (and misleading) identification of her state with that of the frail snowdrop, which "awakes to life, bedew'd with tears" and "trembles, while the ruthless wind / Bends its slim form."[15] Making an analogy between female and flower that goes back to the Greeks and to Petrarch, Robinson's poem represents the snowdrop as a tormented but pure innocent who struggles to survive under harsh conditions and dies "unshelter'd and unknown" as the "*rival*" and "gaudy *Crocus* flaunts its pride" (23, 22, 21). With only a rival and no sympathizing other, the snowdrop remains unrecognized, but in the final stanza Robinson, as the speaker, gives the snowdrop the empathetic recognition it has lacked. In so doing, she asserts her own need for recognition, as well as her power to bestow recognition on an "unknown." In this light, the words "rival" and "unknown" are especially significant; they layer the narrative of fragile woman with a literary narrative that reveals Robinson's anxiety about her own reputation and, in a sense, opens the door for Coleridge's poem. Up against prideful rivals—conservative writers like William Gifford or Richard Polwhele, who sought to destroy Robinson's authority as a writer—she remains unknown, but as she has written a poem for the snowdrop, she has set up the situation for a poem to be written for her, an exchange that might produce the sympathetic connection to the other that will affirm her poetic authority.

Significantly, Robinson's *Ode to the Snow-drop* first appeared in her novel *Walsingham* (1797) as a poem written by the eponymous protagonist. The poem

---

[14]     Michael Ferber suggests in *The Dictionary of Literary Symbols* (Cambridge: Cambridge University Press, 1999) that it is the Romantic poets who take the traditional association of the flower with a selection or "bouquet" of poems and connect it to the poet (76).

[15]     *Mary Robinson: Selected Poems*, ed. Judith Pascoe (Toronto: Broadview Press, 2000), lines 2, 9–10. All quotations of Robinson's poetry unless otherwise noted will be from this edition, hereafter cited as *MR*. Quotations of Samuel Taylor Coleridge's poems are from *Poetical Works*, ed. J. C. C. Mays, 3 vols. in 6 parts, (Princeton: Princeton University Press, 2001), 1.1 (Reading Text), 2.1 (Variorum Text), hereafter cited as *PW*.

provides the transition from Walsingham's happy childhood when he is the expected heir and his "every wish was anticipated, every word was law," to the beginning of his traumatic story of disaster and disinheritance that begins with his loss of his uncle, Sir Edward, and centers on his intense rivalry with his cousin Sidney, who displaces him. Without a sympathetic other, Walsingham's whole life becomes determined by this rivalry.[16] As his identification with the snowdrop suggests, Walsingham sees himself as victimized by circumstance, and, like Robinson, he seeks a sympathizing response to validate his plight. The cross-dressed Sidney can fulfill that need, if Walsingham can recognize his connection to her and sacrifice his egotism. Though that moment only comes when Sidney is revealed as a woman at the novel's close (of course, they marry), the body of the novel stresses both characters' unstable, androgynous identities.[17] Walsingham is, in some sense, Robinson in drag, just as Sidney is a woman in drag. Because Sidney appears as male, Walsingham mistakenly discounts his ambivalent emotional response to her, when it is her very feminine masculinity, their shared sensibility, which should appeal to his. By making a sensitive male character the author of her poem, Robinson thus articulates, in a form that troubles gendered identities, her authorial need for the sympathetic response of an associating mind—a shared sensibility— that bridges gender and authorizes the poet.

When Coleridge's *The Apotheosis; or, the Snow-drop* appeared in *The Morning Post* at the beginning of 1798, it would have been read by the reading public as a response to Robinson's novel as well as to her *Ode to the Snow-drop*. During this exchange both writers used a variety of pseudonyms that, though never crossing gender, reveal their mutual experimentation with different poetic identities. Daniel Stuart first hailed Robinson's novel on 2 December 1797. Four days later an "Editorial Notice" appeared addressed "To Correspondents": "We have many favours which wait only for room, particularly much Poetical Correspondence. The beautiful lines by Albert [Coleridge], further extracts from Mrs. Robinson's excellent novel [Walsingham], &c &c will appear tomorrow we hope." The following day, 7 December, Coleridge's poem, *Lines to an Unfortunate Woman, in the Back Seats of the Boxes at the Theatre*, was published under the pseudonym Albert. More than likely, this poem would have registered with Robinson as it showed Coleridge's sympathy for fallen women, especially in the context of the theater. On the same day, Tabitha Bramble, one of Robinson's personas, is commended by an anonymous editor for "the elegance of [her] stile, and the richness of [her] imagination," and more poems from Albert, "whose beautiful lines grace our Paper," are promised. On 14 December Wordsworth's poem *The*

---

[16]    *Walsingham; or the Pupil of Nature,* ed. Julie Shaffer (Toronto: Broadview Press, 2003), 58. In fact, it is Walsingham's failure to see in Sidney this sympathetic other that causes all his problems, including thinking he has lost all the women he loves to Sidney, mistakenly raping someone, being accused of gambling, being challenged to a duel, and shooting someone.

[17]    Shaffer, Introduction to *Walsingham*, 25.

*Convict*, which had been submitted by Coleridge, appeared under the pseudonym "Mortimer." Right before *The Apotheosis*, Coleridge published *The Vision of the Maid of Orleans, A Fragment*" under his own name (26 December, 148 lines of which would go on to be lines 127–277 of the *Destiny of Nations*) and several political poems on body parts under the pseudonym "Laberius."[18]

Finally, on 3 January 1798, *The Apotheosis; or, the Snow-drop* materialized in print under the Italian pseudonym "Francini." *The Morning Post* responded with an Editorial Notice on 4 January: "Mrs. Robinson's WALSINGHAM has never received a more gratifying tribute of praise than the *beautiful poem*, by FRANCINI, in our paper of yesterday; such a commendation is honourable, as flowing from the pen of classical elegance, and true poetic inspiration." David Erdman suggests that this notice was written by Coleridge, but his grounds for doing so are unclear.[19] If Coleridge did write this notice, it is interesting that he is praising his own praise of Robinson. It suggests his motives here are as much about self as other. Given that Robinson was the editor of the poetry section at this point, it seems quite possible that the notice could also have been written by Robinson. Either way, by responding to *Walsingham*, Coleridge's poem exposes its interest in destabilizing gender conventions and implies the other's importance for "true poetic inspiration." If Coleridge never explicitly acknowledges Walsingham in the poem, it is Robinson as Walsingham, masculine and feminine poet, partaking of the sublime and beautiful, who lurks behind the poem's address.

Coleridge's *Apotheosis* provides exactly the sympathizing response that Robinson's poem demands; it creates a complex lyrical exchange and reveals Coleridge's and Robinson's shared sensibility. Coleridge's poem revises and responds to Robinson's on several levels. It responds to her content, first, by valorizing her poetic immortalization of the snowdrop, and, second, by raising Robinson, as Laura, to a deified poetic status. It also revises Robinson's rhyme scheme and stanza pattern by changing her six-line stanzas to eight and using the rhyme scheme of *The Ancient Mariner* for the second quatrain, but it keeps intact her iambic tetrameter and final line of trimeter. Finally, it weaves their poems together through shared imagery, in particular that of the snowdrop and eolian harp. More specifically, Coleridge's emotional connection to Robinson allows him to cross poetic gender boundaries. It is not an unambivalent response, as Susan Luther has elegantly shown; rather, it is full of undercurrents and "uneasy with the associations of myrtle and laurel, LOVE and FANCY, activity and passivity, poesy and oblivion, 'imitative sympathy' and 'potent sorcery,' uneasy with 'feelings unreproved.'" In particular, the punning on "LAURA lie" and Lorelei perhaps implies that Coleridge feels seduced into

---

[18]     See "Verse Contributions by Coleridge and Wordsworth" in Appendix D of Coleridge's *Essays on His Times*, ed. David Erdman (Princeton: Princeton University Press, 1978), 285–6.

[19]     Ibid., 285–6.

unfamiliar and treacherous territory.[20] However, Robinson's designation here as "Laura" is also a reference to her Della Cruscan pseudonym, Laura Maria, and to Petrarch's Laura. Coleridge is not in fact trapped in Robinson's imagery and language; instead, his engagement with Robinson's poem not only allows him to inhabit new poetic territory and dress in the language of sensibility (a kind of cross-dressing if you will), but it also allows him to explore questions of poetic agency without the same kind of rivalry he would feel with another male poet, to write in "imitative sympathy" without loss of self.[21] *Apotheosis* takes on the flowery, affective and ornamental language of the Della Cruscans in a self-conscious manner that not only praises Robinson in her own earlier style but also allows Coleridge to experiment with the erotically charged artifice of that style of verse.[22] Coleridge's exclamations and flattery, his use of the language of sensibility and Della Cruscan imagery in this poem, seem far from the language of the more significant conversation poems of this time. And yet, it is precisely the conversation poems that they recall, despite the lack of first person speaker. As Jerome McGann suggests, the conversation poem evolved out of Coleridge's response to and movement away from the Della Cruscans.[23] In making Robinson and her poem the source of inspiration, in giving himself over to her, Coleridge authorizes his own poetry.

Coleridge's dialogue with Robinson begins through his parallel sympathy for the snowdrop, a sympathy that is mediated by the "potent sorceries of [her] song" (6). If it seems that the speaker is going to play the chivalrous role, however, that gesture is displaced onto Laura, whose acute sensibility is emphasized: "She gaz'd till all the body mov'd / Interpreting the spirit's thought" (11–12). Her "witching rhymes" (18) have led the speaker to recognize the snowdrop's worth and have saved the snowdrop by immortalizing it. Describing the sympathetic response that is the basis of Robinson's poem and her poetry more generally, Coleridge reveals his sympathy with Robinson as a poet of reputation. His poem imitates hers in

---

[20]    Luther, 401, 402. Picking up on this cue, Erdman claims that, in this poem, Coleridge is "trapped in Perdita's paraphernalia" ("Lost Poem Found: The Cooperative Pursuit and Recapture of an Escaped Coleridge 'Sonnet' of 72 Lines," *Bulletin of the New York Public Library* 65 [1961]: 267). Brian Haman in conversation also pointed out to me the connection between "Laura lie" and Lorelei.

[21]    *Apotheosis*, 15. Fulford does not see Coleridge as trapped either; rather, he sees him exploring the possibilities of feminizing the sublime (*Romanticism and Masculinity*, 116).

[22]    Note here that the very act of poetic exchange between a male and female poet in which the central focus is poetic agency and the natural world functions to reveal the poet's artifice are themselves aspects of the Della Cruscan style. For more on Della Cruscan style, see Judith Pascoe, *Romantic Theatricality: Gender, Poetry, and Spectatorship* (Cornell: Cornell University Press, 1997); Jerome J. McGann, *The Poetics of Sensibility: A Revolution in Literary Style* (Oxford: Clarendon Press, 1996), chapter 9: "The Literal World of the Della Cruscans." McGann represents the Della Cruscans as the embodiment of the poetry of sensibility.

[23]    McGann, esp. 19–23 and 88–90.

order to uphold her poetic authority and affirms her reputation to produce such an apotheosis. But, of course, it is only through his poem that the snowdrop is brought to the "Pierian climes" (20), "mid laurels ever green" (23). In this first part of the poem, Coleridge literally inhabits Robinson's poem and raises its imagery to a dream-like sublime landscape of the mountaintop ("Pierian climes" in stanza 3, the "vast summit" in stanza 5) where a breeze of inspiration plays the tree branches like an eolian harp ("A sea-like sound the branches breathe, / Stirr'd by the breeze that loiters there" [41–2]).

In this landscape, a natural setting most often associated with Romantic poetry, the poem shifts its focus from the imagery of Robinson's snowdrop to Laura/Robinson, producing a second apotheosis, that of Robinson. This apotheosis happens in a fairy-like dreamland of Coleridge's creation in which natural and spiritual, magical and mythological elements mix. Graced by "LOVE and FANCY" (33), Laura lies in a privileged dream-like state, carried up "that strange unpathway'd steep" to a place where the breeze allows her to "forget the coil of mortal care" (44) and "mists along the margin rise, / As heal the guests who thither come" (46). She appears to be in the perfect state for poetic inspiration, a state that allows her to transcend her bodily illness and to "fit the soul to re-endure / It's [sic] earthly martyrdom" (47–8). In creating this landscape, Coleridge has elevated Laura, literally and figuratively, providing Robinson with a sympathetic response that valorizes her poetry. If this is Robinson's "sublime union of sensibility," however, it is so only insofar as Coleridge has placed her content in his context. In the very act of elevating Robinson, a gesture that seemingly effaces his own poetic ambition, Coleridge creates his own space, inspired by Robinson, but a new landscape that combines their images and becomes the site of his poem. Moreover, rather than giving us Laura as poet, Coleridge presents Laura asleep, creating a literal image of the beautiful in the sublime: "A magic slumber heaves her breast! / Her arm, white wanderer of the harp, / Beneath her cheek is prest!" (54–6). The extravagant exclamation marks in this part of the poem underscore the speaker's intensity of response. But why is he so excited? Is he overcome by her beauty? Is he bothered by her dream-filled sleep? Is he disturbed by the harp's disuse? Is he excited by a music that seems to emanate without origin? The ambiguity of the speaker's response seemingly creates distance between Robinson/Laura and Coleridge as the speaker emphasizes the tension between the music of the harp (her poetry), which is "half-perceiv'd" (61), and the "Remember'd loves," who "light up her cheek" (63), a tension that might be framed as Romantic versus Della Cruscan. If the first part of the poem emphasized "the potent sorceries of [her] songs" (6), the final stanzas seem to represent Robinson as a woman drawn from her art by dreams of love, who the speaker must finally pity.[24]

---

[24]   On Coleridge's use of pity, see Ellison chapters 4 and 5. The last stanza of the poem, with its syntactical awkwardness and its introduction of personified Pity, was added when the poem was published in *The Morning Post* (*PW*, 1.1.424).

Such a reading of the poem's gender politics, which portrays Coleridge as chivalrously distancing himself from Robinson, however, overlooks several key aspects of the poem. First, the emotional intensity of the speaker's response reveals the identification with the other that he and Robinson both felt was necessary to poetic inspiration. Moreover, if these final stanzas attempt to dissociate him from the feminine, the entrance of "Pity" (66), whose personification links her to Robinson's original concern for the snowdrop and who stands in for the speaker, undermines that gesture. As Julie Ellison has suggested, for Coleridge, pity is "the purest form of sympathy" and is strongly associated with the feminine, especially the feminine capacity for comfort and conversation.[25] In reiterating Coleridge's identification with Robinson, then, Pity's entrance at the end suggests the need to analyze further Coleridge's cross-dressing, for while he may have resituated the snowdrop and Robinson, the response, the method, and the language are all reminiscent of Della Cruscan style, a style that was clearly linked, because of its ornamentation and its theatricality, to the feminine.[26] According to both Judith Pascoe and Jerome McGann, the Della Cruscan poetic model, grounded in the ideals of sensibility, is structured by an affective, erotic relationship between heterosexual poetic friends that is entirely fictional. In their responses to one another, Della Cruscan writers like Robert Merry, Hannah Cowley, and Robinson focused most intensely on the other's ability to inspire poetry and, in praising the other poet, created a new landscape that would assert the writer's poetic authority. The very self-authorizing mode of response that Coleridge uses in "Apotheosis," which I analyze above, mimics what Judith Pascoe has shown to be the structure and intent of Robinson's "Ode to Della Crusca."[27] Moreover, despite Coleridge's use of the Romantic breeze trope and the eolian harp, the new landscape of Coleridge's poem is more artificial and ornate than naturalized, a Della Cruscan scene shaped by Coleridge's increasing self-consciousness, perhaps because of his work with Wordsworth on *Lyrical Ballads*, about the insincerity of that kind of poetry. Like the Della Cruscans, Coleridge's concern is less with the natural than with using nature to draw attention to Robinson in his constructed landscape.[28] Its imagery ("the woven arboret," "a sea-like sound the branches breathe," "zephyr-trembling lilies," for example), language (especially the use of adjectival phrases, neologisms, the elisions of letters from words like "reclin'd" and "stirr'd"), and intensity of emotional response reflect the elaborate and emotional style of Robinson's Della Cruscan Odes and her *Sappho and Phaon*. Writing to Robinson, then, rather than for *Lyrical Ballads,* not only honors her poetic authority but also

---

[25]   Ellison, 142–3.

[26]   Both Pascoe and McGann emphasize the obligations of Romanticism to Della Cruscan poetry, a swerve that attempts to disguise these roots because of their artificial and elaborate ornamental style, which many of the Romantics, especially Wordsworth, saw as too theatrical and thus insincere.

[27]   Pascoe, 79.

[28]   See Pascoe, 85; McGann, 77–8.

allows Coleridge to experiment with a feminine style that he and the Romantic poets would later reject and that Robinson also felt became a problem for her poetic reputation.

That *Apotheosis* foregrounds both poets' concerns with poetic authority becomes even clearer when we notice that the image of Laura, asleep while her "uphung" (57) harp makes a "music [that] hovers half-perceived" (61), also overtly recalls Coleridge's *The Eolian Harp* in its 1796 form, *Effusion XXXV*.[29] By reworking imagery from his own poem in this poem to Robinson, Coleridge links their concerns and blends their imagery. If Robinson's passivity seems problematic, it is so only insofar as it is a problem for Coleridge as well, for in *Effusion XXXV* he similarly represents his own passive state of poetic inspiration. Lying amidst murmurings and "witching" sounds, both Coleridge's speaker and Laura/snowdrop inhabit a "Fairy Land" (*Apotheosis*, 23) where the breezes of inspiration play on their bodies, like the breeze playing across the wind-harp. As Coleridge's earlier eolian harp lies in the casement "caressed" by "the desultory breeze," "like some coy maid half yielding to her lover" (14–15), Robinson's harp with "coy reproachfulness complains / In snatches of reluctant sound!" (59–60). The earlier harp makes "such a soft floating witchery of sound" (22), much as Laura murmurs "witching rhymes" in the first part of *The Apotheosis* (18). And, in the second part of *The Apotheosis*, the harp plays, like its counterpart, without its musician. Furthermore, this shared imagery is reinforced by the poems' similar structures. Though the setting of *The Apotheosis* does not have much of the natural imagery of the earlier poem, it begins with a dialogue with another, in this case the snowdrop, and that dialogue leads the speaker to a transcendent moment which is then undercut, in this case by the "sprite" who will "waft her back to earth" rather than by Sara Fricker. The lack of first person here serves to highlight the difference of this conversation from that in *Effusion XXXV*, as it is more overtly shaped by the Della Cruscan style; the apostrophe to the snowdrop foregrounds instead an explicit dialogue with another poet mediated by the convention of the flower poem and imagined through the shared figure of the eolian harp.

Subtle, seemingly gendered, differences in the way the harps are portrayed in *Effusion XXXV* and *The Apotheosis* might be interpreted to suggest that Coleridge wants to differentiate his poetic practice from that of Robinson. For example, rather than creating the visionary moment of *Effusion XXXV*, the music of Laura's harp is "half-perceived, / And only moulds the slumberer's dreams" (61–2) of love. Similarly, though Coleridge's eolian harp becomes a sign for "all of animated nature" (44), Laura's harp seems to reproach her for hanging it up. However,

---

[29]     My interest here is in the earliest published version of *The Eolian Harp, Effusion XXXV. Composed August 20th 1795, at Clevedon, Somersetshire*, which first appeared in Coleridge's *Poems on Various Subjects, 1796* (*PW*, 2.1.316–28). The earlier version does not yet have the five-paragraph structure paralleling it to *Tintern Abbey* and excludes lines 26–33 (the "one Life" passage, 1817). It is not yet framed as a conversation poem but as an effusion, the spontaneous expression of emotion that links it to Della Cruscan poetry.

such differences are neutralized by the fact that Coleridge situates Robinson in a position that parallels his own in *Effusion XXXV*. Like that speaker who "on the midway slope" (34) stretches his limbs and becomes analogous to that "subject lute" (43), Robinson reclines on the mountain, though with eyes fully closed. Her mind does not become a subject lute, except insofar as Coleridge plays her; instead, she foregrounds a problem that Coleridge shared, the question of agency. Coleridge responds to Robinson's anxiety about reputation by bringing in a figure that he used to represent his own poetic authority, the eolian harp, which places that power outside the subject's control. In *Effusion XXXV*, McGann claims, the harp "becomes an emblem of the poem (and poet) of sensibility," and it appears similarly in *The Apotheosis*. But if Coleridge rejects that identification at the end of *Effusion XXXV*, in *The Apotheosis* he deploys it to accentuate the erotic and affective connections to Robinson and her poetry. As Coleridge's poem presents it, the tension for Robinson is between the harp's music and the loves that occupy her dreams, a clear parallel to the tensions the speaker of *Effusion XXXV* feels as he is torn between indulging his reflections and pleasing his wife. At the very moment Coleridge seems to be emphasizing their gender difference, he in fact underscores their similarity, their shared anxieties as poets. Coleridge's poem to Robinson is more than a playful response; it provides him with the opportunity to interweave his poetry with hers in a lyrical exchange that affirms both their reputations. Coleridge, like the "zephyr-trembling lilies" of *Apotheosis* who "bend to kiss their softer selves / That tremble in the stream below," has bent to kiss his softer self in Robinson (50–52). As the image of the lilies kissing their reflection suggests, it is a gesture at once kind and condescending, giving and narcissistic, a gesture that affirms her but also reveals his own delicate (flower-like) sensibility.[30] By portraying Robinson in the language of his own poetry as well as hers, he not only praises her but affirms a shared model of poetic authority grounded in sensibility and symbolized by the eolian harp.

The specific conversation Coleridge generates in *Apotheosis* is, however, only part of a larger web of associations that conveys Robinson's and Coleridge's investment in each other's poetry. This nexus of images both employ—eolian harp, flower, Chatterton as misunderstood genius, nightingale—results from Robinson's and Coleridge's "imitative sympathy" and reveals their "associating mind[s]." Despite these images' conventionality, the repetition and association of them across a range of poems create a series of echoes that highlights the need to read Coleridge and Robinson in conversation with one another, even if they are not explicitly in dialogue. Moreover, their mutual investment in this particular

---

[30]  McGann links the emblem of the kiss to the Della Cruscans and claims that several of the poems from 1792–1794, in particular *Kisses*, *The Sigh*, and *The Kiss* are specifically Della Cruscan. All of these poems were published in the same 1796 volume of poems as the effusions. William Keach suggests in the notes to his edition of Coleridge's poems that the ending of *The Kiss* (lines 14–17) anticipates *The Eolian Harp* (*Coleridge: The Complete Poems*, ed. William Keach [New York: Penguin Books, 1997], 446).

EDINBURGH UNIVERSITY LIBRARY

WITHDRAWN

group of images, especially enabling to insecure poets because they downplay the poet's agency, underscores their shared anxieties about poetic authority. Like the eolian harp, the flower, Chatterton, and the nightingale each offer the poet a model of poetic authority that requires surrendering one's self emotionally to nature or to another for inspiration.

Robinson may already have been responding to Coleridge's connection of fragile flower to poet when she wrote her snowdrop poem, as it appears to be remarkably similar to an earlier Coleridge poem, *On Observing a Blossom on the First of February 1796* (*Watchman*, 11 April 1796). And both Coleridge's and Robinson's poems are revisions of Robert Burns's *To a Mountain Daisy. On Turning One Down, with the Plough, in April--------1786*.[31] As a working class, self-educated Scottish poet, Burns's poetry would have interested them both as a model of the naïve style, a truly natural poetry that flows from the passions without artifice or imitation, and as an example of the poetic success of an individual marginalized by the dominant culture. What all of these poems share is their use of the flower image as a feminized figure of victimization, whose fate is analogous to both a ruined maiden and a misunderstood poet, and a closing identification between the speaker and the flower, in which the speaker sees his/her own state. Though the form of the three poems is distinct, the closing identification of speaker and flower makes the emotional trajectory of the poems parallel, and the analogous identification of the flower with a poet whose reputation has been destroyed reworks the traditional identification of flower and maiden. Especially the linkage of flower, maiden, poet in Coleridge's and Robinson's poems underscores their identification with the oppressed and their interest in the poet as a feminized figure.

The conventional flower poem, a figure going back to Ovid's *Metamorphoses* and to Petrarch, represents the flower as a figure of love or desire. Whereas Ovid's gods turned people into flowers to preserve or escape desire, in the Petrarchan sonnet the beloved is identified with the flower in order to portray her beauty and desirability to the speaker. In these Romantic poems, however, the flower becomes a figure for the speakers' anxieties about self. No longer a figure of desire or love, the flower functions to reveal the fragility of human life and poetic reputation. In

---

31      As Lewis Patton notes in his edition of Coleridge's *The Watchman* (Princeton: Princeton University Press, 1970), 202n.1, Lamb specifically made the connection to Burns in a letter to Coleridge of 31 May 1796. Coleridge also published a second flower poem, *To a Primrose*, around the same time in *The Watchman* (27 April 1796), which he claimed as his own (he took it from *Anthologia Hibernica* 1 [Jan 1793], where it is signed "S------, 14 Feb. 1791"). This poem might have served as the model for both Robinson's *Ode to the Snow-drop* and Coleridge's response. Note in particular the use of the word "gaudy" at line 20 of *To a Primrose*, the same word Robinson uses. Quotations of Robert Burns, *To a Mountain Daisy* are from *Selected Poetry and Prose*, ed. Robert D. Thornton (Boston: Houghton Mifflin, 1966). Robinson also includes a sonnet, *The Snowdrop*, in her 1791 *Poems*, which uses the Della Cruscan imagery of tears and emphasizes the snowdrop's fragile innocence.

all of the poems, the flower must struggle against the victimizing blast of the wind that is not yet the breeze of inspiration. In Burns's poem, the daisy must stand up against "the bitter-biting *North*" (13) wind as Robinson's snowdrop "trembles, while the ruthless wind / Bends its slim form" (*MR*, 9–10) and, even more explicitly, Coleridge's blossom is "gazed upon…with blue voluptuous eye" by the "teeth-chattering Month" who has "borrowed Zephyr's voice" (*On Observing a Blossom*, 4–5, 3, 4). Burns's daisy is unlike the garden's "flaunting flowers" (19) that are protected, because it stays "unseen, alane" (24) in the "stibble-field" (23) in "scanty-mantle clad" (25), lifting its "unassuming head / In humble guise" (27–8) only so "the *share* uptears [its] bed" (29). "Such is the fate," the speaker tells the reader, "of artless Maid…. / By Love's simplicity betray'd" (31, 33) and of "simple Bard…. / Unskilful he to note the card / Of *prudent Lore*" (37, 39–40). The speaker laments that such "*suffering worth*" (42) is driven to this fate "By human pride or cunning" (44). Simplicity and artlessness of both flower and poet contrast with the "cunning" and egotistical show ("flaunting") of those who destroy them.

Much like Burns's daisy, Robinson's snowdrop is "[u]nshelter'd and unknown" (*Ode to the Snow-drop*, 23). Robinson heightens the gender imagery, however, increasing both the sexual violence done to the fragile snowdrop ("The night breeze tears thy silky dress" [18]) and making her exclusion a matter of competitive rivalry with the Crocus to whom the snowdrop is compared ("The gaudy *Crocus* flaunts its pride, / And triumphs where *its* *rival*—died" [21–2]). Though the snowdrop precedes the crocus in spring, the crocus's ability to "flaunt its pride" allows it to succeed. Robinson maintains the sense that the snowdrop is destroyed by prideful egotism, using the verb form of "flaunt" and the word "gaudy" to contrast with the snowdrop's innocent simplicity. Transforming Burns's common daisy and Coleridge's generic blossom to a snowdrop, a fragile and transient, white spring flower symbolizing hope, Robinson heightens the sense of the flower's innocence, increasing its symbolism. In addition, Robinson makes the connection between flower as betrayed maiden and misunderstood poet implicit rather than explicit as in Burns's poem; the word "rival" changes the connotation of "unknown," recasting it as an issue of fame. Robinson's flower subtly becomes the female poet whose reputation is destroyed on sexualized grounds, as the phallic crocus symbolizes her most threatening rivals, Gifford and Polwhele. In contrast, Coleridge uses Burns's analogies more explicitly and adds one of his own. The issue for Coleridge is society's oppressive indifference: Robinson's and Burns's violated maiden becomes "some sweet girl of too too rapid growth" who is "Nipped by consumption mid untimely charms" (*On Observing a Blossom*, 10–11); Burns's "simple Bard" becomes Chatterton, "Bristowa's bard, the wondrous boy! / An amaranth, which Earth scarce seemed to own, / Till disappointment came, and pelting wrong / Beat it to Earth!" (12–15). Coleridge adds as his final comparison "Poland's hope, /… killed in the opening bud" (16-17), a reference to the Poles' failed rebellion to stop the Russians' partition of Poland in 1794. These "Dim similitudes / Weaving in moral strains" (19–20), as the speaker calls them, increase the moral tenor and the larger social context of Coleridge's poem.

In all three poems, the expressed sympathy for the flower as both maiden and poet critically connects the plight of the two, whose innocent simplicity is betrayed and overcome by a selfish and proud public. This link is especially important because the flower becomes a means for each speaker to reflect on his/her own state. For the male poets, the last lines of the poems reveal the speaker's recognition of his feminized position as poet and of his mortality. In Robinson's case, the last lines underscore her sense of social exclusion both as a fallen woman (given her past in the theater and her affair with the Prince of Wales) and as a poet. The identification of misunderstood poet and fallen woman highlights their similar plights in an unfeeling world. As I have suggested above, one element that most likely heightened Robinson's and Coleridge's interest in one another was a mutual concern for the oppressed state of women and their shared sense of the public indifference toward poets.[32] Not only did Coleridge think Robinson a fine poet, "a woman of undoubted genius," but he expressed concern for her misrepresentation.[33] In the same letter, written just after Robinson's death, he asked Southey to include her poem, *Jasper*, in the *Annual Anthology*. In a later letter to Maria Elizabeth, Robinson's daughter, who was gathering poetry to appear with her mother's work in the compilation *The Wild Wreath*, Coleridge also expressed concern that Robinson's poetry (as well as his own!) would appear with that of men whose reputations were dubious and who, at one point, had slighted her mother.[34] Robinson, likewise, had spent the last years of her life championing poets misunderstood by the public (see the preface to *Sappho and Phaon*, 1796), asserting the rights of women as writers and thinkers (*Letter to the Women of England*, 1799 and *The Natural Daughter*, 1799), and building her own reputation as a Romantic poet. Her *Lyrical Tales* responded to *Lyrical Ballads* in part to help build the fame of Coleridge and Wordsworth and in part to augment her own fame.

The ends of the three flower poems emphasize the speakers' senses of their own transient positions in the world as each speaker differently identifies with the flower. If Burns's speaker guiltily crushes the daisy, who "met [him] in an evil hour" (2), in the end he recognizes himself in the daisy and, in mourning her fate, mourns his own. Speaking to himself in the second person, he exclaims:

> Ev'n thou who mourn'st the *Daisy's* fate,
> *That fate is thine*—no distant date;
> Stern Ruin's *plough-share* drives, elate,

---

[32]    On Coleridge's sympathy for fallen women, see Taylor, chapter 4: "Blank Faces and Fear of Ruin" in *Erotic Coleridge*. On his support of the rights of woman, see her "Coleridge, Wollstonecraft, and the Rights of Woman."

[33]    25 January 1800, *Collected Letters*, 1:562. Coleridge also said to Southey, "Ay! that woman has an Ear" (28 February 1800, *Collected Letters*, 1:576).

[34]    Coleridge to Maria Elizabeth Robinson, 27 December 1802, *Collected Letters*, 2:904–6. See Byrne, 394–5 for more on this exchange.

Full on thy bloom,
Till crush'd beneath the *furrow's* weight,
Shall be thy doom!" (49–54)

Robinson's identification with the flower similarly shifts the focus to Robinson herself, but whereas Burns's poem seems to move outward to a concern with human mortality more generally, Robinson's individualizes and sentimentalizes her response. This identification highlights her sense of isolation and shifts the context; the reader feels the speaker's anxiety that "no sunny beam [will] gild her grave" (24) as she has "known the cheerless hour… / [Has] felt the chilling, wint'ry gale, / And WEPT and SHRUNK" (32–5), rejected because of poverty, disability, and infamy.

Whereas Robinson uses the flower to intensify pity for snowdrop and speaker and perhaps to naturalize her position, Coleridge employs the blossom as the means to escape self. Both variants of *On Observing a Blossom* reflect the speaker's sense of dis-ease and anxiety. The version first published in *The Watchman*, 11 April 1796, ties that anxiety specifically to Coleridge's wife's threatened miscarriage and his fear for her life. Though a later version revises this passage to focus on "anxious self," the earlier version emphasizes Coleridge's concern for a suffering woman, literally and figuratively.[35] More importantly, both versions recall the imagery of Coleridge's effusions, especially XXXV, the early form of *The Eolian Harp*, which also appeared in April 1796. Thinking to have escaped his anxiety by reflecting on the blossom Coleridge writes, "And the warm wooings of this sunny day / Tremble along my frame, and harmonize / Th'attempered brain, that ev'n saddest thoughts / Mix with some sweet sensations, like harsh tunes / Play'd deftly on a soft-ton'd instrument" (*On Observing a Blossom*, 24–8). The harp image reframes the reflection on the blossom in a poetic context; the speaker's body played by the "warm wooings" (24) recalls the "subject Lute" of *Effusion XXXV*, but here the harp imagery underscores the speaker's discontent. This last series of images is striking in its conflicting range of emotions; if the "sweet sensations" that play across the "attempered organ" parallel the "soft-toned instrument," his "saddest thoughts" are transformed into "harsh tunes" (26–8). Here, the speaker's identification with the flower reveals, as in *Effusion XXXV*, his "unregenerate" (55), "attempered" (26) mind, his sense of the "harsh" (27) quality of his own verse.

Written at about the same time, these two poems, with their shared eolian harps, stress Coleridge's interest in a poetic authority derived from the poet's passive responsiveness to outside influences, especially nature. The harp imagery recurs frequently in his early poetry as a figure for his relation to nature and his concerns

---

[35]    Lines 21–3 of the original version read, "I've stolen one hour / From black anxiety that gnaws my heart / For her who droops far off on a sick bed." In a later version, this line becomes, "I've stolen one hour / From anxious self, Life's cruel task-master!"

about poetic authority and gender difference in particular.[36] McGann suggests that, in the poetry of the 1790s, Coleridge uses the harp as a metaphor for a spontaneous poetry of sensibility in which the poet and poem function passively like the harp, a metaphor that, as I have shown above, he also clearly connected to Robinson. Though the eolian harp has come to be read as the quintessential Romantic image since Coleridge's poem of that name, the Della Cruscans also flirted with this image in a nascent form, using it to represent a poetry of intense, sympathetic, and spontaneous responsiveness to nature and to the other. As McGann points out, "the eighteenth-century discourse of sensibility seized the eolian harp as a non-conscious tool for revealing the vital correspondences that pour through the material world."[37] In *Lines to Anna Matilda* (*The British Album*, I:86–8), for example, Della Crusca (Robert Merry) identifies Anna Matilda's (Hanna Cowley's) poetry with an eolian harp: "Let but thy lyre impatient seize, / Departing Twilight's filmy breeze, / That winds th'enchanting chords among, / *In ling'ring labyrinth of song*."[38] Similarly, in *Ode to Della Crusca*, a poem whose structure I have suggested above Coleridge might be imitating in *Apotheosis*, Robinson represents her heart as an eolian harp (though she doesn't call it that), as it "revibrates" (3) to Robert Merry's "ever-witching song" (2) as "With magic thrilling touch / Till ever'y nerve, with quiv'ring throb divine" (4–5). Like Coleridge's bodily "frame" (25) in *On Observing a Blossom* and the speaker's "indolent and passive brain" (33) in *Effusion XXXV*, which respond like the harp caressed by the wind, Robinson's heart trembles and quivers with the inspiration of Merry's poetry. In each of these cases, the poetic body functions as a kind of harp across which the winds of inspiration play, making an outside force the source of poetic authority.

Coleridge would certainly have been aware of the harp's significance in Della Cruscan poetry, as he sought to revise its significance in changing *Effusion XXXV* to *The Eolian Harp*. As mentioned previously, without the "One Life" passage, which may have resulted from Wordsworth's influence and which provides a spiritual unity to "the shapings of the unregenerate mind" (55), the earlier poem was not yet the philosophical reflection it later became; instead, it was an

---

[36]   Coleridge's epigraph to the 1796 *Poems on Various Subjects* cites four lines from Bowles that make the lyre (not yet the eolian harp) a figure for those poems. He also uses the image of the eolian harp in *Ode on the Departing Year* (December 1796) and stanzas one and seven of *Dejection: An Ode* (*Morning Post*, 4 October 1802) to differing effects.

[37]   McGann, 21. James Thomson was the first English poet to exploit this symbol in *The Castle of Indolence* (lines 352–60) and his *Ode on Aeolus's Harp*. For more on Coleridge's response to the Della Cruscans, see also Byrne, 246–7.

[38]   Significantly, the next lines of this verse include two of the other images that Robinson and Coleridge experiment with in these earlier poems, the nightingale and the flower: "Anon, the amorous *Bird of Woe*, / Shall steal the tones that quivering flow, / And with them soothe the sighing woods, / And with them charm the slumb'ring floods; / Till, all exhausted by the lay, / He hang in silence on the spray, / Drop to his idol flow'r beneath, / And, 'midst her blushes, cease to breathe" (qtd. in McGann, 82).

exploration of the Della Cruscan emphasis on the poet's receptive sensibility, as it is acted on by outside forces. Naming the eolian harp and giving it a divine energy, Coleridge extends this idea of poetic receptivity even further and wonders "what if all of animated nature / Be but organic harps" (36–7).[39] This gesture connects poet, poem, nature through the figure of the eolian harp, turning each into instruments who derive their power from the unseen, spiritual winds that blow upon them. Thus Sara's entrance at the end of the poem becomes the means not only to check the pantheistic impulse but also to control Coleridge's extension of Della Cruscan sensibility. If in *Apotheosis* Coleridge links the eolian harp to the feminine (and female) Robinson, however, in *The Eolian Harp* he opposes the female, figured as the reproving Sara, to that poetic image. In this case, Sarah represents the properly domestic as the poem transforms the feminine, erotically receptive image of the poet, embodied in the parallel between the dreaming Robinson of *Apotheosis* and his somnolent speaker, into the chastised, subservient, and thus feminized, husband. This final image suggests, then, Coleridge's erotic, poetic, and spiritual unease with such imaginings.

It seems significant, then, that Robinson first overtly frames the harp as an *eolian* harp in Sonnet XIV of *Sappho and Phaon*, which was published in October 1796, just six months after Coleridge's *Effusion XXXV* and *On Observing a Blossom*.[40] Though the image of the harp recurs frequently in Robinson's earlier poetry to signify her intense poetic sensibility, her use of an eolian harp in the sonnet sequence registers an important shift in the poem and in her oeuvre, as she also articulates a poetic philosophy for the first time in this sequence.[41] Asserting

---

[39]     See McGann, chapter 2: "Coleridge's 'Eolian Harp,'" 19–23, and Magnuson, "'The Eolian Harp' in Context," *Studies in Romanticism* 24 (1985): 3–20. According to Magnuson, the 1796 *Effusion* has a more playful role than *The Eolian Harp*, being "presented as one of many effusions of the moment" (11). McGann argues that Coleridge later rejected the identification of poet/poem and harp because it would make the poet into a magician, usurping the powers of God (22–3).

[40]     Michael Ferber points out that "Aeolian lyre" would most likely "refer to Sappho and Alcaeus, whose lyrics were in the Aeolian dialect" (7). Robinson may be playing with this allusion, but she clearly makes her lyre an eolian harp like Coleridge's. Note also that Alcaeus was a pseudonym that Coleridge later adopted in responding to Robinson (via one of Wordsworth's poems) in *Alcaeus to Sappho* (*Morning Post*, 24 November 1800). For a reading of this poem, see my "From *Lyrical Ballads* to *Lyrical Tales*."

[41]     See in particular Robinson's *Ode to Della Crusca* (1791), *Ode to the Muse* (*World* 1788; *Fashionable Advertiser* 1791), *To the Muse of Poetry* (1791), *Ode to the Harp of Louisa* (*Oracle*, 15 January 1793), and *Ode to Genius* (*Oracle*, 7 December 1793). Written in the Della Cruscan style, these poems make the harp a symbol of Robinson's poetic powers and of poetry more generally. Though it is not yet the eolian harp because more consciously played by the poet, the harp figure combines the sublime and the beautiful, reason and passion; it is primarily associated with the feminine and sympathetic receptiveness to others; and it embodies the ecstasy which Robinson associates with inspiration. *Ode to the Harp of Louisa* creates a disjunction between memorializing Laura, the subject of the poem,

the importance of sensibility in poetic practice and its grounding in feminine experience, Robinson argues "the philosophical case of poetry *in the discourse of poetry*" and claims, through her portrayal of Sappho as a figure of poetic power and impassioned reason, the importance of both passion and reason in that discourse.[42] In her "Introductory Account of Sappho," following her preface, Robinson portrays Sappho as the model poet of sensibility whose poems have a "vivid glow of sensibility" and are "possessed of none of the artificial decorations of a feigned passion; they [are] the genuine effusions of a supremely enlightened soul, labouring to subdue a fatal attachment" (*MR*, 152). While Robinson emphasizes the emotional responsiveness associated with the Della Cruscans, she rejects here the "artificial decorations of a feigned passion" of their poetic exchanges and stresses instead "genuine effusions," using Coleridge's word. Grounding her poetry in the "legitimate sonnet" of Milton, Robinson argues for a poetry whose authority comes from the poet's emotional responsiveness to forces outside herself (in Sappho's case, to Phaon), which Robinson associates with the feminine, and she embodies that philosophy in her sonnet sequence. As McGann has suggested, this manifesto "puts her at odds with the two dominant (and masculinist) theories of poetry articulated in the volatile 1790s," represented by Gifford's *Baviad* (1791), which satirizes the Della-Cruscans, and Wordsworth's Preface to *Lyrical Ballads* (1800), which rejects the theatricality of the Della Cruscans and "restores poetry . . . to its 'manly' [though still emotional] heritage."[43]

Robinson might well have read Coleridge's 1796 poems and would have recognized in that volume Coleridge's exploration of Della Cruscan sensibility, imagery, and language. While I cannot argue for a direct influence, Robinson's consciousness of her place in poetic circles at the time and the shared imagery I have traced above suggest that she would already have started to see Coleridge as a poetic ally. Certainly, she is playing with the eolian harp image in this sequence, much as Coleridge does, in order to explore its implications in a poetry of sensibility. In the opening sonnet, Robinson speaking through Sappho claims that "blest Poesy! with godlike pow'rs [was given] / To calm the miseries of man" (9–10), but by Sonnet IV, "Mute, on the ground [her] Lyre neglected lies, / The Muse forgot" (5–6) because Phaon's presence distracts and disorders Sappho's senses. Struggling between reason and passion, she sets out to woo Phaon, but fears already the failure of her poetic powers. She thus turns in Sonnet XIV to address directly an alternative source of poetic authority, the eolian harp, and demands that it "prompt my Phaon's dreams with tend'rest lays" (5), accompanied by the sorrowful songs of Philomel ("he"?), before night descends.[44] The eolian harp's independence has the potential to affect Phaon's unconscious; its ability

---

and memorializing her harp that might prefigure the division in Coleridge's portrayal of Robinson at the end of *The Apotheosis*.

[42]  McGann, 98. See chapter 10: "Mary Robinson and the Myth of Sappho," 94–116.

[43]  McGann, 98–9.

[44]  See Luther (402) for another reading of this sonnet.

to act without an agent is, paradoxically, its source of power because its poetry seems inspired directly from nature. By embodying her sensibility in the harp, Sappho suggests her poetry is naturally created from outside herself and is thus a spontaneous emotional response that she does not control. The harp's "dulcet" (9) music creates a dream-like atmosphere in which the "sunny people" (12) are lulled into a kind of suspended state, reminiscent of the speaker in Coleridge's *Effusion XXXV*. The "sunny people" contrast with "the wise" who seek to disrupt the "little world" of love (13). If the eolian harp can have this lulling effect on Phaon, Sappho can protect "the breast of Love" (14) from the stings that might wound it; she can create this other state in which Phaon will recognize her love through the power of poetry. The eolian harp (and the poetry it produces), then, becomes the means for her to possess Phaon, to give his cheek the rapturous glow that will indicate his love for her, but it also stands in here for a poetry of sensibility, whose force has an unconscious bodily effect. Robinson's harp may seem far from Coleridge's, and yet they share the same murmurous sounds, the same twilight moment that creates a sense of otherworldliness. As the speaker of Coleridge's poem is lulled by the harp's music, so Sappho hopes to lull Phaon to draw him into her world. In both cases, the eolian harp functions as a figure for the expression of a poetic power founded in sensibility and emotional interconnection with another. Robinson's poem reveals a sympathy with Coleridge's that, if not imitative, implies a shared interest in poetic authority that takes its origins not from emotion recollected in tranquility but from the poet's passive surrendering of him/herself to powerful, spontaneous emotions evoked by forces (nature, another poet, or a similarly responsive individual) outside him/herself. Such a model could offer poets like Robinson and Coleridge, who saw themselves as outsiders to mainstream literary circles, a means to establish a poetic authority that was less threatening both to themselves and to others because less centered on the self's active role in producing poetry.

The image of the harp connects another pair of Coleridge's and Robinson's poems, their similarly titled Monodies to Chatterton (Robinson's *Monody to the Memory of Chatterton* and Coleridge's *Monody on the Death of Chatterton*), which further reveal their earlier shared poetic practice. It is not surprising, in light of my analysis of the eolian harp above and given that Chatterton was a fellow poet, that both poets would use the harp in these poems, if only in passing, as a figure for poetic expression with the full emotional impact of sensibility. For Robinson, "the fine raptures of poetic fire" must "vibrate on the trembling lyre," just as "unpitied pangs the mind can move" and "sorrow claims the kind embalming tear, / Or worth oppress'd excites a pang sincere," in order for "some kindred soul" (her) to "pour the song sublime / And with the cypress bough the laurel twine."[45] Making

---

[45]   Robinson's *Monody to the Memory of Chatterton* is quoted from *The Poetical Works of the Late Mrs. Mary Robinson*, ed. Maria Robinson (London, 1806, 1824; rpt. Providence: Brown University Women Writers Project, 1990), 137–40. These quotes are from lines 89, 90, 87, 92–3, 93–4. This edition will be cited hereafter as *PWMR*.

a correspondence between sympathy and poetry, between emotional intensity and poetic fire, Robinson emphasizes how sensibility creates "the song sublime." Coleridge claims a similar power when he sympathizes with Chatterton, whom he calls "Sweet harper of time-shrouded minstrelsy," and turns "Sublime of Hope" to "the cottaged dell" where "the wizard passions weave a holy spell" to conclude his poem (*Monody on the Death of Chatterton*, 141, 122, 125). What we might read here in both poets work is an early attempt on the part of each to create, through identification with another poet, "the sublime union of sensibility."

Furthermore, in both Monodies, the parallel identifications with Chatterton as a misunderstood genius reveal not only each poet's correspondences with Chatterton but also with one another. Like the flower poems, these Monodies on Chatterton champion his fragility and marginalization, but do so in order to highlight the current neglect of poetic genius. Just as Coleridge establishes himself by praising Robinson in *Apotheosis*, Coleridge and Robinson use their emotional response to Chatterton to establish their own poetic authority. Moreover, Chatterton has special interest for both because his poetic authority was established through the Thomas Rowley poems, poems in which he not only responded to another poet but became that poet. That is, Chatterton's poetic authority came through a force outside himself by imitating other poets, a practice that both Coleridge and Robinson employed. As Beth Lau argues about John Clare and Keats, who "paradoxically had to establish his legitimacy by proving his derivativeness," impersonation was a way of establishing their otherwise "tenuous authority"; these poets "sought legitimacy through a kind of self-loss."[46]

Significantly, Coleridge revised his *Monody on the Death of Chatterton* to appear in the 1796 edition of his *Poems,* along with his effusions.[47] As the poem functions to memorialize Chatterton, it also situates Chatterton within a tradition of neglected poets and emphasizes his concern for the oppressed. Magnuson describes the poem as "primarily an expression of Coleridge's identification with Chatterton and a protest against society's neglect of poets and literature, which

---

[46]    Lau, "Protest, 'Nativism,' and Impersonation in the Works of Chatterton and Keats," *Studies in Romanticism* 42 (2003): 535, 533, 535.

[47]    J. C. C. Mays sorts out the confusion of Coleridge's many revisions of "Monody on the Death of Chatterton" in his notes to *PW*. He suggests one consider the poem "in three basic forms: a school exercise in the form of an irregular Pindaric ode dating from 1790, a Romantic ode written at Bristol and Cambridge in 1794 and successively expanded and modified in subsequent collections, and an elegy in couplets dating from 1829–34" (*PW*, 2.1.166). David Fairer also distinguishes the earlier two versions, identifying the 1790 version with Chatterton's satirical elegies and the 1794 version with what Beth Lau calls a "sentimental image, which characterized Chatterton as a young, frail, blighted flower and victim of oppressive forces." See David Fairer, "Chatterton's Poetic Afterlife, 1770–1794: A Context for Coleridge's *Monody,*" in *Thomas Chatterton and Romantic Culture,* ed. Nick Groom (New York: St. Martin's Press, 1999), 228–52 and Beth Lau, "Class and Politics in Keats's Admiration of Chatterton," *Keats-Shelley Journal* 53 (2004): 30.

serves Coleridge's own search for financial support."[48] The 1796 version of the poem, written in 1794, transforms the earlier Pindarics into a Romantic ode colored by traces of sensibility, and it increases the connection with Chatterton, upholding the genius of Chatterton's art and stressing the speaker's anxiety about his own poetic abilities. Chastising his country for its neglect of genius, Coleridge demands, "Is this the land of song-ennobled line? / Is this the land, where Genius ne'er in vain / Pour'd forth his lofty strain?" (23–5). He worries, however, "Lest kindred woes persuade a kindred doom: / For oh! big gall-drops, ... / Have blackened the fair promise of my spring" (113–15). Coleridge's identification with Chatterton here underscores his anxiety about his ability to withstand such harsh criticism and hardship as the earlier poet endured. The poem details the act of suicide in order to ward it off, for the end of the poem is, as in *On Observing a Blossom*, Coleridge's attempt to leave behind such morbid thoughts, this time literally in a planned escape to America, "where Susquehana pours his untamed stream" (159). There, he will erect a tomb to Chatterton, and they can "greet with smiles the young-eyed Poesy" (132).[49]

Coleridge's poem responds to Chatterton's death more complexly than I have time to address here, and Paul Magnuson has carefully traced its intertextual and historical contexts; what interests me is its relationship to Robinson's *Monody to the Memory of Chatterton*. Her poem appeared much earlier in the *Oracle* in May 1791, and lines 21–32 are also excerpted in *Walsingham* (170–71). Walsingham presumably writes these lines as he arrives in Bristol, identifying his despondency at Isabella's supposed dishonoring with Chatterton's despair. He compares Chatterton to "the pale primrose" who "scarce wakes to beauty ere it feels decay; / While baleful weeds their hidden poisons pour, / Choke the green sod and wither every flower" (29–32), an image that recalls Robinson's *Ode to the Snow-drop*, the poem Coleridge published as *To a Primrose* in *The Watchman*, 27 April 1796 (see note 30), and Walsingham's own concern with Isabella's deflowering. Like Coleridge, Robinson is erecting a monument in verse to Chatterton that expresses her own anxieties about poetic authority and yet at the same time asserts her poetic

---

48    Paul Magnuson, "Coleridge's Discursive 'Monody on the Death of Chatterton,'" *Romanticism on the Net* 17 (February 2000), <http://users.ox.ac.uk/~scat0385/17monody.html> (accessed 24 September 2005).

49    John Keats's early sonnet on Chatterton, *Oh Chatterton! How very sad thy fate!* should be mentioned here as continuing in this vein with his representation of Chatterton as "a half-blown flower, which cold blasts amate." See Claude Lee Finney, *The Evolution of Keats's Poetry*, 2 vols. (Cambridge: Harvard University Press, 1936), 1:55, for an analysis of Keats's heavy reliance on Coleridge's *Monody* as a source. For more on Keats's relationship to Chatterton see Lau, "Class and Politics in Keats's Admiration of Chatterton"; "Protest, 'Nativism,' and Impersonation in the Works of Chatterton and Keats," 519–39; "The Ventriloquized Self in Keats and Chatterton," in *Inventing the Individual: Romanticism and the Idea of Individualism*, ed. Larry H. Peer (Provo: Brigham Young University Press, 2002), 125–33.

power: "Yet shall the Muse, to gentlest sorrow prone, / Adopt his cause, and make his griefs her own" (9–10). Just as she emphasizes the snowdrop's suffering, here she underlines Chatterton's isolation, saved only by his verse and the possibility of fame. The poem's repetition of negatives ("not," "nor," "No") articulates the poet's deprivation. Her poem sets out to preserve Chatterton's verse, arguing for his immortality through its "dazzling lustre" that will "claim a brighter wreath than wealth can give" (103, 104). Having herself experienced disdain and hardship, Robinson attempts to use her poetic authority, still in its earlier stages, to save Chatterton's name, a name that she notes is "borrow'd" and that "gain'd by Fiction what was due to Fame" (57–8). Though Chatterton's Rowley poems were deemed forgeries, Robinson, who herself had been writing under the pseudonym Laura Maria in the 1780s and whose authorial fame was being fed by public fictions of her sexual history, might have felt a sympathy with Chatterton that went beyond his interest to her as a misunderstood poet.

Of course, many Romantic poets shared an investment in Chatterton as Wordsworth's "marvellous boy," whose poetry embodied the power of imagination, despite its forged status.[50] While I am not suggesting that Coleridge and Robinson respond directly to one another, I do want to propose that, given their other associations, the parallel seems striking and can shed further light on their interrelated poetic concerns. In addition to their shared interest in Bristol, Chatterton's and Robinson's birthplace, the Monodies represent a collective anxiety about poetic fame and the slighting of genius, as much a reflection on their own poetic authority as on Chatterton's genius.[51] Though Robinson's poem seems less politicized than Coleridge's and more confident in its poetic authority (appropriately, since Robinson was the more established poet when she wrote her Monody), the poems share the language of sensibility in their personal expressions of grief. Coleridge later wrote off his poem as juvenilia, perhaps because its language resembles that of the Della Cruscans. According to Magnuson, "both versification and allusions link Coleridge's 'Monody' to the literature of sensibility." In fact, Thelwall wrote Coleridge that the poem suffered because it was of the "Della Crusca school which blurs almost every one of your poems—I mean the frequent accent upon adjectives and weak words—'Escap'd the *sore* wounds [l. 11]—'Sunk to the *cold* earth' [l. 32]—'Love glittering, thro' the *high* tree branching wide' [l. 99]—'When most the *big* soul feels' [l. 101]—'Anon upon some *rough* rock's fearful brow' [l. 106]—'But dare no longer on the *sad theme* muse' [l. 112]— all occur in the first eight pages."[52] Coleridge responded to Thelwall by calling

---

<sup>50</sup>    The epithet "marvellous boy" is from Wordsworth's *Resolution and Independence.*

<sup>51</sup>    Southey was also from Bristol as was Sara Fricker. In 1795, Coleridge and Southey had planned their pantisocracy on College Green near where Robinson was born (Byrne, 4). In 1796, Coleridge had also sought subscriptions for *The Watchman* in Bristol.

<sup>52</sup>    Cited in Magnuson, "Monody." Robinson also later rejected her Della Cruscan poetry and mocks it in *Walsingham.*

"the Della-crusca place of Emphasis" "absurd": "where we wish to point out the *thing,* & the *quality* is mentioned merely as decoration."[53] Thelwall suggests that Coleridge's poetry prior to *Lyrical Ballads* is struggling to separate itself from that of the Della Cruscans; its influence "blurs" his poems. What Coleridge and Thelwall object to is the detraction from the thing itself: the adjective seeks to specify the thing but, in fact, has the opposite effect. The object becomes covered with its descriptors, ornamented like a Christmas tree. The adjectives attempt to heighten emotion and instead bring with them an element of theatricality. Coleridge's Monodies on Chatterton share this quality as well as two elements of the conversation poem that McGann suggests arose from the experience of sensibility: "spontaneity and a continuity of mental action."[54] It is possible, given that Coleridge was aware of and experimenting with Della Cruscan ideas and language, that in revising his earlier version he may have recalled Robinson's more personal Monody. It seems worth noting that in the 1796 version he removed the Gray epigraph which their poems originally shared, he strengthened the personal response and increased his use of couplets, and he included a stanza where he sees Chatterton's "wasted form" and "hurried steps" (64). (Robinson hears Chatterton's "wandering shade complain" and sees his "phantom" in Bristol Cathedral [73, 76].) Finally, in a note to the 1796 Monody, which he and Cottle decided not to publish, Coleridge comments specifically on Chatterton's forgery, his ability "to ingeniously counterfeit styles."[55] In light of the complex citation practices of his *Biographia Literaria* and the allusiveness of his Monody, this interest appears pointed. He and Robinson clearly shared an interest in experimenting with the poetic styles of others as they worked to make their own. These early Monodies may serve, then, as an indication of future poetic practice. Like Chatterton himself, they seek to gain authority by speaking through the voice or persona or style of someone else who is more established or respected, forging their own authorship by imitating another's.

Coleridge's shape-shifting may be seen in the juxtaposition of *The Apotheosis* with his other 1798 poems, those in *Lyrical Ballads*. By the time of *Lyrical Ballads*, Coleridge, under the influence of another powerful poet, Wordsworth, had divided loyalties and was intent on redefining his poetic concerns to fit his role in that volume. The change in Coleridge's thinking can be traced by comparing his two nightingale poems, *The Nightingale, A Conversation Poem*, published in *Lyrical Ballads*, and an earlier poem, *To the Nightingale* (1795). The nightingale poems, however, also provide another set of poems that connect Coleridge to Robinson and further indicate their shared poetic development. For not only does Coleridge's earlier nightingale poem use the same image of the white-armed lady with her harp that appears in *Apotheosis* but, in Sonnet XIV of *Sappho and Phaon*, Robinson explicitly associates the eolian harp with the nightingale. This association recalls

---

53  Coleridge, *Collected Letters*, 1:216.
54  McGann, 19.
55  Cited in Magnuson, "Monody."

a much earlier poem of Robinson's, written during her Della Cruscan phase, her *Ode to the Nightingale* (*Oracle*, 11 December 1789, published under Laura Maria).[56] Of course, the nightingale is a literary motif with a long history again going back to the Greeks (in particular Ovid and Sappho) that includes Milton (*Il Penseroso*), but it is with Robinson that it starts to take on its Romantic overtones and with Coleridge that it takes its Romantic form. The nightingale's importance for Robinson, its double connection with poetry and love, is made explicit in her citation of the opening sonnet of Milton's 1645 sonnets in her preface to *Sappho and Phaon*: "Whether the Muse, or Love call thee his mate, / Both them I serve, and of their train am I" (*MR*, 145). While it is Keats who most explicitly responds to Robinson's poem, especially in his recontextualizing of her word "Forlorn," Coleridge's poems can be read as an indirect response to the ornamental language of the Della Cruscans so prominent in Robinson's ode, the very language he was trying out in his effusions of 1796. His poems are both a reconfiguring of the traditional representation of the nightingale as a melancholy bird as well as an extension of the presentation of self in Robinson's poem.

Robinson's early poem takes up the convention of the nightingale as a figure for poetry and situates it in a Della Cruscan landscape of ornamental language and surface adjectives, yet its focus on the self in nature, however stylized, makes it a pre-Romantic poem. The bird is represented as a sympathetic figure, as one who has lost its mate, as the speaker projects her own sense of loss, her "forlorn" state, onto the bird (82–4). The speaker questions the bird's wandering, listens to its tale, and wanders herself until she is forced by resistless pain to stop. Much like Keats, the speaker attempts to unite with the bird, but whereas Keats's nightingale offers a joyous escape from self, Robinson's bird affirms the speaker's melancholy. As they "chaunt [their] woes" (66) together, the nightingale's "strain" allows the speaker to crown herself with "a weeping wreath" of "thorns" (61, 70, 68), an act that valorizes her suffering and her poetry. But even these "melting Strains" (77) cannot release her from her "tyrant sorrow" (78), to which she finally returns. Just as Keats's bird serves only to remind him of his own bodiliness, so too the speaker's connection to the bird, her poetry, cannot overcome the very thing she wishes to escape. Written several years before Robinson began in earnest to assert her authority as a poet, the poem is rife with adjectival phrases and contracted words that create a Della Cruscan landscape adorned with "filmy vapours" (7) and "silv'ry dews" (68) where nightingale and speaker mourn "beside the willow-margin'd stream" (11) and beneath a "waning Crescent" (71). Nonetheless, the poem also provides an important indication of Robinson's later poetic concerns. In addition to her use of her own sorrows to sell her poetry, the poem reveals a

---

[56]    Robinson also published a *Second Ode to the Nightingale* immediately following this one in her 1791 *Poems*. The second ode's Della Cruscan landscape has several Romantic elements, including a speaker observing an increasingly naturalized landscape, a breeze trope, and rustic imagery more associated with Wordsworth's early poems. The speaker rejects "gaudy glitt'ring scenes" for the nightingale's "obliterating pow'rs."

poetic authority that is achieved, paradoxically, through a kind of self-loss.[57] The speaker's identification with the nightingale produces a strong emotional response that is the source of her poetic power. Like the figure of the harp, though less fully elaborated, the nightingale emphasizes the externality of poetic inspiration, the self-surrender to a natural source that is necessary to composition. Her identification with the nightingale here parallels her later identification with the snowdrop, and her speaker seems an emotional precursor to the reflective subject of Coleridge's conversation poems.

If Coleridge's nightingale poems reflect on Robinson's, they also reveal his progression away from the language of sensibility. *To the Nightingale* dates from the period (1794–1796) when, McGann claims, Coleridge was under the influence of the Della Cruscans.[58] The poem praises the nightingale's song over "the delicious airs / That vibrate from a white-arm'd lady's harp / What time the languishment of lonely love / Melts in her eye" (19–22), an image that resonates with Laura's portrayal in *Apotheosis* as well as the speaker's lovelorn state in Robinson's *Ode to the Nightingale*. The preference of the nightingale over the lady's harp significantly situates Coleridge's poem in line with a history of poets (in particular Milton, whom he quotes in line 17) and a history of poetry about the nightingale to which he refers in the first nine lines. The poem begins with a consciousness of its own belatedness, a consciousness of using a well-worn poetic figure for the "love-lorn." But Coleridge sets out to differentiate his nightingale from the bird of other poets, as he emphasizes "I *do* hear thee" (10) and often "hymn thy name" (15). The poetry of the nightingale is "sweeter" (19) than that of the lady, whose poetry is not situated in the natural or the mythical realm but instead is a feminized poetry of sensibility that derives from the "languishment of lonely love" (21). Coleridge's poem further asserts its difference from previous works by using the nightingale not as a figure of the lovelorn but as a foil for the intimate relationship of marriage. Rejecting, perhaps ironically, one final association of the nightingale—the myth of Philomel's rape by her brother-in-law— Coleridge ends the poem by asserting the domestic when he reidentifies the bird with the voice of Sara, promising him the name of husband, as the sweetest poetry still. The poem thus establishes a hierarchy of poetry through its figures that prioritizes the intimate voice of marriage and the direct apprehension of nature over that of the Bards, of myth, or the artifice of the Lady. Rejecting what the speaker considers false literary traditions, Coleridge's *To the Nightingale* provides a response to Robinson's poem on several levels: it critiques the poetic convention of using the nightingale as a figure of melancholy; it rejects the kind of poetry symbolized by the Lady with her harp, a figure Coleridge clearly associates with Robinson; and it offers the domestic as a solution to the lovelorn's agony, the wife's voice as a substitute for the nightingale's strain.

---

[57]    See Jacqueline Labbe, "Selling One's Sorrows: Charlotte Smith, Mary Robinson, and the Marketing of Poetry," *The Wordsworth Circle* 25 (1994): 68–71.

[58]    McGann, 89.

If the earlier poem can be read as an attempt by Coleridge to reconfigure conventional poetic imagery, Coleridge's later conversation poem explicitly marks the distance that he intends to place in 1798 between the conversation poem and sentimental poetry like Robinson's. Significantly, *The Nightingale* is the only conversation poem in *Lyrical Ballads*, and as such it is more like Wordsworth's poems than the more supernatural ones that Coleridge was supposed to be contributing to the volume. If earlier he borrowed Della Cruscan language and images, here he uses Wordsworthian ones.[59] This poem has been read variously as a place for Coleridge's working through of his poetic anxiety and as a poetic manifesto for Coleridge's poetry in *Lyrical Ballads*.[60] According to Susan Luther, Coleridge's poem is an "endeavor to reformulate, restructure, and refine not only lyric language, but the figure of the poet," holding in tension the conversational persona with that of the lyrist. It establishes not only a complex dialogue with Milton's work but also with Wordsworth's that shows, she argues, the "recuperative power of successive revision."[61] I will not rehearse Luther's argument here but want to suggest that another figure in this dialogue may be Robinson, whose ode can also be read through its relationship to Milton. Let me briefly indicate how Coleridge's poem might be critiquing Della Cruscan uses of the nightingale like Robinson's by looking at two moments in the poem. In the first part of the poem, the speaker, out for an evening walk with friends, critiques the traditional portrayal of the nightingale as "melancholy," claiming that "in nature there is nothing melancholy" (15). Instead, some "night-wandering man" (16), much like Robinson's night-wandering female speaker, has projected his own sorrow onto the nightingale and named it as such. This leads the speaker to critique the whole history of poets who have "echoe[d] the conceit" (23) and to redefine the poet's task as "a different lore" (41): "so his song / Should make all nature lovelier, and itself / Be lov'd like nature!" (32–4). Articulating a creed far from the artifice and theatricality of the Della Cruscan's erotically charged poetic exchanges, Coleridge goes on to chastise those "youths and maidens most poetical / Who lose the deep'ning twilight of the spring / In ball-rooms and hot theatres," who "still full of meek sympathy must heave their sighs / O'er Philomela's pity-pleading strains" (35–9). Robinson's association with the *bon ton* and the theatre would certainly include her in this "most poetical" group, whose poetry, "full

---

[59]    Mays points out the poem is full of "Wordsworthian associations and echoes" (*PW*, 1.1.521). The self-mocking poem that Coleridge wrote to accompany the poem when he sent it to Wordsworth, *To William Wordsworth, with* The Nightingale (10 May 1798), self-consciously affirms this connection, as he claims the poem "makes its own inglorious harmony" with, as Mays translates, "Aeolian farting" (1.1.521).

[60]    See Timothy P. Enright, "Sing, Mariner: Identity and Temporality in Coleridge's 'Nightingale,'" *Studies in Romanticism* 33 (1994): 481–501 and Susan Luther, "'A Different Lore': Coleridge's 'The Nightingale,'" *The Wordsworth Circle* 20 (1989): 91–7 as two examples.

[61]    Luther, "'A Different Lore': Coleridge's 'The Nightingale,'" 96, 95.

of ... sympathy," "sighs" over the nightingale's "pity-pleading strains," a Della Cruscan phrase to be sure. In the course of the poem, Coleridge sets out to create a new poetic dialogue among himself and Dorothy and William Wordsworth by revising the poetic tradition of the nightingale, but the very act of revision affirms his connection to an earlier poetic dialogue with Robinson and the Della Cruscans. For though Robinson's poem might be said to lose "the deep'ning twilights of the spring" (36) in its course, it also begins by imagining the nightingale in its natural haunts, not in its mythic setting. Moreover, if Coleridge seeks to recenter poetry in a man conversing with his friends, in the second half of the poem he returns to the image of the harp and the Lady, here refigured as "a most gentle maid" (69), who is "(Even like a Lady vow'd and dedicate / To something more than nature in the grove)" (72–3). It is this muse-like maid who mediates the Moon's waking of the "wild" grove of nightingales into "choral minstrelsy, / As if one quick and sudden Gale had swept / An hundred airy harps!" (80–82). Though the comparison of nightingale to eolian harp here imagines a poetry inspired solely by nature, the resurfacing of a harp in connection with an inspiring lady retains the trace of its representation in Coleridge's and Robinson's earlier nightingale poems. If the grove of nightingales can be read as a figure for Romantic poetry, Robinson's and Coleridge's earlier dialogue must be considered as part of its history, for much like the nightingales "they answer and provoke each other's songs— / With skirmish and capricious passagings, / And murmurs musical" (58–60).

The overlapping images I have traced here suggest an even more complex relationship between Robinson and Coleridge than scholars have thus far articulated, one that Robinson clearly pushed but that was also mutually beneficial. Robinson and Coleridge shared an investment in reconfiguring traditional poetic imagery and a concern for poetic reputation that began as early as 1796 and if not sublime was at least "associating," an "imitative sympathy" that was the source of a productive, if short-lived, lyrical exchange. While Coleridge may later have turned away from the figure of the eolian harp, in 1796 both he and Robinson imagined it to be a symbol for a poetry grounded in sensibility. Highly aware of the fragility of poetic reputation and anxious to establish themselves, both poets saw the eolian harp as a fitting image of poetic inspiration: the poet could passively surrender him/herself to emotions spontaneously evoked by forces outside themselves (nature, another poet, a marginalized other like Chatterton). Both wanted to downplay poetic agency, and, paradoxically, saw their identification with others as a source of poetic authority. Thus, images like the nightingale, the flower, and Chatterton associated with poetry, vulnerability, otherness, and marginality provided a means to emphasize their sensitivity to others and to the natural world. If the flower revealed the poet as a feminized figure, Chatterton provided an image of neglected poetic genius as well as a model for successfully forging one's own authority by imitating another's. Both harp and nightingale embodied their receptiveness to nature. Where the images of the eolian harp and flower reveal Robinson's and Coleridge's mutual experimentation with the ornamental Della Cruscan style that they both later rejected, the nightingale and Chatterton poems emphasize their shared concern for neglected genius as well as both poets's movements toward the more natural settings and self-reflection we have come to associate with Romanticism. Their parallel, and at times overlapping, exploration of these four images thus reveals a process of lyrical exchange, whose culmination was their work at the *The Morning Post* (1797–1800), but which began earlier as both poets sought to authorize their reputations as important poets.

Though Robinson claims in her *Memoirs* never to have met that "associating mind" she sought, a few pages later she imparts the story of her daughter's first words, spoken while they are imprisoned for debt during her married life with Mr. Robinson. Though she does not say so, it is her "mother's tale" offered as a response to and revision of Coleridge's "father's tale" at the end of his *The Nightingale*.[62] Where Coleridge's son Hartley is hushed by the awesome sight of the moon, Robinson's little girl responds to the moon slipping behind a cloud with the words her nurse has used to discipline her: "all gone."[63] Though the children's responses to the natural world are markedly different, that Robinson chooses to rewrite Coleridge's scene in her *Memoirs*, as she seeks to write her story, underscores her sense of their shared project. Though she never mentions his name throughout, it is clearly Coleridge, as the above analysis suggests, who has been the "associating mind" she claims never to have found. What is "all gone" from Robinson's *Memoirs* is Coleridge's shaping presence, but he hovers even there, like the music of Laura's harp, "half-perceiv'd."

## Works Cited

Bolton, Betsy. "Romancing the Stone: 'Perdita' Robinson in Wordsworth's London." *ELH* 64 (1997): 727–59.

Burns, Robert. *Selected Poetry and Prose*. Edited by Robert D. Thornton. Boston: Houghton Mifflin, 1966.

Byrne, Paula. *Perdita: The Literary, Theatrical, Scandalous Life of Mary Robinson*. New York: Random House, 2004.

Clemit, Pamela. "Coleridge, Godwin and Mary Robinson: The Identity of 'C.'" *The Friends of Coleridge, TLS*—Letters (18 February 2005). <http://www.friendsofcoleridge.com/TLS2.htm> (accessed 24 September 2005).

Coleridge, Samuel Taylor. *Coleridge: The Complete Poems*. Ed. William Keach. New York: Penguin Books, 1997.

—. *The Collected Letters of Samuel Taylor Coleridge*. Ed. Earl Leslie Griggs. 6 vols. Oxford: Clarendon Press, 1956.

---

[62]   Paula Byrne also notices this connection in her recent biography (57–8).

[63]   For another reading of this moment in Robinson's *Memoirs,* see Chris Cullens, "Mrs. Robinson and the Masquerade of Womanliness," in *Body and Text in the Eighteenth Century*, eds. Veronica Kelly and Dorothea von Mucke (Stanford: Stanford University Press, 1994), 266–89.

—. *Poetical Works*. Ed. J. C. C. Mays. 3 vols. in 6 parts. Princeton: Princeton University Press, 2001.

—. *Specimens of the Table Talk of S. T. Coleridge*. Ed. Henry N. Coleridge. London: J. Murray, 1835. Project Gutenberg, Ebook #8489. <ftp://ibiblio.org/pub/docs/books/gutenberg/etext05/8tabc10.txt> (accessed July 2005).

—. "Appendix D: Verse Contributions by Coleridge and Wordsworth." In *Essays on His Times*. Ed. David Erdman. Princeton: Princeton University Press, 1978.

—. *The Watchman*. Ed. Lewis Patton. Princeton: Princeton University Press, 1970.

Cross, Ashley. "From *Lyrical Ballads* to *Lyrical Tales*: Mary Robinson's Reputation and the Problem of Literary Debt." *Studies in Romanticism* 40 (2001): 547–70.

Cullens, Chris. "Mrs. Robinson and the Masquerade of Womanliness." In *Body and Text in the Eighteenth Century*. Ed. Veronica Kelly and Dorothea von Mucke. Stanford: Stanford University Press, 1994. 266–89.

Curran, Stuart. "Mary Robinson's *Lyrical Tales* in Context." In *Re-Visioning Romanticism: British Women Writers, 1776–1837*. Ed. Carol Shiner Wilson and Joel Haefner. Philadelphia: University of Pennsylvania Press, 1994. 17–35.

Ellison, Julie. *Delicate Subjects: Romanticism, Gender, and the Ethics of Understanding*. Ithaca: Cornell University Press, 1990.

Enright, Timothy P. "Sing, Mariner: Identity and Temporality in Coleridge's 'Nightingale.'" *Studies in Romanticism* 33 (1994): 481–501.

Erdman, David. "Lost Poem Found: The Cooperative Pursuit and Recapture of an Escaped Coleridge 'Sonnet' of 72 Lines." *Bulletin of the New York Public Library* 65 (1961): 249–68.

Fairer, David. "Chatterton's Poetic Afterlife, 1770–1794: A Context for Coleridge's *Monody*." In *Thomas Chatterton and Romantic Culture*. Ed. Nick Groom. New York: St. Martin's Press, 1999. 228–52.

Ferber, Michael. *The Dictionary of Literary Symbols*. Cambridge: Cambridge University Press, 1999.

Finney, Claude Lee. *The Evolution of Keats's Poetry*. 2 vols. Cambridge: Harvard University Press, 1936.

Fulford, Tim. "Mary Robinson and the Abyssinian Maid: Coleridge's Muses and Feminist Criticism." *Romanticism on the Net* 13 (February 1999). <http://users.ox.ac.uk/~scat0385/kublarobinson.html> (accessed 25 August 1999).

—. *Romanticism and Masculinity: Gender, Politics, and Poetics in the Writing of Burke, Coleridge, Cobbett, Wordsworth, DeQuincey, and Hazlitt*. New York: Palgrave, 1999.

Jackson, H. J. "Coleridge's Women, or Girls, Girls, Girls Are Made to Love." *Studies in Romanticism* 32 (1993): 577–600.

Labbe, Jacqueline. "Selling One's Sorrows: Charlotte Smith, Mary Robinson, and the Marketing of Poetry." *The Wordsworth Circle* 25 (1994): 68–71.

Lau, Beth. "Class and Politics in Keats's Admiration of Chatterton." *Keats-Shelley Journal* 53 (2004): 25–38.

—. "Protest, 'Nativism,' and Impersonation in the Works of Chatterton and Keats." *Studies in Romanticism* 42 (2003): 519–39.

—. "The Ventriloquized Self in Keats and Chatterton." In *Inventing the Individual: Romanticism and the Idea of Individualism*. Ed. Larry H. Peer. Provo: Brigham Young University Press, 2002. 125–33.

Ledbetter, Kathryn. "A Woman of Undoubted Genius: Mary Robinson and S. T. Coleridge." *Postscript* 11.1 (1994): 43–9.

Luther, Susan. "'A Different Lore': Coleridge's 'The Nightingale.'" *The Wordsworth Circle* 20 (1989): 91–7.

—. "A Stranger Minstrel: Coleridge's Mrs. Robinson." *Studies in Romanticism* 33 (1994): 391–409.

McGann, Jerome. *The Poetics of Sensibility: A Revolution in Literary Style*. Oxford: Clarendon Press, 1996.

Magnuson, Paul. "Coleridge's Discursive 'Monody on the Death of Chatterton.'" *Romanticism on the Net* 17 (February 2000). <http://users.ox.ac.uk/~scat0385/17monody.html> (accessed 24 September 2005).

—. "'The Eolian Harp' in Context." *Studies in Romanticism* 24 (1985): 3–20.

Mellor, Anne K. *Romanticism and Gender*. New York: Routledge, 1993.

Pascoe, Judith. "Mary Robinson and the Literary Marketplace." In *Romantic Women Writers: Voices and Countervoices*. Ed. Paula R. Feldman and Theresa M. Kelley. Hanover, NH: University Press of New England, 1995. 252–68.

—. *Romantic Theatricality: Gender, Poetry, and Spectatorship*. Ithaca: Cornell University Press, 1997.

Robinson, Daniel. "From 'Mingled Measure' to 'Ecstatic Measures': Mary Robinson's Poetic Reading of 'Kubla Khan.'" *The Wordsworth Circle* 26 (1995): 4–7.

Robinson, Mary. *Mary Robinson: Selected Poems*. Ed. Judith Pascoe. Toronto: Broadview Press, 2000.

—. *Memoirs of the Late Mrs. Robinson, Written by Herself*. Ed. Maria E. Robinson. 4 vols. London: R. Phillips, 1801.

—. *The Poetical Works of the Late Mrs. Mary Robinson*. Ed. Maria Robinson. London, 1806, 1824. Rpt. Providence: Brown University Women Writers Project, 1990.

—. *Walsingham; or the Pupil of Nature*. Ed. Julie Shaffer. Toronto: Broadview Press, 2003.

Sisman, Adam. "Coleridge, Mary (Perdita) Robinson, and 'Kubla Khan.'" *The Friends of Coleridge, TLS*—Letters (2 December 2004). <http://www.friends of coleridge.com/KublaKhan.htm> (accessed 24 September 2005).

Taylor, Anya. "Coleridge on Persons in Dialogue." *Modern Language Quarterly* 50 (1989): 357–74.

—. "Coleridge, Wollstonecraft, and the Rights of Woman." In *Coleridge's Visionary Languages: Essays in Honour of J. B. Beer*. Ed. Tim Fulford and Morton D. Paley. Cambridge: D. S. Brewer, 1993. 83–98.

—. *Erotic Coleridge*. New York: Palgrave Macmillan, 2005.

Vargo, Lisa. "The Claims of 'real life and manners': Coleridge and Mary Robinson." *The Wordsworth Circle* 26 (1995): 134–7.

# Chapter 3
# Romantic Ambivalence in *Frankenstein* and *The Rime of the Ancient Mariner*

Beth Lau

Readers of *Frankenstein* know that Mary Shelley was familiar with Coleridge's *Rime of the Ancient Mariner*, since she quotes the work twice in her novel. Early on in the 1818 edition, Robert Walton tells his sister that he is "going to unexplored regions, to 'the land of mist and snow;' but I shall kill no albatross, therefore do not be alarmed for my safety."[1] In the 1831 text, the passage is expanded as Walton explains, "or if I should come back to you as worn and woful as the 'Ancient Mariner?' You will smile at my allusion; but I will disclose a secret. I have often attributed my attachment to, my passionate enthusiasm for, the dangerous mysteries of ocean, to that production of the most imaginative of modern poets."[2] In both the 1818 and 1831 editions, Victor Frankenstein quotes lines 446–51 of *The Ancient Mariner*—

> Like one who, on a lonely road
>   Doth walk in fear and dread,
> And, having once turn'd round, walks on,
>   And turns no more his head;
> Because he knows a frightful fiend
>   Doth close behind him tread—

to describe his state of mind as he walks the streets of Ingolstadt the morning after bestowing life on his creature (*1818*, 35–6; *1831*, 59).[3] In addition to these two

---

[1]    Mary Shelley, *Frankenstein*, ed. J. Paul Hunter (New York: Norton, 1996), 11. All references to the novel are to this, the 1818 edition, unless otherwise noted. When it is necessary to distinguish this from other editions, it will be referred to as *1818*.

[2]    *Frankenstein, or The Modern Prometheus*, ed. M. K. Joseph (New York: Oxford University Press, 1969), 21. Quotations of the 1831 text of the novel are from this edition, hereafter referred to as *1831*.

[3]    Mary Shelley slightly misquotes the passage by writing "who" instead of "that" for line 446. Her use of "lonely" instead of "lonesome" in the same line suggests that she was citing the poem from the first edition of *Lyrical Ballads*, which is the only edition that has "lonely" instead of "lonesome" for this passage. See the text and notes for *The Rime of the*

direct quotations in the novel, Mary Shelley's 1831 Introduction to *Frankenstein* contains a clear allusion to Coleridge's poem. Describing the vision that originated the novel, Shelley writes, "I saw the hideous phantasm of a man stretched out, and then, on the working of some powerful engine, show signs of life and stir with an uneasy, half vital motion" (*1831*, 9). This passage echoes lines 385–8 of *Ancient Mariner* where the ship "'gan stir, / With a short uneasy motion— / Backwards and forwards half her length / With a short uneasy motion."[4]

Despite these conspicuous references to *The Ancient Mariner*, remarkably few critics have examined intertextual parallels between *Frankenstein* and Coleridge's poem. Several scholars have noted Coleridge's importance for Mary Shelley. Robert Kiely claims that "of all the romantic influences on [Mary Shelley's] mind and work, [Percy] Shelley's undoubtedly stimulated, but Coleridge's comforted; Shelley's provided confusion and enchantment, Coleridge's provided psychological and moral consolation." Emily Sunstein also states that "of all Godwin's friends Coleridge probably had the greatest influence on Mary." John Beer concludes that Mary Shelley's quotations of *Ancient Mariner* in *Frankenstein* "show how intimately the images and language of Coleridge's poem had entered her imagination," and Beer notes several parallels between the two works.[5] Articles

---

*Ancient Mariner* in Samuel Taylor Coleridge, *Poetical Works*, ed. J. C. C. Mays, 3 vols. in 6 parts (Princeton: Princeton University Press, 2001), 1.1 (Reading Text), 2.1 (Variorum Text) and also Jack Stillinger's clear presentation of variants in *Coleridge and Textual Instability: The Multiple Versions of the Major Poems* (New York: Oxford University Press, 1994), 176. In this essay, I quote from the first, 1798 version printed in *Poetical Works* as that closest to the one Mary Shelley would have known when composing her novel, though I refer to the title of the poem by its later spelling (*The Rime of the Ancient Mariner* rather than 1798's *The Rime of the Ancyent Marinere*).

[4]    John Beer notes this allusion to *The Rime of the Ancient Mariner*, which is not documented by either J. Paul Hunter or M. K. Joseph in their editions of the novel ("Mary Shelley, *Frankenstein*," in *A Companion to Romanticism*, ed. Duncan Wu [Oxford: Blackwell, 1998], 233). Hunter notes another possible allusion to *The Rime of the Ancient Mariner* in *Frankenstein*: he considers Victor's reference to the "burning thirst" he experiences when he is adrift at sea, just before landing in Ireland, to be indebted to Coleridge's poem (*1818*, 119n.4). William Veeder (*Mary Shelley and* Frankenstein: *The Fate of Androgyny* [Chicago: University of Chicago Press, 1986], 106) argues for another possible allusion, which I discuss below. Mary Shelley also quotes line 386 of *Ancient Mariner* in a 9 September 1823 letter to Leigh Hunt, describing her journey to England on board a ship: "though the Engine gave a 'short uneasy motion' to the vessel, the water was so smooth that no one on board was sick" (*The Letters of Mary Wollstonecraft Shelley*, ed. Betty T. Bennett, 3 vols. [Baltimore: The Johns Hopkins University Press, 1980–1988], 1:377).

[5]    Robert Kiely, *The Romantic Novel in England* (Cambridge: Harvard University Press, 1972), 170; Emily W. Sunstein, *Mary Shelley: Romance and Reality* (Baltimore: The Johns Hopkins University Press, 1989), 51; Beer, 233, 227–8, 234–5.

by Sarah Webster Goodwin and Michelle Levy, however, are among the few that provide detailed comparisons of *Ancient Mariner* and *Frankenstein*.[6]

Coleridge has perhaps been overlooked in intertextual studies of *Frankenstein* because the novel is most frequently discussed in relation to the works of Mary Shelley's family: her husband Percy Bysshe Shelley and her parents William Godwin and Mary Wollstonecraft.[7] In addition, *Frankenstein* is often interpreted as

---

[6]    Sarah Webster Goodwin, "Domesticity and Uncanny Kitsch in 'The Rime of the Ancient Mariner' and *Frankenstein*," *Tulsa Studies in Women's Literature* 10 (1991): 93–108; Michelle Levy, "Discovery and the Domestic Affections in Coleridge and Shelley," *Studies in English Literature, 1500–1900* 44 (2004): 693–713. Another work that compares *Ancient Mariner* and *Frankenstein*, along with Wordsworth's *The Prelude*, is Eugene Stelzig's "Always/Never on the Way Home: Reflections on the Romantic Self and the Family," *Mid-Hudson Language Studies* 12 (1989): 46–53. Leslie Ann Minot and Walter S. Minot offer an in-depth study of affinities between Coleridge and Mary Shelley, but they argue that *Christabel* rather than *The Rime of the Ancient Mariner* is the Coleridge work "most relevant to Shelley's central purposes in *Frankenstein*" ("*Frankenstein* and *Christabel*: Intertextuality, Biography, and Gothic Ambiguity," *European Romantic Review* 15 [2004]: 24).

[7]    Critics who read *Frankenstein* as a commentary on or response to Percy Bysshe Shelley and his works include P. D. Fleck, "Mary Shelley's Notes to Shelley's Poems and *Frankenstein*," *Studies in Romanticism* 6 (1967): 226–54; Kiely, 160–64; Christopher Small, *Ariel Like a Harpy: Shelley, Mary and* Frankenstein (London: Victor Gollancz, 1972), 100–121; Paul A. Cantor, *Creature and Creator: Myth-making and English Romanticism* (Cambridge: Cambridge University Press, 1984), chap. 4, especially 108, 116–17, 130; Veeder, 92–8, 112–23, and *passim*; Margaret Homans, *Bearing the Word: Language and Female Experience in Nineteenth-Century Women's Writing* (Chicago: University of Chicago Press,, 1986), 100–19; Anne K. Mellor, *Mary Shelley: Her Life, Her Fiction, Her Monsters* (New York: Methuen, 1988), especially chap. 4; Elisabeth Bronfen, "Rewriting the Family: Mary Shelley's *Frankenstein* in its Biographical/Textual Context," in Frankenstein: *Creation and Monstrosity*, ed. Stephen Bann (London: Reaktion, 1994), 16–38. Katherine Hill-Miller cites other sources (*"My Hideous Progeny": Mary Shelley, William Godwin, and the Father-Daughter Relationship* [Newark: University of Delaware Press, 1995], 215–16n.10).

Studies of *Frankenstein* in relation to William Godwin and his works include Small, 68–99; Gay Clifford, "*Caleb Williams* and *Frankenstein*: First-Person Narrative and 'Things as They Are,'" *Genre* 10 (1977): 601–17; U. C. Knoepflmacher, "Thoughts on the Aggression of Daughters," in *The Endurance of* Frankenstein: *Essays on Mary Shelley's Novel*, ed. George Levine and U. C. Knoepflmacher (Berkeley and Los Angeles: University of California Press, 1979), 88–119; A.D. Harvey, "*Frankenstein* and *Caleb Williams*," *Keats-Shelley Journal* 29 (1980): 21–7; David Seed, "'Frankenstein': Parable or Spectacle?" *Criticism* 24 (1982): 327–40; Veeder, especially 13, 125–7, 132–5, 158, 168–71, 215–16; William St. Clair, *The Godwins and the Shelleys: A Biography of a Family* (Baltimore: The Johns Hopkins University Press, 1989), 434–8; Marilyn May, "Publish and Perish: William Godwin, Mary Shelley, and the Public Appetite for Scandal," *Papers on Language and Literature* 26 (1990): 489–512; Pamela Clemit, *The Godwinian Novel: The Rational Fictions of Godwin, Brockden Brown, Mary Shelley* (Oxford: Oxford University Press, 1993);

a condemnation and correction of masculine Romanticism. As Goodwin remarks, "Relatively scant attention has been paid to the novel's rich allusions to 'The Rime of the Ancient Mariner,' largely because they have been understood in the most accessible terms as part of Mary Shelley's indictment of the male Romantic poet." A typical view is that expressed by Irene Tayler and Gina Luria when they write, "*Frankenstein* may be read as Romantic Woman's ultimate judgment on the alienated artist of male romanticism."[8] I argue that, far from being a target of disapproval, Coleridge was a profoundly sympathetic and congenial figure to Mary Shelley whose beliefs, themes, and literary techniques resonated with and helped shape her own. In particular, both writers express profound ambivalence toward ambition and intimate, especially family relationships and employ a variety of defensive strategies to simultaneously address and deflect disturbing implications in their works.

---

Pamela Clemit, "*Frankenstein, Matilda,* and the Legacies of Godwin and Wollstonecraft," in *The Cambridge Companion to Mary Shelley*, ed. Esther Schor (Cambridge: Cambridge University Press, 2003), 26–44; Bronfen; Hill-Miller, *passim*; and Beer, 230–31.

Critics who explore *Frankenstein* in connection to Mary Wollstonecraft and her works include Marc Rubenstein, "'My Accursed Origin': The Search for the Mother in *Frankenstein*," *Studies in Romanticism* 15 (1976): 165–94; Janet M. Todd, "Frankenstein's Daughter: Mary Shelley and Mary Wollstonecraft," *Women and Literature* 4 (1976): 18–27; Sandra M. Gilbert and Susan Gubar, *The Madwoman in the Attic: The Woman Writer and the Nineteenth-Century Literary Imagination* (New Haven: Yale University Press, 1979), 222–3, 673n.30; Bronfen; Hill-Miller, 93–7; William D. Brewer, "Mary Wollstonecraft and Mary Shelley: Ideological Affinities," in *Jane Austen and Mary Shelley and Their Sisters*, ed. Laura Dabundo (Lanham, MA: University Press of America, 2000), 97–107; Clemit, "*Frankenstein, Matilda,* and the Legacies of Godwin and Wollstonecraft." Betty T. Bennett analyzes all of Mary Shelley's works in relation to those by P. B. Shelley, Godwin, and Wollstonecraft, stressing the affinities in their political views (*Mary Wollstonecraft Shelley: An Introduction* [Baltimore: The Johns Hopkins University Press, 1998]). My argument is not that Coleridge's works are more important to Mary Shelley than those of her parents or husband but that they constitute another significant influence that has received insufficient attention.

   [8]   Goodwin, 99; Irene Tayler and Gina Luria, "Gender and Genre: Women in British Romantic Literature," in *What Manner of Woman: Essays in English and American Life and Literature*, ed. Marlene Springer (New York: New York University Press, 1977), 121. Many of the critics cited in note 7 who explore *Frankenstein*'s allusions to Percy Shelley and his works read the novel as a criticism of Percy Shelley and male Romanticism generally (see especially Fleck, Cantor, Homans, Veeder, Mellor, *Mary Shelley*, and Bronfen). Another influential critic who argues that *Frankenstein* is a critique of male Romanticism is Mary Poovey, *The Proper Lady and the Woman Writer: Ideology as Style in the Works of Mary Wollstonecraft, Mary Shelley, and Jane Austen* (Chicago: University of Chicago Press, 1984), chap. 4. Those who specifically cite Coleridge as one of the male Romantics whose point of view conflicts with Mary Shelley's include Gilbert and Gubar, 235; Poovey, 261n.16; and Mellor, *Mary Shelley*, 70–71, 77–9.

The factual record of Mary Shelley's contact with Coleridge and his works can be briefly summarized. Coleridge read *Political Justice* and met William Godwin in 1794. Although Coleridge objected to Godwin's atheism and denigration of domestic affections,[9] the two men visited, corresponded, read each others' works, and influenced one another in important ways. Especially in the period of 1799–1801, Coleridge visited Godwin frequently in London and sent "kisses for Mary and Fanny [Imlay Godwin]" in his letters.[10] Godwin credited Coleridge with helping to develop his appreciation of poetry and in general enlarging his sympathies or "poetic and physiopathic feelings."[11] Indeed, he claimed that Coleridge was one of "the four principal oral instructors to whom I feel my mind indebted for improvement" and for a while considered writing Coleridge's biography.[12] A story survives that when Mary was a child, she and young Claire Clairmont hid under the sofa in order to hear Coleridge recite *The Rime of the Ancient Mariner*. Mrs. Godwin ordered them to bed, but Coleridge interceded on their behalf and they were allowed to hear the recitation.[13] After arriving home from Ramsgate on 19 December 1811, Mary with her family attended the remaining lectures in Coleridge's 1811–1812 series on Shakespeare and Milton.[14] On 23 January 1813, after returning from Scotland along with Christy Baxter, Mary attended the opening night of Coleridge's *Remorse* and also "saw a good deal of Coleridge himself" at this time.[15] In her girlhood and adolescence Mary Shelley therefore was frequently exposed to Coleridge—the man, his conversation, and his writings—and Sunstein claims that as a teenager Mary regarded Coleridge as one of her favorite modern authors.[16]

Mary Shelley's interest in Coleridge did not abate after she met and became involved with Percy Bysshe Shelley in 1814. Percy Shelley had admired Coleridge's poetry for some time; as a schoolboy at Eton he "developed the eccentricity of muttering bits of *Macbeth* and *Ancient Mariner* under his breath," and on 5 October 1814 he thrilled Mary Shelley and Claire Clairmont with a "melodramatic reading" of *The Ancient Mariner* and Wordsworth's *The Mad Mother*.[17] There is considerable evidence that the Shelleys were studying Coleridge in the years leading up to and

---

[9]    See Nicholas Roe, *Wordsworth and Coleridge: The Radical Years* (Oxford: Clarendon Press, 1988), 11, 93, 115–17.

[10]    *The Collected Letters of Samuel Taylor Coleridge*, ed. Earl Leslie Griggs, 6 vols. (Oxford: Clarendon Press, 1956–1971), 1:621; see also 1:588.

[11]    Coleridge, *Letters*, 1:588; quoted and discussed in Sunstein, 25.

[12]    St. Clair, 225, 227.

[13]    Sunstein, 40; Mellor, *Mary Shelley*, 11.

[14]    Sunstein, 51.

[15]    Sunstein, 58; see also St. Clair, 339.

[16]    Sunstein, 59.

[17]    Richard Holmes, *Shelley: The Pursuit* (New York: Putnam, 1975), 30, 257; see also Scott McEathron, "Death as 'Refuge and Ruin': Shelley's 'A Vision of the Sea' and Coleridge's 'The Rime of the Ancient Mariner,'" *Keats-Shelley Journal* 43 (1994): 170–92.

including *Frankenstein*'s composition. Mary Shelley's journal records that on 6 January 1815, "S reads Ode to France aloud and repeats [recites from memory] the poem to tranquility."[18] A manuscript also survives, which Donald Reiman dates from the period February 1815 to March 1816, in which Mary Shelley has written out from memory Coleridge's *France: An Ode* ("Ode to France" in Mary Shelley's manuscript) and *Fire, Famine and Slaughter*.[19] John Polidori also noted in his journal for 1 June 1816 that Mary Shelley recited "Coleridge on Pitt," or *Fire, Famine and Slaughter*, in Geneva; it must have been an impassioned performance, since Polidori said it "persuade[d him that Coleridge] is a poet."[20] Charles Robinson has assembled evidence of the Shelley circle's frequent reading of Coleridge's *The Friend* from October 1814 through September 1816.[21] Mary Shelley's reading list for 1815 lists "Coleridge's Poems," probably either the 1797 or 1803 edition of *Poems, by S. T. Coleridge. To Which Are Now Added Poems by Charles Lamb and Charles Lloyd* (*Journals*, 1:90). Her journal for 26 August 1816 notes that "several books arrive among others Coleridges Christabel which Shelley reads aloud to me before we go to bed" (*Journals*, 1:131). In addition, Percy Shelley had a species of fit at Villa Diodati in the summer of 1816 after Byron recited lines from *Christabel* describing Geraldine's loathsome bosom. After hearing the lines, according to Polidori, Shelley looked at Mary and "thought of a woman he had heard of who had eyes instead of nipples" and ran shrieking from the room.[22]

Byron had heard *Christabel* recited by Sir Walter Scott and was tremendously impressed by the poem, as he told Coleridge in a letter of October 1815.[23] In a note to *The Siege of Corinth* (1816), he praised *Christabel* as a "wild and singularly original and beautiful poem."[24] As Coleridge explains in his Preface to *Kubla Khan*, the poem was published "at the request of a poet of great and

---

[18]    *The Journals of Mary Shelley, 1814–1844*, ed. Paula R. Feldman and Diana Scott-Kilvert, 2 vols. (Oxford: Clarendon, 1987), 1:59. The *Ode to Tranquillity* remained a favorite with Mary Shelley. She slightly misquotes line 16 ("The bubble floats before, the sceptre stalks behind") in an 18 January 1824 journal entry (2:472) and at one point intended to use another passage from the poem as an epigraph for chapter two of her novel *Lodore* (see Mary Shelley, *Letters*, 2:196).

[19]    Donald Reiman, ed., *Shelley and His Circle, 1773–1822*, vol. 7 (Cambridge: Harvard University Press, 1986), 1–12.

[20]    Qtd. in Reiman, 10.

[21]    Charles E. Robinson, "The Shelley Circle and Coleridge's *The Friend*," *English Language Notes* 8 (1971): 269–74.

[22]    Qtd. in Reiman, 11. See also Holmes, *Shelley*, 328–30. According to Richard Monckton-Milnes, Mary Shelley was the source of Percy's vision, since Percy had learned from her that Coleridge originally meant for Geraldine to have "two eyes in her bosom" (qtd. in Sunstein, 112).

[23]    Leslie A. Marchand, *Byron: A Biography*, 3 vols. (New York: Knopf, 1957), 2:542–3.

[24]    Byron, *The Complete Poetical Works*, ed. Jerome J. McGann, 7 vols. (Oxford: Clarendon Press, 1980–1993), 3:486.

deserved celebrity," meaning Byron (*Poetical Works*, 1.1:511). Byron helped get Coleridge's *Remorse* accepted by the Drury Lane Committee in 1812, and in 1815 and 1816 Byron exchanged a number of letters with Coleridge and also donated £100 to a fund for his relief.[25] Among the group gathered in Geneva the summer *Frankenstein* was conceived, Coleridge was in high favor, and his poems and prose works were frequently read and recited. The Shelleys' interest in Coleridge appears to have continued throughout 1817 while *Frankenstein* was being written and revised, since the reading list for 1817 includes "Coleridge's Lay Sermon" or *The Statesman's Manual* for Mary (Percy read it in 1816) and "Coleridges Biographica [sic] Literaria" for Percy (Mary Shelley, *Journals* 1:98, 102). There is no question that Mary Shelley was deeply interested in Coleridge and familiar with many of his works and that her interest had been shared and fostered by family members and friends since her infancy. That she continued to read and admire Coleridge's works in later life is attested by the fact that she added further references to Coleridge and *The Ancient Mariner* in the 1831 edition of *Frankenstein*,[26] as well as by references to Coleridge in her letters and journals from the 1820s through the 1840s (a number of which are cited in this essay).

It is therefore not surprising that Mary Shelley quotes from *The Ancient Mariner* in *Frankenstein* or that the novel shares many similarities in theme, conflict, imagery, and narrative technique with Coleridge's poem. My argument, however, is not simply that Coleridge influenced Mary Shelley but that the two writers were profoundly akin in their temperaments and outlooks. Even when Mary Shelley may not have been directly influenced by Coleridge's work, she expresses concerns and employs literary techniques similar to those of the elder writer.

One central parallel between *The Rime of the Ancient Mariner* and *Frankenstein* is that both feature ambitious "overreacher" characters who reject social ties and commit crimes again nature. The Ancient Mariner leaves behind the familiar community represented by the "Harbour," "Kirk," and "Light-house" (21–4) and embarks on a bold journey to new territories, reminiscent of Magellan's or Captain Cook's voyages of discovery—or Robert Walton's daring expedition to the North Pole to "[ascertain] the secret of the magnet" (*Frankenstein*, 8).[27]

---

[25]    Marchand, 2:267–8, 580, 597; Warren Stevenson, "Byron and Coleridge: The Eagle and the Dove," *Byron Journal* 19 (1991): 114–27.

[26]    Minot and Minot argue that the increased references to Coleridge in the 1831 edition of *Frankenstein* improve the novel, making for "a tighter narrative patterning, particularly with regard to the use of doubles and foils" (24).

[27]    Leon Waldoff, citing John Livingston Lowes and D. W. Harding, remarks the ambitious, anti-social nature of the Mariner's journey and its similarity to those of Magellan and Captain Cook ("The Quest for Father and Identity in 'The Rime of the Ancient Mariner,'" *Psychoanalytic Review* 58 [1971]: 440). Levy associates the Mariner's voyage with eighteenth-century British imperial expansion and cites others who have developed this argument (693, 710n.8).

The Mariner then asserts his dominance over the animal kingdom and rejects a proffered relationship when he kills the friendly albatross. Victor Frankenstein violates nature by rudely "penetrat[ing] into [her] recesses" (28) in his obsessive pursuit of scientific knowledge, and he usurps nature's laws by creating life in his laboratory. His work is anti-social in that he pursues it alone and does not visit or even write to his family while he is engaged in it.

Both *The Ancient Mariner* and *Frankenstein* also espouse morals that condemn selfish ambition and advocate a loving, harmonious co-existence with people and other living things. This message is conveyed in the Mariner's lines, "He prayeth well who loveth well / Both man and bird and beast" (612–13), as well as in his statement that "O sweeter than the Marriage-feast, / 'Tis sweeter far to me, / To walk together to the Kirk / With a goodly company" (601–4) in communal worship. Victor Frankenstein tells Walton to "Seek happiness in tranquillity and avoid ambition" (152). He also admonishes Walton that "If the study to which you apply yourself has a tendency to weaken your affections … then that study is certainly unlawful, that is to say, not befitting the human mind" (33). Robert Walton, unlike Victor, writes to his sister and longs for a friend while engaged in his quest for knowledge and glory, and he turns back from his expedition when his crew feels unsafe. He thereby avoids Victor's crime and gives up or at least tempers ambition with loving concern for others. As Walton himself says, directly comparing his situation to that of the Ancient Mariner, he "kill[s] no albatross" on his journey to "'the land of mist and snow'" (11) but instead respects the needs and rights of other beings.

Mary Shelley's vision in *Frankenstein* of the dangers of egotistical ambition and the need for maintaining human ties has been characterized as an attack on male Romantic individualism and an expression of what psychologist Carol Gilligan terms an "ethic of care," which "gives priority to the good of the family and the community rather than to the rights of the individual" as is typical in the male "ethic of justice."[28] Coleridge, however, clearly shared Mary Shelley's reservations about egotistical self-assertion and her belief in the importance of supportive human relationships. One of Shelley's central points about relationships in fact is strikingly similar to an idea that recurs again and again in Coleridge's writings. Robert Walton, in expressing to his sister his longing for a friend, emphasizes the way in which an ideal friend would "repair the faults of your poor brother" and "endeavour to regulate my mind" (10). Walton later expresses similar ideas to Victor Frankenstein; he wants a friend to sympathize with him but also to "direct me by his counsel" (16). In the 1831 edition, Victor's reply clearly sums up the definition of friendship Walton is articulating. "'I agree with you,' replied the stranger; 'we are unfashioned creatures, but half made up, if one wiser, better, dearer than ourselves—such a friend ought to be—do not lend his

---

[28]     Anne K. Mellor, "Possessing Nature: The Female in *Frankenstein*," in *Romanticism and Feminism*, ed. Anne K. Mellor (Bloomington: Indiana University Press, 1988), 229. See also Mellor, *Mary Shelley,* 86–7.

aid to perfectionate our weak and faulty natures" (*1831*, 28). In his narrative of his idyllic childhood, Victor emphasizes the ways in which Clerval and Elizabeth balance and complete him by exposing him to interests and personality traits lacking in his own character. As Victor says about Elizabeth in the 1818 text, "although there was a great dissimilitude in our characters, there was a harmony in that very dissimilitude" (20).

As Robert Kiely notes, "In her treatment of friendship, Mary [Shelley] shows the Coleridgean side of herself."[29] Unlike Percy Shelley, who in works such as *Alastor* and the essay "On Love" tends to characterize the ideal soul mate as a being strikingly similar to oneself, Coleridge emphasizes the way that friends, which include partners of the opposite sex, complete the individual by supplying qualities he or she lacks.[30] Both Anthony Harding and J. Robert Barth extensively document this dimension of Coleridge's thinking about relationships, which appears again and again in both his public and his private writings.[31] For example, in the seventh of his 1811–1812 lectures on Shakespeare and Milton, Coleridge declares that "It is inevitable to every noble mind whether man or woman to feel itself of itself imperfect and insufficient, not as an animal merely but altogether as a moral being.... The Creator has ordained that one should possess what the other does not and the union of both is the most complete ideal of the human character that can be conceived—In everything blending the similar with the dissimilar is the secret of all pure delight—Who should dare then to stand alone and vaunt himself in himself sufficient?" Similarly, in lecture eight Coleridge says, "The individual has by this time learnt the greatest & best knowledge of the human mind that we are in ourselves imperfect and another truth of perhaps equal importance that there exists in nature a possibility of uniting two beings each identified in their nature but distinguished in their separate qualities so that each should retain what distinguishes them & at the same time acquire the qualities of that which is contradistinguished to them." In addition, Coleridge referred to the idyllic love of Adam and Eve before the fall as "a union of opposites, a giving and receiving mutually of the permanent in either, a completion of each in the other."[32]

---

[29]    Kiely, 167.

[30]    Veeder discusses Percy Shelley's rejection of the ideal of complementarity between lovers and his preference for relationships in which the beloved is a projection of oneself (99–102). In chapter 1, Veeder identifies a variety of sources for Mary Shelley's belief in the ideal of complementarity and balance in love relationships but does not consider Coleridge as a possible source or like-minded contemporary writer.

[31]    Anthony John Harding, *Coleridge and the Idea of Love: Aspects of Relationship in Coleridge's Thought and Writing* (Cambridge: Cambridge University Press, 1974); J. Robert Barth, S. J., *Coleridge and the Power of Love* (Columbia: University of Missouri Press, 1988).

[32]    Coleridge, *Lectures 1808–1819 On Literature*, ed. R. A. Foakes, 2 vols. (Princeton: Princeton University Press, 1987), 1:314, 333; 2:428. The last quotation is from an unidentified lecture.

So similar to Coleridge's are Mary Shelley's statements on the balancing and completing function of friends that one assumes she must have directly encountered the latter's ideas. No clear source has been identified, however, that could have informed her comments in the first edition of *Frankenstein*. Coleridge's 1811–1812 lectures are one obvious possibility, but Mary was in Ramsgate for her health when the lectures began and returned to London only on 19 December, whereas lectures seven and eight quoted above were delivered on 9 and 12 December, respectively.[33] Mary might have heard these lectures summarized by her father, who was attending regularly, or by another family friend such as Henry Crabb Robinson, who wrote a report of lecture seven for the *Morning Chronicle* and praised it in his diary.[34] Mary also might have read one of the newspaper summaries of the lectures that she missed, several of which appeared. Or, since Coleridge expressed his ideas about friendship and love in many writings throughout his life, he also may have brought up these topics frequently in conversation, so that she could have heard him express them or have heard her father report them after conversing with Coleridge. It is significant that in March 1835 Mary Shelley copied into her journal a passage from Coleridge's *The Improvisatore*, which includes the following remarks about love. "Above all," Coleridge writes and Mary Shelley copies, "it supposes a soul which, men in the pride & summertide of life, even in the lustihood of health & strength, had felt oftenest & prized highest … I mean that willing sense of the unsufficingness of the self for itself, which predisposes a generous nature to see, in the total being of another, the supplement & completion of its own" (*Journals*, 2:547). Even if she had never read or heard Coleridge's ideas before, it is telling that she responded to them when she did encounter them in print.[35]

The messages advocating community and love, however, are undercut in both *The Rime of the Ancient Mariner* and *Frankenstein* in significant ways. Most conspicuously, in these works that preach the importance of relationships, the central characters experience radical, irremediable solitude. The dominant impression of both works, I would argue, is not of the interconnectedness of all living beings but of the Mariner, "Alone, alone, all all alone, / Alone on the wide wide Sea!" (232–3) and the outcast Creature, "dependent on none, and related to none," "wretched, helpless, and alone" (86, 87). Victor Frankenstein too regards himself as uniquely miserable and isolated from all others in his guilt and remorse (e.g., 57–9, 106, 109–10). The sustaining relationships with spouses, families, and communities advocated in poem and novel are not available to the central

---

[33]   See Bennett, 14; Coleridge, *Lectures*, 1:300, 324.

[34]   Coleridge, *Lectures*, 1:300–301, 318–19.

[35]   My argument to this point agrees with that of Levy, who stresses the importance of relationships for tempering expansionist impulses in both Coleridge and Shelley. In what follows, however, my essay diverges from Levy's by noting ambivalence in Coleridge's and Shelley's treatment of domestic affections and ambition.

characters, and one could surmise that those relationships are idealized precisely because they are perceived as unattainable.[36]

Certainly Coleridge and Shelley experienced tremendous loneliness in their own lives; their journals are filled with lamentations about their solitary states. "It was the will of Providence that I should pursue my pilgrimage *alone*," Coleridge writes.[37] "Loneliness has been the curse of my life," Mary Shelley similarly remarks (*Journals*, 2:543). In another entry, Coleridge addresses his "dear" notebook as the "Sole Confidant of a breaking Heart, whose social nature compels *some* Outlet.... I have not a soul on earth to whom I can reveal [his inmost thoughts]—and yet 'I am not a God, that I should stand alone' and therefore to you, my passive, yet sole ... kind, friends I reveal them."[38] Similarly, in her first entry after Percy Shelley's death, Mary writes, "Now I am alone! Oh, how alone! ... White paper—wilt thou be my confident [*sic*]? I will trust thee fully, for none shall see what I write" (2:429). In another journal entry of 21 October 1838, after describing her retiring personality and the tragedies of her life, Shelley concludes, "all this has sunk me in a state of loneliness no other human being ever before I beleive [*sic*] endured— Except Robinson Crusoe" (2:555). Finally, an entry from Shelley's journal for 16 April 1841 consists solely of the following lines: "Alone—alone—all—all alone / Upon the wide, wide sea— / And God will not take pity on / My soul in agony!" (2: 573).[39] A sense of radical isolation—of being incomplete and lacking the other who would supply one's missing half—is one of the central affinities between Coleridge and Shelley, and it is also one of the most pervasive and haunting elements of *Ancient Mariner* and *Frankenstein*. The fact that Shelley quoted the stanza on solitude in her journal leaves no doubt that she responded deeply to this dimension of Coleridge's poem.[40]

The morals that advocate nurturing family and community relationships are undermined in *The Ancient Mariner* and *Frankenstein* in other ways. Not only are many characters alone in both works, but the relationships that are presented are fraught with conflict, hostility, pain, and resentment. These terms characterize all

---

[36]    Jean Hall makes a similar point ("*Frankenstein*: The Horrifying Otherness of Family," *Essays in Literature* 17 [1990], 182–4).

[37]    Quoted from an unpublished notebook entry by Harding, 125.

[38]    *The Notebooks of Samuel Taylor Coleridge*, vols. 1–3 ed. Kathleen Coburn, vol. 4 ed. Kathleen Coburn and Merton Christensen, vol. 5 ed. Kathleen Coburn and Anthony John Harding (Princeton: Princeton University Press, 1957–2002), 3:#3325.

[39]    Shelley slightly misquotes lines 232–5 of *The Ancient Mariner*. Her version is most similar to the *Lyrical Ballads* text of the poem (all four editions), line 234 of which reads "and Christ would take no pity on," as opposed to "And never a saint took pity on" in later versions (Coleridge, *Poetical Works*, 1.1:196, 2.1:519; Stillinger, *Coleridge and Textual Instability*, 170).

[40]    Stelzig emphasizes the major characters' isolation and inability to unite or reunite with families in both *Ancient Mariner* and *Frankenstein*. For Stelzig, *Frankenstein* is even more radical in its depiction of solitude and homelessness than *Ancient Mariner* (52).

of the Mariner's and the Creature's relationships with others and on some level virtually all of Victor Frankenstein's as well. Many critics have interpreted various problematic relationships in both works as expressions of conflicted feelings toward mother, father, and sibling figures. For example, the killing of the albatross in *The Rime of the Ancient Mariner* has been interpreted as a matricide, a patricide, and a fratricide. The albatross is maternal in that it is associated with food and protection. It is paternal in that it is associated with God the father. The Mariner's killing of the albatross also parallels Cain's murder of his brother Abel, and the Mariner's subsequent wandering resembles Cain's punishment for his crime. The fact that fratricide is featured in Coleridge's *Osorio* and *The Wanderings of Cain*, both written in the same year as *The Ancient Mariner* (1797), lends further support to the latter interpretation. Critics frequently relate the poem's depiction of troubled family relationships to Coleridge's own conflicted feelings toward his mother, his younger brother Frank, and his older brother George, who became a father figure after his natural father died when Coleridge was eight years old. David Miall identifies the source of the Mariner's guilt over shooting the albatross as Coleridge's repressed childhood belief that he was somehow responsible for his father's sudden death and would be punished for it.[41]

*Frankenstein* also conveys ambivalence toward mothers, fathers, and siblings who have been associated with figures in Mary Shelley's own life. Most of the characters in the novel, like Shelley herself, lack mothers, and the parallel between Victor Frankenstein's abandonment of his Creature the moment it comes to life and Mary Wollstonecraft's death shortly after giving birth to her daughter is hard to ignore. Just as the Mariner's reaction to the shooting of the albatross has been

---

[41]    David Miall, "Guilt and Death: The Predicament of *The Ancient Mariner*," *Studies in English Literature, 1500–1900* 24 (1984): 633–53. David Beres interprets the killing of the albatross as a matricide ("A Dream, a Vision, and a Poem: A Psychoanalytic Study of the Origins of *The Rime of the Ancient Mariner*," *International Journal of Psychoanalysis* 32 [1951]: 97–116). Diane Hoeveler considers the shooting of the albatross a patricide ("Glossing the Feminine in 'The Rime of the Ancient Mariner,'" *European Romantic Review* 2 [1992]: 152–3), and Leon Waldoff reads the poem as the expression of Oedipal struggles with various father figures. Critics who connect the story of Cain and Abel to *Ancient Mariner* include John Livingston Lowes, *The Road to Xanadu: A Study in the Ways of the Imagination* (Boston: Houghton Mifflin, 1927), 237–8, 254–60; Humphrey House, *Coleridge: The Clark Lectures, 1951-1952* (London: Rupert Hart-Davis, 1953), 84–5, 98; Susan Eilenberg, *Strange Powers of Speech: Wordsworth, Coleridge, and Literary Possession* (New York: Oxford University Press, 1992), 45–6, 49; and R. A. Foakes, "Coleridge, Violence, and 'The Rime of the Ancient Mariner,'" *Romanticism* 7 (2001): 41–57. Others who analyze conflicted feelings toward mother, father, and brother figures in Coleridge's life and work include Max F. Schultz, "Coleridge Agonistes," *JEGP* 61 (1962): 268–77; Norman Fruman, *Coleridge: The Damaged Archangel* (New York: George Braziller, 1971), especially 22, 362–3, 405–6, 409, 548–9n.26, 565n.119, 566n.127, 566n.129; and Thomas McFarland, "Coleridge's Anxiety," in *Coleridge's Variety: Bicentenary Studies*, ed. John Beer and L. C. Knights (Pittsburgh: University of Pittsburgh Press, 1975), 134–65.

interpreted as a reflection of Coleridge's traumatized response to his father's death, the Creature's intense pain as well as his anger at his parent for abandoning him has been read as a reflection of Shelley's own troubled feelings toward her mother: guilt from the sense of being responsible for her death and anger over her mother's neglect. As Gilbert and Gubar note, "Shelley … like all orphans, must have feared that she had been deliberately deserted by her dead parent."[42]

Like *The Ancient Mariner*, which depicts God as both a loving and a punishing father figure,[43] *Frankenstein* contains both idealized benevolent fathers (Alphonse Frankenstein and old DeLacey) and cruel, neglectful fathers, the latter of which outnumber the former. The most conspicuous example of a neglectful father is Victor Frankenstein himself, who abandons his "child" immediately after its birth and thereafter expresses only disgust and hatred toward it. As U. C. Knoepflmacher notes, the novel is filled with references to other cruel, unjust fathers, including "the father whose 'dying injunction' forbade Walton to embark on a sea-faring life; Henry Clerval's father, who insists that his son be a merchant rather than a poet; the 'inexorable' Russian father who tries to force his daughter into a union she abhors; and the treacherous Turkish father who uses Safie to obtain his freedom yet issues the 'tyrannical mandate' that she betray Felix." Laura Claridge argues that even the apparently benign Alphonse Frankenstein and father DeLacey are flawed, irresponsible parents. The novel's conflicted treatment of fathers has frequently been allied with Mary Shelley's notoriously complex relationship with her own father, William Godwin, who at the time when *Frankenstein* was composed had cut off all communication with his daughter.[44]

Sibling rivalry is also rampant in the novel. Felix DeLacey is a rival brother figure to the Creature, in that Felix bars him from access to the beloved father. The Creature's killing of William Frankenstein can likewise be read as an expression of anger and jealousy at a rival brother, since the Creature apparently thinks William is Victor's son and therefore his own half brother. Knoepflmacher links the Creature's reactions to both Felix and William to Mary Shelley's childhood resentment of her half brother William Godwin, Junior, who as Godwin's only male child usurped her special place in her father's regard. Victor Frankenstein's creation of a being who destroys his family has been traced to his resentment, after years of being an only child, over having to share his parents' attention with natural and adopted siblings (the latter of whom can include Justine and Clerval

---

[42]    Gilbert and Gubar, 244. Other critics who explore Mary Shelley's ambivalent feelings toward her mother (and stepmother) and the reflection of these feelings in *Frankenstein* include Rubenstein; Knoepflmacher, 108–10; Veeder, 166–8; Mellor, *Mary Shelley*, 12–13; and Hill-Miller, 19–20, 24–5, 32–40, 93–7.

[43]    See Hoeveler, 152–4.

[44]    Knoepflmacher, 104; Laura P. Claridge, "Parent-Child Tensions in *Frankenstein*: The Search for Communion," *Studies in the Novel* 17 (1985): 14–26. For Mary Shelley's conflicts with her father and their resonance in *Frankenstein* see also the sources cited in note 7, especially Veeder and Hill-Miller.

as well as Elizabeth). William Crisman, who develops this argument, identifies many other characters in the novel who experience troubled sibling relationships, including Alphonse Frankenstein, the supposedly saintly Elizabeth, and even Robert Walton, whose relationship with his sister Margaret is usually regarded as a model of loving intimacy. "Mary Shelley," Crisman writes, "seems to imagine mutually supportive sibling relations only with great difficulty."[45] Her problematic relationship with her half-sister Claire Clairmont, who accompanied her when she eloped with Percy Shelley and thereafter was often an unwanted presence in their domestic arrangements, is another example of sibling tension in the author's life. While they ostensibly celebrate the family, both *Ancient Mariner* and *Frankenstein* depict discord and hostility in parent-child and sibling relationships, which may in part reflect the authors' conflicted feelings toward their own family members.

In other ways, poem and novel portray close relationships as oppressive and burdensome, far from the nurturing completion of the Coleridgean ideal. The image of the dead albatross hanging around the Mariner's neck powerfully conveys a situation of unwanted, horrifying connection to another being. Mary Shelley draws upon this image from Coleridge's poem when she has Victor Frankenstein say about his impending marriage to Elizabeth: "Could I enter into a festival with this deadly weight yet hanging round my neck, and bowing me to the ground" (104). The "deadly weight" refers to Victor's promise to create a mate for the Creature, as well as to the oppressive burden of the Creature generally, whom Victor persistently but unsuccessfully tries to ignore and disown. Veeder believes that Victor's reference to the "deadly weight hanging about [his] neck" also refers to Elizabeth; the passage, Veeder argues, reflects Victor's horror at the prospect of marriage and the intimacy with Elizabeth this would entail.[46] Thus the novel, as Jean Hall has noted, "projects two polarized versions of relationship: relationship as idealized by the benevolent family, whose structure naturally supports the individual and grounds his or her identity, and relationship as entanglement, invasion, [and] inexplicable perversity that disintegrates the benevolent self. By

---

[45]    Knoepflmacher, 93–4. William Crisman, "'Now Misery Has Come Home': Sibling Rivalry in Mary Shelley's *Frankenstein*," *Studies in Romanticism* 36 (1997): 27–41; the passage quoted in on 39. Claridge also points out tensions in Walton's relationship with his sister, though for Claridge Margaret is a mother figure (16). Another essay that claims *Frankenstein* presents the nuclear family in a negative light is Adam Komisaruk's "'So Guided by a Silken Cord': *Frankenstein*'s Family Values," *Studies in Romanticism* 38 (1999): 409–41. Komisaruk argues that Shelley's novel provides a critique of the bourgeois family by linking "the cult of the domestic affections" to "the politics of self-interest" in capitalist economics (423). Goodwin regards both *Ancient Mariner*'s and *Frankenstein*'s treatment of domesticity as chiefly negative. For Goodwin, Shelley portrays home "as the site of destruction" and "repressed violence" (101), and Life-in-Death in *Ancient Mariner* is "the castrating female, that secret, fearful presence at the heart of the home" (95).

[46]    Veeder, 106. Minot and Minot make a similar point (39–41).

turns Mary Shelley welcomes the ties that bind, or abhors them."[47] A comparably ambivalent attitude toward intimate relationships suffuses *The Ancient Mariner* and, I would argue, formed one of the elements of the poem that drew Mary Shelley to it.

In addition, both works express ambivalence about self-assertion and ambition. In *Ancient Mariner*, such ambivalence is conveyed by the fact that the crew at first condemns the Mariner for shooting the albatross but immediately afterward praises his deed. In addition, the Mariner's experience can be viewed as positive in that it makes those who undergo it, whether literally in the Mariner's case or vicariously as in the Wedding Guest's, "sadder but ... wiser" (624). Foakes argues that the Mariner's killing of the albatross, like Cain's murder of his brother, is "an assertion of his individuality that marks him off as special" and that the poem "powerfully registers the paradox that most of us wish to assert the self, to be distinctive, to transgress, and at the same time cannot face isolation, but need to share with others a place in a community."[48] Although *Frankenstein* may appear to be, as Levy states, a cautionary tale that "teach[es] the dangers of ambition and the need for restraint,"[49] it too contains passages that complicate its perspective. Most significantly, Victor Frankenstein's final speech, which initially states a clear-cut moral, ends by seriously qualifying it. "Seek happiness in tranquillity, and avoid ambition," Victor tells Walton, "even if it be the apparently innocent one of distinguishing yourself in science and discoveries. Yet why do I say this? I have myself been blasted in these hopes, yet another may succeed" (152). Lawrence Lipking states that the novel's "irresolution" on the "theme of hubris.... reaches an almost comic impasse" in this passage. "Right at the point of renouncing his sins," Lipking notes, "the hero takes it back."[50] In another late episode, Victor chastises Walton's crew for their lack of courage when they insist on returning home and rallies them to continue their "glorious expedition" and prove the superiority of human will over nature's elements (149). This speech is similar to one Walton makes at the beginning of the 1831 edition of the novel, when he declares, "Why not still proceed over the untamed yet obedient element? What can stop the determined heart and resolved will of man?" (*1831*, 23). Walton himself, though he agrees to return to England in compliance with his crew's demands, does so unwillingly and bitterly regrets abandoning his "hopes of utility and glory" (150). Instead of recanting their early attitudes toward ambition, Victor and Walton seem just as committed to fame and heroic deeds at the end of the novel as they were at the beginning.[51]

---

[47]   Hall, 184.

[48]   Foakes, 51.

[49]   Levy, 706.

[50]   Lawrence Lipking, "*Frankenstein*, the True Story; or, Rousseau Judges Jean-Jacques," in Mary Shelley, *Frankenstein*, ed. J. Paul Hunter (New York: Norton, 1996), 329.

[51]   Kiely argues that the novel conveys mixed messages about individualism and ambition. According to Kiely, the two competing themes in *Frankenstein* are "that man

The ostensible moral of *The Ancient Mariner* and *Frankenstein*—that solitary self-assertion is a crime that should and will be punished—is further undermined by a number of elements that qualify the overreacher's guilt, diminish his responsibility for his crime, or otherwise confuse the work's point of view toward its central characters and their actions. One way in which the Mariner's and Victor Frankenstein's responsibility for their crimes is eroded is the fact that each is extremely passive. William Wordsworth was the first to remark that the Mariner "is continually acted upon" instead of being an active agent himself.[52] From the outset of the voyage, when his ship is blown off course, the Mariner is at the mercy of natural and supernatural forces that move or arrest, punish or relieve him, all with virtually no resistance or influence on the Mariner's part. So passive is the Mariner that one even wonders if his initial aggressive act of shooting the albatross was really his own decision or the result of some power compelling him to do what he had no wish to do, as is the case with Geraldine in *Christabel*.[53] Moreover, the inexplicable nature of the Mariner's crime—the absence of motive for his shooting of the bird—interferes with our condemnation of the deed. It is difficult to judge someone when you have no idea why he committed an action and when the person doesn't even seem to know himself.[54]

Victor Frankenstein also is frequently depicted as passive, helpless to the fate or destiny that rules his life.[55] Like the Mariner, Victor commits a deed that causes most of the tragedy in the novel but the motives for which are highly unclear. This action is Victor's abrupt, illogical abandonment of his Creature the moment it comes to life.[56] Why, one wonders, does the Creature look so ugly to him when it

---

discovers and fulfills himself through others and destroys himself alone" and "that genius, even in its failures, is unique, noble, and isolated from other men by divine right" (172).

[52]     In a "Note to the Ancient Mariner" in the 1800 edition of *Lyrical Ballads*. See William Wordsworth and Samuel Taylor Coleridge, *Lyrical Ballads*, ed. R. L. Brett and A. R. Jones (London: Methuen, 1963), 277.

[53]     Minot and Minot discuss the evidence that Geraldine herself may be "the innocent victim of an evil enchantment" (37) and compare the ambiguity over who is the victim and who the perpetrator of wrongdoing in *Christabel* to a similar ambiguity in *Frankenstein*.

[54]     Stillinger makes a similar point (*Coleridge and Textual Instability*, 67–8).

[55]     Poovey extensively documents the novel's, especially the 1831 text's, depiction of Victor Frankenstein as a "passive victim of powerful forces" (135; see also 133–7). Mellor (*Mary Shelley*, 170–74) argues that references to fate added to the 1831 text downplay Victor's responsibility for his actions in a way that was absent in the 1818 version. Although Victor Frankenstein's references to fate are more frequent in 1831, they are also common in the 1818 text (see, for example, 17, 21, 23, 28, 125–6, 142). The evidence indicates that Shelley further developed this dimension of Victor's character in 1831 but that it was present in the novel from the start.

[56]     This, I would argue, is the central "crime" in the novel, more akin to the Mariner's killing of the albatross than Victor's creation of life, since it involves the betrayal of a vulnerable, trusting being. This action is also more responsible for the deaths that ensue than the act of bringing the Creature to life. There is no reason to believe that the Creature would

comes to life and not when he is putting it together; how can he run out of the room and then out of the house without wondering where the Creature will go and what it will do? The answers to these major questions about Victor's thought processes are never provided, no more than the Mariner's motives for shooting the albatross are spelled out, and we therefore have trouble determining exactly what crime each man should be accused of.

Another explanation for these irrational behaviors is that either the characters or their creators are unable to understand or do not wish to examine too closely the impulses behind them. Goodwin comments that "Both Coleridge and Shelley are writing in these works about something they do not clearly understand, which means that repression is an important component of their writing." Waldoff remarks about the fact that, in *The Ancient Mariner*, both the shooting of the albatross and the blessing of the water snakes happen "unaware": this is "the way unconscious defenses work." Hill-Miller notes the "implausible and unconvincing" nature of the explanations Victor offers for why he abandoned his creature and concludes, "There is clearly some other deep-seated and unarticulated taboo at work in Victor Frankenstein's imagination."[57] *The Ancient Mariner* and *Frankenstein* are highly ambivalent works, which address aggressive, anti-social impulses the authors find both attractive and appalling, which they want to explore and yet fear to acknowledge or confront. By depicting actions that reverberate with significance and have tremendous consequences in the works while withholding any account of the actors' motives, Coleridge and Shelley can maintain a delicate balance of both engaging and avoiding the issues implied by these deeds.

The ability to both explore controversial issues and distance themselves from these is maintained in both works in other ways. Shelley complicates and obscures her point of view by employing multiple narrators, all of whom engage our sympathies.[58] *The Rime of the Ancient Mariner* also employs multiple narrators, particularly in its later versions when the gloss and Latin epigraph were added. Jack

---

have become a murderer if Victor had cared for him, since his nature initially was kind and gentle. One should also recall that, according to Mary Shelley's 1831 Introduction, the novel originated with the scene of Victor's rejection of the Creature. What thrilled Shelley with horror was the moment when the creator found his work abhorrent. John Clement Ball believes that Shelley regards "abandonment after the fact as a greater crime than the initial creation" ("Imperial Monstrosities: 'Frankenstein,' the West Indies, and V. S. Naipaul," *Ariel* 32.3 [2001]: 42.)

[57]    Goodwin, 104; Waldoff, 447; Hill-Miller, 65. According to Hill-Miller, Victor is recoiling from the incest taboo, in that the Creature represents his dead mother brought back to life. For another psychological explanation of the lack of motive for the Ancient Mariner's shooting of the albatross, see Miall, 640–42.

[58]    I disagree with critics such as Bronfen who believe that Victor Frankenstein is drawn "exclusively in pejorative colours" (30–31). As Kiely (156–8) and Lipking (317) note, Victor is admired, often in glowing terms, by all the other characters, including the Creature, who mourns Victor's death at the end of the novel. In addition, as is the case with the Ancient Mariner, Victor undergoes such appalling suffering that he enlists many

Stillinger notes that Coleridge's successive revisions to the poem made it "almost overauthored." The speakers or authorial voices in the poem in its 1817 and later versions include "the Mariner telling his story, the poet-narrator describing the Mariner and his story, the pious and scholarly commentator in the margins, and a now-legendary figure named S. T. Coleridge, Esq., putting it all together," and all of these figures "exert their conflicting claims on the reader's eye, ear, reason, [and] emotions."[59] Sarah Dyck notes four different perspectives in *The Ancient Mariner*: that of the Mariner, the Wedding Guest, the "minstrel balladeer" who narrates the poem, and the antiquarian editor who provides the gloss and Latin epigraph. According to Dyck, none of these perspectives is privileged and the reader is "expected, or challenged, to draw his own conclusions."[60] Confronted with such a proliferation of narrative voices, the reader of both Coleridge's and Shelley's works has difficulty determining who speaks for the author. As a result the authors cannot be blamed for or identified with disturbing implications in the works, such as their sympathy with bold, ambitious deeds and defiance of authority or social codes; their hostility toward family members and dread of intimate relationships; and the profound sense of alienation they express. Mary Poovey argues that multiple narrators in *Frankenstein* allow Shelley to avoid "having to take a single, definitive position on her unladylike subject," to "express and efface herself at the same time and … to satisfy her conflicting desires for self-assertion and social acceptance."[61] As we have seen, however, Coleridge's *Ancient Mariner* is similarly ambiguous and may even have instructed Shelley on techniques for dispersing and deflecting her points of view.

Mary Shelley's account of the origin of *Frankenstein* in her 1831 Introduction removes the author from responsibility for her work in various ways. According to Shelley, the illustrious men at Geneva, especially Byron and Percy Shelley, proposed the idea of writing ghost stories and urged Mary to think of a topic. The idea that finally occurred to her was inspired by Byron's and Percy Shelley's

---

readers' sympathies especially since (again like the Mariner) most of the action is presented from his perspective.

[59]     Stillinger, *Coleridge and Textual Instability*, 70, 73.

[60]     Sarah Dyck, "Perspective in 'The Rime of the Ancient Mariner,'" *Studies in English Literature, 1500–1900* 13 (1973): 591. Mary Shelley could not have read the version of *The Ancient Mariner* that contained the gloss when she composed *Frankenstein*, but the poem even in its early form was complex in its narrative strategies, featuring three of the four authors Stillinger mentions (the Mariner, the poet, and S. T. Coleridge) and three of the perspectives Dyck distinguishes (Mariner's, Wedding Guest's, and minstrel-balladeer's). Shelley of course could have been familiar with the marginal glosses by the time she revised *Frankenstein* for the 1831 edition. Beer states that *Frankenstein* follows *Ancient Mariner* in its use of "three distinct tellers … the Mariner, the narrator of the ballad and the compiler of the marginal glosses." Beer also calls this "interplay of narrators" a characteristic Romantic technique which reflects "the interplay of different strains of thought … that came into existence during the time of the French Revolution" (227–8).

[61]     Poovey, 131.

conversation and came to her as an involuntary vision. "My imagination," Mary Shelley writes, "unbidden, possessed and guided me, gifting the successive images that arose in my mind with a vividness far beyond the usual bounds of reverie" (*1831*, 9). Shelley's account of the trancelike inspiration of *Frankenstein* and the influence of others in motivating her to write, as well as her disparagement of her novel as a "hideous progeny" (*1831*, 10), all disassociate the author from the shocking implications of her story and from the assertive act of composition itself.[62]

Poovey contrasts Mary Shelley's insecure sense of herself as a writer with that of "many of her male contemporaries."[63] Coleridge, however, employed almost exactly the same strategies Mary Shelley displays in her Introduction to downplay his own responsibility and disassociate himself from works that could be considered shocking or unconventional. As Knoepflmacher notes, Shelley's account of her waking dream of "the pale student of unhallowed arts" that formed the inspiration for her novel "recalls Coleridge's own distancings from an 'unhallowed' and possibly demonic imagination" in his Preface to *Kubla Khan*.[64] *Kubla Khan* presents a bold vision of the artist as a godlike being who draws inspiration from dark forces in the lower depths of consciousness as well as from the sunnier regions of rationality. The Preface to the poem, however, disparages the work and absolves the author of responsibility for it. In the first place, the poem is subtitled "A Vision in a Dream," making it two removes from a conscious, deliberate work of art. Coleridge also labels the poem a fragment, implying not only that the work is slight because unfinished but also that any disturbing elements in the present piece may have been offset by later passages in the finished work and therefore should not be judged apart from the larger, missing context. Coleridge claims too that he published the work only because Byron urged him to do so; he himself considers *Kubla Khan* a mere "psychological curiosity" rather than a legitimate poem. There then follows the notorious account of the poem having come to him "in a profound sleep" after reading *Purchas's Pilgrimage* and, when he awoke, having passively recorded the lines that had been given to him "without any sensation or consciousness of effort" (*Poetical Works*, 1.1:511). Nearly all of the elements that distance the author from her work in Shelley's Introduction are present in Coleridge's Preface to *Kubla Khan*: disparaging the work as curious or

---

[62]     Critics who comment on these and other defensive strategies in Shelley's 1831 Introduction include Poovey, 137–41; Rubenstein, 180–82; Homans, 116–17; and Hall, 185–8.

[63]     Poovey, 140.

[64]     Knoepflmacher, 97. Marilyn Butler says that Mary Shelley's account of *Frankenstein*'s conception "may well be lifted from Coleridge's equally creative description … of the dream origins of 'Kubla Khan'" (Introduction, *Frankenstein, or, The Modern Prometheus*, by Mary Shelley, ed. Butler [Oxford: Oxford University Press, 1998], xxiii). I quote from Coleridge's Preface as printed in the first, 1816 version of *Kubla Khan*, which is the reading text in *Poetical Works* (1.1.511–12).

bizarre; crediting others, including in both cases Lord Byron, for the creation or appearance of the work in public; and describing the work's composition as an involuntary process.[65]

We have strong evidence that Mary Shelley knew and admired *Kubla Khan*. On 26 August 1816 she noted in her journal that Coleridge's *Christabel* had arrived in Geneva with a shipment of books (1:131), by which she means the volume that contained *Christabel*, *Kubla Khan*, and *The Pains of Sleep*. Since Byron urged Coleridge to publish the poem, he is also likely to have spoken of it highly to the Shelleys when they talked of Coleridge that summer. Finally, in a journal entry of 2 December 1834 Mary Shelley, explaining that her imagination has been her chief consolation in a life of suffering, calls it "my treasure—my Kubla Khan—my Stately pleasure ground through which a mighty river ran down to a sunless sea" (2:543). Shelley clearly was familiar with Coleridge's poem and relished its depiction of the artistic imagination. It is also likely that she was drawn to the complex defensive strategies employed in Coleridge's Preface.

Before leaving this topic, one can note that the 1800, 1802, and 1805 versions of *The Rime of the Ancient Mariner* subtitle the ballad "A Poet's Reverie."[66] Like "A Vision in a Dream," "A Poet's Reverie" has the effect not only of disparaging the work as slight and inconsequential but also suggests that it was composed involuntarily, in a dream-like state. Coleridge also referred to the poem in conversation as "a work of pure Imagination," downplaying its conscious or rational nature.[67] Such apologetic and dismissive remarks about his poems were common for Coleridge. He introduced *The Three Graves* in the *Sibylline Leaves* volume (actually titled "Continuation of *The Three Graves*, by William Wordsworth") much as he did *Kubla Khan* by saying, "The Author has published the following humble fragment, encouraged by the decisive recommendation of more than one of our most celebrated living Poets" and "Its merits, if any, are exclusively Psychological."[68] The Preface to the *Sibylline Leaves* volume refers

---

[65]    Elisabeth Schneider makes many of these points about elements of Coleridge's Preface that serve to downplay the author's responsibility for or deflect criticism from the poem that follows (*Coleridge, Opium, and* Kubla Khan [1953; rpt. New York: Octagon Books, 1966], 22, 24–7, 107–9).

[66]    See Coleridge, *Poetical Works*, 2.1:509; Stillinger, *Coleridge and Textual Instability*, 158.

[67]    See Coleridge, *Table Talk*, ed. Carl Woodring, 2 vols. (Princeton: Princeton University Press, 1990), 1:149. Miall makes similar points about the phrases "a work of pure Imagination" and "A Poet's Reverie" (637).

[68]    Coleridge, *Poetical Works* 1.1:336–7. Minot and Minot cite this passage to illustrate Coleridge's "curious public relationship to his work," in that he desired recognition but also drew attention to his "shortcomings" as a poet (32). Minot and Minot relate Coleridge's ambivalent attitude toward himself as a poet to Victor Frankenstein's similarly conflicted self-image as a creator, in that he desires to be known and praised for his creation but then finds it hideous and disowns it as soon as it comes to life.

disparagingly to "the fragmentary and widely scattered state" of the poems it includes. *Reflections on Having Left a Place of Retirement* was first published with the subtitle "A Poem, which affects not to be Poetry," and to a friend Coleridge characterized *Fears in Solitude* as "a sort of Middle thing between Poetry & Oratory."[69] Far from forming a contrast to Mary Shelley's insecure sense of herself as a writer, Coleridge presents his work and himself as a writer in almost exactly the same way Shelley does.

If Coleridge and Shelley suffered from insecurity, however, they also knew how to use passivity and self-effacement to their advantages. Poovey argues that Mary Shelley's presentation of herself as a modest, demure figure instead of as a confident writer actually afforded her "precisely the grounds she needed to sanction her artistic career."[70] By claiming that she had no literary ambition or high regard for her own works, Shelley paradoxically felt sanctioned to persist in the unladylike practice of writing and publishing books. Similarly, Coleridge could publish a bold, original poem like *Kubla Khan* by dismissing it as a fragmentary psychological curiosity or *The Ancient Mariner* by disparaging it as "A Poet's Reverie" or "a work of ... pure Imagination." Similarly, he could write distinguished poems such as *Dejection: An Ode* and *To William Wordsworth* whose ostensible subject is Coleridge's failure or inferiority as a poet. Richard Holmes in fact argues that Coleridge created an enabling identity of himself as a failed poet, which distinguished him from the successful Wordsworth and served to release his creative energies.[71] Coleridge and Shelley may have been to some extent handicapped by their insecurities, but they also managed to adapt their insecurities to empowering literary self-images.

Similar adaptive or passive-aggressive strategies are employed by characters in *The Ancient Mariner* and *Frankenstein*. Waldoff points out how, paradoxically, the Mariner gains power over others after accepting a submissive role toward the father figures in the poem (God, the Storm Blast, Death, and the Polar Spirit). His attempt to assert his identity by shooting the albatross and thereby defying the father fails utterly, but as a passive conveyor of the message he has been taught, the Mariner come to possess "strange power[s] of speech" (*Ancient Mariner*, 587) and a commanding presence that arrests and transforms younger men like the wedding guest.[72] Victor Frankenstein, as previously noted, is largely passive, but the Creature has often been interpreted as his alter ego who punishes family members

---

[69]    Jack Stillinger cites and discusses these instances of Coleridge presenting himself as "a writer who is not wholly serious in his endeavors and perhaps not even competent" (*Coleridge and Textual Instability*, 108–9). See also Coleridge, *Poetical Works*, 1.1:469; 2.1:353.

[70]    Poovey, 142.

[71]    Richard Holmes, *Coleridge: Early Visions* (New York: Viking, 1990), 296, 300–302.

[72]    Waldoff, 448–9.

and friends toward whom Victor harbors repressed hostility.[73] The demure, selfless women in *Frankenstein* also engage in a kind of passive aggression toward Victor. When Justine resigns herself to an unjust execution and Elizabeth declares she would rather share Justine's fate than be the unknown murderer, Victor writhes in an agony of remorse and contrasts his own corrosive guilt to these women's spotless natures (57–8, 61). As Knoepflmacher remarks, "Passivity, used correctly, as Mary Shelley knew … can be as powerful a weapon as rage."[74]

If one needs another example of how their inner conflicts and insecurities aided Coleridge and Shelley as artists, one can say that these anxieties and tensions, however troubling to both in their personal lives, contributed to the complex, fascinating, inexhaustible nature of *The Rime of the Ancient Mariner* and *Frankenstein*. Although all distinguished works of literature lend themselves to a variety of interpretations, these two works are remarkable—and remarkably similar—for the unusual multiplicity and diversity of interpretations they have generated. Moreover, this very indeterminacy and ambivalence mark both poem and novel as Romantic works. As Lipking argues, writers of "the Romantic mainstream … were far from single-minded.… Indeed, one way of characterizing the age would emphasize its internal divisions or self-contradictions."[75]

The many significant parallels between *Frankenstein* and *The Rime of the Ancient Mariner* indicate that Coleridge, whom Robert Walton calls "the most imaginative of modern poets" (*1831*, 21), should be acknowledged as an important figure in Mary Shelley's imaginative life. The far-ranging similarities between Coleridge's and Shelley's works also challenge the idea that Mary Shelley rejected "masculine Romanticism" and endorsed an opposing set of beliefs.[76] Instead, Shelley's novel, with its rich tensions and ambiguities—its condemnation of and covert sympathy with ambitious acts of creation and self-assertion; its simultaneous celebration

---

[73]    As Crisman remarks, the idea that the Creature is Victor Frankenstein's alter ego or double and that "the murders are also Victor's murders" is "an assumption so old in *Frankenstein* criticism that it no longer needs extensive proof" (30, 29).

[74]    Knoepflmacher, 111.

[75]    Lipking, 321. Others who claim that *Frankenstein*'s and *The Ancient Mariner*'s conflicts and open-endedness mark them as Romantic works include Kiely, 173, and L. J. Swingle, "On Reading Romantic Poetry," *PMLA* 86 (1971): 978, 980. Jack Stillinger claims that an author's self-divisions often produce rich "uncertainties, doubts, ambiguities, and contradictions" in his or her work, qualities that for Stillinger characterize the most accomplished and lasting (i.e., canonical) literary works but that especially characterize those from the Romantic and later periods ("The Story of Keats," in *The Cambridge Companion to Keats*, ed. Susan J. Wolfson [Cambridge: Cambridge University Press, 2001], 246–60; rpt. in Stillinger, *Romantic Complexity: Keats, Coleridge, Wordsworth* [Urbana: University of Illinois Press, 2006], 118, 123; Preface, *Romantic Complexity*, viii).

[76]    The terms "masculine Romanticism" and its counterpart "feminine Romanticism" are employed by Anne K. Mellor, who argues that they identify two separate literary traditions within the Romantic period (*Romanticism and Gender* [New York: Routledge, 1993], 3 and *passim*).

and undermining of intimate relationships; and the many distancing devices and defensive strategies built into its narrative and introduction—are consistent with the work of at least one major male Romantic poet: Samuel Taylor Coleridge. The case of Mary Shelley and Coleridge suggests that the Romantic movement is less divided along gender lines than has often been claimed and that the works of both male and female Romantic writers can be illuminated by acknowledging and exploring affinities between them as well as by the more common practice of emphasizing their differences. Instead of viewing Mary Shelley and other Romantic women writers as being in conflict with the male poets, one can perceive common ground among these writers by recognizing shared conflicts in all of their works. Indeed, dynamic conflict and ambivalence are hallmarks of Romantic literature written by both men and women.

## Works Cited

Ball, John Clement. "Imperial Monstrosities: 'Frankenstein,' the West Indies, and V. S. Naipaul," *Ariel* 32.3 (2001): 31–58.

Barth, J. Robert, S.J. *Coleridge and the Power of Love*. Columbia: University of Missouri Press, 1988.

Beer, John. "Mary Shelley, *Frankenstein*." *A Companion to Romanticism*. Ed. Duncan Wu. Oxford: Blackwell, 1998. 227–36.

Bennett, Betty. *Mary Wollstonecraft Shelley: An Introduction*. Baltimore: The Johns Hopkins University Press, 1998.

Beres, David. "A Dream, A Vision, and a Poem: A Psychoanalytic Study of the Origins of *The Rime of the Ancient Mariner*." *International Journal of Psychoanalysis* 32 (1951): 97–116.

Brewer, William D. "Mary Wollstonecraft and Mary Shelley: Ideological Affinities." In *Jane Austen and Mary Shelley and Their Sisters*. Ed. Laura Dabundo. Lanham: University Press of America, 2000. 97–107.

Bronfen, Elisabeth. "Rewriting the Family: Mary Shelley's *Frankenstein* in its Biographical/Textual Content." Frankenstein: *Creation and Monstrosity*. Ed. Stephen Bann. London: Reaktion, 1994. 16–38.

Butler, Marilyn. Introduction. *Frankenstein, or, The Modern Prometheus*. By Mary Shelley. Ed. Marilyn Butler. Oxford: Oxford University Press, 1994. ix–li.

Byron, Lord, George Gordon. *The Complete Poetical Works*. Ed. Jerome J. McGann. 7 vols. Oxford: Clarendon Press, 1980–1993.

Cantor, Paul A. *Creature and Creator: Myth-making and English Romanticism*. Cambridge: Cambridge University Press, 1984.

Claridge, Laura P. "Parent-Child Tensions in *Frankenstein*: The Search for Communion." *Studies in the Novel* 17 (1985): 14ᴸ–26.

Clemit, Pamela. "*Frankenstein, Matilda*, and the Legacies of Godwin and Wollstonecraft." In *The Cambridge Companion to Mary Shelley*. Ed. Esther Schor. Cambridge: Cambridge University Press, 2003. 26–44.

—. *The Godwinian Novel: The Rational Fictions of Godwin, Brockden Brown, Mary Shelley*. Oxford: Oxford University Press, 1993.

Clifford, Gay. "*Caleb Williams* and *Frankenstein*: First-Person Narrative and 'Things as They Are.'" *Genre* 10 (1977): 601–17.

Coleridge, Samuel Taylor. *Lectures 1808–1819 On Literature*. Ed. R. A. Foakes. 2 vols. Princeton: Princeton University Press, 1987.

—. *The Collected Letters of Samuel Taylor Coleridge*. Ed. Earl Leslie Griggs. 6 vols. Oxford: Clarendon Press, 1956-1971.

—. *The Notebooks of Samuel Taylor Coleridge*. Ed. Kathleen Coburn, Merton Christensen, and Anthony John Harding. 5 vols. Princeton: Princeton University Press, 1957–2002.

—. *Poetical Works*. Ed. J. C. C. Mays. 3 vols. in 6 parts. Princeton: Princeton University Press, 2001.

—. *Table Talk*. Ed. Carl Woodring. 2 vols. Princeton: Princeton University Press, 1990.

Crisman, William. "'Now Misery Has Come Home': Sibling Rivalry in *Frankenstein*." *Studies in Romanticism* 36 (1997): 27–41.

Dyck, Sarah. "Perspective in 'The Rime of the Ancient Mariner.'" *Studies in English Literature, 1500–1900* 13 (1973): 591–604.

Eilenberg, Susan. *Strange Powers of Speech: Wordsworth, Coleridge, and Literary Possession*. New York: Oxford University Press, 1992.

Fleck, P. D. "Mary Shelley's Notes to Shelley's Poems and *Frankenstein*." *Studies in Romanticism* 6 (1967): 226–54.

Foakes, R. A. "Coleridge, Violence, and 'The Rime of the Ancient Mariner.'" *Romanticism* 7 (2001): 41–57.

Fruman, Norman. *Coleridge: The Damaged Archangel*. New York: George Braziller, 1971.

Gilbert, Susan M., and Sandra Gubar. *The Madwoman in the Attic: The Woman Writer and the Nineteenth–Century Literary Imagination* (New Haven: Yale University Press, 1979).

Goodwin, Sarah Webster. "Domesticity and Uncanny Kitsch in 'The Rime of the Ancient Mariner' and *Frankenstein*." *Tulsa Studies in Women's Literature* 10 (1991): 93–108.

Hall, Jean. "*Frankenstein*: The Horrifying Otherness of Family." *Essays in Literature* 17 (1990): 179–89.

Harding, Anthony John. *Coleridge and the Idea of Love: Aspects of Relationships in Coleridge's Thought and Writing*. Cambridge: Cambridge University Press, 1974.

Harvey, A. D. "*Frankenstein* and *Caleb Williams*." *Keats–Shelley Journal* 29 (1980): 21–7.

Hill-Miller, Katherine C. *"My Hideous Progeny": Mary Shelley, William Godwin, and the Father–Daughter Relationship*. Newark: University of Delaware Press, 1995.

Hoeveler, Diane Long. "Glossing the Feminine in 'The Rime of the Ancient Mariner.'" *European Romantic Review* 2 (1992): 145–62.

Holmes, Richard. *Coleridge: Early Visions*. New York: Viking, 1990.

—. *Shelley: The Pursuit*. New York: Putnam, 1975.

Homans, Margaret. *Bearing the Word: Language and Female Experience in Nineteenth–Century Women's Writing*. Chicago: University of Chicago Press, 1986.

House, Humphrey. *Coleridge: The Clark Lectures, 1951–1952*. London: Rupert Hart–Davis, 1953.

Kiely, Robert. *The Romantic Novel in England*. Cambridge: Harvard University Press, 1972.

Knoepflmacher, U. C. "Thoughts on the Aggression of Daughters." In *The Endurance of Frankenstein: Essays on Mary Shelley's Novel*. Ed. George Levine and U. C. Knoepflmacher. Berkeley and Los Angeles: University of California Press, 1979. 88–119.

Komisaruk, Adam. "'So Guided by a Silken Cord': *Frankenstein*'s Family Values." *Studies in Romanticism* 38 (1999): 409–41.

Levy, Michelle. "Discovery and the Domestic Affections in Coleridge and Shelley." *Studies in English Literature, 1500–1900* 44 (2004): 693–713.

Lipking, Lawrence. "*Frankenstein*, the True Story: or, Rousseau Judges Jean–Jacques." *Frankenstein*. By Mary Shelley. Ed. J. Paul Hunter. New York: Norton, 1996. 313–31.

Lowes, John Livingston. *The Road to Xanadu: A Study in the Ways of the Imagination*. Boston: Houghton Mifflin, 1927.

McEathron, Scott. "Death as 'Refuge and Ruin': Shelley's 'A Vision of the Sea' and Coleridge's 'The Rime of the Ancient Mariner.'" *Keats-Shelley Journal* 43 (1994): 170–92.

McFarland, Thomas. In "Coleridge's Anxiety." *Coleridge's Variety: Bicentenary Studies*. Ed. John Beer and L. C. Knights. Pittsburgh: University of Pittsburgh Press, 1975. 134–75.

Marchand, Leslie A. *Byron: A Biography*. 3 vols. New York: Knopf, 1957.

May, Marilyn. "Publish and Perish: William Godwin, Mary Shelley, and the Public Appetite for Scandal." *Papers on Language and Literature* 26 (1990): 489–512.

Mellor, Anne K. *Mary Shelley: Her Life, Her Fiction, Her Monsters*. New York: Methuen, 1988.

—. "Possessing Nature: The Female in *Frankenstein*." *Romanticism and Feminism*. Ed. Anne K. Mellor. Bloomington: Indiana University Press, 1988. 220–32.

—. *Romanticism and Gender*. New York: Routledge, 1993.

Miall, David. "Guilt and Death: The Predicament of *The Ancient Mariner*." *Studies in English Literature, 1500–1900* 24 (1984): 633–53.

Minot, Leslie Ann, and Walter S. Minot. "*Frankenstein* and *Christabel*: Intertextuality, Biography, and Gothic Ambiguity." *European Romantic Review* 15 (2004): 23–49.

Poovey, Mary. *The Proper Lady and the Woman Writer: Ideology as Style in the Works of Mary Wollstonecraft, Mary Shelley, and Jane Austen*. Chicago: University of Chicago Press, 1984.

Reiman, Donald H., ed. *Shelley and His Circle, 1773–1822*. Vol. 7. Cambridge: Harvard University Press, 1986.

Robinson, Charles E. "The Shelley Circle and Coleridge's *The Friend*." *English Language Notes* 8 (1971): 269–74.

Roe, Nicholas. *Wordsworth and Coleridge: The Radical Years*. Oxford: Clarendon Press, 1988.

Rubenstein, Marc. "'My Accursed Origin': The Search for the Mother in *Frankenstein*." *Studies in Romanticism* 15 (1976): 165–94.

St. Clair, William. *The Godwins and the Shelleys: A Biography of a Family*. Baltimore: The Johns Hopkins University Press, 1989.

Schneider, Elisabeth. *Coleridge, Opium, and* Kubla Khan. 1953. Rpt. New York: Octagon Books, 1966.

Schultz, Max F. "Coleridge Agonistes." *Journal of English and Germanic Philology* 61 (1962): 268–77.

Seed, David. "'Frankenstein': Parable or Spectacle?" *Criticism* 24 (1982): 327–40.

Shelley, Mary. *Frankenstein*. Ed. J. Paul Hunter. New York: Norton, 1996.

—. *Frankenstein, or, The Modern Prometheus*. Ed. M. K. Joseph. New York: Oxford University Press, 1969.

—. *The Journals of Mary Shelley, 1814–1844*. Ed. Paula R. Feldman and Diana Scott–Kilvert. 2 vols. Oxford: Clarendon Press, 1987.

—. *The Letters of Mary Wollstonecraft Shelley*. Ed. Betty T. Bennett. 3 vols. Baltimore: The Johns Hopkins University Press, 1980–1988.

Small, Christopher. *Ariel Like a Harpy: Shelley, Mary and* Frankenstein. London: Victor Gollancz, 1972.

Stelzig, Eugene. "Always/Never on the Way Home: Reflections on the Romantic Self and the Family." *Mid–Hudson Language Studies* 12 (1989): 46–53.

Stevenson, Warren. "Byron and Coleridge: The Eagle and the Dove." *Byron Journal* 19 (1991): 114–27.

Stillinger, Jack. *Coleridge and Textual Instability: The Multiple Versions of the Major Poems*. New York: Oxford University Press, 1994.

—. *Romantic Complexity: Keats, Coleridge, Wordsworth*. Urbana: University of Illinois Press, 2006.

Sunstein, Emily W. *Mary Shelley: Romance and Reality*. Baltimore: The Johns Hopkins University Press, 1989.

Swingle, L. J. "On Reading Romantic Poetry." *PMLA* 86 (1971): 974–81.

Tayler, Irene, and Gina Luria. "Gender and Genre: Women in British Romantic Literature." In *What Manner of Woman: Essays in English and American Life and Literature*. Ed. Marlene Springer. New York: New York University Press, 1977. 98–123.

Todd, Janet M. "Frankenstein's Daughter: Mary Shelley and Mary Wollstonecraft." *Women and Literature* 4 (1976): 18–27.

Veeder, William. *Mary Shelley and* Frankenstein: *The Fate of Androgyny*. Chicago: University of Chicago Press, 1986.

Waldoff, Leon. "The Quest for Father and Identity in 'The Rime of the Ancient Mariner.'" *Psychoanalytic Review* 58 (1971): 439–53.

Wordsworth, William, and Samuel Taylor Coleridge. *Lyrical Ballads*. Ed. R. L. Brett and A. R. Jones. London: Methuen, 1963.

# Chapter 4
# "Something must be done": Shelley, Hemans, and the Flash of Revolutionary Female Violence

Susan J. Wolfson

On 9 June 1821, under "Literary Intelligence," *Literary Gazette* announced that the Royal Society of Literature prize has been awarded to "a lady, of celebrity in the Literary world—Mrs. HEMANS; who has, we understand, produced a beautiful poem … likely to add to her fame." Just below was news that "The publisher of Shelley's Queen Mab, has been indited by the Society for the Suppression of Vice. It is dreadful to think, that for the chance of a miserable pecuniary profit, any man would become the active agent to disseminate principles so subversive of the happiness of Society."[1] The fellowship of Felicia Hemans's fame with Percy Shelley's infamy was not the accident of this *Gazette.* The poets had a long interest in each other—though not without ambivalence.

Born as Britain primed for a war with France that would rage until 1815 (he, in late summer 1792; she, just after the autumnal equinox of 1793), they never met, at least in person. But as an Eton lad Shelley was captivated by Hemans's first volume (1808); and Hemans took *Alastor* (1814) to heart, relaying it into her *Tales, and Historic Scenes, in Verse* (1819), even as she tracked the abuses of Shelley's political poetry in *The Quarterly Review* and the scandals and controversies roiling across the next decade. By the time George Gilfillan was pairing the two for Victorian readers, they had become siblings in a poetic mythology:

> Like him, dropping fragile, … like him, the victim of exquisite nervous organization; … so strikingly alike, as to seem brother and sister, in one beautiful, but delicate and dying family. Their very appearance must have been similar. How like must the girl, Felicia Dorothea Browne, with the mantling bloom of her cheeks, her hair of a rich golden brown, and the ever varying expressions of her brilliant eyes, have been to the noble boy Percy Bysshe Shelley, when he came first to Oxford, a fair-haired, bright-eyed enthusiast, on whose cheek and brow, and in whose eye was already beginning to burn a fire, which ultimately enwrapped his whole being in flames![2]

---

[1]  *Literary Gazette,* 9 June 1821, 362.
[2]  *Tait's Edinburgh Magazine*, new series 14, June 1847, 362.

For all the delicacy, Gilfillan's Shelley still has fire, but how refined is the sister-poet, who in the decades when they were reading each other was wrapping female "nervous organization" in forms vibrantly passionate, sometimes violent. For his part, Shelley was distressed that Felicia Dorothea Browne, "certainly a tyger,"[3] seemed so enamored of sanguinary war. For her part, she was sorry about his skepticism, though never about the poetry. In 1828, with Shelley's name a scandal, Mrs. Hemans still felt her pulse beating to his. Concerned by some friends' objections to her using his verse as an epigraph, she wrote to her publisher William Blackwood, hoping to erase Shelley's signature but wanting to keep his verse, twelve lines of it, married to hers.[4]

From his cousin Thomas Medwin, who had met young Felicia Browne, Eton-lad Shelley heard of "the grace, and charming simplicity and naiveté of this interesting girl"; her *Poems* "made a powerful impression" of talents and likely promise (*FH*, 526). An exchange of letters ensued, until Mrs. Browne, getting wind of some heterodoxy, put an end to it. In a last letter to "amiable Felicia" from mid-March 1811 (just before expulsion from Oxford for that pamphlet on *The Necessity of Atheism*), Shelley not only defended his views, but also urged his correspondent to reflect with more moral consideration on one glaring fault:

> I examined the grounds upon which Theism is founded, they appeared to me weak, thro' deficiency of proof I became an Atheist. I read, I repeated your Poems I admired them, it gave me much regret, to find among so many beauties one fault, one glaring fault, I wrote to you, I informed you of it your letter entirely removed the only cause of complaint, a fear that you approved of fatal sanguinary wars. (*FH*, 527–8)

Felicia Browne was one of many caught up the national romance of chivalry reborn in the Peninsular War. Though her 1808 *Poems* was hardly a war-whoop, the scattered stamps of approval hit Shelley with dismaying glare: *The Spartan Mother and Her Son* ("Adieu! my mother, if with glory crown'd / Home I return not, scarr'd with many a wound, / I'll bravely fall in battle's rushing tide"); *The Ruined Castle* ("Here glory's crimson banner waving spread"; "Ah! where is now the warrior's ardent fire?"), *To Patriotism* ("Britannia's sons inspire / With all thy

---

[3]   To classmate and fellow-atheist T. J. Hogg, July 1811; *Shelley and His Circle, 1773–1822*, ed. Kenneth Neill Cameron, vol. 2 (Cambridge: Harvard University Press, 1961), 847.

[4]   Explaining that the poem was already in press, Blackwood assured her that Shelley's name would "not signify" negatively, because for "all his follies and impieties" Shelley was "a true poet"; *Felicia Hemans: Selected Poems, Letters, & Reception Materials*, ed. Susan Wolfson (Princeton: Princeton University Press, 2000), 495–6. For Hemans's reading and echoing of Shelley's poetry, see the index. Unless otherwise indicated, quotations of Hemans's poetry, correspondence, etc. follow this edition, cited as *FH*.

energy and fire: / Teach them to conquer or to die"), and *To My Younger Brother, on His Entering the Army* ("bless our noble fuzileer").[5]

Her next volume, the same year, was *England and Spain; or, Valour and Patriotism,* no mere lyric but a fierce celebration, across 28 pages of 530 heroic couplets, of the alliance against Napoleon, with a long view of British history as synonymous with glorious warfare. The title-page epigraph is brandished from Pope's *Iliad* (12.283–4): "His sword the brave man draws / And asks no omen but this country's cause." If Miss Browne could draw no man's sword, she drew her pen, leaguing with the feminine spirits of Muse, Liberty, and Freedom:

> Rise, Freedom, rise! …
> Queen of the lofty thought, the gen'rous deed,
> Whose sons unconquer'd fight, undaunted bleed,
> Inspiring Liberty!
>
> When ev'ry heart is fir'd, each pulse beats high,
> To fight, to bleed, to fall, for Liberty.[6]

So wrapped and rapt is the poet by the virtual battlefield of *England and Spain* that she manages to let slip a report of the material muse of war, Commerce, to be defended with blood. "Wave the dread banner, seize the glitt'ring lance! / With arm of might assert thy sacred cause" (p. 2) turns out to be a call in the cause of imperial hegemony, another warrior-*she* charged with spiritual fire:

> fearless Commerce, pillar of thy throne,
> Makes all the wealth of foreign climes thy own;
> From Lapland's shore to Afric's fervid reign,
> She bids thy ensigns float above the main;
> Unfurls her streamers to the fav'ring gale,
> And shows to other worlds her daring sail;
> Then wafts their gold, their varied stores to thee,
> Queen of the trident! empress of the sea!
> For this thy noble sons have spread alarms,
> And bade the zones resound with BRITAIN's arms! (p. 5)

Amiable Felicia freely admitted her "decided predilection for everything *military*" in March 1811 to the family friend who helped get these first two volumes

---

[5]   Felicia Dorothea Browne, *Poems* (London: T. Cadell and W. Davies, 1808), pp. 14, 42, 43, 64, 65.

[6]   *England and Spain; or, Valour and Patriotism* (London: T. Cadell and W. Davies, 1808), pp. 12, 22.

published.[7] In the apostrophe to this regal Queen (her national double), human blood enters the ledger as credits to valour and patriotism—the sort of thing that Shelley found a glaring fault, especially for economic profit:

> He bleeds! he falls! his death-bed is the field!
> His dirge the trumpet, and his bier the shield!
> His closing eyes the beam of valour speak,
> The flush of ardour lingers on his cheek;
> Serene he lifts to heaven those closing eyes … (p. 11)

About her brother George, wounded and harrowed in this war, she wrote in April 1809, "Deeply as I feel for the sufferings my dearest Brother must have endured, still I can hardly regret that he has received a wound in so glorious a cause, and as a trophy of so brilliant a victory; it will ever be his pride that he has bled in the service of his country."[8]

What Hemans caught in *Alastor* was a form of female brilliance, Shelley's poetry of the passionate incandescence of the female body: "the solemn mood / Of her pure mind kindled through all her frame /A permeating fire" (161–3), writes Shelley of a veiled dream maid.[9] Hemans's poetry of 1819 kindles this fire into public, historical agency, beyond the recall of men's dreams or dreads:

> Such wild and high expression, fraught
> With glances of impassion'd thought,
> As fancy sheds in visions bright,
> O'er priestess of the God of Light!
> And the dark locks that lend her face
> A youthful and luxuriant grace,
> Wave o'er a cheek, whose kindling dyes
> Seem from the fire within to rise …

This radiant impassionata is the vengeful eponym of *The Widow of Crescentius* (1.145–2). Sparked in domestic affection ("the Widow of"), her fire burns away distinction of private and public, personal and political. If in the wake of the French Revolution, Edmund Burke insisted that "we begin our public affections in our families" and that "love to the whole is not extinguished by this subordinate

---

[7]    Francis Nicholson, "Correspondence," *Memoirs and Proceedings of the Manchester Literary and Philosophical Society* 54.9 (1910): 27.

[8]    Nicholson, 13–14.

[9]    Quotations from Shelley, unless otherwise indicated, follow *Shelley's Poetry and Prose*, ed. Donald Reiman and Neil Fraistat, 2nd ed. (New York: Norton, 2002); prose is cited by page number.

partiality,"[10] Hemans works the argument in reverse: disaffection from the civic whole may begin when power extinguishes domestic ties and may take its most disturbing form in figures of female violence against the patriarchs. This widow will murder a husband-killing Emperor, whose death-throes are stoked with her fire:

> Gazing with stern vindictive smile,
> A feverish glow of triumph dyed
> His burning cheek, while thus he cried:
> "Yes! these are death pangs!—on thy brow
> Is set the seal of vengeance now!" (2.253–8)

Also reversing the customary gender scheme, Hemans has a *she* (dressed as a minstrel boy, no less) gazing with triumphant pleasure on a *he*. Tellingly, although the word *stern* throbs in the plot of triumph with heartache—"Oh! there are sorrows which impart / A sternness foreign to the heart" (2.145–6); "my fate / Hath made me stern as desolate" (2.293–4)—and to an ultimately fatal conclusion, the word was all still too "frequent and irksome" in *Tales and Historic Scenes* for the liking of the *London Literary Gazette*.[11]

Hemans's stern *Tales* greeted readers in May 1819, the month when Shelley was writing "Something must be done" for Beatrice's voice in Act 3 of *The Cenci*, after her father raped her. He was still "writing the Cenci, when the news of the Manchester Massacre reached us," and the events "aroused in him emotions of indignation and compassion," Mary Shelley recalls.[12] Writing to his publisher, Shelley pours his emotions into lines he'd already written for Beatrice: "Something must be done.... What yet I know not."[13] When *The Cenci* appeared in England in 1820, it was (in turn) post-Peterloo discourse, setting Manchester into a history of oppressions as old as the Renaissance, as recent as the Revolution-priming *ancien régime*.[14] It wouldn't be until after the Reform Bill of 1832 that Leigh Hunt felt he could publish the poet's first response, *The Masque of Anarchy* (a courtly re-

---

[10] *Reflections on the Revolution in France* (1790); 10th ed. (London: J. Dodsley, 1791), 290.

[11] 18 September 1819, 594–5. The reviewer may have been irked, too, by the gender-liberal applications of the word, attached to women not only in the strength of affections but also of transgressive resolve.

[12] "Note on Poems of 1819," *The Poetical Works of Percy Bysshe Shelley* (London: Edward Moxon, 1839), 3:205; hereafter *1839*.

[13] *Letters of Percy Bysshe Shelley*, ed. F. L. Jones, 2 vols. (Oxford: Clarendon Press, 1964), 2:117.

[14] Even as reviewers focused on blasphemy and depravity, they got the social text, not "blind to the fact that the inadequacies of the Roman nobility and church were not uniquely Italian"; Stuart Curran, *Shelley's "Cenci"* (Princeton: Princeton University Press, 1970), 10.

titling of Shelley's *Mask)* and hail it as a "*political anticipation*" (his italics) of an inevitable spirit of reform, accomplished without any violence:

> the poet recommends that there should be no active resistance, come what might; which is a piece of fortitude, however effective, which we believe was not contemplated by the Political Unions: yet, in point of the spirit of the thing, the success he anticipates has actually occurred, and after his very fashion... . The battle was won without a blow.[15]

By 1832 this cheer was, in turn, post-*Cenci* discourse. But in the crises of 1819, *The Cenci* and *The Mask of Anarchy* mark an impasse in Shelley's indignation between violent and visionary courses of action—so, too, in Hemans's records and histories of women, which repeatedly stage violent female confrontations with male tyrannies, in a poetry of seemingly inescapable death sentences for women.

*The Cenci* is infused with gender politics: because her torment and retaliation are inseparable from their formation in, and by, corrupt patriarchy, "Beatrice Cenci" is a figure for England in 1819 no less than of the Italian Renaissance. So too Hemans's sorority in *Tales* and *Records of Woman*: if the sites are other cultures, other times, the themes return home with symbolic lore. For both poets, gender is a flashpoint rhetoric of male oppressions and female grievances; and for both, the disordering of the feminine in retaliatory or revolutionary actions arises as a sensational disturbance within, and against, the political text. The Romantic fellowship of Shelley and Hemans is tightly wound around their turbulent romances of women inflamed by transformative passion.

* * *

Beatrice's "something must be done" constellates in *The Cenci* in reciprocity to deeds of patriarchal tyranny.[16] In his opening scene Shelley presents Count Cenci boasting away to Cardinal Camillo of craving some "deed to act / Whose horror might make sharp an appetite / Duller than mine—I'd do,—I know not what" (1.1.100–102). Scarcely pausing over "what I have decreed to do," he summons

---

[15]   Percy Bysshe Shelley, *The Masque of Anarchy. A Poem*, Preface by Leigh Hunt (London: Edward Moxon, 1832), x–xi.

[16]   For the verbal pattern, see Curran, 133–4. Having translated "Sodomy was the least and Atheism the greatest of [the Count's] vices," Mary Shelley found the fulfillment of the Count's attempts "by force & threats to debauch his daughter" too "horrible. & unfit for publication"; *Relation of the Death of the Cenci* (from an Italian ms. conveyed to her from the Palazzo Cenci archives), in Betty T. Bennett, ed., *The Bodleian Shelley Manuscripts*, vol. X (New York: Garland Press, 1992), 174–5, 182–3. For "the systematic betrayal of Beatrice" by "fathers—familial, political and religious," a scheme Shelley heightened from this source, see Eugene Hammond, "Beatrice's Three Fathers: Successive Betrayal in Shelley's *The Cenci*," *Essays in Literature* 8 (1981): 25–6, 32n.5.

"manhood's purpose stern" to bellow, at the close of Act I: "It must be done; it shall be done, I swear!" (1.3.172–8). With more than Macbeth ardor, he thrills, "Would that it were done!" to close the next scene (2.1.193). When *would* becomes *done*, the word *Parricide* first sounds, coming to Beatrice not as a determination, or even in audition of vague possibility, but in a syntax of horrific conceptual contradiction, borne by the indirection of simile:

> Like Parricide …
> Misery has killed its father: yet its father
> Never like mine … O, God! What thing am I? (3.1.36–8)

Ravaged by a father who is no father, from a human subject, *I*, down to a *thing*, Beatrice (as G. H. Lewes grasped) speaks "Parricide" as a figure of traumatic repression.[17] Yet as she mutters, "I have no father" (39–40), the cancellation gets set, in Shelley's historicism, as awful prediction.[18]

Primed by Shelley's assurances in his *Preface* that he has shunned the aesthetic indulgence of "a detached simile" (143), a reader has to register the force-field that shifts from what was "done" by the father into an imperative future, an *I* recovered in a determined *Aye*:

> I shall go mad. Aye, something must be done;
> What yet I know not … something which shall make
> The things that I have suffered but a shadow
> In the dread lightning which avenges it;
> Brief, rapid, irreversible, destroying
> The consequence of what it cannot cure. (3.1.86–91)

In the mask of this maddened woman, Shelley envisions things as they are blasted into shadows by a vengeance with the force of primal nature—as if Beatrice were twin to Shakespeare's King Lear fuming at the "unnatural" daughters he has unwisely empowered:

> I will have such revenges on you both
> That all the world shall—I will do such things—
> What they are, yet I know not; but they shall be
> The terrors of the earth. (2.4.278–81)[19]

---

[17]    She "means that the intensity of her misery has absorbed all consciousness of its cause (father)"; *Westminster Review* 35 (1841): 338.

[18]    For the simile as latent plot, see William Jewett, *Fatal Autonomy* (Ithaca: Cornell University Press, 1997), 151.

[19]    The Arden Edition of *King Lear*, ed. Kenneth Muir (1972; New York: Methuen, 1980).

But how different are the politics in *The Cenci,* where it is a daughter's rage at an unnatural father, still in power, with the regal support of every institution, temporal and divine.

If it takes a female mask for Shelley to invoke categorical, violent opposition, its arc of parricide is also a crux, tracing not just revolutionary hope but a recent historical horror, a vast image out of French-Revolution Spiritus Mundi. Parricide was the lynchpin of Burke's infernal trinity of "Regicide, and parricide, and sacrilege" in his *Reflections on the Revolution in France,* where the status quo ante is rendered as if it were sacred scripture:

> we have consecrated the state, that no man should approach to look into its defects
> or corruptions but with due caution; that he should never dream of beginning its
> reformation by its subversion; that he should approach to the faults of the state as
> to the wounds of a father, with pious awe and trembling sollicitude. By this wise
> prejudice we are taught to look with horror on those children of their country
> who are prompt rashly to hack that aged parent in pieces.[20]

Six years on, in the first of his *Two Letters ... on the Proposals for Peace with the Regicide Directory of France,* looking with horror at a state where "children are encouraged to cut the throats of their parents,"[21] Burke gendered his history:

> out of the tomb of the murdered Monarchy in France, has arisen a vast,
> tremendous, unformed spectre, in a far more terrific guise than any which ever
> yet have overpowered the imagination and subdued the fortitude of man. Going
> straight forward to it's end, unappalled by peril, unchecked by remorse, despising
> all common maxims and all common means, that hideous phantom overpowered
> those who could not believe it was possible she could at all exist ... (6–7)

Ronald Paulson reads the specter shape of terror as Milton's Death reborn,[22] but Burke's phantom is stripped of Milton's republican politics (his Death bears "the likeness of a Kingly Crown") and emphatically re-sexed. It is a *she* set against the civil "fortitude of man" (*overpowered* sounds twice): "No man, in a publick or private concern, can divine by what rule or principle her judgments are to be directed" (96), let alone countenance the new idea "that women had been too long under the tyranny of parents and of husbands"—a system Burke prefers to call "guardianship and protection" (103).

With a numeral famous from Burke's celebrated outrage at the failure of chivalry in the fall of the French queen, "I thought ten thousand swords must have

---

[20]    *Reflections on the Revolution in France,* 114, 143.

[21]    *Two Letters Addressed to a Member of the Present Parliament, on the Proposals for Peace with the Regicide Directory of France* (London: F. and C. Rivington, 1796), 105.

[22]    *Representations of Revolution (1789–1820)* (New Haven: Yale University Press, 1983), 72; see *Paradise Lost,* 2.666 *ff.*

leaped from their scabbards to avenge even a look that threatened her with insult" (*Reflections*, 86), Mary Shelley reciprocally crafted Victor Frankenstein's worst nightmare about his poor Creature's plea for "justice due" in the form of a female companion: "she might become ten thousand times more malignant than her mate, and delight, for its own sake, in murder and wretchedness." And she might revolt against her patriarchal assignment: "He had sworn to quit the neighbourhood of man, and hide himself in deserts; but she had not; and she, who in all probability was to become a thinking and reasoning animal, might refuse to comply with a compact made before her creation."[23] In this spectral *might*, justice is denied to abject grievance. Beatrice at her most monstrous is a sequel to this nightmare, as if Victor's phantasm were her herald.[24]

Burke's appeal to sentiment and domestic affection owed some of its affective power to England's regard of old, ailing George III as the tender father of his people, a vulnerable but still titled king in 1819.[25] Shelley's is parricide with a difference. Beatrice is vulnerable to the unchecked monster of patriarchy itself, a regime in which a father's rape cannot be named or tried but "parricide" is ever under surveillance, discussion, and prosecution. The Count accuses his wife of teaching their son "Parricide with his alphabet" (2.1.132). The Pope, officially neutral in "the great war between the old and young," yet mindful of his own "white hairs and tottering body," inclines to the father's cause: "Children are disobedient, and they sting / Their fathers' hearts to madness and despair" (2.2.32–9). *The Cenci*'s final sounding of *parricide* is this Pope's extravagant citation of Paolo Santa Croce's murder of his mother, to gain his inheritance:

> Parricide grows so rife
> That soon, for some just cause no doubt, the young
> Will strangle us all, dozing in our chairs.
> Authority, and power, and hoary hair
> Are grown crimes capital. (5.4.20–24)

The source's word was "Matricide" (*Relation*, X:216–17). Shelley changed the gender to sharpen the edge of Papal policing.

---

[23]    *Frankenstein; or, The Modern Prometheus*, 1818; ed. Susan J. Wolfson (New York: Longman, 2006), 114, 129.

[24]    Mary Shelley worked in fellowship with her husband on *The Cenci*. After she transcribed *Relation* in May 1818, Percy urged her to undertake a tragedy, but she felt unable. As he did so in 1819, they frequently "talked over" its composition ("Note on The Cenci," *1839*, 3:274; Mary here misremembers the date of transcription as 1819). Percy meant to have her *Relation* set as prefix to his play (*Relation*, X:18). It wasn't, but she did include it in her one-volume *Poetical Works of Percy Bysshe Shelley* (London: Edward Moxon, 1839 [d. "1840"]).

[25]    See John Barrell, "Sad Stories: Louis XVI, George III, and the Language of Sentiment," in *Refiguring Revolutions,* ed. Kevin Sharpe and Steven Zwicker (Berkeley: University of California Press, 1998), 78–9.

A student of Greek tragedy, Shelley knew that parricide was a prohibition primed by hardwired inhibition. "That word parricide, / Although I am resolved, haunts me like fear," he has abused son Giacomo Cenci shudder (3.1.340–41). The safety-catch on the surge to political liberation is this male psychological identification. The deed done, Giacomo cannot shake off "remorse" (5.1.2): "It was a wicked thought, a piteous deed, / To kill a old and hoary-headed father" (9–11). Even the hired assassins recoil with a Burkean horror ("those children of their country who are prompt rashly to hack that aged parent in pieces") that bristles with Macbeth-regicide:

> *Olimpio*. We dare not kill an old and sleeping man;
> His thin grey hair, his stern and reverent brow,
> His veined hands crossed on his heaving breast,
> And the calm of innocent sleep in which he lay,
> Quelled me. Indeed, indeed, I cannot do it. (4.3.9–13)

> *Marzio*.                              … my knife
> Touched the loose wrinkled throat, when the old man
> Stirred in his sleep, and said, "God! hear, O, hear,
> A father's curse! What, art thou not our father?"
> And then he laughed. I knew it was the ghost
> Of my dead father speaking through his lips,
> And could not kill him. (4.3.16–22)

The oedipal haunting throws into sharp relief Beatrice's simultaneous morphing into Lady Macbeth, a twinning that undoes the argument of justice, poisoning the aura of revolution.

Yet it is an index of Shelley's political conflict that all around this climactic event, he is using Beatrice to advance *parricide* into a critical question, from its first event in her post-rape simile ("Like Parricide …" [3.1.37]) to her refusal to confess in a system that has a criminal lexicon for what she has "done" but no name, except the negative "unutterable," for what was done to her (5.3.81), no "word that might make known / The crime," as she complains to her confidant Orsino (3.1.154–5). "Cenci has done an outrage to his daughter," is all he can whisper to Giacomo (3.1.348). If "Days of outrage" would be Mary Shelley's phrase for the political crises of England in 1819 (*1839*, 3:205), at this dramatic crisis "outrage" is a blank sign of excess that can recoil only in "half conjectures," "obscure hints," whispered talk, "darkly guessing, stumbling" (3.1.350–58).[26]

---

[26]   Though to English eyes and ears, *outrage* seems etymological as "out-rage," the root is French *outré* (in excess); even so, "out-rage" is a long-standing folk etymology. Whether in delicacy or in horror, Shelley's *Preface* is so evasive at times as to put excess in doubt. To write that the Count's hatred of Beatrice "shewed itself … under the form of an incestuous passion" and provoked "what she considered a perpetual contamination both

In defiance of this regime of signification, Beatrice declares to her arresting officer, "I am more innocent of parricide / Than is a child born fatherless" (4.4.113–14). To Leigh Hunt the plea was continuous with the first traumatic simile-site of the word.[27] Yet as he and others recognized, the declaration is more than a local plea: it is a public challenge to the law per se. Even Giacomo feels a sympathy for Beatrice's "avenging such a nameless wrong / As turns black parricide to piety" (5.1.44–5). As much as her deed, her opposition becomes a site of trial, first in Act 5, then in a long history of critical judgment.[28] To the judge's legal aggression, "Art thou not guilty of thy father's death?" (5.3.77), Beatrice turns the question back on the court, to interrogate the laws by which she is being tried:

> Or wilt thou rather tax high judging God
> That he permitted such an act as that
> Which I have suffered, and which he beheld;
> Made it unutterable, and took from it
> All refuge, all revenge, all consequence,
> But that which thou has called my father's death?
> Which is or is not what men call a crime,
> Which either I have done, or have not done … (5.3.78–85)

These last words play audibly against that opening scene, where the Count speaks to the Cardinal in chilling, casual immunity to "what men call crime" (1.1.68). An awful detail in *Relation* is Beatrice's last plea for audience: "she placed her head under the axe which at one blow was divided from her body as she was repeating the 2nd verse of the psalm *De profundis*, at the words *fiant aures tuae*."[29]

---

of body and mind" (141) is to allow us to think it was all mental drama, just forms and considerations, with no certain deed.

27 In *The Indicator*, Hunt protested that objections to a "lie" failed to grasp the language of a "horrid dream" in "contradiction" to nature (42 [26 July 1820]: 331–2). In *Lord Byron and Some of his Contemporaries* (London: Henry Colburn, 1828), Hunt proposed that in Beatrice's voice, a "liberal and masculine" Shelley conveys a "horror at the violation of principle. The reader refuses to think that a daughter has slain a *father,* precisely because a dreadful sense of what a father ought not to have done has driven her to it, and because [the reader] sees that in any other situation she would be the most exemplary of children" (367–8).

28 "We cannot attach the criminality of parricide to her," G. H. Lewes writes for the defense; "Common notions of right and wrong … do not here apply" (339). Others pile on to indict pernicious mistakes, sophistry, even hypocrisy (e.g., Robert Whitman, "Beatrice's 'Pernicious Mistake' in *The Cenci*," *PMLA* 74 (1959): 249–53; Stephen Behrendt, *Shelley and His Audiences* [Lincoln: University of Nebraska Press, 1989]; Stuart Sperry, *Shelley's Major Verse* [Cambridge: Harvard University Press, 1988], &c &c &c).

29 X:234–5; "Out of the depths have I cried unto thee, O Lord. / Lord, hear my voice: *let thine ears* be attentive to the voice of my supplications" (Psalm 130, King James Bible; emphasis mine).

Shelley might have mobilized this last call to a Father beyond time and history into a devastating politics of utopia; but one of the most arresting complications of *The Cenci* is the way its gender politics recede at the act of parricide. The political question—what's rotten in the state of Rome?—gets eclipsed by a question of character: what's the fault in Beatrice? Her hard zeal, moreover, implies another politics that many readers feel called to iterate: violent revolution, even against monstrous tyranny, can be only another monstrosity.[30] Beatrice becomes her father's daughter we're told, from first reviews to latest analyses.[31] Shelley's seemingly most tendentious interpolation in the *Relation* in this respect is the next scene: the arrival of the Papal Legate with a warrant for the Count's arrest to "answer charges of gravest import" (4.4.11–13). Yet this *lex ex machina* is less a solution to than the crux of Shelley's political question. Did Beatrice jump a system that would have reformed, checked the tyrant, purged its monster? Or is the warrant only the latest exercise of Papal fund-raising?[32] What is the implied political allegory of this moment: patience? impending reform? or delusion?

Even with displacements onto the Italian Renaissance and its female agents of retaliation, Shelley couldn't decide. Opposite fiery Edmund Kean (for whom he wrote the part of the Count), he hoped to cast Eliza O'Neill as Beatrice, having been "deeply moved ... by the graceful sweetness, the intense pathos, and sublime vehemence of passion she displayed" on stage; "She was often in his thoughts

---

[30]     Even though she patterns political grievances, argues Michael Scrivener, her actions plot "a series of dilemmas" about violence in the name of "innocence"; *Radical Shelley* (Princeton: Princeton UP, 1982), 188–9. To Behrendt, Shelley is caught in a conflict between his "subversive intent" in writing Beatrice as the voice of a suffering populace ready "to contemplate violent revolution" (against, implicitly, "the Regency establishment") and the error of investing in her course of action (147, 152–3).

[31]     *Literary Gazette* dismissed her sad resignation ("Whatever comes, my heart shall sink no more ..." etc. [5.4.78–89]) with alliteration that William Safire might envy: "the dying infidelity of that paragon of parricides" (1 April 1820, 210). To *Monthly Review*, "incest committed by a father, and murder perpetrated by a daughter" were to be weighed equally (2nd series, 94 [February 1821], 162). So, too, in a long twentieth-century trial, among recent judgments one finds: "she becomes her father's child" (Sperry, 135); "plotting her father's murder and in employing assassins," she "adopts the behavior she has condemned in others" (Behrendt, 151). For mordant rebuttal to the invoking of "objective ethical standard," see Curran, 141, especially n.13. Even *Relation* is more sympathetic: "At length these unhappy women finding themselves without hope of relief [in several supplications to the Pope]—driven by desperation resolved to plan [the Count's] death" (X:184–5).

[32]     Shelley's *Preface* proposes this interpretation: "The Pope, among other motives for severity, probably felt that whoever killed the Count Cenci deprived his treasury of a certain and copious source of revenue" (141). For skepticism about the impending justice signified by the warrant, see Curran, 141–2.

as he wrote," recalled Mary Shelley.[33] The play closes in a scene that returns Beatrice from political vehemence to domestic pathos, speaking of "doing" now in resignation to a death-sentence:

> … Here, Mother, tie
> My girdle for me, and bind up this hair
> In any simple knot; aye, that does well.
> And yours I see is coming down. How often
> Have we done this for one another; now
> We shall not do it any more. My Lord,
> We are quite ready. Well, 'tis very well. (5.4.159–65)

In another elaboration of *Relation*,[34] Shelley writes the scene with literacy in iconographies of female hair. Unbound, wanton hair evokes Medusa, Eve, and in political radiance, Cassandra and the French Revolutionary Goddesses, all primed for (if not achieving) power. This scene of final binding up (for beheading) is a reordering grace synonymous with the order of death.

Thus Shelley restores Beatrice from the ravages of rape—"How comes this hair undone?" she cries just after (3.1.6)—to domestic decorum, and aligns her with the famous portrait at the Colonna Place given rapturous ekphrasis near the end of the *Preface*, and engraved for the 1819 publication: "she seems sad and stricken down in spirit… . Her head is bound with folds of white drapery from which the yellow strings of her golden hair escape, and fall about her neck"—a little erotic frisson amid the "fixed and pale composure" (144). *Relation* reports the Pope's fear that his judges had been confused by this hair-power: "like threads of gold and because they were extremely long she used to tie it up & when afterwards she loosened it the splendid ringlets dazzled the eyes of the spectator" (X:242–3); in perfect reciprocity, the Papal rigor is a "torture of the hair" (X:208–9)—a taming that seems almost Persean. *Relation* concludes in horrid details of her execution that play to this Medusa myth: "the blow gave a violent motion to her body & discomposed her dress" (the language suggests a second rape); then the Perseus-display of the trophy-head: "The executioner raised the head to the view of the people, and … the cord by which it was suspended slipt from his hold & the head fell to the ground shedding a great deal of blood" (X:234–5).

But if Medusa (golden style) is thus vanquished, her full story returns her to another, exculpatory twinship with Beatrice. As Shelley knew from Ovid (*Metamorphoses* Book 4), she was raped by a god, then punished by having her famously golden hair transformed into a nest of male-petrifying snakes. Hers is thus an equivocal power, one the Romantic generation, argues Jerome McGann, understood as "a symbol of cultural, sometimes, revolutionary, change."[35] Late in 1819, as a virtual sequel to *The*

---

[33]    "Note on The Cenci"; *1839*, 2:276–7. For P. B. Shelley's hopes to cast Eliza O'Neill, see his letter to T. L. Peacock; c. 20 July 1819, *Letters*, 2:102–3.

[34]    There, Beatrice and Lucretia help each other only with their garments (X:224–5).

[35]    "The Beauty of the Medusa," *Studies in Romanticism* 2 (1972): 4, 7.

*Cenci*, Shelley wrote *On the Medusa of Leonardo da Vinci, in the Florentine Gallery*, a sublime complication of "horror" at her power and rapture at the "beauty" of her suffering: [36]

> Yet it is less the horror than the grace
>    Which turns the gazer's spirit into stone;
> . . . . . . . . . . . . . . . . . . . . . . . . . . . . .
>    'T is the melodious hue of beauty thrown
> Athwart the darkness and the glare of pain,
> Which humanizc and harmonize the strain.

In Italy, too, Shelley heard a generally humanizing conversation on Beatrice, "a romantic pity" for her sufferings "and a passionate exculpation of the horrible deed" (*Preface*, 141)—a vector to be reversed in England, where the Tory press linked her "crimes" to Shelleyan politics.

*The Cenci* is composed of this array of ambivalences. Shelley's *Preface* advertises a character-tragedy, in which Beatrice may be anatomized as a moral failure. At the same time he is at pains to resist the moralizing frames that would defeat "a dramatic purpose," and rehearses the "dogmas" in order, seemingly, to deny the maxims full interpretive authority:

> Undoubtedly, no person can be truly dishonoured by the act of another, and
> the fit return to the most enormous injuries is kindness and forebearance, and
> a resolution to convert the injurer from his dark passions by peace and love.
> Revenge, retaliation, atonement, are pernicious mistakes. (141–2)

This rehearsal sounds rote, as if merely to set the stage for a defense of dramatic poetry:

> If Beatrice had thought in this manner she would have been wiser and better;
> but she would never have been a tragic character.... It is in the restless and
> anatomizing casuistry with which men seek the justification of Beatrice, yet feel
> that she has done what needs justification; it is in the superstitious horror with
> which they contemplate alike her wrongs and their revenge; that the dramatic
> character of what she did and suffered, consists. (142)

Yet this defense of dramatic value has a problematic intertext in Shelley's remarks on Milton's Satan in another preface he was writing, across the same time, for *Prometheus Unbound*: "The character of Satan engenders in the mind a pernicious casuistry which leads us to weigh his faults with his wrongs and to excuse the

---

[36]    Mary Shelley made this the first of the "Miscellaneous Poems" in *Posthumous Poems of Percy Bysshe Shelley* (London: John and Henry L. Hunt, 1824), 139–40 (my text); see also *1839*, 3:195–6.

former because the latter exceed all measure" (207)—that excess which is "outrage" in *The Cenci*. It's not that Beatrice Unbound is Satanic; it's that her political case threatens to perplex distinction of cause and casuistry.

The force of this pernicious casuistry may be an unspoken motivation for the stabilizing text that precedes the *Preface* to *The Cenci,* Shelley's *Dedication to Leigh Hunt, Esq.*—in effect a male compact in implicit contrast to female parricide. Shelley honors their solidarity "in that patient and irreconcilable enmity with domestic and political tyranny and imposture which the tenor of [Hunt's] life has illustrated," and proposes a brotherhood in antithesis to the "sad reality" of Beatrice's course of action. No one, he says in this public vindication of Hunt, is

> more gentle, honourable, innocent and brave ... of more exalted toleration for all who do and think evil, and yet himself more free from evil.... In that patient and irreconcilable enmity with domestic and political tyranny and imposture which the tenor of your life has illustrated, and which, had I health and talents should illustrate mine, let us, comforting each other in our task, live and die. (140)

Yet as he was writing these words in Italy, in mid-August 1819,[37] events erupting in England the very same week would pose a test of this resolve, not in the least because, when he learned of these outrages, Shelley felt a political fellowship with Beatrice the parricide.

On 16 August, about 100,000 Manchester workers gathered at St. Peter's Field for peaceful demonstrations and to hear Henry "Orator" Hunt voice their grievances, and were set upon by a pack of saber-wielding local yeomanry, in likely complicity with the London home office. The radical press broadcast the scandal of the female victims, and Shelley reacted as Beatrice. "The torrent of my indignation has not yet done boiling in my veins," he fumed to his publisher Ollier on 6 September, having just read of the events in Leigh Hunt's *Examiner;* "I wait anxiously [to] hear how the Country will express its sense of this bloody murderous oppression of its destroyers. 'Something must be done.... What yet I know not'" (*Letters,* 2: 117). When he writes to his friend Peacock on the 21st, however, he has cooled down a bit, and shifts his Beatrice-syntax, now without quotation marks, away from what the *Preface* calls her "pernicious mistakes" (142):

> I have received all the papers you sent me, & the Examiners regularly, perfumed with muriatic acid. What an infernal business this of Manchester! What is to be done? Something assuredly. H. Hunt has behaved I think with great spirit & coolness in the whole affair. (21 September 1819; *Letters,* 2:120)

---

[37]   Though the published byline of *The Cenci* is *"Rome,* May 29, 1819" (when Shelley was in the city of the play's events), it is in August that he tells Hunt, "I mean to dedicate it to you" (*Letters,* 2:112).

Instead of an imperative, "what is to be done" is now a question. Though Henry Hunt was arrested and brought to trial in London, he called down no lighting bolt of revolution.[38]

*The Cenci* is hardly so consolidated, and the chief symptom is the welter of genres Shelley brings into play, in sequence, or superimposed, under the pressure of conflicted political thinking: classical tragedy (family curse), Shakespearean tragedy (Italian style), Jacobean tragedy, gothic melodrama (Italian-Catholic style), Enlightenment cultural critique, revolutionary tract, atheist polemic (Shelley style), even *Clarissa* (Mary was reading it in 1818–1819[39]). *The Mask of Anarchy* is more formally coordinated: it is a dream vision of atrocious then ideal politics, and its climax is an inspirational ballad-anthem of stern but nonviolent protest:

> Stand ye calm and resolute,
> Like a forest close and mute,
> With folded arms and looks which are
> Weapons of unvanquished war. (319–22)

The sudden death of Anarchy (just prior) is the allegorical corollary to the theme of this song, the magical effect of patient female fortitude in the theater of male tyranny—a regime for which *Anarchy* is Shelley's polemical synonym. A "maniac maid" lies down before the rushing army of tyrants; "her name was Hope, she said: / But she looked more like Despair" (86–8). Unlike the desperate parricides of *The Cenci*, or the harridans of Burke's gothic, this maid pities her father as history in arrest: "My father Time is weak and grey / With waiting for a better day" (90–91). Risking political martyrdom, this aggrieved daughter is saved by a miracle of rare device:

> When between her and her foes
> A mist, a light, an image rose,
> Small at first, and weak, and frail
> Like the vapour of a vale:
>
> Till as clouds grow on the blast,
> Like tower-crowned giants striding fast
> And glare with lightnings as they fly,
> And speak in thunder to the sky,

---

[38]     "Hunt identified himself as a law-abiding, God-fearing, Christian reformer who was as horrified by Carlile's outrages as by the government," notes Scrivener (225); radical Richard Carlile was an eyewitness to Peterloo. Shelley hoped that it would be "the higher orders" that would lead reform politics, but he wasn't confident: "I wonder & tremble.—" (24 August 1819; *Letters*, 2: 115).

[39]     See *The Journals of Mary Shelley,* ed. Paula R. Feldman and Diana Scott-Kilvert (1987; Baltimore: The Johns Hopkins University Press, 1995), April 1818 and August 1819 (205, 293).

> It grew—a Shape arrayed in mail
> Brighter than the Viper's scale,
> And upborne on wings whose grain
> Was as the light of sunny rain.
>
> On its helm, seen far away,
> A planet, like the Morning's, lay,
> And those plumes its light rained through
> Like a shower of crimson dew. (102–17)

This Shape seems kin to Shelley's Medusa—"mailed radiance," a "tempestuous loveliness of terror," "brazen glare," a "thrilling vapour of the air" (*On the Medusa*, 140). But there is no horror for men. Rather, Hope can now rise with "quiet mien" (129) and hear a song, as if from a sympathetically leagued mother Earth (138–46), its theme a renovated history for all men:

> "Men of England, heirs of Glory,
> Heroes of unwritten story,
> Nurslings of one mighty Mother,
> Hopes of her, and one another ..." (147–50)

In the political dream-vision that succeeds the sad reality of *The Cenci*, the feminine is cast as the repository of a myth of transformative revolution without violence.[40]

Across the late Regency and the decade that preceded the Reform Bill, Hemans was resorting to various historical displacements to dramatize tyranny in figures of male treachery and female revenge, often in spectacular transgression of "feminine" character.[41] Her *Tales, and Historic Scenes* is a macrotext, within which *The Widow of Crescentius* and *The Wife of Asdrubal* are allied chapters. Unlike the widow's revenge, the wife's has no historical effect. But allied with the destruction of a city-state (not just one tyrant), it's a political rhetoric for readers in 1819, fresh from a quarter century of war, in which Napoleon's sieges were notoriously brutal. Hemans's scene is Carthage, a feminine figure beyond mere convention: "Her walls have sunk, and pyramids of fire / In lurid splendor from her domes aspire" (3–4). For his safety, governor Asdrubal has secretly traded the city

---

[40]    While I appreciate Anne Janowitz's focus on the female figurings of Shelley's "communitarian poetics," I can't see such insubstantial visionary figures advancing "a fierce and autonomous female interventionism" that "enacts the productive links of communitarianism and women's liberation"; "A Voice from across the Sea: Communitarianism at the Limits of Romanticism," in *The Limits of Romanticism*, ed. Mary Favret and Nicola Watson (Bloomington: Indiana University Press, 1994), 92–3.

[41]    My discussion here draws somewhat from my different contexts of discussion in *Borderlines* (Palo Alto: Stanford University Press, 2006), 58–67 and 307–9.

to the invading Romans. His wife, sons, and patriots hold out in the citadel, and as conquest impends, torch it and die. Just before this climax, the wife appears on the roof, to berate the cad, stab their sons before his eyes, and throw the bodies into the flames, with a taunt of patriarchal defeat: "thou, their sire, / In bondage safe, shalt yet in them expire" (57–8).

Hemans gives the triumph a gender reassignment. Asdrubal is feminized down to a trophy in a "Roman triumph" (48), while his wife, "sternly beauteous in terrific ire" (18), stages an aesthetic sublime of political fury, "a strange and fierce ascendancy" (22):

> The flames are gathering round intensely bright,
> Full on her features glares their meteor-light,
> But a wild courage sits triumphant there,
> The stormy grandeur of a proud despair;
> A daring spirit, in its woes elate,
> Mightier than death, untameable by fate.
> The dark profusion of her locks unbound,
> Waves like a warrior's floating plumage round;
> Flush'd is her cheek, inspired her haughty mien,
> She seems th' avenging goddess of the scene. (23–32)

She could have been auditioning for Beatrice Cenci, reading Act 5. As with Beatrice, domestic relations turn political, stern, violent, and fatal all at once: "Is that a mother's glance, where stern disdain / And passion awfully vindictive, reign?" asks the poet (34–5). The political act is not parricide but infanticide, wrapped in the derealizing horrifics of supernatural spectacle: the climax of this historic scene is the wife's "frantic laugh" and "frenzied glance on high" just before "midst rolling flames" she "is lost to mortal eye" (65–8).

The real politics of infanticide is a recurrent theme for Hemans, however, and not always historically displaced. *Modern Greece* (1817) pauses at Suli and, a decade or so on, this scene returns in *The Suliote Mother* (1825). The history is a famous event from 1803, when Suli women, in alarm as the Turkish army advances on their mountain fasthold, their men already lost to a failed rout, hurled themselves with their children into a chasm to avoid rape, murder, or enslavement. *Modern Greece* puts the turbulent domestic affections in the public sphere, with the women (as Felicia Browne might have wanted to be) as fellow-warriors for Liberty:

> woman mingled with your warrior-band.
> Then on the cliff the frantic mother stood
> High o'er the river's darkly-rolling wave,
> And hurl'd, in dread delirium, to the flood,
> Her free-born infant, ne'er to be a slave.

> For all was lost—all, save the power to die
> The wild indignant death of savage liberty. (494–500)

Reprising this female politics of death, *The Suliote Mother* opens on an icon of savage liberty:

> She stood upon the loftiest peak,
>   Amidst the clear blue sky,
> A bitter smile was on her cheek,
>   And a dark flash in her eye. (1–4)

That dark flash is both defiance and, for historically knowing readers, a flash forward to this iconic Mother's "act of desperation" (says Hemans in a note), one accompanied, in caustic pathos, with a virtual national anthem: "Freedom, young Suliote! for thee and me!" (40).

The injustice of Beatrice's fate in *The Cenci* reflexively projects justice at another time and another place, and the hope of Shelley's *The Mask* is similarly projective beyond the historical moment of 1819, with the rhetorical axis of both works positioning readers for this appeal. Looking back over history, Hemans's political rhetoric is differently calibrated, with a recurring equation of suicide with female resistance that says, in effect, that there is no hope in historical time. *The Bride of the Greek Isle* is a *Record* of spectacular but impotent female rebellion. Pirate-slavers disrupt the wedding, murder the groom and abduct the bride. That night, Eudora's mother, straining to see the pirate ship, is startled by a "rushing flame" of Satanic aura: it is "like a glittering snake, / That coils up a tree" (191) and has "redden'd the stars with its wavy glare" (196). But it is the Bride-no-more who appears as its agent and icon, a savage female liberty, with unbound hair, and a brand

> Blazing up high in her lifted hand!
> And her veil flung back, and her free dark hair
> Sway'd by the flames as they rock and flare,
> And her fragile form to its loftiest height
> Dilated, as if by the spirit's might,
> And her eye with an eagle-gladness fraught,—
> Oh! could this work be of woman wrought?
> Yes, 'twas her deed!—by that haughty smile
> It was her's!—She hath kindled her funeral pile! (204–12)

Unveiled, unbound, eagle-glad, she is at one with the retaliatory dynamo. Hemans's elaborations exceed mere revenge. When she writes, in lines just prior, "Man may not fetter, nor ocean tame / The might and wrath of the rushing flame!" (189–90), it is about more than fire. It is an apocalypse in which a woman like Beatrice Cenci, doomed to sexual violence, wins release from the fetters of men.

But Hemans's cultural grammar is there, too, writing the death sentence in time and history. "The slave and his master alike" escape (201), while the bride stays on the burning deck: "Proudly she stands, like an Indian bride / On the pyre" (215–16). This proud romance is the infamous patriarchal imposition on widows that the Raj found so horrific that it would outlaw it in 1829, the year after *Records of Woman* was published. In the macrotext of *Records,* female rage is always self-consuming, and we're never certain whether this is Hemans's necessary frame of containment or her political point about female fate in a world of male-ordered tyrannies.

In *The Indian City*, Maimuna, a Mecca-bound Muslim widow, is wrought to a "work of power" (121) after her son is murdered by Brahmin children for trespassing onto holy ground.

> [She] proudly flung from her face the veil,
> And shook the hair from her forehead pale,
> And 'midst her wondering handmaids stood,
> With the sudden glance of a dauntless mood.
> Ay, lifting up to the midnight sky
> A brow in its regal passion high,
> With a close and rigid grasp she press'd
> The blood-stain'd robe to her heaving breast,
> And said—"Not yet—not yet I weep,
> Not yet my spirit shall sink or sleep,
> Not till yon city, in ruins rent,
> Be piled for its victim's monument." (125–36)

The kindling gaze, the unveiled face, and unbound hair spell impending violence, here a "Moslem war," and are invoked with Shelleyan poetic power. Hemans loved *Ode to the West Wind* for "the elevation of ... thought," and "even at [its] wildest, ... the exquisite charms of ... imagery and versification."[42] Shelley's *Ode* ends in burning prayer:

> by the incantation of this verse,
> Scatter, as from an unextinguished hearth,
> Ashes and sparks, my words among mankind!
> Be through my lips to unawakened Earth
> The trumpet of a prophecy! (65–9)

Hemans gives Maimuna this voice, not in some visionary future, but in time and history:

---

[42]   So reports her friend, Henry Chorley, *Memorials of Mrs. Hemans* (London: Saunders and Otley, 1836), 1:296.

> Maimuna from realm to realm had pass'd,
> And her tale had rung like a trumpet's blast.
> There had been words from her pale lips pour'd,
> Each one a spell to unsheath the sword. (161–4)

She has the power of the Shape on the fields of Peterloo, but with an immediate historical agency that converts *words* to *sword*:

> … her voice had kindled that lightning flame;
> She came in the might of a queenly foe,
> Banner, and javelin, and bended bow;
> But a deeper power on her forehead sate—
> *There* sought the warrior his star of fate;
> Her eye's wild flash through the tented line
> Was hail'd as a spirit and a sign,
> And the faintest tone from her lip was caught,
> As a Sybil's breath of prophetic thought. (170–78)

Yet all this power rides on the arc of Hemans's reading of female fate: Maimuna's destruction of the Brahmin city is a "Vain, bitter glory!" (179). She turns "from her sad renown, / As a king in death might reject his crown" (185–6), and soon makes good on the fatal analogy.

For Hemans, the imagination of women with violent political agency had to take routes into a supernatural idiom that courts Burke's gothic horrors, and return routes to domestic spheres and affections. Shelley is a fellow Romantic here. In the regime of Rome, Beatrice welcomes "the grave" as what is "just"—the only "alleviation of worst wrongs" (5.4.111–15). Her embrace of death is a romance wrought by patriarchal tyranny. Shattered by the fear that her "father's spirit" will rape her ever in the hereafter—"wind me in his hellish arms, and fix / His eyes on mine, and drag me down, down, down! / For was he not alone omnipotent / On earth, and ever present?" (5.4.60, 66–9)—Beatrice finds composure in invoking Death as maternal care:

> wind me in thine all-embracing arms!
> Like a fond mother hide me in thy bosom,
> And rock me to the sleep from which none wake. (5.4.116–18)

The death of the rebellious female, or put another way, the politics of revolt staged as female defeat, is a question as knotty for Shelley as for Hemans. Both hesitate before violent revolution as a fatal course, but both are caught, and caught up, in a shadowy context: the historical persistence of gender symbolism in the dark havoc of injustice and oppression. When Shelley has Beatrice cry out, "I shall go mad. Aye, something must be done; / What, yet I know not," he already knew what would be done and defeated, in fellowship with Hemans's mad women—angered and crazed by their tortures—in the toils of their fatal sanguinary wars.

## Works Cited

Barrell, John. "Sad Stories: Louis XVI, George III, and the Language of Sentiment." *Refiguring Revolutions: Aesthetics and Politics from the English Revolution to the Romantic Revolution.* Ed. Kevin Sharpe and Steven N. Zwicker. Berkeley: University of California Press, 1998. 75–98.

Behrendt, Stephen C. *Shelley and His Audiences*. Lincoln: University of Nebraska Press, 1989.

Browne, Felicia Dorothea [later Hemans]. *Poems*. London: T. Cadell and W. Davies, 1808.

—. *England and Spain; or, Valour and Patriotism*. London: T. Cadell and W. Davies, 1808.

Burke, Edmund. "Letter I: On the Overtures of Peace." *Two Letters Addressed to A Member of the Present Parliament, on the Proposals for Peace with the Regicide Directory of France by the right honourable Edmund Burke.* London: Rivington, 1796.

—. *Reflections on the Revolution in France*. 1790. 10th ed. London: J. Dodsley, 1791.

Cameron, Kenneth Neill, ed. *Shelley and His Circle, 1773–1822*. Vol. 2. Cambridge: Harvard University Press, 1961.

Chorley, Henry F. *Memorials of Mrs. Hemans, with Illustrations of her Literary Character from her Private Correspondence.* 2 vols. London: Saunders and Otley, 1836.

Curran, Stuart. *Shelley's "Cenci": Scorpions Ringed with Fire.* Princeton: Princeton University Press, 1970.

Gilfillan, George. "Female Authors. No. I—Mrs. Hemans." *Tait's Edinburgh Magazine*, new series 14 (June 1847): 359–63.

Hammond, Eugene R. "Beatrice's Three Fathers: Successive Betrayal in Shelley's *The Cenci.*" *Essays in Literature* 8 (1981): 25–32.

Hemans, Felicia. *Felicia Hemans: Selected Poems, Letters, & Reception Materials.* Ed. Susan J. Wolfson. Princeton University Press, 2000.

Hunt, Leigh. "The Destruction of the Cenci Family, and Tragedy on that Subject." *The Indicator* 41 (19 July 1820): 321–8, and 42 (26 July 1820): 329–36. This is Hunt's own translation of the Italian account, and preview of Shelley's play.

—. "Mr. Shelley." *Lord Byron and Some of His Contemporaries.* 2nd ed. 2 vols. London: Henry Colburn, 1828. 1: 294–406.

Janowitz, Anne. "'A Voice from across the Sea': Communitarianism at the Limits of Romanticism." In *The Limits of Romanticism: Essays in Cultural, Feminist, and Materialist Criticism.* Ed. Mary A. Favret and Nicola J. Watson. Bloomington: Indiana University Press, 1994. 83–100.

Jewett, William. *Fatal Autonomy: Romantic Drama and the Rhetoric of Agency.* Ithaca: Cornell University Press, 1997.

Lewes, George Henry [G.H.L.]. *The Westminster Review* 35.2 (April 1841): 303–44.

*Literary Gazette, and Journal of the Belles Lettres, Arts, Sciences, etc."* 167. 1 April 1820. *"The Cenci."* 209–10.

———. 9 June 1821. "Literary Intelligence." 362.

*London Literary Gazette*, 18 September 1819. Review of Hemans's *Tales, and Historic Scenes, in Verse.* 593–5.

McGann, Jerome J. "The Beauty of the Medusa: A Study in Romantic Literary Iconology." *Studies in Romanticism* 2 (1972): 3–25.

*Monthly Review* 2d series 94. February 1821. On *The Cenci,* 161–8.

Nicholson, Francis. "Correspondence between Mrs. Hemans and Matthew Nicholson." *Memoirs and Proceedings of the Manchester Literary and Philosophical Society* 54.9 (1910): 1–40.

Paulson, Ronald. *Representations of Revolution (1789–1820).* New Haven: Yale University Press, 1983.

Scrivener, Michael Henry. *Radical Shelley: The Philosophical Anarchism and Utopian Thought of Percy Bysshe Shelley.* Princeton: Princeton University Press, 1982.

Shelley, Mary Wollstonecraft. *Frankenstein; or, The Modern Prometheus.* 1818. Ed. Susan J. Wolfson. New York: Longman, 2006.

——. *The Journals of Mary Shelley.* Ed. Paula R. Feldman and Diana Scott–Kilvert. 1987; Baltimore: The Johns Hopkins University Press, 1995.

——, ed. *Posthumous Poems of Percy Bysshe Shelley.* London: John and Henry L. Hunt, 1824.

——, trans. *Relation of the Death of the Cenci.* Ed. Betty T. Bennett. *The Bodleian Shelley Manuscripts.* 23 vols. Gen. ed. Donald Reiman. New York, Garland Press, 1992. 10:157–272.

——, ed. *The Poetical Works of Percy Bysshe Shelley.* 4 vols. London: Edward Moxon, 1839.

——, ed. *The Poetical Works of Percy Bysshe Shelley.* London: Edward Moxon, 1839 (d. "1840").

Shelley, Percy B[ysshe]. *The Cenci. A Tragedy, in Five Acts.* Italy: for C. and J. Ollier, 1819.

——. *Letters of Percy Bysshe Shelley.* Ed. Frederick L. Jones. 2 vols. Oxford: Clarendon Press, 1964.

——. *The Masque of Anarchy. A Poem.* Preface by Leigh Hunt. London: Edward Moxon, 1832.

——. *Shelley's Poetry and Prose.* Ed. Donald H. Reiman and Neil Fraistat. 2nd ed. New York: Norton, 2002.

Sperry, Stuart M. *Shelley's Major Verse.* Cambridge: Harvard University Press, 1988.

*Tait's Edinburgh Magazine*, new series 14 (June 1847): 362.

Whitman, Robert. "Beatrice's 'Pernicious Mistake' in *The Cenci.*" *PMLA* 74
        (1959): 249–53.
Wolfson, Susan J. *Borderlines: The Shiftings of Gender in British Romanticism.*
        Stanford: Stanford University Press, 2007.

*[handwritten annotation at top:]* as our spectrum widens due to archives being digitised it seems likely that we will discover more writers who will not fall into the next categories

# Chapter 5

## Spiritual Converse:
# Hemans's *A Spirit's Return* in Dialogue with Byron and Shelley

Alan Richardson

*[handwritten annotations:]* canonisation has hitherto always dns – these continuities between f and m are staged in the ease of B on the site of the body

*[handwritten annotation left margin:]* the historiographical error of generalising from a few examples

Yearning in vain for the "full and deep communion of kindred natures," the poet goes on to scorn the "common, every-day intercourse of human beings": "how poor it is—how heartless!—how much more does it oppress the mind with a sense of loneliness, than the deepest solitude of majestic nature!" Byronic sentiments, to be sure. But the "ardent spirit" here panting, "as the captive for the free air of Heaven," for the "mingling of thought with thought" is not Lord Byron, but Felicia Hemans.[1] A reminder, if we still need one, that Hemans did not always write under cover of the domestic affections, but could on occasion, at least in manuscript, show a disdain for quotidian, household "intercourse" worthy of Childe Harold. Evidence, too, for the affinities that link Hemans to her male contemporaries— most prominently Byron and Percy Shelley—affinities that scholars and critics have only begun to explore.[2]

*[handwritten annotation right margin:]* track the feminist turn

Reading Hemans in relation to the male poets who long dominated the scholar's Romantic canon represents a new phase in criticism, not only of Hemans, but of Romantic-era women's poetry generally. As recently as 1995, Isobel Armstrong could advocate a critical strategy that would exclude such readings, in favor of what Armstrong herself characterizes as a "one-sided" approach to women's poetry "in isolation from male poetry." "The next step," she adds, "will be to look at the interaction of the two—but let us postpone this until women's work is known better."[3] More than a decade later, it seems fair to say that scholars of

---

[1]   Undated letter by Hemans quoted in Harriet Browne Hughes, "Memoir of Mrs. Hemans," in *The Works of the Late Mrs. Hemans, with a memoir by her sister ……* 7 vols. (Philadelphia: Lea and Blanchard, 1840), 1:128–9.

[2]   See Jerome McGann, *The Poetics of Sensibility* (Oxford: Clarendon Press, 1996), 174–94; Susan Wolfson, "Hemans and the Romance of Byron," in *Felicia Hemans: Reimagining Poetry in the Nineteenth Century*, ed. Nanora Sweet and Julie Melnyk (Basingstoke: Palgrave, 2001), 155–80; and Adriana Craciun, "Romantic Satanism and the Rise of Nineteenth-Century Women's Poetry," *New Literary History* 34 (2004): 699–721.

[3]   Isobel Armstrong, "The Gush of the Feminine: How Can We Read Women's Poetry of the Romantic Period?" in *Romantic Women Writers: Voices and Countervoices*, ed. Paula R. Feldman and Theresa M. Kelley (Hanover: University Press of New England, 1995), 32.

the period are still getting to know this large body of long-neglected poetry. Yet, postponing critical study of the "interaction" between male and female poets of the era no longer seems a viable option.

How, for instance, could we begin to understand *A Spirit's Return*, one of Hemans's finest poems, without sustained reference to Byron and Shelley? The poem, in fact, insists upon such attention, beginning with its epigraph, taken from the signature work of Byron's "Satanic" phase, *Manfred*: "This is to be a mortal, / And seek the things beyond mortality!"[4] These lines, spoken in *Manfred* by "a Spirit," alert the reader of Hemans's poem to a series of allusions to what might be termed "Spirit" poems by both Byron and Shelley, ringleaders of Southey's "Satanic school." In addition to *Manfred*, these poems include *Alastor; or the Spirit of Solitude*, the *Hymn to Intellectual Beauty* ("SPIRIT fair"), and the *Ode to the West Wind* ("Be thou, Spirit fierce, my spirit!"). Along with a number of direct allusions to these poems, Hemans takes over from her male contemporaries a familiar thematic cluster—involving solitude, necromancy, voice, doomed passion, and the sublime—in order to turn it to her own ends. Throughout *A Spirit's Return*, Hemans engages in intertextual conversation with Byron and Shelley, and yet her spirit poem ultimately develops in a unique direction of her own, building on but also crucially departing from the works she alludes to, borrows from, emulates, and criticizes.

Perhaps because of its extensive engagement with male Romantic poetry, *A Spirit's Return* has received surprisingly little attention from scholars to date—surprising, because Hemans herself spoke of this poem as one of her greatest single works. Harriet Browne Hughes, her sister, declared that Hemans preferred *A Spirit's Return* to "any thing else she had written" to date, and quotes Hemans's own acknowledgment that her "friends" had found in it "a greater power" than Hemans had ever demonstrated.[5] Henry Chorley, in his memoir of Hemans, provides identical quotations, adding to the latter one a kind of disclaimer on Hemans's part: "but if there be, as my friends say, a greater power in it than I had before evinced, I paid dearly for the discovery, and it almost made me tremble as I sounded 'the deep places' of my soul."[6] Modern criticism has done scant justice

---

    4    *Manfred*, II.4.158–9. For the sake of convenience, all quotations from the canonical Romantic poets follow the texts in David Perkins, ed., *English Romantic Writers*, 2nd ed. (Fort Worth: Harcourt Brace, 1995). Longer poems are cited by line, *Manfred* by act, scene, and line. I also quote from Perkins's text of *A Spirit's Return*, which proves more reliable than the text in *Felicia Hemans: Selected Poems, Letters, Reception Materials*, ed. Susan Wolfson (Princeton: Princeton University Press, 2000). (Wolfson, for example, misprints "hast" for "hadst" in line 18 and "behind" for "beheld" in line 102.) Wolfson's headnote and notes to the poem, however, are invaluable.

    5    Hughes, 1:214.

    6    Henry F. Chorley, *Memorials of Mrs. Hemans, with illustrations of her literary character from her private correspondence*, 2 vols. (New York: Saunders and Otley, 1836), 2:130.

to Hemans's achievement in this poem, however: the few critics who notice it at all do not seem to like it very much. Anthony Harding, for one, describes the poem rather mordantly as an "instructive instance" of the male "absorption and obliteration of woman's existence" without even a note of the "tragic" to redeem it.[7] Reading *A Spirit's Return* as a poem in critical dialogue with the spirits—and the Spirits—of *Manfred* and *Alastor* may help account for Hemans's own high estimation of it and, I hope, rediscover a measure of that poetic "power" that once so impressed her inner circle of readers.

The poem begins by evoking not the younger male Romantics but the high Romanticism of their elder contemporaries. The opening line—"Thy voice prevails; dear Friend, my gentle Friend!"—both launches the poem's thematics of voice (and vocal power) and establishes its generic allegiance to the "conversation poem" established by Coleridge (in poems like *The Nightingale* and *Frost at Midnight*) and Wordsworth (most notably in *Tintern Abbey*, with its address to the speaker's sister as his "dear, dear Friend"). Like these foundational conversation poems, with their silent but insistently present auditors, *A Spirit's Return* hovers strategically between monologue and dialogue, the speaker's words shaped (and indeed inspired) by an awareness of the auditor's expectations and reactions, and yet leaving the auditor effectively mute. The speaker may hear an occasional response, but the reader never does. Already, however, Hemans's engagement with the examples of her male contemporaries features both emulation and a certain amount of creative revisionism, as she reverses the usual gender dynamics—active male speaker and silent female auditor as in *The Eolian Harp*, and *Tintern Abbey*—by featuring a muted male auditor and a forceful female speaker.

Or is the speaker male? First time readers of the poem might well assume so, at least through its first seventy lines.[8] The epigraph from *Manfred*, along with a growing cluster of verbal echoes and thematic allusions, would seem initially to establish the speaker as a well-known Romantic type: the solitary, moody, anti-social, iconoclastic, and passionate male protagonist. The very premise of the poem—the reluctant offer to unseal a "long-shut heart" at the behest of the "Friend" (2)—recalls Manfred's half-forced confession of his own impassioned history to the Witch of the Alps (II.2.49–121). Like Manfred, the speaker of *A Spirit's Return* stood "companionless" "even in youth" (23); like the kindred poet-protagonist of Shelley's *Alastor*, the speaker was early doomed to a "silent hearth" (28). (Compare the *Alastor* poet's "cold fireside and alienated home" [76]).

---

[7]    Anthony John Harding, "Felicia Hemans and the Effacement of Woman," in *Romantic Women Writers: Voices and Countervoices*, ed. Paula R. Feldman and Theresa M. Kelley (Hanover: University Press of New England, 1995), 141.

[8]    Michael Williamson similarly notes, in his overview of the poem, that "it appears briefly as if Hemans has written a cross-gendered monologue about a male 'Romantic' protagonist, like Shelley's Alastor" ("Impure Affections: Felicia Hemans's Elegiac Poetry and Contaminated Grief," in *Felicia Hemans: Reimagining Poetry in the Nineteenth Century*, ed. Nanora Sweet and Julie Melnyk [Basingstoke: Palgrave, 2001], 31).

Hemans phrases her own version of characteristic Romantic alienation—"For me the silver cords of brotherhood / Were early loosed" (25–6)—in terms that almost beg the reader to impose a masculine identity on the speaker (otherwise, why not the bonds of sisterhood?). Like Manfred, and like the speaker of Shelley's *Hymn to Intellectual Beauty* ("I called on poisonous names"), Hemans's speaker turns to necromancy: "My life's lone passion, the mysterious quest / Of secret knowledge" (36–7). The speaker's simile for the state of mind accompanying all this—"Making my quick soul vibrate as a lyre" (39)—recalls the "long-forgotten lyre" in *Alastor* (42) (and its frame poet's own search for secret knowledge), the *Hymn to Intellectual Beauty* ("music by the night wind sent / Through strings of some still instrument"), and, more dimly, the *Ode to the West Wind* ("Make me thy lyre, even as the forest is"). Indeed, the Aeolian lyre or wind harp is perhaps the male Romantic poet's most cherished piece of furniture, and can be traced back at least to Coleridge's *Eolian Harp*; Hemans has already primed the reader for such high Romantic associations with her reference to the wind's "Aeolian breath" a bit earlier in the poem (14).

Finally, Hemans's speaker asserts in this early section of the poem a sort of intellectual and linguistic self-confidence that may seem more familiar from the male canon than from what has been termed "feminine" Romanticism:

> Midst the bright silence of the mountain-dells
> In noontide-hours or golden summer-eves,
> My thoughts have burst forth as a gale that swells
> Into a rushing blast, and from the leaves
> Shakes out response. (41–5)

Not that the Shelleyan veil is any easier to pierce through in this poem than it typically is in Shelley:

> O thou rich world unseen!
> Thou curtain'd realm of spirits!—thus my cry
> Hath troubled air and silence—dost thou lie
> Spread all around, yet by some filmy screen
> Shut from us ever? (45–9)

As in Shelley, too, the limitations of human language grow evident as the speaker strives to push pass those limits, wishfully assuming the mantle of poet-prophet:

> Cold, weak and cold,
> Is Earth's vain language, piercing not one fold
> Of our deep being!—Oh, for gifts more high!
> For a seer's glance to rend mortality!
> For a charm'd rod, to call from each dark shrine,
> The oracles divine! (55–60)

No "charm'd rod" is forthcoming, although the speaker will discover over the course of the poem a voice and a language far more powerful than quotidian speech. The point, though, is that the speaker *wants* theses things, to rend the veil, to compel response, to speak with oracular authority; to wield the rod; in short, to be one of the guys.

Soon after this moment, however, the reader finds cause to abandon any assumption of a male speaker. It's not so much that the speaker now "woke to love"—after all, Manfred and the *Alastor* poet also share the experience of a consuming, doomed romantic passion. But, perhaps startlingly to a reader who has been following the allusions to Byron and Shelley, the beloved is explicitly gendered as male: "There was no music but his voice to hear" (73). Hemans teases us up to the last moment—the previous line, "Save the *one* Being to my centred thought," seems calculated to evoke the parallel of Astarte in *Manfred*: "Yet there was one" (II.2.103). And the reiteration of the speaker's term for the silent auditor, "gentle Friend!" (63), may also be intended to encourage the reader to gender the Friend female. One modern critic, in fact, persists in taking the auditor as female even after the male identity of the speaker's "one" beloved object is revealed.[9] But that cannot be, as the extended utterance represented by the poem constitutes, or rather starts out as, an explanation by the speaker for her inability to return the auditor's own forlorn passion.

> Thou knew'st me not in life's fresh vernal noon—
> I would thou hadst!—for then my heart on thine
> Had pour'd a worthier love. (17–19)

The auditor, gentle man that he is, will presumably abandon his romantic pursuit of the speaker now that he learns he has a rival for her affections, the hardest of all rivals to displace: a dead one.

The beloved's death plays a crucial role in the poem; that it permanently dashes the auditor's hopes is merely incidental. It renders the beloved—who was never available to the speaker in any case, thanks to some mysterious bar between them or between their families—something of an *homme fatal*. For rather than freeing the speaker to pursue other, more eligible men, his death instead plunges her into not hapless grief but rather a renewed and still more intense immersion in necromancy, seeking (like Manfred before her) to summon her beloved, through some powerful "spell" (142), back from the dead. Unlike Manfred, however, she does not seem to need any demonic aid in order to do so, and even more unlike Manfred, she actually gets to have a long, substantive conversation with the returned Spirit.

The speaker's awakening to love, then, results in anything but the self-denying effacement that some readers have presumed; rather, it leads to her strongest acts of self-assertion in the poem. Although recent critics have seen Hemans's (however

---

[9]    Williamson, 31.

uneasy) relation to "female domesticity" as the master key to understanding her poetic achievement, Hemans herself advanced a quite different theory: "In the best of everything I have done, you will find one leading idea—*Death*: all thoughts, all images, all contrasts of thoughts and images, are derived from living much in the valley of that shadow."[10] In *A Spirit's Return*, the beloved's death removes even the possibility that the speaker's love may result in domestic happiness, while pulling her well beyond the confines of the domestic sphere. For proper ladies did not then wear out the night summoning up ghosts with magic words, though déclassé aristocratic poets evidently did.

The beloved's death also leads, in advance of any supernatural special effects, to the speaker's first experience of the sublime:

> we dream not of love's might
> Till Death has robed with soft and solemn light
> The image we enshrine!—Before *that* hour,
> We have but glimpses of the o'ermastering power
> Within us laid!—*then* doth the spirit-flame
> With sword-like lightening rend its mortal frame;
> The wings of that which pants to follow fast
> Shake their clay-bars, as with a prison'd blast, —
> The sea is in our souls!

This is the sublime of Longinus, not an alternative female or feminine version; that last phrase, "the sea is in our souls," might serve as a textbook illustration for the Longinian sublime, or even as a definition of it.[11] The momentary extinction of the habitual self by an "o'ermastering power" as described here constitutes a hallmark of the sublime, *not* evidence for the speaker's "absorption" by an idealized male other. And the effect of this experience on the speaker is not disempowerment; not at all.

What happens next in the poem might best be summarized by borrowing John Anderson's phrase (from his persuasive reading of *The Forest Sanctuary*), "the

---

    10    Hughes, 1:280. For important discussions of Hemans's vexed relation to the ideology of domesticity as the central concern of her poetry, see Marlon Ross, *The Contours of Masculine Desire* (Oxford: Clarendon Press, 1989), 289–309; Anne K. Mellor, *Romanticism and Gender* (New York: Routledge, 1993), 123–43; and Susan J. Wolfson, "'Domestic Affections' and 'the spear of Minerva': Felicia Hemans and the Dilemma of Gender," in *Re-Visioning Romanticism: British Women Writers, 1776–1837*, ed. Carol Shiner Wilson and Joel Haefner (Philadelphia: University of Pennsylvania Press, 1994), 128–66.

    11    For influential discussions of a "feminine" or "female" sublime, see Barbara Freeman, *The Feminine Sublime* (Berkeley and Los Angeles: University of California Press, 1995) and Patricia Yeager, "Toward a Female Sublime," in *Gender and Theory*, ed. Linda Kauffman (New York: Blackwell, 1989), 191–212.

triumph of voice."[12] For the speaker, emboldened by her discovery of the sublime depths within her, and impelled by her desire to reach through to her beloved, finds a voice that actually can rend the veil between the living and the dead. The lines that recount her efforts to cast a spell powerful enough to summon her beloved's spirit are as confident and self-assertive as any in male Romantic poetry:

> I tell thee that a power
> There kindled heart and lip; —a fiery shower
> My words were made; —a might was given to prayer,
> And a strong grasp of passionate despair,
> And a dread triumph!—Know'st thou what I sought?
> For what high boon my struggling spirit wrought?
> —Communion with the dead!—I sent a cry,
> Through the veil'd empires of eternity,
> A voice to cleave them! (131–9)

The passage begins to echo Manfred's own spell for conjuring Spirits ("By the strong curse that is within my soul, / The thought which is within me and around me" [I.47–8)]) but with the mingled powers of love and of poetic language added to the sheer force of despair:

> By the mournful truth,
> By the lost promise of my blighted youth,
> By the strong chain a mighty love can bind
> On the beloved, the spell of mind on mind;
> By words, which in themselves are magic high,
> Arm'd and inspired, and wing'd with agony;
> By tears, which comfort not, but burn, and seem
> To bear the heart's blood in their passion-stream;
> I summon'd, I adjured! (139–47)

All that seems missing is a touch of Romantic Satanism, which Hemans duly supplies—"Awake, appear, reply" (154)—echoing the famous triplet with which Satan himself summons his prostrate confederates in *Paradise Lost* ("Awake, arise, or be forever fallen" [1.330]).

More allusions to the Satanic school follow. Manfred's "tyrant-spell" draws its authority from the dark planet that rules his destiny, "a star condemned, / The burning wrack of a demolished world, / A wandering hell in the eternal space" (I.44–6), phrases that can't help but evoke Milton's Satan. The speaker of *A Spirit's Return* has her own version of "that planet" (163), "a large lone star, / Now

---

John M. Anderson, "The Triumph of Voice in Felicia Hemans's *The Forest Sanctuary*," in *Felicia Hemans: Reimagining Poetry in the Nineteenth Century*, ed. Nanora Sweet and Julie Melnyk (Basingstoke: Palgrave, 2001), 55–73.

burning o'er yon western hill afar" (159–60). (The poem is set at the hour of dusk; if this is the evening star, or Venus, then it is also, of course, the morning star, or Lucifer.) Sitting "beneath that planet," having "wept [her] woe to stillness," the speaker does not utter forth additional conjurations, does not really do anything, except to gaze "unconsciously" at the quiet landscape around her. It is at this moment that the Spirit finally comes to her, unbidden. The scene is modeled on that in the climactic fifth stanza of Shelley's *Hymn*:

> While yet a boy I sought for ghosts, and sped
>   Through many a listening chamber, cave and ruin,
>   And starlight wood, with fearful steps pursuing
> Hopes of high talk with the departed dead.
> I called on poisonous names with which our youth is fed;
>     I was not heard—I saw them not—
>     When musing deeply on the lot
> Of life, at that sweet time when winds are wooing
>   All vital things that wake to bring
>   News of birds and blossoming—
>   Sudden, thy shadow fell on me;
> I shrieked, and clapped my hands in ecstacy!

Like Shelley's represented youthful self, the speaker of *A Spirit's Return* breaks through to the transcendent realm not when actively pursuing or attempting to summon her beloved back from death, but in a moment of calm, half-conscious musing in a peaceful natural setting. Hemans's speaker, however, attains precisely that which Shelley's past self had apparently given over: high talk (rather than sublime, but wordless and evanescent, contact) with a disembodied Spirit.

This imagined scenario, "suggested," according to Chorley, "by a fire-side conversation," provided Hemans with the impetus for the poem.

> It had long been a favorite amusement to wind up our evening by telling ghost stories. One night, however, the store of thrilling narratives was exhausted, and we began to talk of the feelings with which the presence and the speech of a visitant from another world (if, indeed, a spirit *could* return,) would be most likely to impress the person so visited. After having exhausted all the common varieties of fear and terror in our speculations, Mrs. Hemans said she thought the predominant sensations at the time must at once partake of awe and rapture.[13]

Awe and rapture—the two leading terms in the lexicon of the sublime—displace the "common," stock Gothic responses to a ghostly encounter. But Hemans's response does not only represent a significant revision of the Gothic tradition; more specifically, it contains in embryo the revisionary response to *Manfred* that

---

[13]    Chorley, 2:57–8.

will do so much to help shape *A Spirit's Return*. *Manfred*, after all, reaches its dramatic crisis (at the end of Act II) with the anti-hero's abortive interview with the revenant spirit of his own beloved, Astarte. Manfred, on this occasion, feels nothing like common fear or terror; but neither does he feel awe, exactly, and certainly not rapture. His response is definitive of his Byronic egotism. He "cannot speak to her," but wants her to talk to, and to talk about, him: "Forgive me or condemn me" (II.4.105). When Astarte remains silent, he resorts to something uncomfortably like pathetic begging ("Say that thou loath'st me not") and repeated commands to "speak to me!" Revealingly, the first of the seven words he manages to wring from Astarte is his own name ("Manfred!"), followed by a telegraphic message ("Tomorrow ends thy earthly ills") and a hasty "Farewell!" (152). There is no dialogue; Manfred's responses, questions, and further demands elicit only another "Farewell" and a last reiteration of "Manfred!"

Manfred's ghostly rendezvous, then, all but parodies the narcissism evident throughout his obsession with Astarte ("She was like to me in lineaments ..." [II.2.105]). It eventuates in Manfred becoming "convulsed," leading to the caustic Spirit's comment that provides the epigraph to *A Spirit's Return* ("This is to be a mortal / And seek the things beyond mortality" [II.2.158–9]). The scene must have been the most notorious example, within what Hemans and her circle would have called "modern" poetry, of a literary treatment of the situation that she and her friends were discussing by the fire, over the course of their domestic, English version of the evening ghost-story sessions at Villa Diodati that inspired another woman's creative dialogue with two generations of Romantic poets, *Frankenstein*. And already, thinking aloud to her friends, Hemans has found the key to her departure from Byron and, to a lesser extent, from Shelley as well: she will provide a representation of tranformative "spiritual communion,"[14] neither wordless as in Shelley's *Hymn*, nor tragically short-circuited as in his *Alastor*, but robust, extended, and articulate.

Easier said than done. Hemans, again according to Chorley, worried that she had "sacrificed too much in the apparition scene, to the idea that sweetness and beauty might be combined with supernatural effect,"[15] though for this reader the conceit of a marmoreal repose ("something awfully serene, / Pure, — sculpture-like" [178–9]) works well enough. The primary concern of the passage, however, is not to convey the sense of "Greek statuary" that Hemans later spoke of.[16] Rather, it aims to dialogize an impossible relation—that between living and dead lovers—that for Byron in *Manfred* had remained hopelessly, almost absurdly one-sided. True enough, Hemans's speaker suffers the painful realization that the relation has become unequal for what might be termed structural reasons, the "sick feeling that in *his* far sphere / *My* love could be as nothing!" (187–8). This might be (and has been) taken as an instance of self-abnegation. Notice, though, how studiously it

---

[14]   Chorley, 2:58.
[15]   Chorley, 2:67.
[16]   Chorley, 2:67.

inverts the Byronic egotism of Manfred, who can imagine himself loved or reviled by Astarte but not comparatively unimportant to her. And, closely following on this first swerve from Byronism, comes another, as the speaker actually manages to have a revealing, extended conversation with her Spirit:

> But he spoke—
> How shall I tell thee of the startling thrill
> In that low voice, whose breezy tones could fill
> My bosom's infinite? (189–92)

Taking in the thrilling voice of her ghostly lover, the speaker does not lose her own voice, but rather engages in what Hemans calls "glorious intercourse" (201). "I questioned of the dead— / Of the hush'd, starry shores their footsteps tread— / And I was answer'd" (205–7). Simply from the point of view of an adept in the magical arts, who has earlier deployed "secret knowledge" in a quest to reach through to the "curtain'd realm of spirits," she succeeds beyond her wildest Shelleyan hopes. She asks her surprisingly forthcoming ghost about the afterworld, about the post-mortem status of earthly memories, about the persistence of human love: "I ask'd, and I was answer'd" (213). If anything like "absorption" is taking place in this scene, the speaker is doing the absorbing: "I drank in *soul*!" (205). And along with this internalization of the other (more typical of male than of female Romantic-era poetics) comes an equally unexpected sense of possession: "One full fraught hour of Heaven, / To earthly passion's wild implorings given, / Was made my own" (221–3).

The visionary gleam soon fades, as fade it must. The hour ends and the "radiant guest" departs, with a final variant on *Manfred*: "'Farewell, / On earth we meet no more'" (216–17). (Compare Astarte: "Tomorrow ends thy earthly ills. / Farewell" [II.4.152–3].) "What now is left?," the speaker asks, voicing the silent auditor's implicit question, obliterating as well any lingering hopes he may still cling to of gaining her affections. "A faded world, of glory's hues bereft, / A void, a chain" (226–7). Hers is a familiar (male) Romantic dilemma, one that all but renders her a female Childe Harold:

> I dwell, 'midst throngs, apart,
> In the cold silence of the stranger's heart;
> A fix'd, immortal shadow stands between
> My spirit and life's far-receding scene;
> A gift hath sever'd me from human ties. (226–30)

What differentiates her sense of human isolation from the cynical brooding of a Harold, however, is precisely that notion of a "gift"—not a curse, as in *Manfred*, not an irremediable sense of loss, as in *Alastor* or *Childe Harold*, but something closer to the lonely but ennobling feeling of election that one finds in Wordsworth or, for that matter, in Milton. As Chorley recalls the genesis of the poem, the one—"favored above all men" —who had shared in such a "strange and spiritual communion" would afterwards be, not depressed, but "raised … too high for common joy to enliven."[17] Nor does the speaker feel despair so much as a deferred hope, one that takes a distinctly Shelleyan expression: "the wing'd flower-seed meets / A soil to rest in" (254–5). This phrase recalls the "winged seeds" of the *Ode to the West Wind*, the more insistently in a passage that begins by invoking spring's "awakening voice" and the breeze that "summons *me* to go" (238, 242). The implication of the allusion is clear: if Winter comes, can Spring be far behind?

Perhaps the most striking feature of Hemans's deviation from *Manfred* and *Alastor* concerns the optimistic tone of her speaker toward the end, which builds on the premonition of rebirth that aligns *A Spirit's Return* more closely to Shelley's *Ode*. Unlike Manfred, who finally despairs of ever finding Astarte in the afterlife, or the *Alastor* poet, who awakens from his swoon to wander disconsolately and aimlessly and seems not even to hope for reunion, Hemans's speaker fully expects to "dwell" with her beloved Spirit in what might be termed post-domestic bliss. This difference might constructively be read in terms of Hemans's repudiation of a Byronic cynicism regarding human relations in general and erotic ones in particular. It simultaneously represents an extension of Shelleyan idealism in its preference for spiritual congress over earthly (including domestic) attachments. In this poem, that is, Hemans proves more impatient of the earthly sphere and its limitations, and consequently more committed to a spiritual, transcendent alternative (though hardly an orthodox one) than Wordsworth or Byron, while seeming far more sanguine about the possibility of a higher, post-mortem eros than even Shelley does in his most typical poems. The contrast with Wordsworth's *Laodamia*, another Romantic "Spirit" poem hovering in the background, is instructive: while Laodamia does manage to summon and to speak extensively with her dead husband, Protesilaus, the two talk at cross purposes the entire time, she begging him to remain while he insists that she look beyond her earthly desire for him. Laodamia then demonstrates her utter failure to understand her husband's spiritual counsels by dying at his (immaterial) feet as he disappears, an act deemed equivalent to a "wilful" suicide (159). (And therefore, one presumes, relegating Laodamia to an afterlife apart from her husband and far from the Elysian Fields.) Hemans's speaker, on the other hand, evinces no desire to weakly cling to her Spirit's presence and stoically wears out her natural years on earth, content (if by no means happy) to wait for what she knows is an inevitable spiritual reunion.

To grasp the full force of this poem's conclusion, however, it pays to consider Hemans's skillful manipulation of figures of address, including the figure of apostrophe, yet another example of how she both draws upon and varies the practice of her male contemporaries. As noted above, the "conversation poem" relies by definition on various figures of address, used to signal and respond to the presence of the silent auditor. Whether these figures constitute instances of apostrophe remains a matter of some debate: when the speaker addresses his sister

---

[17]    Chorley, 2:58.

in *Tintern Abbey* or his infant son in *Frost at Midnight* is he "turning" (as apostrophe demands) from a default auditor (the reader) to address someone else?[18] In a case like *A Spirit's Return*, which *begins* by addressing the auditor, and which might be taken to constitute one prolonged address, the explicit evocations of the auditor's presence would not seem examples of apostrophe per se. But then, what should one make of the addresses to the beloved Spirit?

Apostrophes to the dead or absent, to personified abstractions or inanimate beings, play a notorious role within the male Romantic canon; they have been taken as characteristic of the high Romantic ode, just as more familiar addresses ("dear Friend") characterize the conversation poem.[19] Frequently, of course, one finds both sorts of address within the same poem. The *Dejection* ode, for example, includes both addresses to the unnamed "Lady" ("friend devoutest of my choice") and to the wind ("Mad Lutanist"); *Tintern Abbey* apostrophizes both the speaker's sister and the Wye river ("O sylvan Wye"). Some poststructuralist readers have found the more abstract sort of apostrophe, in its blatant poeticality, intentionally excessive or even "embarrassing,"[20] although Romantic-era readers and reviewers do not seem to have taken much exception to them. Byron's notoriously lordly apostrophe to the ocean in *Childe Harold* ("Roll on, thou deep and dark blue Ocean—roll!" [4.179]), though it might seem the most embarrassing Romantic apostrophe of them all, struck Hemans herself as "magnificent."[21] In *A Spirit's Return*, Hemans makes use of the entire spectrum of the figure of address, from the domestic ("sweet Friend") to the sublime ("O thou rich world unseen"), and innovatively manipulates the figure of apostrophe in order to bring closure to the poem.

The deftness with which Hemans manipulates figures of address in *A Spirit's Return* grows out of her implicit recognition of the triadic structure of such figures. Poststructuralist critics, most notably Paul de Man and Jonathan Culler, who view the figure of apostrophe as linguistically deviant and discursively disruptive, describe it as a two-way, dyadic relation (or spectacularly dysfunctional relation) between the poetic speaker and the apostrophized subject, typically absent, dead, inanimate, or a personified abstraction. Yet for classical rhetoricians, as well as for

---

[18]     See Douglas J. Kneale, "Romantic Aversions: Apostrophe Reconsidered," in *Rhetorical Traditions and British Romantic Literature*, ed. Don Bialostosky and Lawrence D. Needham (Bloomington: Indiana University Press, 1995), 149–66, and my response to Kneale in "Apostrophe in Life and in Romantic Art: Everyday Discourse, Overhearing, and Poetic Address," *Style* 36 (2002): 363–85.

[19]     See the classic discussions of apostrophe by Jonathan Culler (*The Pursuit of Signs: Semiotics, Literature, Deconstruction* [Ithaca: Cornell University Press, 1981], 135–54) and Paul De Man ("Autobiography as De-Facement," 1979; rpt. in *The Rhetoric of Romanticism* [New York: Columbia University Press, 1984], 67–92) and my discussion in "Apostrophe."

[20]     Culler, 135.

[21]     Hughes, 145. Indeed, Hemans works a number of variations on this apostrophe (e.g., "Father of waves! roll on!") into her *Indian Woman's Death-Song*.

the Bakhtin group and for cognitive linguists today, apostrophe involves a three-way relation among the poetic speaker, the addressee or "hero" of the apostrophe, and a "side participant" or witness who actually does hear the apostrophe, no matter to whom or to what the apostrophe is nominally addressed.[22] Such figures are by no means recondite and reserved exclusively for "high" literature. Quintilian offers, as the paradigmatic example of apostrophe, the "diversion of our words to address some person other than the judge" in a case of rhetorical pleading.[23] (Imagine a lawyer momentarily turning to address the victim's bereaved spouse in presenting her summation at the end of a murder trial.) A more quotidian example might be a startled pedestrian shouting at a speeding car, "why can't you slow down!," more for the benefit of fellow pedestrians in the crosswalk than for the driver, already distant with windows closed and sound system blasting. In each case, the point of the address is to convey an attitude to the "side participant"—the judge or jury, the other pedestrians—rather than to the nominal addressee.

The initial figure of address in *A Spirit's Return* serves, as we have seen, to place the silent auditor in a privileged, affectionate relation with the speaker: "Thy voice prevails; dear Friend, my gentle Friend!" The first instances of apostrophe ("O thou rich world unseen!" [45]; "O, my soul" [84]) seem, by contrast, "merely" rhetorical, uttered for the benefit of the auditor who now functions as "side-participant" in a triadic linguistic relation. The speaker, that is, addresses the "world unseen" not in order to communicate with it, but in her efforts to rouse conviction in the "gentle" auditor. But as the poem continues, something unexpected yet entirely appropriate begins to happen. The addresses to the auditor become less intimate and more challenging, even a little bullying. "Oh! deem thou not" (129), "Believe it not!" (159), "with *fear?*—Oh! *not* with fear!' (187). At the same time, the beloved Spirit, who at first seems to exemplify the absent or dead apostrophic subject of poststructuralist rhetoric, becomes more and more real and intimate, culminating in that remembered hour of "communion with eternity" (214). By the close of the poem, the Spirit has drawn near again and altogether displaces the "gentle Friend" as the poem's addressee, seeming by now more real (to the speaker, and perhaps to the reader as well) than the increasingly irrelevant Friend who effectively disappears from view. The poem's concluding eight lines are addressed exclusively to the Spirit, now firmly ensconced in the "thou" position:

> shall not *I*, too, be,
> My spirit-love! upborne to dwell with thee?
> Yes! by the power whose conquering anguish stirr'd
> The tomb, whose cry beyond the stars was heard,
> Whose agony of triumph won thee back
> Through the dim pass no mortal step may track,

---

[22]   Richardson, 366–9.

[23]   *Institutio Oratoria*, trans. H.E. Butler, 4 vols. (Cambridge: Harvard University Press, 1921), 2:41.

> Yet shall we meet!—that glimpse of joy divine,
> Prov'd thee for ever and for ever mine! (255–62)

De Man, understanding apostrophe in dyadic terms, speculates that the poet's wish to make the dead speak again harbors the "latent threat" that the "living are struck dumb, frozen in their own death."[24] Here, however, apostrophe seems to give vibrant existence both to the speaker and to her "spirit-love"; it is the (rhetorical) third participant and (romantic) third wheel, the poem's silent auditor, who gets dumbstruck and frozen out at the end.

When asked about the most significant contemporary influences upon her writing career, Hemans chose two poets from what scholars a decade ago would have been termed the canonical Romantic tradition. "I have heard her say," reports Chorley, "that Wordsworth and Shelley were once the spirits contending to obtain the mastery over her: that the former soon gained the ascendancy is not, I think, to be wondered at; for much as she delighted in Shelley, she pitied him still more." Immediately, Byron enters the equation as well: "In defining the distinction between the genius of Wordsworth and that of Byron, I remember her saying, that it required a higher power to still a tempest than to raise one."[25] In *A Spirit's Return*, Hemans draws significantly on all three poets, elaborating a scenario she found powerfully but inadequately expressed in *Manfred* while borrowing elements of Wordsworth's (and Coleridge's) "conversation" poems and Shelley's supernatural poems. Yet she uniquely extends the masculine tradition in representing a successful rather than painfully abortive attempt at spiritual converse. The speaker's shifting relation to her male auditor might even be seen to mirror the poet's relation to her male contemporaries. The speaker begins in earnest conversation with her persistent admirer, only to effectively lose sight of him by the end as she turns instead to her spirit-love. The poet begins by emulating the dialogic poetics of Wordsworth and Coleridge, developing a scenario codified by Byron and Shelley, eventually turning aside or diverging from her models in choosing to represent what in *Manfred* and *Alastor* tragically resists representation: the "glorious intercourse" between questing human subject and her spirit-lover. Reading *A Spirit's Return* in relation to the poetry of her male contemporaries both enriches our sense of Hemans's poetic achievement and deepens our appreciation of the masculine Romantic tradition while underscoring its neglected possibilities.

---

[24]    De Man, 78.
[25]    Chorley, 2:217.

## Works Cited

Anderson, John M. "The Triumph of Voice in Felicia Hemans's *The Forest Sanctuary.*" In *Felicia Hemans: Reimagining Poetry in the Nineteenth Century*. Ed. Nanora Sweet and Julie Melnyk. Basingstoke: Palgrave, 2001. 55–73.

Armstrong, Isobel. "The Gush of the Feminine: How Can We Read Women's Poetry of the Romantic Period?" In *Romantic Women Writers: Voices and Countervoices*. Ed. Paula R. Feldman and Theresa M. Kelley. Hanover: University Press of New England, 1995. 13–32.

Chorley, Henry F. *Memorials of Mrs. Hemans, with illustrations of her literary character from her private correspondence*. New York: Saunders and Otley, 1836. 2 vols.

Craciun, Adriana. "Romantic Satanism and the Rise of Nineteenth–Century Women's Poetry." *New Literary History* 34 (2004): 699–721.

Culler, Jonathan. "Apostrophe." *The Pursuit of Signs: Semiotics, Literature, Deconstruction*. Ithaca: Cornell University Press, 1981. 135–54.

De Man, Paul. "Autobiography as De–Facement." 1979. Rpt. in *The Rhetoric of Romanticism*. New York: Columbia University Press, 1984. 67–92.

Freeman, Barbara. *The Feminine Sublime*. Berkeley and Los Angeles: University of California Press, 1995.

Harding, Anthony John. "Felicia Hemans and the Effacement of Woman." In *Romantic Women Writers: Voices and Countervoices*. Ed. Paula R. Feldman and Theresa M. Kelley. Hanover: University Press of New England, 1995. 138–49.

Hemans, Felicia. *Felicia Hemans: Selected Poems, Letters, Reception Materials*. Ed. Susan J. Wolfson. Princeton: Princeton University Press, 2000.

Hughes, Harriet Browne. "Memoir of Mrs. Hemans." In *The Works of the Late Mrs. Hemans, with a memoir by her sister….* 7 vols. Philadelphia: Lea and Blanchard, 1840. 1:27–317.

Kneale, J. Douglas. "Romantic Aversions: Apostrophe Reconsidered." In *Rhetorical Traditions and British Romantic Literature*. Ed. Don Bialostosky and Lawrence D. Needham. Bloomington: Indiana University Press, 1995. 149–66.

McGann, Jerome J. *The Poetics of Sensibility: A Revolution in Literary Style*.

Macovski, Michael. *Dialogue and Literature: Apostrophe, Auditors, and the Collapse of Romantic Literature*. Oxford: Oxford University Press, 1994.

Oxford: Clarendon Press, 1996.

Mellor, Anne K. *Romanticism and Gender*. New York: Routledge, 1993.

Perkins, David, ed. *English Romantic Writers*. 2nd ed. Fort Worth: Harcourt Brace, 1995.

Quintilian. *Institutio Oratoria*. Trans. H. E. Butler. 4 vols. Cambridge: Harvard University Press, 1921.

Richardson, Alan. "Apostrophe in Life and in Romantic Art: Everyday Discourse, Overhearing, and Poetic Address." *Style* 36 (2002): 363–85.

Ross, Marlon. *The Contours of Masculine Desire: Romanticism and the Rise of Women's Poetry*. Oxford: Oxford University Press, 1989.

Williamson, Michael T. "Impure Affections: Felicia Hemans's Elegiac Poetry and Contaminated Grief." In *Felicia Hemans: Reimagining Poetry in the Nineteenth Century*. Ed. Nanora Sweet and Julie Melnyk. Basingstoke: Palgrave, 2001. 19–35.

Wolfson, Susan J. "'Domestic Affections' and 'the spear of Minerva': Felicia Hemans and the Dilemma of Gender." In *Re–Visioning Romanticism: British Women Writers, 1776–1837*. Ed. Carol Shiner Wilson and Joel Haefner. Philadelphia: University of Pennsylvania Press, 1994. 128–66.

——. "Hemans and the Romance of Byron." In *Felicia Hemans: Reimagining Poetry in the Nineteenth Century*. Ed. Nanora Sweet and Julie Melnyk. Basingstoke: Palgrave, 2001. 155–80.

Yeager, Patricia. "Toward a Female Sublime." In *Gender and Theory*. Ed. Linda Kauffman. New York: Blackwell, 1989. 191–212.

# Chapter 6
# William Wordsworth and Felicia Hemans

Julie Melnyk

In the summer of 1830, two major Romantic poets, William Wordsworth and Felicia Hemans, would finally meet. In their meeting, the first generation of Romanticism would engage with the second, the male poet with the female, and both would be inspired by the encounter. While Wordsworth was writing little poetry in this late stage of his career, his relationship with Hemans would serve as inspiration for a poetic tribute to her in his important late poem, *Extempore Effusion Upon the Death of James Hogg* (1835). For Hemans, the meeting would give new direction to her poetic career. In Wordsworth she would find a new paradigm that allowed her to embrace a domestic and religious vision even as she reclaimed for herself a vatic voice.

## The Visit and Wordsworth's Response

In 1830, William Wordsworth, 60 years old, was living at Rydal Mount with his wife and sister. While he wrote few new poems, especially compared with the extraordinary productivity of his early maturity, he continued to revise his earlier work and issue new editions. He also received a steady stream of visitors, which over the course of the next years would become a flood: friends and acquaintances, pilgrims coming to pay homage to this living monument of English poetry, and also younger poets, hoping to meet the man whose poems had defined English Romanticism and inspired other poets to imitation, extension, and, inevitably, reaction.

One of these younger poets, Felicia Hemans, spent two weeks at Rydal Mount in June and July of 1830 and then remained in the Lake District for several more weeks, paying Wordsworth occasional visits. Though the poets had never before met face to face, they had read one another's work. Hemans had expressed her admiration for Wordsworth's poetry in an 1826 letter to Maria Jane Jewsbury, who had sent her a collection of his poems:

> I would not write to you sooner, because I wished to tell you that I had really
> studied these poems, and they have been the daily food of my mind ever since I
> borrowed them. There is hardly any scene of a happy, though serious, domestic

life, or any mood of a reflective mind, with the spirit of which some one or other of them does not beautifully harmonize.[1]

Although she identifies him as "the true <u>Poet of Home</u>," she initially singles out his political poems for special praise, as well as *The Narrow Glen, Corra Linn, Song for the Feast of Brougham Castle, Yarrow Visited,* and *The Cuckoo.* She also reports having read "Ecclesiastical Sketches" (in later editions called *Ecclesiastical Sonnets*) "with deep interest."[2] In *Records of Woman, with Other Poems,* she includes a poem in tribute, *To Wordsworth,* where she praises him as

> True bard and holy!—thou art ev'n as one
> Who, by some secret gift of soul or eye,
> In every spot beneath the smiling sun,
> Sees where the springs of living waters lie. (25–8)[3]

The visit itself, however, was needed to turn admiration into inspiration for both poets.

Wordsworth received his visitor graciously, and in a letter to Samuel Rogers (30 July 1830) he writes, "We like Mrs. Hemans much—her conversation is what might be expected from her Poetry, full of sensibility—and she enjoys the Country greatly."[4] A later letter written in August is more equivocal:

> Her conversation, like that of many literary Ladies, is too elaborate and studied—
> and perhaps the simplicity of her character is impaired by the homage which has
> been paid her—both for her accomplishments and her Genius.[5]

Hemans may in fact have been trying too hard to impress the older poet; in a letter of 22 June 1830 she records her "nervous fear at the idea of presenting myself to Mr. Wordsworth."[6] Hemans, however, found herself entirely delighted with the company of the great writer:

> I am charmed with Mr. Wordsworth himself; his manners are distinguished
> by the frank simplicity which I believe to be ever the characteristic of real
> genius; his conversation perfectly free and unaffected, yet remarkable for power
> of expression and vivid imagery; when the subject calls forth any thing like

---

[1]    Susan J. Wolfson, ed., *Felicia Hemans: Selected Poems, Letters, Reception Materials* (Princeton: Princeton University Press, 2000), 492.

[2]    Wolfson, ed., *Felicia Hemans,* 492.

[3]    Paula R. Feldman, ed., *Records of Woman With Other Poems* (Lexington: University of Kentucky Press, 1999), 118.

[4]    Wolfson, ed., *Felicia Hemans,* 556.

[5]    Wolfson, ed., *Felicia Hemans ,* 557.

[6]    Wolfson, ed., *Felicia Hemans,* 504.

enthusiasm, the poet breaks out frequently and delightfully, and his gentle and affectionate playfulness in the intercourse with all the members of his family, would of itself sufficiently refute Moore's theory in the Life of Byron, with regard to the unfitness of genius for domestic happiness.[7]

According to Hemans's letters, the two poets enjoyed walks in the mountains and discussions of literature. Wordsworth recited poetry to her, lines from Spenser, Milton, Burns, and much of his own work. Hemans repeatedly praises his kindness to her and emphasizes her affection and admiration for him; as she tells H. F. Chorley, "I begin to talk with him as with a sort of paternal friend."[8]

Wordsworth, too, saw their brief time together as the foundation of a friendship. After her death, he records in a letter both his admiration and some telling reservations:

> I think highly of that Lady's genius—but her friends, and I had the honor of being one of them—must acknowledge with regret, that her circumstances, tho' honorably to herself, put her upon writing too often and too much—she is consequently diffuse; and felt herself under the necessity of *expanding* the thoughts of others, and hovering over their feelings, which has prevented her own genius doing justice to itself, and diminished the value of her productions accordingly.[9]

Wordsworth here seems to recognize a fundamental difference between his own poetics of self-exploration and Hemans's representation of multiple voices from diverse cultures and historical periods, and he ably describes Hemans's poetics, which crucially involve the representation of the thoughts and feelings of others, though without recognizing the independent value of this kind of poetry or the difference made by gender.[10]

Nevertheless, admiration was clearly dominant in his poetic reaction to Hemans's death. In 1835, he was inspired to write *Extempore Effusion Upon the Death of James Hogg*, one of his more important later poems. Here he records the passing of a generation of poets, all of whom had died in the previous three years,

---

[7]    Wolfson, ed., *Felicia Hemans*, 504.

[8]    Wolfson, ed., *Felicia Hemans*, 505.

[9]    Wolfson, ed., *Felicia Hemans*, 558.

[10]    A similar dynamic, but with gender roles reversed, existed between Robert and Elizabeth Barrett Browning. Robert Browning's dramatic monologues, like Hemans's poetry, depend upon the exploration of the thoughts and feelings of others, and Elizabeth Barrett Browning felt that Robert Browning's own thoughts and feelings ought to be more directly represented in his poetry: "having thought so much and so deeply on life and its ends," he should, she urged, convey his ideas "in the directest and most impressive way, the mask thrown off however moist with breath" (qtd. in Paul Turner, introduction to *Men and Women 1855*, by Robert Browning [Oxford: Oxford University Press, 1972], xiv).

mourning in turn the deaths of Hogg, Scott, Coleridge, Lamb, and finally Crabbe, before turning to Hemans, dead at the age of 41:

> As if but yesterday departed,
> Thou [Crabbe] too art gone before; but why
> O'er ripe fruit, seasonably gathered,
> Should frail survivors heave a sigh?
>
> Mourn rather for that holy Spirit,
> Sweet as the spring, as ocean deep;
> For Her who, ere her summer faded,
> Has sunk into a breathless sleep. (33–40) [11]

Though "summer" here clearly refers to her early death, it may be that he also associates her with that summer at Rydal Mount and that significant visit. She is placed in the company of men he regards as true poets, and she is the only woman to whom Wordsworth pays such poetic tribute.

Wordsworth found inspiration in Hemans's poetry and death for this late poem, one of the few that he was to write, even though he would live another 20 years after their meeting.[12] Hemans, however, though she would live only five more years, was still writing prolifically and was also at a turning point in her career; this meeting with William Wordsworth would change the direction of her future career profoundly and permanently.

### Hemans's Reaction and Wordsworth's Influence

When she visited Wordsworth in 1830, Felicia Hemans was 37 years old, facing a period of personal and professional crisis. The 1820s had been a productive and successful decade for Hemans, who had become one of the best-known and most popular poets in England. Although in the first stage of her career she had written ambitious, politically-engaged poetry, such as *The Restoration of the Works of Art to Italy* (1816) and *Modern Greece* (1817), in the 1820s she had turned to affectional poetry, writing mostly shorter lyrics with subject matter that remained

---

[11]     William Wordsworth, *Extempore Effusion Upon the Death of James Hogg*, in *William Wordsworth: The Oxford Authors*, ed. Stephen Gill (Oxford: Clarendon Press, 1984), 371.

[12]     It is also possible that his revisions of *Ecclesiastical Sonnets* in the next decade owed something to Hemans and her appreciation of that work, though the immediate inspiration for the revisions, which is well-documented, does not concern Hemans. For more on these revisions, see Abbie Findlay Potts's extensive introduction to her edition of *The Ecclesiastical Sonnets of William Wordsworth: A Critical Edition* (New Haven: Yale University Press, 1922.)

acceptably feminine, though international and transhistorical in scope, culminating in *Records of Woman* (1828). Her identity as an affectional poet through this period was underwritten by her own supportive domestic establishment. She had long been separated (probably by mutual agreement) from her husband and the father of her five sons, Captain Hemans, now resident in Italy; her household during these years was centered on her mother, and this matriarchal home provided crucial psychological, physical, and ideological support. Although in the poems of this period home and happy domestic life are regularly displaced to past or future or distant land, Hemans's sense of herself as a poet of the home depended on her own experience of harmonious domesticity in a female-headed household.

But Hemans's mother fell ill in 1826 and died early in 1827; in 1828, Hemans's brother, who had formerly lived nearby, took his family to settle in Ireland, her two eldest sons went to Rome to live with their father, and Hemans and the other three boys left their Welsh home to settle near Liverpool. Hemans had to cope not only with the devastating loss of her mother and the consequent break-up of her household, but also with the loss of support for her own identity as a domestic poet. She was adrift, looking for a new direction and a new justification for her poetry.

Then, in January of 1830 came a further psychological blow, the publication of Thomas Moore's *Letters and Journals of Lord Byron: With Notices of His Life*. Throughout her career, Byron had been the strongest poetic presence in Hemans's poetry, as Susan Wolfson's analysis in "Hemans and the Romance of Byron" amply demonstrates. Though she often contested his conclusions and feminized his ideas, she returned again and again to his work in her epigraphs, her heroines, and her themes. For much of her life, she even wore a brooch containing a lock of his hair. Two revelations in Moore's biography, however, put an end to this one-sided "romance." One came in an 1820 letter to Murray included in the volume in which Byron dismisses the work of "bluestocking" women poets. In fact, he had mentioned Hemans by name in this letter, though Moore suppressed so specific a reference to a living poet; Hemans, however, recognized the reference all too clearly. More devastating, though, were the details revealed about Byron's private life, which Moore attempted to justify by claiming that poetic genius is incompatible with domestic happiness. This claim, of course, doubly told against Hemans: against her most fundamental beliefs and against any claims of her own to genius. Hemans took off the brooch and never wore it again;[13] her poetic relationship with Byron was at an end, and she felt rejected by a man she had seen as model and even mentor.

It was at this crucial point in her poetic career that Hemans traveled to the Lake District to meet William Wordsworth and, as it turns out, to discover a new poetic paradigm. Perhaps the first indication of Wordsworth's growing influence

---

[13]    Susan J. Wolfson, "Hemans and the Romance of Byron," in *Felicia Hemans: Reimagining Poetry in the Nineteenth Century*, ed. Nanora Sweet and Julie Melnyk (Basingstoke: Palgrave, 2001), 155, 173–4.

in Hemans's life comes in the letters that she writes from the Lake District that summer of 1830. Her initial reactions, as in the letter quoted above, indicate that she sees in Wordsworth a poet whose example refutes Moore's claims about the incompatibility of poetry and domestic life. In a letter of 25 June she quotes Wordsworth himself as saying with reference to the claim, "It is not because they possess genius that they make unhappy homes, but because they do not possess genius enough."[14] Very often when she writes about Wordsworth, her thoughts seem to turn to Byron, as though the two are linked in her mind. She begins to see in Wordsworth a replacement for Byron, who had implicitly rejected her and her poetics: Wordsworth is a new poetic model whose work she can emulate, engage, contest, and return to time after time. While she had viewed her relationship with Byron as a kind of poetic romance, however, her attitude toward Wordsworth seems instead that of an admiring daughter for a kind and supportive father, a "paternal friend."

But what did this new poetic model offer Hemans? Was she, like many rejected lovers, merely looking for the first available substitute, or was there something in Wordsworth's poetics that held a particular attraction for her? One attraction, of course, might have been the fact that Byron had explicitly denigrated and defined himself against Wordsworth, notably in *Don Juan*; in choosing a Wordsworthian paradigm, Hemans moved decisively away from her earlier Byronic inspiration.

However, Hemans's turn to Wordsworth sprang from deeper sources, connected both to her frustration with the restraints imposed by affectional poetry and to the nature of her own poetic crisis. Stephen Gill refers to the early Victorian perception of Wordsworth both as "high-priest of Nature and as domestic being at home amongst the Lakes,"[15] and it is precisely this combination that appealed to Hemans at this point in her career. His retired, harmonious home-life refuted Moore's assertions, even as his poetry, particularly his early work, embodied the high Romantic ideal of poet as Seer, a human being in contact with the divine—a divine spirit that the aging Wordsworth now generally interpreted as the Christian God. The Wordsworthian model thus offered Hemans the possibility of reconciling the domestic, the religious, and the vatic.

Although the classic image of the Wordsworthian Romantic is the solitary Wanderer, his poems are populated with other people and develop themes such as maternal love and childhood innocence that Hemans's affectional poetry also emphasizes. The focus in Wordsworth's poems is typically the poet's own psychology, his reaction to meetings with others, whereas Hemans's poetry, as Wordsworth noted, is often more concerned with "*expanding* the thoughts of others, and hovering over their feelings." Still, Hemans may well have felt an affinity with the more clearly social Wordsworth poems. Moreover, the later Wordsworth had become (notoriously) more conservative and more orthodox in his Christianity. Hemans's encounter with the older Wordsworth in 1830 allowed her to recuperate

---

[14]   Wolfson, ed., *Felicia Hemans*, 506.

[15]   Stephen Gill, *Wordsworth and the Victorians* (Oxford: Clarendon Press, 1998), 10.

the vatic poetry of his early maturity for a new age and for a woman poet by extending and expanding the tendencies of Wordsworth's own poetic development toward a more Christian and even more domestic vision. Thus, Hemans recovered for the woman poet the prophetic voice of Romanticism that her affectional poetry had sacrificed in its attempts to carve out an acceptably feminine poetic sphere.

The full impact of the Wordsworthian paradigm, and the shift away from the Byronic, is evident in Hemans's next major volume of poetry, *Scenes and Hymns of Life* (1834). In fact, the shift is clear from the opening page, where she dedicates the volume to Wordsworth. An initial, overly fulsome dedication was vetoed by the elder poet in a clearly uncomfortable letter:

> I must say that a *public* testimony in so high a strain of admiration is what I cannot but shrink from . . . I am emboldened to express a wish that you would instead of this Dedication in which your warm and kind heart has overpowered you, simply inscribe them to me, with such expression of respect or gratitude as would come within the limits of the rule which . . . will naturally suggest itself.[16]

Hemans therefore settled for this less extravagant dedication: "To William Wordsworth, Esq., in token of deep respect for his character and fervent gratitude for moral and intellectual benefit derived from reverential communion with the spirit of his poetry, this volume is affectionately inscribed by Felicia Hemans."[17] Here Hemans resorts to religious language—"reverential communion"—to represent the depth of her engagement with Wordsworth's spiritual poetics.

While the dedication clearly indicates her new poetic model, the shift from Byronic to Wordsworthian paradigm is also marked in the move from international to English sources of inspiration. In *Records of Woman, With Other Poems* (1828), Hemans's last major volume before her encounter with Wordsworth, the Byronic internationalism is clear: only 11 of the 57 poems (less than 20%) take inspiration from English history, culture, or landscape; 5 have an American setting; and fully 27 (about 47%) are set in foreign lands. (I do not include in the count of foreign settings those that focus on an English character abroad.) Many of these "foreign" poems focus on the same places that Byron often celebrated in his poetry, including "oriental" poems and ones set in Italy and Greece. Fifteen of Hemans's epigraphs in the volume are actually in their original European languages, and six are derived from Byron's own works, while only two come from Wordsworth (including one of the epigraphs to the volume as a whole). In contrast, *Scenes and Hymns of Life* focuses, like so much of Wordsworth's poetry, on English landscape and culture: all fifteen of the epigraphs derive from British authors, including seven from

---

[16]    Wolfson, ed., *Felicia Hemans*, 556.

[17]    Felicia Hemans, *The Poetical Works of Mrs. Hemans*, The "Grosvenor" Poets (London: William Collins), 607. All subsequent quotations from *Scenes and Hymns of Life* are taken from this edition.

Wordsworth and none at all from Byron.[18] Moreover, ten of the 23 poems (about 43 per cent) are clearly English in their inspiration, two are American, and only four (17 per cent) are definitely foreign. Even among the "foreign" poems, one is a sympathetic portrayal—with an epigraph from Wordsworth—of a Royalist father and daughter awaiting execution during the French Revolution, and two focus on Protestant martyrdom in the Alps; Byron's favorite authors and countries are gone, replaced by British authors and English history and landscape.

Gone, too, are the Byronic heroines of *Records of Woman*. Susan Wolfson has described how Hemans transmuted alienated Byronic heroes into heroines who are similarly separated from their communities, not because of their alienated souls, but because of "suffering wrought by ruptured bonds, between husband and wife, mother and child."[19] These women react violently and passionately to these ruptures. For instance, of the six poems in *Records of Woman* that take their epigraphs from Byron, four contain such passionate heroines: Arabella Stuart, torn from the arms of her love, teeters on the verge of suicidal madness in her prison cell; Eudora, *The Bride of the Greek Isle*, exacts a suicidal revenge on her captors by setting fire to their ship and dying in the conflagration; Ulla, the eponymous heroine, calls to the spirit of her drowned lover and ends by throwing herself into a wild, Byronic ocean; and Maimuna, the mother in *The Indian City*, "instigates a pan-Moslem war"[20] in revenge for her son's murder at the hands of Hindus.

No such heroines appear in *Scenes and Hymns of Life*, which instead emphasizes Wordsworthian themes of spiritual and poetic insight derived from "incidents and situations from common life."[21] Perhaps inspired by the example of Wordsworth in his Preface to *Lyrical Ballads*, Felicia Hemans, too, marked this major shift in her poetics with a Preface in which she explicitly states her new poetic aims:[22]

> I trust I shall not be accused of presumption for the endeavour which I have here made to enlarge, in some degree, the sphere of religious poetry, by associating with its themes more of the emotions, the affections, and even the purer imaginative enjoyments of daily life, than may have been hitherto admitted within the hallowed circle.

---

[18]    The other sources are as follows: Shakespeare (2); Thomas Campbell (2); Alexander Wilson (2); William Howitt (1); and William Cowper (1).

[19]    Wolfson, "Hemans and the Romance of Byron," 163.

[20]    Wolfson, "Hemans and the Romance of Byron," 166.

[21]    William Wordsworth, 1802 Preface to *Lyrical Ballads*, in *William Wordsworth: The Oxford Authors*, 596.

[22]    Hemans, *Poetical Works*, 607. *Scenes and Hymns of Life* was the first of Hemans's volumes to include such a Preface, written in the first person; prefatory material in earlier volumes generally took the form of epigraphs from the work of other writers.

> It has been my wish to portray the religious spirit, not alone in its meditative joys and solitary aspirations (the poetic embodying of which seems to require from the reader a state of mind already separated and exalted), but likewise in those active influences upon human life, so often called into victorious energy by trial and conflict, though too often also, like the upward-striving flame of a mountain watch-fire, borne down by tempest-showers, or swayed by the current of opposing winds.

Hemans's first paragraph sets out her project of domesticating religious poetry and, simultaneously, of reclaiming for domestic poetry the possibility of religious transcendence. Just as Wordsworth's poetry connected the commonplace with the transcendent, achieving spiritual insight from ordinary life, here Hemans connects traditional affectional themes—"the emotions, the affections . . . of daily life"—with religious insight. In both cases, the poet becomes the interpreter who can convey the spiritual reality incarnated in the physical and social world. The second paragraph defines ways in which her poems will move beyond traditional Romantic themes, insisting, in a way that seems to combine Romantic and Victorian emphases, on the equal importance of contemplative and active spirituality. While she intends her volume to include the kind of "meditative joys and solitary aspirations" around which so many of Wordsworth's early poems develop, she also emphasizes a more communally engaged and active spirituality. This social spiritual ideal may also have been inspired by the later Wordsworth's poetry and ideas, but in these poems Hemans combines his inspiration with her own experience as a woman and an affectional poet.

While, as the Preface makes clear, Wordsworth's influence pervades *Scenes and Hymns of Life*, his presence is most clearly marked in the seven poems that take their epigraphs from his work. The first of these is the third poem in the volume, *Cathedral Hymn*, which takes its epigraph from Book 3, Sonnet 45 of *Ecclesiastical Sonnets*. This 1822 volume presents the history of the Church of England in sonnets, beginning with the introduction of Christianity to the British Isles. Sonnets 43-45 in Book 3, inspired by King's College Chapel, Cambridge, were among the first he wrote but appear late in the volume, where Wordsworth explores the present significance and function of the Anglican Church in English society. Sonnet 43 begins with a defense of the chapel and its builders against charges of excessive expense and elitism. Then it hymns the beauty of the chapel with its "lofty pillars," "branching roof," and "ten thousand cells / Where light and shade repose."[23] Finally, Wordsworth turns to the chapel's auditory qualities, the way that music echoes, "wandering on as loth to die." The next poem, Sonnet 44, elaborates on the visual and auditory qualities of the chapel, describing first its stained-glass windows with portraits of "Martyr, or King, or Eremite," shedding

---

[23]     William Wordsworth, *The Ecclesiastical Sonnets of William Wordsworth: A Critical Edition*, ed. Abbie Findlay Potts. All subsequent quotations from these sonnets are taken from this edition.

their "sleepy light," and then its music: "every stone is kissed / By sound, or ghost of sound, in mazy strife; / Heart-thrilling strains." Sonnet 45, from which Hemans took her epigraph, turns to the way that sacred places offer both comfort and inspiration.

> They dreamt not of a perishable home
> Who thus could build. Be mine, in hours of fear
> Or grovelling thought, to seek a refuge here;
> Or through the aisles of Westminster to roam;
> Where bubbles burst, and folly's dancing foam
> Melts, if it cross the threshold; where the wreath
> Of awe-struck wisdom droops: or let my path
> Lead to that younger Pile, whose sky-like dome
> Hath typified by reach of daring art
> Infinity's embrace; whose guardian crest,
> The silent Cross, among the stars shall spread
> As now, when She hath also seen her breast
> Filled with mementos, satiate with its part
> Of grateful England's overflowing Dead.

In this sonnet Wordsworth moves from King's College Chapel to Westminster Abbey and on to St. Paul's Cathedral, describing how each elevates and soothes, not only by suggesting Eternity but also through the presence of history— "mementos"—and particularly the mementi mori constituted by the tombs. In earlier Wordsworth poems, such consolation would almost certainly have come from Nature, but here the poet has turned from Nature to Culture for inspiration.

In *Cathedral Hymn*, Hemans picks up on the presence of the past in her unnamed Cathedral: "A temple shadowy with remembrances / Of the majestic past" (2–3). Like Wordsworth in Sonnet 44, she describes the stained glass which casts over all "a colouring of heroic days … wandering back / To other years" (4, 6–7). She then turns to the tombs and other mementos of past glories: "the helms of antique chivalry" (16); "the forms, in pale proud slumber carved, / Of warriors on their tombs" (18–19). She even imagines the music of the past ringing in the Cathedral, "where the high anthems of old victories / Have made the dust give echoes" (22–3). Rather than seeing these historical artifacts as central to the Cathedral's meaning, however, she dismisses them, awakened to the present by the sight of the Cross:

>                         Hence, vain thoughts!
> Memories of power and pride, which long ago,
> Like dim processions of a dream, have sunk
> In twilight-depths away. Return, my soul!
> The Cross recalls thee. Lo! the blessed Cross!
> High o'er the banners and the crests of earth
> Fixed in its meek and still supremacy! (23–9)

Wordsworth evokes the Cross on St. Paul's Cathedral as a "guardian crest"; Hemans recalls instead a Cross within the church and, echoing Wordsworth's language, sees it as conquering all merely human crests. The vanity of earthly power and its symbols expressed here is a recurrent theme in Hemans's work, seen in such poems as *The Effigies* and *The Image in Lava*. In the next lines the poet's attention moves from the cross, the symbol of human suffering and Christian hope, to the congregation, "the throng of beating human hearts, / With all their secret scrolls of buried grief, / All their fullness of immortal hope!" (30–32) Then, like Wordsworth in Sonnets 43 and 44, Hemans moves on to the sounds of the Cathedral. These sounds, however, are specifically identified as *voices* raised together in song.

> Hark! how the flood
> Of the rich organ-harmony bears up
> Their voice on its high waves!— a mighty burst!
> A forest-sounding music! Every tone
> Which the blasts call forth with their harping wings
> From gulfs of tossing foliage, there is blent:
> And the old minster—forest-like itself—
> With its long avenues of pillared shade,
> Seems quivering all with spirit, as that strain
> O'erflows its dim recesses, leaving not
> One tomb unthrilled by the strong sympathy
> Answering the electric notes. Join, join, my soul!
> In thine own lowly, trembling consciousness,
> And thine own solitude, the glorious hymn. (33–46)

The rest of the poem—lines 47 to 124—records the words of the hymn sung by the congregation. Here, instead of the relatively empty and peaceful church of Wordsworth's sonnets, filled with wordless music and historical echoes, Hemans portrays a cathedral full of people singing, the poet as one among many worshippers. In fact, as I have argued at length elsewhere, the singing with and on behalf of the community enables and vindicates the woman poet's voice.[24] Interestingly, while Wordsworth turned from natural to cultural and historical sources of consolation in his sonnets, Hemans moves back towards an earlier Wordsworthian motif of sacredness and spirit in Nature. Taking up the brief suggestion of organic form in his Sonnet 43 ("branching roof"), she transforms the Cathedral into a forest. The sounds of the voices become those of the wind through the trees, and the voices seem to bring the tree-like pillars themselves to life.

Finally, Wordsworth ends Sonnet 45 with the commemorative function of the English church, seeing in the future of St. Paul's the accumulation of yet more

---

[24]     See my article "Victorian Religious Women Writers and Communal Identities," *Australasian Victorian Studies Journal* 10 (2004): 70–90.

"mementos" of the past. Hemans, too, refers to the church's tombs in the final lines both of the description of the cathedral quoted above and of *Cathedral Hymn* itself, but she shifts the focus from the dead as memorials of the past to their present and future life. The end of the first section of the poem, possibly inspired by lines from Wordsworth's Sonnet 44 ("every stone is kissed / By sound, or ghost of sound, in mazy strife; / Heart-thrilling strains"), describes how sound echoes from the tombs: "that strain / O'erflows its dim recesses, leaving not / One tomb unthrilled by the strong sympathy / Answering the electric notes" (41–4). The echoes from the tombs suggest that they—or their occupants—are alive, joining the song of the living congregation. The final lines of the hymn—"Let the hymn pierce the sky, / And let the tombs reply! / For seed, that waits the harvest-time, is there" (122–4)—look forward even more explicitly to the resurrection of the dead housed in those tombs.

Hemans's *Cathedral Hymn* clearly takes its inspiration from *Ecclesiastical Sonnets*, as she takes up Wordsworth's theme of the inspirational power and sensory appeal of English churches. Hemans shifts the focus more toward the present and future, however, treating the dead not as relics of the past—though relics still able to offer inspiration in the present—but as people who will eventually be restored to life. She also peoples Wordsworth's nearly empty chapel with suffering, singing human beings, who bring the church itself to life. Moreover, in placing herself among the congregation, in writing their words of corporate worship, she justifies her own public poetic voice. In some ways, Hemans's revisions represent an extension of Wordsworth's own increasingly orthodox Christian commitments, but they are vital for her as a woman poet, for whom the claim to a vatic voice is more difficult.

The poem immediately following, *Wood Walk and Hymn*, balances Hemans's portrayal of formal worship within the Cathedral—albeit one like a living forest—with one of worship in a real forest—albeit one described in ecclesiastical terms. This poem is clearly inspired by Wordsworth's own poetry of sacred Nature. It takes its epigraph from *Nutting* ("Move along these shades / In gentleness of heart: with gentle hand / Touch—for there is a spirit in the woods") and serves as both homage and reply to Wordsworth's poem. The hymn that concludes the poem responds directly to the earlier poem's closing injunctions, significantly in the voice of the Romantic child, attuned to Nature and its spiritual revelations.

> Yes! lightly, softly move!
> There *is* a power, a presence in the woods;
> A viewless being that, with life and love,
> Informs the reverential solitudes:
> The rich air knows it, and the mossy sod—
>     Thou—*Thou* are here, my God!

Like the older Wordsworth himself, Hemans here Christianizes the early Wordsworth's often pantheistic poetry, partly to bring it into conformity with her own religious beliefs, but also, as I argue elsewhere, to make room in the Romantic tradition for herself as a Christian and as a woman poet.[25]

These two consecutive poems clearly demonstrate Wordsworth's powerful influence on Hemans's late work. The next poem in the volume, *Prayer of the Lonely Student*, however, represents Hemans's most sustained and crucial engagement with Wordsworthian ideas. It addresses a problem repeatedly taken up in Wordsworth's poetry: the loss of immediacy of response to and joy in Nature as the poet matures. This theme appears centrally in *Tintern Abbey*, *Ode: Intimations of Immortality*, and *The Excursion* Book Fourth ("Despondency Corrected"). In all three explorations of loss and gain, Wordsworth treats the loss as permanent, though counterbalanced by increased wisdom or human understanding, or by a renewed enjoyment through memory or vicarious pleasure. Hemans's treatment, by contrast, does hold out the possibility of a full restoration of joy and poetic vision, and in the epigraph she uses Wordsworth's own words to suggest the possibility:

> Soul of our souls! and safeguard of the world
> Sustain—THOU only canst—the sick at heart;
> Restore their languid spirits, and recall
> Their lost affections unto Thee and thine. (*Excursion*, IV.28–32)

Hemans will connect this restoration and return to God with a further restoration of the sense of "splendour in the grass and glory in the flower" (Wordsworth, *Ode: Intimations of Immortality*, 181). It is significant that she takes her epigraph from *The Excursion* rather than from the earlier works; here an older and more orthodox William Wordsworth has already begun the process of Christianizing the poetic *vates*, a process that Hemans will pursue in two poems in this volume, *Prayer of the Lonely Student* and *A Poet's Dying Hymn*, which also takes its epigraph from this same passage of *The Excursion*.[26]

Though Hemans's initial reference is to the more orthodox later poem, the form of *The Prayer of the Lonely Student*, an irregular English ode, indicates a heavier debt to Wordsworth's Immortality Ode, as its opening lines attest:

> Night—holy night—the time
> For mind's free breathings in a purer clime!
> Night!—when in happier hour the unveiling sky
>     Woke all my kindled soul
> To meet its revelations, clear and high,

---

[25]  See my article "Hemans's Later Poetry: Religion and the Vatic Poet," in *Felicia Hemans: Reimagining Poetry in the Nineteenth Century*, ed. Nanora Sweet and Julie Melnyk (Basingstoke: Palgrave, 2001), 74–92.

[26]  Stephen Gill notes that in the Victorian period "*The Excursion* was regarded as Wordsworth's great work," celebrated, along with *Ecclesiastical Sonnets*, for its "moral tendency" (Gill, *Wordsworth and the Victorians*, 2, 19).

> With the strong joy of immortality!
> Now hath strange sadness wrapped me, strange and deep—
> And my thoughts faint, and shadows o'er them roll,
> E'en when I deemed them seraph-plumed, to sweep
>     Far beyond earth's control. (1–10)

This passage introduces the Wordsworthian theme of loss. Wordsworth's Ode, though it makes reference to Nature "by night or day," focuses on a joyous May morning; Hemans chooses instead a cloudy night. Her footnote indicates that the poem was partly inspired by a lecture by William Hamilton, the astronomer royal, which she heard in November 1832.[27] But the nighttime setting also tends to mute the pantheism of Wordsworth's description, focusing attention immediately on the Heavens and, in particular, the stars:

> Wherefore is this? I see the stars returning,
> Fire after fire in heaven's rich temple burning:
> Fast shine they forth—my spirit-friends, my guides,
> Bright rulers of my being's inmost tides;
> They shine—but faintly, through a quivering haze (11–15)

The stars correspond to the "visionary gleam" of Wordsworth's poem, now, if not fled, then dimmed and diminished. For the speaker they are sacred fires, spiritual presences, even the soul's moon, governing its movements. In the next lines, Hemans echoes *Tintern Abbey* in the student's account of development from child to youth:

> Oh! Is the dimness *mine* which cloud those rays?
> They from whose glance my childhood drank delight!
> A joy unquestioning—a love intense—
> They that, unfolding to more thoughtful sight
> The harmony of their magnificence,
> Drew silently the worship of my youth
> To the grave sweetness on the brow of truth. (16–22)

As in Wordsworth's poems, the speaker's feeling for the stars changes as s/he grows, taking on an increasing intellectual component, but in Hemans the sense of loss is more muted; the thought seems more something added to the joy and love, rather than something qualifying them.

At the beginning of the Immortality Ode, Wordsworth sees others experiencing privileged joys that he once knew and can no longer share, but none are adult humans: the joyful are Birds, Lambs, the "Shepherd Boy," "the Babe"; adults are perforce excluded from the fullness of this experience, though they may be able

---

[27]    Hemans, 619.

to re-experience it through memory. The poet's lengthy philosophical interlude (line 58—"Our birth is but a sleep and a forgetting"—to line 170—"and hear the mighty waters rolling evermore") accounts for this loss and leads to the eventual reconciliation with loss and a sense of recompense. Hemans's speaker, though, imagines other adults who still can perceive the "revelations, clear and high":

> Shall they shower blessing with their beams Divine,
> Down to the watcher on the stormy sea,
> And to the pilgrim toiling for his shrine
> Through some wild pass of rocky Apennine,
>   And to the wanderer lone
>   On wastes of Afric thrown,
>     And not to *me*? (23–9)

The blessings and the guidance of the stars, which the speaker has lost, are clearly still available to other people. Early in the Ode Wordsworth's contemplation of the joys of others lead him to his central questions: "Whither is fled the visionary gleam? / Where is it now, the glory and the dream?" Similarly, Hemans moves immediately to a slightly different series of questions:

>         Am I a thing forsaken?
>     And is the gladness taken
> From the bright-pinioned nature which hath soared
> Through realms by royal eagle ne'er explored,
> And, bathing there in streams of fiery light,
> Found strength to gaze upon the Infinite?
>
> And now an alien! Wherefore must this be?
>     How shall I rend the chain?
>     How drink rich life again
> From those pure urns of radiance, welling free? (30–39)

The speaker recalls the earlier gladness as well as the vatic power with which it was connected: the "strength to gaze upon the Infinite." The questions themselves echo Wordsworth's concerns: her "chain" recalls the "inevitable yoke" and the "prison bars" that gradually enclose "the growing Boy"; "radiance, welling free" is also Wordsworthian, recalling both the flowing light of line 69 and the "radiance" that is "taken from my sight" in lines 178–9 of the Ode. While Wordsworth's questions barely suggest the possibility of a recovery of the "glory and the dream," Hemans's final questions are much more pointedly seeking a remedy. Hemans's answer to the speaker's questions is not long in coming: "Father of Spirits! let me turn to Thee!" (40). What has dimmed the radiance and blocked the revelation is pride, and to recover the "visionary gleam" the speaker must return to Christian humility.

Oh! If too much exulting in her dower,
  My soul, not yet to lowly thought subdued,
Hath stood without Thee on her hill of power—
  A fearful and a dazzling solitude!
And therefore from that haughty summit's crown
To dim desertion is by Thee cast down;
Behold! thy child submissively hath bowed—
          Shine on him through the cloud! (41–8)

Hemans's description of the soul on the hill seems inspired by a passage from Book Four of *The Excursion*, in which the Wanderer recounts the youthful exaltation in Nature which he has now lost:

Still, it may be allowed me to remember
What visionary powers of eye and soul
In youth were mine; when, stationed on the top
Of some huge hill—expectant, I beheld
The sun rise up
      . . . . . . . . . . . . . . . . . . . . . . . .
            then, my spirit was entranced
With joy exalted to beatitude. (110–14; 118–19)

In Wordsworth there is no sense that the dimming of radiance in nature results from the soul failing to acknowledge God's power, but Hemans condemns the poet's solitude and self-assertion, both stumbling-blocks to women's identification with the Romantic *vates*, as sinful and as ultimately destructive of the poetic vision. Now recognizing that humility, not pride, is fundamental to Christian vatic power, in the next lines Hemans's speaker faces another source of dejection and failure of inspiration: a fear that one's work will go unappreciated and unrecognized. Although this fear could seem to reflect pride or egoism in its desire for recognition, in Hemans it is expressed, using biblical imagery, as a kind of exile from home and from human sympathy:

Or if it be that, like the ark's lone dove,
My thoughts go forth, and find no restingplace,
No sheltering home of sympathy and love
In the responsive bosoms of my race,
And back return, a darkness and a weight,
Till my unanswered heart grows desolate—
*Yet*, yet sustain me, Holiest! (55–61)

Since Hemans's earlier work was sustained by her supportive and appreciative domestic circle, the crisis here may reflect her own crisis of vocation as that support evaporated; the resolution, however, is a higher sense of vocation:

> —I am vowed
>
> To solemn service high;
> And shall the spirit, for thy tasks endowed,
> Sink on the threshold of the sanctuary,
> Fainting beneath the burden of the day,
>
>> Because no human tone
>> Unto the altar-stone
>
> Of that pure spousal fane inviolate,
> Where it should make eternal truth its mate,
> May cheer the sacred, solitary way? (61–70)

Here the human love that in *Records of Woman* so often failed to provide security or lasting happiness—and sometimes ended in Byronic alienation and suicide—is replaced by divine love and a "marriage" to eternal truth. The affectional vocation with its dependence on human emotion gives way to an explicitly vatic and religious vocation. The work to which the speaker is called requires no recognition—it is "its own high recompense" (83), a word that echoes the resolution of *Tintern Abbey*, where Wordsworth finds "abundant recompense" (89) for the loss of his passionate, unmediated love of Nature.

For Hemans's speaker, though, the reaffirmation of religious vocation leads immediately to a restoration of the vatic vision:

> The dimness melts away
>> That on your glory lay
> O ye majestic watchers of the skies!
>> Through the dissolving veil,
>> Which made each aspect pale,
> Your gladdening fires once more I recognise;
>> And once again a shower
>> Of hope, and joy, and power,
> Streams on my soul from your immortal eyes. (84–92)

The glory in the stars, unlike "the glory in the flower" for Wordsworth's speaker, is fully restored. Here the poetic revelations, the intimations of immortality, come not from a lingering memory of contact with the Divine before birth but instead from continued contact with God. Still, the speaker recognizes in the restored vision a Wordsworthian difference between past and present:

> And if that splendour to my sobered sight
> Come tremulous, with more of pensive light—
> Something, though beautiful, yet deeply fraught
> With more that pierces through each fold of thought
>> Than I was wont to trace
>> On heaven's unshadowed face—
> Be it e'en so! (93–9)

The splendour has not been lost, but it now seems more "pensive," just as Wordsworth's adult vision includes "the joy / Of elevated thoughts" (*Tintern Abbey*, 95–6). Moreover, the "something" that Hemans's speaker now perceives is clearly related to *Tintern Abbey*'s own "something far more deeply interfused" (97).

The conclusion of the poem both affirms the sense of religious vocation and emphasizes the need for humility in the would-be vates seeking eternal truth:

> . . . be mine, though set apart,
> Unto a radiant ministry, yet still
> A lowly, fearful, self-distrusting heart,
> Bowed before Thee, O Mightiest! Whose blessed will
> All the pure stars rejoicingly fulfill. (99–103)

Here Hemans's prayer to God for a "lowly, fearful, self-distrusting heart" recalls Wordsworth's similar request in *Ode to Duty*: "Give unto me, made lowly wise, / The spirit of self-sacrifice" (60–61), though he goes on to ask for "the confidence of reason" (62) rather than continued "self-distrust." In addition, both poems emphasize the link between human and celestial obedience to a higher power, the will of God or that of the "Stern Daughter of the Voice of God" (*Ode to Duty*, 1). Wordsworth, though, makes no explicit connection between submission to divine command and poetic inspiration, whereas Hemans presents the two as inextricably linked.

In *Tintern Abbey*, the Intimations Ode, and *Ode to Duty*, Wordsworth speaks in his own voice; in her poem, however, Hemans creates a mask, not even a poet but a "lonely student." Hemans's use of a mask indicates how difficult it remained for a woman poet to claim a vatic voice, even one that was substantially Christianized or feminized; the social expectations that created the separate sphere of affectional poetry continued to generate anxiety when a woman broached the High Romantic tradition. Nevertheless, in this poem Hemans carefully leaves the gender of the student unspecified (though most readers would probably assume that he was male), and the student is clearly called to the same kind of ministry as the vatic poet: the search for and communication of eternal truth. Through her mask, Hemans engages with Wordsworth's poetry and themes to explore what it means for a person—woman or man—to be both a Christian poet and a Romantic vates.

Hemans died the year after *Scenes and Hymns of Life* was published, but there is evidence that Wordsworth's influence on her poetry persisted to the end. At her death she was working on an ambitious poem to be entitled *The Christian Temple*, a work which would continue exploring religious themes but would also mark a return to poetry concerning large public issues characteristic of her early work. Though we cannot know what the finished work would have been like, its themes suggest a continuing engagement with Wordsworth and his *Ecclesiastical Sonnets*, and its ambition suggests the sense of high poetic and prophetic vocation that she found in his poetry.[28]


## Conclusions

Analyzing the interactions between these two Romantic poets, male and female, changes the way we approach their work. It clarifies the nature of the religious turn in Hemans's late work, placing it in a poetic as well as a personal context and illuminating a little-studied period of her career. But it also affects our readings of Wordsworth. Seeing his work and life through Hemans's poetry reminds us that our dominant critical narrative of his career, which sees his later poetry as a falling off from the genius of his early maturity, is not the only way—perhaps not the most fruitful way—of reading Wordsworth. Victorian readers, as Stephen Gill has demonstrated, much preferred the later Wordsworth, who offered them (as they read him) religious instruction, consolation, and inspiration. Writing in the transitional 1830s, Hemans similarly valued Wordsworth's later works with their more orthodox religious and moral tone, but, crucially, she also comprehended the importance of the earlier, more radical work. Perhaps through her example we too can recover an appreciation of the whole of Wordworth's career as a source of insight and inspiration.


## Works Cited

Feldman, Paula R., ed. *Records of Woman With Other Poems*. By Felicia Hemans. Lexington: University of Kentucky Press, 1999.

Gill, Stephen. *William Wordsworth: A Life*. Oxford: Clarendon Press, 1989.

—. *Wordsworth and the Victorians*. Oxford: Clarendon Press, 1998.

Hemans, Felicia. *The Poetical Works of Mrs. Hemans*. The "Grosvenor" Poets. London: William Collins.

Melnyk, Julie. "Hemans's Later Poetry: Religion and the Vatic Poet." In *Felicia Hemans: Reimagining Poetry in the Nineteenth Century*. Ed. Nanora Sweet and Julie Melnyk. Basingstoke: Palgrave, 2001. 74–92.

—. "Victorian Religious Women Writers and Communal Identities." *Australasian Victorian Studies Journal* 10 (2004): 70–90.

Turner, Paul. Introduction to *Men and Women 1855*. By Robert Browning. Oxford: Oxford University Press, 1972.

---

[28]    If Hemans saw *The Christian Temple* as the culmination of her poetic career, she may have been influenced in her choice of title by the imagery in Wordsworth's 1814 Preface to *The Excursion*, in which he likens his poem to an "ante-chapel" and his projected magnum opus *The Recluse* to "the body of a gothic church" (William Wordsworth, *The Excursion: A Poem* (New York: C. S. Francis,1850), x).

Wolfson, Susan J., ed. *Felicia Hemans: Selected Poems, Letters, Reception Materials*. Princeton: Princeton University Press, 2000.

—. "Hemans and the Romance of Byron." In *Felicia Hemans: Reimagining Poetry in the Nineteenth Century*. Ed. Nanora Sweet and Julie Melnyk. Basingstoke: Palgrave, 2001. 155–80.

Wordsworth, William. *The Ecclesiastical Sonnets of William Wordsworth: A Critical Edition.* Ed. Abbie Findlay Potts. New Haven: Yale University Press, 1922.

—. *The Excursion: A Poem*. New York: C. S. Francis, 1850.

—. *William Wordsworth*: *The Oxford Authors*. Ed. Stephen Gill. Oxford: Oxford University Press, 1984.

Chapter 7

# "Does not it make you think of Cowper?": Rural Sport in Jane Austen and Her Contemporaries

Barbara K. Seeber

In *Mansfield Park*, Rushworth's plan to "have the avenue at Sotherton down" (55) leads Fanny Price to comment to Edmund "in a low voice": "Cut down an avenue! What a pity! Does not it make you think of Cowper? 'Ye fallen avenues, once more I mourn your fate unmerited'" (56).[1] William Cowper ranked highly in Jane Austen's estimation; the "Biographical Notice of the Author" states that her "favourite moral writers were Johnson in prose, and Cowper in verse," and in the *Memoir*, J.E. Austen-Leigh records: "Amongst her favourite writers, Johnson in prose, Crabbe in verse, and Cowper in both, stood high."[2] It is surprising then, as William Deresiewicz points out, that Cowper, "whom virtually everyone acknowledges as a major influence, has scarcely ever been investigated as such," an oversight which he attributes to the "bias ... against ... poetry."[3] Deresiewicz's *Jane Austen and the Romantic Poets* reads *Mansfield Park*, *Emma*, and *Persuasion* in the context of Coleridge, Wordsworth, Scott, and Byron, but does not include Cowper. While in Deresiewicz's account of an "early" versus "major" phase, Cowper is an influence Austen eventually outgrew, he is neglected by critics situating the novelist in relation to women's writing and feminist thought. For example, Claudia Johnson implies that when *Sense and Sensibility*'s Marianne Dashwood reads Cowper, Austen merely uses the poet as a screen for her novel's feminism: "Clearly, Austen

---

[1]  Austen's novels are cited from *The Novels of Jane Austen*, ed. R.W. Chapman, 3rd ed., 6 vols. (Oxford: Oxford University Press, 1988).

[2]  Henry Austen, "Biographical Notice of the Author," in vol. 5 of *The Novels of Jane Austen*, ed. R.W. Chapman, 3rd ed. (Oxford: Oxford University Press, 1988), 7. James Edward Austen-Leigh, *Memoir of Jane Austen* (Oxford: Clarendon Press, 1963), 89.

[3]  William Deresiewicz, *Jane Austen and the Romantic Poets* (New York: Columbia University Press, 2004), 162. There are brief references to Cowper in Jocelyn Harris's *Jane Austen's Art of Memory* (Cambridge: Cambridge University Press, 1989), Frank Bradbrook's *Jane Austen and Her Predecessors* (Cambridge: Cambridge University Press, 1966), and Mary Lascelles's *Jane Austen and Her Art* (Oxford: Clarendon Press, 1939), but there appears to be only one detailed examination of Austen's allusions to Cowper: John Halperin's "The Worlds of *Emma*: Jane Austen and Cowper," *Jane Austen: Bicentenary Essays*, ed. John Halperin (Cambridge: Cambridge University Press, 1975): 197–206.

can, in a sense, get away with a character like Marianne because she suppresses her antecedents—Marianne reads Scott and Cowper, not Hays or Wollstonecraft."[4] This essay, in contrast, follows Fanny Price's lead and thinks through Cowper's influence on Austen, specifically his depiction of hunting and shooting, and the connections between the Romantic poets and Austen's work (both early and late). The Romantic poets followed Cowper in opposing rural sport on a number of grounds, and Austen further developed their argument by establishing parallels between the position of women and animals in patriarchal society. Austen's status within the Romantic canon has been a contested one, and this essay, by focusing on the representation of rural sport, contributes to the growing body of scholarship demonstrating affinities between Austen and the Romantic poets.[5] This is not to reduce Austen to sameness, but to argue that she participates in the community of "Fellow Romantics."

William Cowper's emphasis on the sentience and individuality of animals is characteristic of the emerging discourse of animal rights in the eighteenth century. The anti-hunting argument of *The Task* is based on three major points, the chief of which is animals' ability to feel pain: rural sport is "detested" because it "owes its pleasures to another's pain" and "feeds upon the sobs and dying shrieks / Of harmless nature" (3.326–9).[6] Animals "suffer torture" (6.390) to "make ... [man]

---

[4]     Deresiewicz argues that while the early novels (*Northanger Abbey*, *Sense and Sensibility*, and *Pride and Prejudice*) "are essentially straightforward marriage plots, intricately designed but morally and emotionally unambiguous" (1), the later three novels offer "something ... more: deeper, denser, more complex, more confounding" (1), an improvement attributed to Austen's "encounter" (4) with Wordsworth, Coleridge, Scott, and Byron. She "responded not to a movement, but to four powerful individual talents, just as she had earlier responded to some of the leading talents of the mid– to late eighteenth century—Richardson, Johnson, Cowper, Burney" (2–3). Claudia L. Johnson, *Jane Austen: Women, Politics, and the Novel* (Chicago: University of Chicago Press, 1988), 61.

[5]     See Anne K. Mellor's "Why Women Didn't Like Romanticism: The Views of Jane Austen and Mary Shelley" (*The Romantics and Us: Essays on Literature and Culture*, ed. Gene W. Ruoff [New Brunswick: Rutgers University Press, 1990], 274–87) for an influential articulation of Austen as an anti-Romantic writer. A number of critics, however, challenge such a view of Austen. For example, see special issues of *The Wordsworth Circle* (1976, 1979) and studies such as Edward Neill's *The Politics of Jane Austen* (London: Macmillan, 1999), Deresiewicz's *Jane Austen and the Romantic Poets*, William H. Galperin's *The Historical Jane Austen* (Philadelphia: University of Pennsylvania Press, 2003), and essays by Beth Lau such as "Jane Austen and John Keats: Negative Capability, Romance and Reality" (*Keats–Shelley Journal* 55 [2006]: 81–110), "Placing Jane Austen in the Romantic Period: Self and Solitude in the Works of Austen and the Male Romantic Poets" (*European Romantic Review* 15 [2004]: 255–67), "Jane Austen, *Pride and Prejudice*" (*A Companion to Romanticism*, ed. Duncan Wu [Oxford: Blackwell, 1998], 219–22), and Lau's essay in this collection.

[6]     William Cowper's poetry is cited from *The Poems of William Cowper*, ed. John D. Baird and Charles Ryskamp (Oxford: Clarendon Press, 1995).

sport" (6.386). Secondly, *The Task* depicts rural sport as unthinking activity, for "a mind / Cultur'd and capable of sober thought" (3.323–4) will "love the country … for … its silence and its shade" (3.321–2), not the "clamours of the field" (3.326). It is the hunter's "supreme delight / To fill with riot, and defile with blood" (3.306–7) the "scenes form'd for contemplation, and to nurse / The growing seeds of wisdom" (3.301–2). And thirdly, Cowper implies that rural sport leads to cruelty towards humans:

> The heart is hard in nature, and unfit
> For human fellowship, as being void
> Of sympathy, and therefore dead alike
> To love and friendship both, that is not pleased
> With sight of animals enjoying life,
> Nor feels their happiness augment his own. (6.321–6)

While the hunter "gratif[ies] the frenzy of his wrath" (6.387), the poet imagines an animal world where "the bounding fawn … darts across the glade / When none pursues, through mere delight of heart, / And spirits buoyant with excess of glee" (6.327–9) and the horse "skims the spacious meadow at full speed, / Then stops and snorts, and, throwing high his heels, / Starts to the voluntary race again" (6.331–3). *The Task* endows the treatment of animals with ethical and poetic significance: the speaker "deem[s] the toils / Of poetry not lost, if verse of mine / May stand between an animal and woe, / And teach one tyrant pity for his drudge" (6.725–8).

Cowper attempts to represent animals as individuals in several of his works. In an essay published in *The Gentleman's Magazine*, he "describe[s]" his three pet hares, Puss, Tiney, and Bess, "as having each a character of his own": "We know indeed that the hare is good to hunt and good to eat, but in all other respects poor Puss is a neglected subject." After observing and recording the behavior of the three animals, Cowper concludes, "my intimate acquaintance with these specimens of the kind has taught me to hold the sportsman's amusement in abhorrence; he little knows what amiable creatures he persecutes, of what gratitude they are capable, how cheerful they are in their spirits, what enjoyment they have of life."[7] The attribution of individuality to animals also is evident in *Epitaph on an Hare*. Tiney was "surliest of his kind":

> Though duly from my hand he took
> His pittance ev'ry night,
> He did it with a jealous look,
> And, when he could, would bite. (9–12)

---

[7]     William Cowper, *The Gentleman's Magazine*, June 1784, in vol. 5 of *The Letters and Prose Writings of William Cowper*, ed. James King and Charles Ryskamp (Oxford: Clarendon Press, 1986), 42, 40, 43.

The poem is notable for not sentimentalizing the hare, and its memorializing of Tiney's habits and pleasures contributes to an anti-hunting argument. Similarly, *Epitaphium Alterum*, evoking ancient epitaphs and asking the reader to reflect on her own mortality, gives seriousness to the life and death of Puss, one of Cowper's hares.

While David Perkins suggests that Cowper identified with "persecuted animals and in protesting on their behalf, he was using them as surrogates," he also admits that "no writer in the eighteenth century had more effect than William Cowper in transforming attitudes to animals and stimulating reform. He was quoted over and over in sermons, pamphlets, and in Parliament."[8] For example, Lord Erskine quoted *The Task* in parliament when introducing a bill against animal cruelty and Joseph Ritson quotes the poem to support his *Essay on the Abstinence from Animal Food as a Moral Duty*, which, in turn, influenced Percy Bysshe Shelley.[9] This is not to elide significant differences among Cowper and later Romantic writers. For example, Shelley was vegetarian, while Cowper was not; the latter's world is still anthropocentric: "The sum is this.—If man's convenience, health, / Or safety interfere, his rights and claims / Are paramount, and must extinguish their's" (*Task*, 6.581–3). Nor does Cowper emphasize women's social position, while Austen clearly does. But there are important continuities between Cowper and the Romantics.[10] They developed his representation of animals as sentient individuals, his opposition of rural sports and reflection, and his connection between cruelty to animals and cruelty to humans.

Recent studies such as Christine Kenyon-Jones's *Kindred Brutes: Animals in Romantic-Period Writing* and David Perkins's *Romanticism and Animal Rights* demonstrate that representations of animals are linked to political debates of the day; animals stand in as substitutes for the oppressed (slaves, children, working classes) and, at times, writers made radical claims for the extension of rights to animals: "Since animals could be seen to be metonymically or synecdochically

---

[8]     David Perkins, "Cowper's Hares," *Eighteenth-Century Life* 20.2 (1996): 58. Perkins, *Romanticism and Animal Rights* (Cambridge: Cambridge University Press, 2003), 44. Donna Landry's *The Invention of the Countryside: Hunting, Walking and Ecology in English Literature, 1671–1831* (Houndmills: Palgrave, 2001) takes an unsympathetic view of Cowper: "Seeing animals at leisure, expressing themselves and demonstrating the pleasure of freedom, especially freedom from human constraints, does nothing for Cowper so much as consolidate his sense of rational superiority to other humans as well as animals, his own humane benevolence.... . Cowper's advocacy ends with inviting the benevolent ... to feel pleased with themselves" (123–4).

[9]     Christine Kenyon-Jones, *Kindred Brutes: Animals in Romantic-Period Writing* (Aldershot: Ashgate, 2001), 90. Joseph Ritson, *An Essay on Abstinence from Animal Food as a Moral Duty* (London: Richard Phillips, 1802).

[10]     Rachel Trickett explores the influence of Cowper on William Wordsworth in "Cowper, Wordsworth, and the Animal Fable" (*The Review of English Studies* 34.136 [1983]: 471–80). She does not examine hunting or the ecological implications of both poets, but provides useful parallels between the two poets' description of animals.

linked to … oppressed human groups, they were drawn into the debate, and the continuum of better treatment and rights was also, to some extent, applied to them."[11] Samuel Taylor Coleridge's *To a Young Ass, Its Mother Being Tethered Near It* is an example of the latter. The speaker clearly sees the animal as an individuated being with whom he has formed a connection over time: "*oft* with gentle hand I give thee bread, / And clap thy ragged coat, and pat thy head" (3–4; emphasis added).[12] The donkey is represented as experiencing physical and emotional pain: "But what thy dulled spirits hath dismay'd, / That never thou dost sport along the glade? / And … / That earthward still thy moveless head is hung?" (5–8). Moreover, the speaker imagines a mutual exchange: "How *askingly* its footsteps hither bend? / It seems to say, 'And have I then *one* friend?'" (23–24). Rather than dismissing the poem for its anthropomorphism, Onno Oerlemans argues that "the representation of animals in the romantic period can enable us to see that the concept of anthropomorphism, and the consequent prohibition of it, are inherently features of anthropocentrism."[13] For the insistence that animals are *not* like humans is usually in the service of reducing—rather than enlarging—animals' liberty. Furthermore, the poem's anthropomorphism challenges the human-animal divide *and* the social hierarchies which it legitimizes, indeed naturalizes. The speaker of Coleridge's poem addresses the animal as a "poor little Foal of an oppressed race!" (1) and "hail[s]" it "*Brother*" (26). The language clearly resonates with abolitionist politics, and the poem makes a parallel between the position of animals, slaves, and the poor, since the speaker recognizes that the donkey's "piteous … lot" (15)—"Chain'd to a log within a narrow spot, / Where the close–eaten grass is scarcely seen, / While sweet around her waves the tempting green!" (16–18)—mirrors her owner's fate:

> Poor Ass! thy master should have learnt to show
> Pity—best taught by fellowship of Woe!
> For much I fear me that *He* lives like thee,
> Half famish'd in a land of Luxury! (19–22)

Rather than reading the donkey as a safe substitute for oppressed humans or reducing the poem to a misanthropic gesture, Oerlemans claims that the "poem's sympathy for the foal is to be taken literally" even though its "utopianism … will still appear to most of us, no doubt, as embarrassingly naive."[14] Indeed, this

---

[11] Christine Kenyon-Jones, *Kindred Brutes: Animals in Romantic-Period Writing*, 40.

[12] Coleridge's poetry is cited from *The Complete Poetical Works of Samuel Taylor Coleridge*, ed. Ernest Hartley Coleridge, 2 vols. (Oxford: Clarendon Press, 1912).

[13] Onno Oerlemans, *Romanticism and the Materiality of Nature* (Toronto: University of Toronto Press, 2002), 70.

[14] David Perkins, in *Romanticism and Animal Rights*, argues that Coleridge "was partly clowning when he wrote the verse" (109). He attributes the poem to "misanthropy"

is precisely the response that the poem anticipates and repudiates: "I hail thee *Brother*—spite of the fool's scorn!" (26). The Romantics' attempt to re-imagine human-animal relations also is evident in the depictions of hunting and shooting.

While, as Stephen Deuchar explains, rural sport was defended on the grounds that it "was healthy, virtuous, brought beneficial contact with nature, ... was royal, noble, manly and even patriotic,"[15] the Romantic poets tended to take a different view, and when we read Austen in this context striking parallels occur. William Wordsworth's *Hart-Leap Well*, like Cowper's poetry, emphasizes animal sentience and generates sympathy for the hart's "toil along the mountain side" (29), its "desperate race" lasting "thirteen hours" (141) and the "last deep groan his breath had fetched" (43): "What thoughts must through the creature's brain have passed!" (137).[16] The poem's speaker, listening to the shepherd's story, observes that "This beast not unobserved by Nature fell" (159) and gleans the "lesson": "Never to blend our pleasure or our pride / With sorrow of the meanest thing that feels" (175–6). For Perkins, the poem "presents a development of, or into, a state of higher moral sensitivity": "the modern poet, more reflective, sensitive, and aware than Sir Walter, has no wish to hunt, because his insight and feeling connect him more sympathetically with nature."[17] In that sense, *Hart-Leap Well* is similar to Coleridge's *The Rime of the Ancient Mariner*. The mariner's moral that "He prayeth well, who loveth well / Both man and bird and beast. / He prayeth best, who loveth best / All things both great and small" (7.612–15) has been seen as too obvious to be taken seriously. Surely the shooting of the bird must be a symbol of something more important, but Kenyon-Jones reminds us that in a nineteenth-century cultural context, the poem's "power ... should not be underestimated ... to preach effectively the simple moral of kindness to animals" for "as late as 1881 Frederick Thrupp, lithograph illustrator of Coleridge's work, was interpreting the poem in this straightforward spirit in his essay decrying blood sports, 'The Antient [sic] Mariner and the Modern Sportsman.'" Oerlemans argues convincingly that "the strangeness of the poem, its deliberate supernaturalness, can in part be taken as a strategy for making unfamiliar—and thereby allowing us to reconsider—a

---

(111) due to Coleridge's conflicts with his brothers and Robert Southey, and, since the poor owner is weak and the animals are chained and submissive, the poem utters a safe "protest that did not activate fears of revolution" (113). Oerlemans, 83, 84.

[15]     Stephen Deuchar, *Sporting Art in Eighteenth-Century England: A Social and Political History* (New Haven: Yale University Press, 1988), 94.

[16]     Wordsworth's poetry is cited from *William Wordsworth*, ed. Stephen Gill (Oxford: Oxford University Press, 1984). Peter Mortensen's "Taking Animals Seriously: William Wordsworth and the Claims of Ecological Romanticism" (*Orbis Litterarum* 55 [2000]: 296–310) examines *Hart-Leap Well* as a response to Gottfried August Bürger's "Der Wilde Jäger": in the latter the focus "is not that he treats animals poorly, but rather that he treats the poor like animals," whereas in Wordsworth's poem, "the hart's suffering is a subject of ethical interest in itself" (303).

[17]     Perkins, *Romanticism and Animal Rights*, 84.

moral that would be found merely childish by the majority of its readers": "the supernatural aspects of the tale ... have the effect of blurring the boundaries between human and non-human in both directions of the traditional hierarchy."[18] Both Wordsworth and Coleridge portray hunting as cruel and "egoistic self-assertion."[19] And while Perkins claims Wordsworth in *Hart-Leap Well* is partially sympathetic towards Sir Walter (he is a "figure of vitality, joyousness, courage, tenacity, cruelty, lust, egoism, and megalomania"), Oerlemans reads the poem's description of the hunt and Sir Walter as "a parody of hunting and the art which celebrates it": "Sir Walter understands the hunt, and particularly the final great leap of the hart, as a sign of his own power and supremacy."[20]

Like Wordsworth and Coleridge, Austen depicts hunters as self-absorbed and arrogant, and she parodies the self-aggrandizing manner of the hunter. For example, in *Northanger Abbey* Catherine Morland has to bear the "effusions" of John Thorpe's endless conceit" (66):

> He told her ... of shooting parties, in which he had killed more birds (though without having one good shot) than all his companions together; and described to her some famous day's sport, with the foxhounds, in which his foresight and skill in directing the dogs had repaired the mistakes of the most experienced huntsman, and in which the boldness of his riding, though it had never endangered his own life for a moment, had been constantly leading others in difficulties, which he calmly concluded had broken the necks of many. (66)

The hero of "Sir William Mountague" inherits "a handsome fortune, an ancient House & a Park well stocked with Deer." In the space of merely two pages, Sir William falls in love with seven women, becomes engaged to two of them, and then marries a third one, but, forced to choose between a wedding and the opening of the shooting season, opts for the latter: "Sir William was a Shot & could not support the idea of losing such a Day, even for such Cause.... Lady Percival was enraged.... Sir William was sorry to lose her, but ... he knew that he should have been much more greived [*sic*] by the Loss of the 1st of September (*Minor Works*, 41). And *Mansfield Park's* Maria Bertram is "doomed to the repeated details of ... [Rushworth's] day's sport, good or bad, his boast of his dogs, his jealousy of his neighbours, his doubts of their qualifications, and his zeal after poachers" (115). We are reminded of Byron's satire in *Don Juan*: "The hunters fought their fox-hunt o'er again, / And then retreated soberly—at ten" (13.108).[21]

In Wordsworth's *Hart-Leap Well*, the voices of the shepherd and the poet are connected to nature and, hence, opposed to hunting; in Austen, the heroines

---

[18]    Kenyon-Jones, 72. Oerlemans, 86.

[19]    Perkins, *Romanticism and Animal Rights*, 84.

[20]    Perkins, *Romanticism and Animal Rights*, 83–4. Oerlemans, 92.

[21]    Byron's poetry is cited from *The Complete Poetical Works*, ed. Jerome McGann, 7 vols. (Oxford: Clarendon Press, 1980–1993). Citations refer to canto and stanza numbers.

inhabit this position. While Rosemarie Bodenheimer describes Austen as a "parodist" of the "language of response to nature," and Deresiewicz associates a "deeper involvement with nature" only with the later novels, Austen's heroines are consistently connected with nature.[22] Think of Marianne Dashwood's passion for the trees at Norland, Elizabeth Bennet's enthusiasm for a trip to the Lake District, even Catherine Morland's "lov[ing] nothing so well in the world as rolling down the green slope at the back of the house" (14). In *Persuasion*, Anne Elliot seeks solace in nature: she "left the room, to seek the comfort of cool air for her flushed cheeks" and to "walk … along a favourite grove" (25). She "dread[s] the possible heats of September in all the white glare of Bath, and griev[es] to forego all the influence of so sweet and so sad of the autumnal months in the country" (33). At Lyme, Anne "gloried in the sea" and "sympathized in the delight of the fresh-feeling breeze" (102) which, in turn, "restore[s]" her "bloom and freshness of youth" (104). Similarly, in the much-earlier "Catherine, or the Bower," the heroine relies on her bower and its shrubs to "restore her to herself": "it possessed such a charm over her senses, as constantly to tranquillize her mind & quiet her spirits" (*Minor Works*, 193). In *Mansfield Park*, looking at "the brilliancy of an unclouded night, and the contrast of the deep shade of the woods," Fanny Price "feel[s] as if there could be neither wickedness nor sorrow in the world; and there certainly would be less of both if the sublimity of Nature were more attended to, and people were carried out of themselves by contemplating such a scene" (113). At Sotherton, she takes pleasure in contemplating the "sweet wood" (94); we see her reflect on "the sweets of … autumn" and admire the "growth and beauty" (208) of the shrubbery at the Parsonage; and part of her suffering in Portsmouth is the loss of "all the pleasure of spring": "She had not known before, how much the beginnings and progress of vegetation had delighted her" (431–2). Only when walking along the Portsmouth ramparts does she feel joy: "every thing looked so beautiful under the influence of such a sky, the effects of the shadows pursuing each other… . the ever-varying hues of the sea now at high water, dancing in its glee and dashing against the ramparts with so fine a sound" (409).

---

22 Rosemarie Bodenheimer, "Looking at the Landscape in Jane Austen," *Studies in English Literature* 21, no. 4 (1981): 622. Deresiewicz, 19. For other sources on nature in Austen, see Penny Gay's "A Changing View: Jane Austen's Landscape" (*Sydney Studies* 15 [1990]: 47–62), Lisa Altomari's "Jane Austen and Her Outdoors" (*Persuasions* 12 [1990]: 50–53), William C. Snyder's "Mother Nature's Other Natures: Landscape in Women's Writing, 1770–1830" (*Women's Studies* 21.2 [1992]: 143–62), William Stroup's "'I Live Out of the World': The Problem of Nature in *Emma*" (*Wordsworth Circle* 28.3 [1997]: 155–62), Elizabeth Toohey's "*Emma* and the Countryside: Weather and a Place for a Walk" (*Persuasions* 21 [1999]: 44–52), Jonathan Bate's "Culture and Environment: From Austen to Hardy" (*New Literary History* 30 [1999]: 541–60), Mary J. Curry's "'Not a Day Went by Without a Solitary Walk': Elizabeth's Pastoral World" (*Persuasions* 22 [2000]: 175–86), and Robert Kern's "Ecocriticism: What Is It Good For?" (*Isle: Interdisciplinary Studies in Literature and Environment* 7.1 [2000]: 9–32).

Fanny's responsiveness to nature is also evident in her relationship with animals: her "dear old grey pony" (27) is described as "her valued friend" and its death affects Fanny, who "for some time ... was in danger of feeling the loss in her health as well as in her affections" (35). Fanny empathizes with the suffering of animals; when Mary Crawford borrows her horse for an especially long ride, Fanny "began to think it rather hard upon the mare to have such double duty; if she were forgotten the poor mare should be remembered" (68). In both Wordsworth and Austen, connection to nature leads to sympathy for animals, and both clearly debunk the idea that hunting brings humans into connection with and an appreciation of nature. Byron, too, mocks this notion in *Don Juan*:

> ... 'T is perhaps a pity,
> When Nature wears the gown that doth become her,
>      To lose those best months in a sweaty city,
> And wait until the nightingale grows dumber,
>
> . . . . . . . . . . . . . . . . . . . . . . . . . . . . . . . . .
> Ere patriots their true *country* can remember;—
> But there's no shooting (save grouse) till September. (13.48)

In contrast, Don Juan, who "had a kind of inclination, or / Weakness, for what most people deem mere vermin— / Live animals" (10.50), participates in the fox hunt only once: he "ask'd next day, 'If men ever hunted *twice*?'" (14.35). It is telling, too, that in the second canto's shipwreck scene, the starving Don Juan refuses to partake in the eating of his spaniel for almost a week; only on the "sixth day" does he "receive ... (though first denied) / As a great favour one of his fore-paws" and does so "with some remorse" (2.71). The poem's narrator is sympathetic to the plight of the "poor partridge" seeking refuge in "his stubble screen" from the "deadly shots" (16.80). He indicts fishing as "that solitary vice, / Whatever Isaak Walton sings or says: / The quaint, old, cruel coxcomb, in his gullet / Should have a hook, and a small trout to pull it" (13.106).

The opposition between hunting and "contemplation" drawn by Cowper also is developed by the Romantic writers. In this vein, Austen juxtaposes hunting with reading. *Northanger Abbey*'s John Thorpe "never read[s] novels" (48). In *Sense and Sensibility*, Sir John Middleton is characterized by his love for shooting, on the one hand, and, on the other, a "total want of talent and taste" (32).[23] *Mansfield Park*'s Mr. Rushworth also is not a great reader: he struggles with his "two and

---

23     For a detailed reading of *Northanger Abbey* and *Sense and Sensibility*, see my "The Hunting Ideal, Animal Rights, and Feminism in *Northanger Abbey* and *Sense and Sensibility*" in *Lumen* 23 (2004): 295–308. Margaret Anne Doody suggests that *Sense and Sensibility* sets up hunters in "opposition" and "antagonism" to mothers (Introduction to *Sense and Sensibility* [Oxford: Oxford University Press, 1990], xxix). Also see Patricia Jo Kulisheck's "Every Body Does Not Hunt" (*Persuasions* 8 [1986]: 20–24), which makes the point that hunting is "associated with characters who behave improperly" (23). I agree with

forty speeches" (144) in the rehearsing of *Lovers' Vows*. Like Austen, Byron depicts rural sports as an index of intellectual vacuity:

> The gentlemen got up betimes to shoot,
>     Or hunt: the young, because they liked the sport—
> The first thing boys like after play and fruit;
>     The middle–aged, to make the day more short;
> For *ennui* is a growth of English root,
>     Though nameless in our language:—we retort
> The fact for words, and let the French translate
> That awful yawn which sleep can not abate. (13.101)

Byron's two-couplet *To These Fox Hunters in a Long Frost* (1806–1807) succinctly summarizes this view: "Of unlearned men Lord Falkland did say / 'I pity em much on a long rainy day.' / Ye Fox-hunters too are quite as much lost / When winter the ground has clothed in frost."

The Romantics connected the hunter's hierarchical relationship with nature to other social hierarchies. P. B. Shelley considered the game laws as "despotism" and an "insult and outrage of the rights of … fellow-man" as well as condemning the "barbarous and bloody sport from which every enlightened and amiable mind shrinks in abhorrence and disgust." In "Vindication of a Natural Diet," he connects the "brutal pleasures of the chase" with the production of meat, which relies on desensitization: "Is it to be believed that a being of gentle feelings, rising from his meal of roots, would take delight in sports of blood?"[24] Wordsworth's Sir Walter is a Knight, who has at his disposal not only nature but also "vassals" who carry out the commands he "crie[s] out" at them (3–4). Similarly, Austen is keenly aware of the social hierarchies reflected in rural sport. In *Pride and Prejudice*, Charlotte Lucas's young brother fantasizes that if he "were as rich as Mr. Darcy," he "would keep a pack of foxhounds, and drink a bottle of wine every day" (20). In *Mansfield Park*, Henry Crawford lends William Price a horse so he can join the fox-hunt—a privilege meant to ensure his and, more importantly, Fanny's gratitude. Rushworth's "zeal after poachers" (115) also reminds the reader that sporting activities are a class privilege. Byron in *Don Juan* similarly draws attention to the way rural sport reifies class division:

> The mellow Autumn came, and with it came
>     The promised party, to enjoy its sweets.

---

her general point, but our approaches are very much different, and Kulisheck understimates the predominance of the hunting pattern.

[24]    Percy Bysshe Shelley, "On the Game Laws," in *The Prose Works of Percy Bysshe Shelley*, ed. E. B. Murray, vol. 1 (Oxford: Clarendon Press, 1993), 280, 281. "Vindication of a Natural Diet," in *The Complete Works of Percy Bysshe Shelley*, ed. Roger Ingpen and Walter E. Peck, vol. 6 (London: Ernest Benn, 1965), 17, 11.

> The corn is cut, the manor full of game;
>> The pointer ranges, and the sportsman beats
> In russet jacket:—lynx–like in his aim,
>> Full grows his bag, and wonder*ful* his feats.
> Ah, nutbrown Partridges! Ah, brilliant Pheasants!
> And ah, ye Poachers!—'T is no sport for peasants. (13.75)

In canto 16, "There were two poachers caught in a steel trap / Ready for gaol, their place of convalescence" (16.61).

Austen furthers the argument of her contemporaries by emphasizing the position of women as prey. David Perkins point out the erotic associations of the hunt and the "pleasure house" built in its commemoration in *Hart-Leap Well.*[25] The house is also associated with trickery: Sir Walter will employ "a cunning Artist ... to frame / A bason for that fountain in the dell" (61–2). And since the house commemorates the killing of a deer (obviously not a willing participant in the chase), we ought to be suspicious of Sir Walter's "place of love for damsels that are coy" (60). The narrator's description of the hart as "stone-dead / With breathless nostrils stretched above the spring" (77–8) undermines Sir Walter's chivalric language: given Sir Walter's interpretation of a hart fighting for its life as "gallant," his definition of "coy damsels" might be similarly self-serving and elide resistance. Wordsworth does not develop the pleasure-house as a monument to both kinds of hunting, but Austen emphasizes parallels between women and animals in patriarchal society. For example, in *Mansfield Park* Henry Crawford's recreation includes "making a small hole in Fanny Price's heart": "how do you think I mean to amuse myself ... on the days that I do not hunt? ... my plan is to make Fanny Price in love with me" (229). Fanny, having watched his toying with Maria, "cannot think well of a man who *sports* with any woman's feelings" (363; emphasis added). Similarly, in "Catherine, or the Bower," Edward Stanley, a hunter, "sport[s]" (*Minor Works*, 234) with Catherine's affections and the "fears of her Aunt" (*Minor Works*, 229) just because he can; he "possessed an opinion of his own Consequence, & a perseverance in his own schemes which were not to be damped by the conduct of others" (*Minor Works*, 221). And in *Sense and Sensibility*, Willoughby dallies with Marianne for his "own amusement" (320).[26] These parallels struck Austen at an early age. In "Jack and Alice," written by a teenage Austen, Lucy actively pursues the object of her affections, Charles Adams: "I was determined to make a bold push & therefore wrote him a very kind letter, offering him with great tenderness my hand & heart. To this I received an angry ... refusal, but thinking it might be rather the effect of his modesty than anything else, I pressed him again on the subject. But he never answered any more of my

---

[25]   Perkins, *Romanticism and Animal Rights*, 83.

[26]   In *Jane Austen and the Province of Womanhood* (Philadelphia: University of Pennsylvania Press, 1989), Alison G. Sulloway briefly notes that Willoughby "hunted both women and animals" (127).

Letters & very soon afterwards left the Country." When Lucy follows Charles to his estate, she "found ... [herself] suddenly seized by the leg & ... caught in one of the steel traps so common in gentlemen's grounds." Lucy's fate is a striking image of the hunting world: men hunt animals and take on a similarly dominant role in their relationships with women. "Oh! cruel Charles to wound the hearts and legs of all the fair," Alice laments (*Minor Works*, 21–2).

While Austen's link between rural sports and the exploitation of women is most pronounced in the villains and buffoons, the pattern has implications for the novels' concluding marriages. Edmund Bertram's hunting is not an insignificant detail in *Mansfield Park*. Cowper condemns the "cassock'd huntsman" (111) in *The Progress of Error* and the participation of the clergy in rural sports was of some controversy in the eighteenth and nineteenth centuries. Since Fanny quotes *The Task* on the cutting of trees, she presumably also recalls Cowper's denouncement of hunting in the same poem. That Fanny marries a hunter is one of the novel's final ironies and further undermines the resolution. The conclusion to *Persuasion* is similarly compromised. The novel has long been noted for its affinities with Romanticism, but critics have not examined its references to hunting and shooting. *Persuasion* follows the patterns examined in this essay, and in its characterization of Captain Benwick, a reader of Romantic poetry who disdains rural sport, Austen very explicitly engages in a dialogue with her male contemporaries.

Charles Musgrove is noted for his lack of reading and his selfish pursuit of pleasure. His "conversation" is not such to make Anne regret having refused his offer of marriage. Anne "could believe ... that a more equal match [than Mary] might have greatly improved him; and that a woman of real understanding might have given more consequence to his character, and more usefulness, rationality, and elegance to his habits and pursuits. As it was, he did nothing with much zeal, but sport; and his time was otherwise trifled away, without benefit from books, or anything else" (43). Without sport, he is at a loss; he accompanies Captain Harville, who has "business" in Bath, "by way of doing something, as shooting was over" (216). Austen highlights Charles's failure as husband and father, and explicitly opposes rural sport to domestic affection. When Anne first arrives at Uppercross, she finds her sister alone and unwell: "Charles is out shooting. I have not seen him since seven o'clock. He would go, though I told him how ill I was. He said he should not stay out long; but he has never come back, and now it is almost one" (37). Since Mary's "ailments lessened by having a constant companion" (46) in Anne, it is implied that Charles plays a key role in producing his wife's hypochondria. Moreover, even when his son is seriously injured, he is out shooting the next day, and, upon his return, makes the "bold public declaration" to attend the evening party at the Great House: "The child was to be kept in bed, and amused as quietly as possible; but what was there for a father to do? This was quite a female case, and it would be highly absurd in him, who could be of no use at home, to shut himself up" (55). Rural sport, hence, is depicted in opposition to sympathy. On the walk back from Winthrop, Charles abandons both Mary and Anne who "was tired enough to be very glad of Charles's ... arm" to "cut off the heads of some nettles in the hedge with his switch" and "to hunt after a weasel which he had a momentary glance of" (90). As Roger Sales drily comments, Charles's "fondness for hunting weasels and rats is not meant to endear him."[27] Partnered with the petulant beheading of nettles, the killing of animals is depicted as spoiled and pointless, and, moreover, the result of being "out of temper with his wife" (90), suggesting a displaced violence. The last we see of Charles Musgrove is when he takes his leave of Anne and Wentworth for the "sight of a capital gun" (240).

While Charles is single-minded, *Persuasion* also includes male characters who occupy an ambivalent position in relation to rural sport. Charles fears that his cousin, Charles Hayter, will not "value" the hunting privileges of his new living as a curate "as he ought": he "is too cool about sporting" (217). Captain Benwick is characterized by an admiration for the "richness of the present age" (100) of poetry, on the one hand, and a lack of interest in rural sport, on the other, the first perhaps leading to the latter. Benwick is "a reading man" (182) according to Wentworth, and Charles agrees: "Give him a book, and he will read all day long" (132). In the social world *Persuasion* depicts, rural sport demarcates separate spheres: "The Mr. Musgroves had their own game to guard, and to destroy; their own horses, dogs, and newspaper to engage them; and the females were fully occupied in all the other common subjects of house-keeping, neighbours, dress, dancing, and music" (42–3). Wentworth and Charles are "shooting together," while "the sisters in the Cottage were sitting quietly at work" (83). For women, hunting is strictly a spectator activity: the only sporting Louisa and Henrietta do is the "hunting of the Laconia" (66) in the navy lists. Benwick's reticence towards shooting causes considerable anxiety amongst the Musgroves and Admiral Croft. Mary, for one, considers him a "very odd young man":

> I do not know what he would be at. We asked him to come home with us for a day or two; Charles undertook to give him some shooting, and he seemed quite delighted, and for my part, I thought it was all settled; when behold! on Tuesday night, he made a very awkward sort of excuse; "he never shot" and he had "been quite misunderstood." (130)

Admiral Croft feels that his "soft sort of manner does not do him justice" (171) and finds his manner "rather too piano for me" (172), while Anne, defending Benwick, "meant to oppose the too-common idea of spirit and gentleness being incompatible with each other" (172). At the end of the novel, we do hear of Benwick "rat-hunting" at Uppercross from Charles: "We had a famous set-to at rat-hunting all the morning, in my father's great barns; and he played his part so well, that I have liked him the better ever since" (219). The notion of Benwick's performing the

---

27    Roger Sales, "In the Face of All the Servants: Spectators and Spies in Austen," *Janeites: Austen's Disciples and Devotees*, ed. Deidre Lynch (Princeton: Princeton University Press, 2000), 196.

role of a hunter suggests the social pressures on Benwick to fit into the Musgrove circle.[28]

While the Musgroves and Admiral Croft find Benwick "odd," his love for books unites him with the novel's heroine. Not a hunter, he takes on a more egalitarian role not only in terms of his relation with nature but also women. Anne and Benwick's conversations about literature are an exchange, and he "noted down the names of those she recommended, and promised to procure and read them" (101). Books are not the only thing that they have in common; they also share the role of nurse. In the immediate aftermath of Louisa's fall and fear for her life, Henrietta faints and "would have fallen on the steps, but for Captain Benwick and Anne, who caught and supported her between them" (110), and both are instrumental to Louisa's recovery. While Benwick is often seen as Austen's parody of the Romantic poets, Deresiewicz offers an astute alternative:

> A jaundiced view says that his very indulgence in grief and great show of bereavement foretell his rapid inconstancy.... But this view ignores Anne's own response to her fellow mourner. Yes, she later joins Captain Harville in deploring the rapidity with which Benwick gets reengaged, but she not only recognizes the genuiness of his grief, she had encouraged him to overcome it.... Anne recognizes that it is the very strength of Benwick's passion ... not its superficiality, that insures that he will soon fall in love again.[29]

Further, Benwick heals not only himself but also Louisa, whose fall from the Cobb at Lyme results in loss of health and loss of Wentworth. The latter absents himself in a hurry, and it is Captain Benwick who brings her back to life, "sit[ting] at her elbow, reading verses, or whispering to her, all day long" (218). Captain Benwick is associated with Romantic poetry, disdain for rural sports, and the healing of Louisa, who, interestingly, is described by Charles as a startled animal: "she is altered: there is no running or jumping about, no laughing or dancing; it is quite different. If one happens only to shut the door a little hard, she starts and wriggles like a young dab chick in the water" (218).

*Persuasion*'s celebration of nature and its depiction of characters as part of natural cycles and seasons contribute to the novel's anti-hunting statement. In the same manner that Wordsworth's *Hart-Leap Well* posits the enduring presence of nature against the arrogance of Sir Walter's killing of the hart, *Persuasion*'s paean to the sea and "the green chasms between romantic rocks" (95) at Lyme surely reflect negatively on Charles Musgrove's "cutting off the heads of nettles and hunting after weasels." That hunting is in opposition to domestic affection and appreciation of nature is particularly important in a novel with such thematic

---

[28]   Moreover, there is a significant difference between rural sport and the farm management in which Benwick is said to have participated. I would like to thank my colleague Ann Howey for suggesting this point to me.

[29]   Deresiewicz, 134.

emphasis on the process of healing and recovery from pain. In *Mothers of the Nation*, Anne K. Mellor argues that in *Persuasion* "Austen urges an alternative political model, the model of a family politic, a well-managed national household governed by a loving mother who is attentive to the needs of all her dependents"; Anne's role is paramount: she is "the exemplar of domestic management—both in public and at home."[30] In her arranging help for Louisa, her nursing of her injured nephew, her comforting of her invalid friend Mrs. Smith, and her counseling of Captain Benwick, Anne restores physical and emotional life—rather than destroying it.

Why then does Austen's heroine marry a hunter? The rigors of Austen's satirical examination of marriage do not disappear at the novel's closure. On the one hand, the novel holds up a narrative of romantic fulfillment, but on the other, this narrative is subjected to irony: Anne's "prett[y] ... musings of high-wrought love and eternal constancy ... along the streets of Bath" were "almost enough to spread purification and perfume all the way" (192). According to Joseph Kestner, the novel's "grim ... truth" is that "nothing more than circumstance brings Wentworth back to Anne Elliot."[31] Captain Wentworth's rise to prominence in the navy has long been celebrated as the triumph of the "self-made man." It is easy to idealize Wentworth in the context of Austen's satire on the landed gentry, but the contrast of Captain Benwick complicates the picture. Wentworth's hunting activities align him with Charles Musgrove; after meeting each other for the first time, they "seemed all to know each other perfectly, and he was coming the very next morning to shoot with Charles" (58). Louisa's fall from the Cobb leaves Wentworth "in an agony of silence" (109). If ever there is a moment to valorize the hunter as a man of action, Austen passes it up. When he does speak, "the first words which burst from ... [him], in a tone of despair, and as if all his own strength were gone" are "Is there no one to help me?" (110). It is Anne who responds and takes charge of the situation and, as we have seen, Captain Benwick who joins her efforts. While Sir Walter Elliot proves himself unworthy of inherited wealth, we do well to "remember that Wentworth earns his fortune by theft," as Anne Mellor points out: "he literally steals or captures ships ... in acts of war—or equally accurately, in state-licensed piracy. Moreover, he is cavalier about the loss of life that such risk-taking acts of military piracy might incur."[32] Wentworth makes his "handsome fortune" (30) by "successive captures" (29), and once his hunting on the high seas has paid off, he is ready to catch a wife: "it was now his object to marry. He was rich, and being turned on shore, fully intended to settle as soon as he could be properly tempted" (61). In his flirtation with Louisa, Henrietta, and the Hayter girls who also "were apparently admitted to the honour of being in love

---

[30]    Anne K. Mellor, *Mothers of the Nation: Women's Political Writing in England, 1780–1830* (Bloomington: Indiana University Press, 2000), 138, 132.

[31]    Joseph Kestner, "Jane Austen: The Tradition of the English Romantic Novel, 1800–1832," *The Wordsworth Circle* 7 (1976): 308.

[32]    Mellor, *Mothers of the Nation*, 125.

with him" (71), he bears an unflattering resemblance to the seducers in Austen's other novels: Henry Crawford, George Willoughby, and John Wickham. Anne's assessment that he was "wrong in accepting (for accepting must be the word) of two young women at once" (82) is a conservative estimate. Wentworth is at best a compromised hero, and Anne's marriage to him is not an unequivocally happy end; the sardonic description of Charles and Mary's marriage—"upon the whole ... they might pass for a happy couple" (43)—has a broader application in the novel. Kestner argues "Neither Jane Austen nor her contemporaries believed marriage terminated the condition of 'things as they are.'"[33] One part of Austen's social critique of "things as they are" is that the hierarchical laws of hunting also apply to marriage. The novel's concluding marriage does not exist outside the world of hunting, a world which opposes all the positive values in the novel: nature, books, healing, and domestic affection.

J. David Grey's statement in the 1986 *Jane Austen Companion* that Austen "pays little attention to pets and animals" has remained largely unchallenged. Sally B. Palmer writes that "Austen rejects the sentimental anthropomorphism of other Romantic-era writers that attributes noble characteristics and human emotions to animals and attempts to enter into their lives and consciousness. She would be aghast at modern views of the animal kingdom suggesting that animals have rights."[34] I take the opposite view. Like her Romantic contemporaries, Austen casts rural sport as the opposite of contemplation. Like them, she shows how rural sport reifies social hierarchies, and develops this with a focus on women's social position. While she does not make animal sentience an explicit part of her argument the way Cowper, Wordsworth, Coleridge, and Shelley do, the idea that animals are more than Cartesian machines is implied in the heroines' responsiveness to nature. Further, *Northanger Abbey*'s John Thorpe first appears on the scene by "check[ing]" his horse "with a violence which almost threw him on his haunches" (44), an action that establishes his domineering and cruel character, and Fanny, in *Mansfield Park*, clearly thinks of her horse as sentient. Austen does not center any of her texts on the treatment of animals, but she weaves contemporary discourses about rural sport into her narratives. By reading Austen in the context of William Cowper and the male Romantics, we gain a deeper understanding of her social critique and a recognition of her participation in the Romantic discourse of animal rights.

---

[33]    Kestner, 308.

[34]    J. David Grey. "Pets and Animals," *The Jane Austen Companion*, ed. J. David Grey (New York: Macmillan, 1986), 324. Sally B. Palmer, "Slipping the Leash: Lady Bertram's Lapdog," *Persuasions On-Line* 25.1.

## Works Cited

Altomari, Lisa. "Jane Austen and Her Outdoors." *Persuasions* 12 (1990): 50–53.

Austen, Henry. "Biographical Notice of the Author." *The Novels of Jane Austen*. Ed. R. W. Chapman. 3rd ed. Vol. 5. Oxford: Oxford University Press, 1988. 3–9.

Austen, Jane. *Minor Works*. Vol. 6 of *The Novels of Jane Austen*. Ed. R. W. Chapman. 3rd ed. Oxford: Oxford University Press, 1988.

——. *The Novels of Jane Austen*. Ed. R. W. Chapman. 3rd ed. 6 vols. Oxford: Oxford University Press, 1988.

Austen-Leigh, James Edward. *Memoir of Jane Austen*. Oxford: Clarendon Press, 1963.

Bate, Jonathan. "Culture and Environment: From Austen to Hardy." *New Literary History* 30 (1999): 541–60.

Bodenheimer, Rosmarie. "Looking at the Landscape in Jane Austen." *Studies in English Literature* 21 (1981): 605–23.

Bradbrook, Frank. *Jane Austen and Her Predecessors*. Cambridge: Cambridge University Press, 1966.

Byron, Lord. *The Complete Poetical Works*. Ed. Jerome McGann. 7 vols. Oxford: Clarendon Press, 1980–1993.

Coleridge, Samuel Taylor. *The Complete Poetical Works of Samuel Taylor Coleridge*. Ed. Ernest Hartley Coleridge. 2 vols. Oxford: Clarendon Press, 1912.

Cowper, William. *The Poems of William Cowper*. Ed. John D. Baird and Charles Ryskamp. 2 vols. Oxford: Clarendon Press, 1995.

——. *The Gentleman's Magazine*, June 1784. *The Letters and Prose Writings of William Cowper*. Ed. James King and Charles Ryskamp. Vol. 5. Oxford: Clarendon Press, 1986. 40–44.

Curry, Mary J. "'Not a Day Went by Without a Solitary Walk': Elizabeth's Pastoral World." *Persuasions* 22 (2000): 175–86.

Deresiewicz, William. *Jane Austen and the Romantic Poets*. New York: Columbia University Press, 2004.

Deuchar, Stephen. *Sporting Art in Eighteenth-Century England: A Social and Political History*. New Haven: Yale University Press, 1988.

Doody, Margaret Anne. Introduction. *Sense and Sensibility*. By Jane Austen. Oxford: Oxford University Press, 1990. vii–xlvi.

Galperin, William H. *The Historical Jane Austen*. Philadelphia: University of Pennsylvania Press, 2003.

Gay, Penny. "A Changing View: Jane Austen's Landscape." *Sydney Studies* 15 (1990): 47–62.

Grey, J. David. "Pets and Animals." In *The Jane Austen Companion*. Ed. J. David Grey. New York: Macmillan, 1986. 324–5.

Halperin, John. "The Worlds of *Emma*: Jane Austen and Cowper." In *Jane Austen: Bicentenary Essays*. Ed. John Halperin. Cambridge: Cambridge University Press, 1975. 197–206.

Harris, Jocelyn. *Jane Austen's Art of Memory*. Cambridge: Cambridge University Press, 1989.

Johnson, Claudia L. *Jane Austen: Women, Politics, and the Novel*. Chicago: University of Chicago Press, 1988.

Kenyon-Jones, Christine. *Kindred Brutes: Animals in Romantic-Period Writing*. Aldershot: Ashgate, 2001.

Kern, Robert. "Ecocriticism: What Is It Good For?" *Isle: Interdisciplinary Studies in Literature and Environment* 7.1 (2000): 9–32.

Kestner, Joseph. "Jane Austen: The Tradition of the English Romantic Novel, 1800–1832." *The Wordsworth Circle* 7 (1976): 297–311.

Kulisheck, Patrica Jo. "Every Body Does Not Hunt." *Persuasions* 8 (1986): 20–24.

Landry, Donna. *The Invention of the Countryside: Hunting, Walking and Ecology in English Literature, 1671–1831*. Houndmills: Palgrave, 2001.

Lau, Beth. "Jane Austen and John Keats: Negative Capability, Romance and Reality." *Keats-Shelley Journal* 55 (2006): 81–110.

—. "Jane Austen, *Pride and Prejudice*." In *A Companion to Romanticism*. Ed. Duncan Wu. Oxford: Blackwell, 1998. 219–22.

—. "Placing Jane Austen in the Romantic Period: Self and Solitude in the Works of Austen and the Male Romantic Poets." *European Romantic Review* 15 (2004): 255–67.

Lascelles, Mary. *Jane Austen and Her Art*. Oxford: Clarendon Press, 1939.

Mellor, Anne K. *Mothers of the Nation: Women's Political Writing in England, 1780–1830*. Bloomington: Indiana University Press, 2000.

—. "Why Women Didn't Like Romanticism: The Views of Jane Austen and Mary Shelley." In *The Romantics and Us: Essays on Literature and Culture*. Ed. Gene W. Ruoff. New Brunswick: Rutgers University Press, 1990. 274–87.

Mortensen, Peter. "Taking Animals Seriously: William Wordsworth and the Claims of Ecological Romanticism." *Orbis Litterarum* 55 (2000): 296–310.

Neill, Edward. *The Politics of Jane Austen*. London: Macmillan, 1999.

Oerlemans, Onno. *Romanticism and the Materiality of Nature*. Toronto: University of Toronto Press, 2002.

Palmer, Sally B. "Slipping the Leash: Lady Bertram's Lapdog." *Persuasions On-Line* 25.1 (2004).

Perkins, David. "Cowper's Hares." *Eighteenth-Century Life* 20.2 (1996): 57–69.

—. *Romanticism and Animal Rights*. Cambridge: Cambridge University Press, 2003.

Ritson, Joseph. *An Essay on Abstinence from Animal Food as a Moral Duty*. London: Richard Phillips, 1802.

Sales, Roger. "In the Face of All the Servants: Spectators and Spies in Austen." In *Janeites: Austen's Disciples and Devotees*. Edited by Deidre Lynch. Princeton: Princeton University Press, 2000. 188–205.

Seeber, Barbara K. "The Hunting Ideal, Animal Rights, and Feminism in *Northanger Abbey* and *Sense and Sensibility*." *Lumen* 23 (2004): 295–308.

Shelley, Percy Bysshe. "On the Game Laws." Vol. 1 of *The Prose Works of Percy Bysshe Shelley*. Ed. E. B. Murray. Oxford: Clarendon Press, 1993. 280–81.

—. "Vindication of a Natural Diet." Vol. 6 of *The Complete Works of Percy Bysshe Shelley*. Ed. Roger Ingpen and Walter E. Peck. London: Ernest Benn, 1965. 5–20.

Snyder, William C. "Mother Nature's Other Natures: Landscape in Women's Writing, 1770–1830." *Women's Studies* 21.2 (1992): 143–62.

Stroup, William. "'I Live Out of the World': The Problem of Nature in *Emma*." *The Wordsworth Circle* 28.3 (1997): 155–62.

Sulloway, Alison G. *Jane Austen and the Province of Womanhood*. Philadelphia: University of Pennsylvania Press, 1989.

Toohey, Elizabeth. "*Emma* and the Countryside: Weather and a Place for a Walk." *Persuasions* 21 (1999): 44–52.

Trickett, Rachel. "Cowper, Wordsworth, and the Animal Fable." *The Review of English Studies* 34.136 (1983): 471–80.

Wordsworth, William. *Hart-Leap Well*. In *William Wordsworth*. Ed. Stephen Gill. Oxford: Oxford University Press, 1984. 168–73.

Chapter 8

# The Uses and Abuses of Imagination in Jane Austen and the Romantic Poets

Beth Lau

The tradition of regarding Jane Austen as non- or even anti-Romantic is longstanding. In the past her novels were thought to follow an Augustan mode at odds with the Romantic ethos. In addition, Austen's works were considered limited in scope, confined to the private affairs of a few middle-class families in provincial villages and oblivious to the major historical developments of her time such as the French Revolution and Napoleonic wars.[1] Even with the advent of historicist and feminist criticism, which challenged many previous characterizations of Austen as detached from the important social, political, and aesthetic currents of the period, she often has continued to be distinguished from her male contemporaries. Jerome McGann, for example, insists that Austen does not espouse the Romantic ideology. Anne Mellor declares that Austen, along with other "leading women intellectuals and writers of the day," "did *not*" participate in the Romantic "spirit of the age" but instead embraced an alternative ideology that Mellor labels "feminine Romanticism."[2]

---

[1]    Richard Simpson may have initiated this charge when he claimed in 1870 that "Of organized society [Austen] manifests no idea. She had no interest for the great political and social problems which were being debated with so much blood in her day" (*North British Review* 52 [1870], in *Jane Austen: The Critical Heritage*, ed. B. C. Southam, [London: Routledge, 1968], 250). As recently as 2000, the Introduction to the Romantic Period in *The Norton Anthology of English Literature* echoed this opinion, stating that "Jane Austen ... is the only major author who seems to be untouched by the political, intellectual, and artistic revolutions of her age" (*The Norton Anthology of English Literature*, ed. M. H. Abrams, et al., 7th ed., vol. 2 [New York: Norton, 2000], 20). The most direct refutation of the view that Austen's works are limited in scope is Donald Greene's "The Myth of Limitation," in *Jane Austen Today*, ed. Joel Weinscheimer (Athens: University of Georgia Press, 1975), 142–75. It should be noted that the most recent edition of *The Norton Anthology of English Literature* no longer includes the statement quoted above and instead provides a paragraph linking Austen to Wordsworth and the Romantic movement (*The Norton Anthology of English Literature*, ed. Stephen Greenblatt, et al., 8th ed., vol. D [New York: Norton, 2006], 22; the editors of the Romantic period volume are Jack Stillinger and Deidre Shauna Lynch).

[2]    Jerome J. McGann, *The Romantic Ideology: A Critical Investigation* (Chicago: University of Chicago Press, 1983), 18–19, 29–31; Anne K. Mellor, "Why Women Didn't Like Romanticism: The Views of Jane Austen and Mary Shelley," in *The Romantics and*

To be sure, some critics throughout the years have argued for Austen's affinities with one or more of the male Romantic poets. A special issue of *The Wordsworth Circle* (7.4 [Autumn 1976]) was devoted to exploring connections between Austen and her male contemporaries. Nina Auerbach in a series of articles compares Austen's novels to various Romantic works, and Susan Morgan's *In the Meantime* also frequently situates Austen within the context of Romanticism. Clifford Siskin's historicist study of Romanticism argues that Austen does participate in the same major innovation, the naturalization of belief in a developing self, as characterizes Wordsworth's poetry and other key works of the period. Recently, three books have appeared (by Clara Tuite, William Galperin, and William Deresiewicz) that in various ways treat Austen as a Romantic writer and together signal a shift in the tendency to segregate the major novelist of the age from the major poets.[3] The

---

*Us: Essays on Literature and Culture*, ed. Gene W. Ruoff (New Brunswick: Rutgers University Press, 1990), 274. Mellor proposes that Austen and other women writers be classified as feminine as distinguished from masculine Romantics in *Romanticism and Gender* (New York: Routledge, 1993). Surveys of the history of Jane Austen criticism in relation to Romanticism may be found in Susan Morgan, *In the Meantime: Character and Perception in Jane Austen's Fiction* (Chicago: University of Chicago Press, 1980), 24–5; Jay Clayton, *Romantic Vision and the Novel* (Cambridge: Cambridge University Press, 1987), 59–60; Sonia Hofkosh, *Sexual Politics and the Romantic Author* (Cambridge: Cambridge University Press, 1998), 125–6; and William Deresiewicz, *Jane Austen and the Romantic Poets* (New York: Columbia University Press, 2004), 3–4.

[3]    Nina Auerbach, "Jane Austen and Romantic Imprisonment," in *Jane Austen in a Social Context*, ed. David Monaghan (Totowa, NJ: Barnes and Noble, 1981), 9–27; "Jane Austen's Dangerous Charm: Feeling as One Ought About Fanny Price," in *Jane Austen: New Perspectives*, ed. Janet Todd (New York: Holmes and Meier, 1983), 208–23; "O Brave New World: Evolution and Revolution in *Persuasion*," *ELH* 39 (1972): 112–28; Clifford Siskin, *The Historicity of Romantic Discourse* (New York: Oxford University Press, 1988), especially 125–47; Clara Tuite, *Romantic Austen: Sexual Politics and the Literary Canon* (Cambridge: Cambridge University Press, 2002); William H. Galperin, *The Historical Austen* (Philadelphia: University of Pennsylvania Press, 2003); William Deresiewicz, *Jane Austen and the Romantic Poets*. See also, among others, essays by Stuart Tave, "Jane Austen and One of Her Contemporaries," in *Jane Austen: Bicentenary Essays*, ed. John Halperin (Cambridge: Cambridge University Press, 1975), 61–74; Gene W. Ruoff, "The Sense of a Beginning: *Mansfield Park*," *The Wordsworth Circle* 10 (1979): 174–86; Doucet Devin Fischer, "Byron and Austen: Romance and Reality," *The Byron Journal* 21 (1993): 71–9; Rachel M. Brownstein, "Romanticism, a Romance: Jane Austen and Lord Byron, 1813–1815," *Persuasions* 16 (1994): 175–84; Peter Knox-Shaw, "*Persuasion*, Byron, and the Turkish Tale," *Review of English Studies* 44 (1993): 47–69; and Laura Dabundo, "A Marriage of True Minds: Communities of Faith in Wordsworth and Austen," *The Wordsworth Circle* 35 (2004): 69–72. I myself have argued for Austen's affinities with one or more of the male Romantic poets in "Jane Austen, *Pride and Prejudice*," in *A Companion to Romanticism*, ed. Duncan Wu (Oxford: Blackwell, 1998), 219–26; "Placing Jane Austen in the Romantic Period: Self and Solitude in the Works of Austen and the Male Romantic Poets," *European Romantic Review* 15 (2004): 255–67; "*Sense and Sensibility* and *Tintern*

present essay seeks to contribute to this goal of firmly integrating Austen within the Romantic movement and canon. I argue this claim from two directions: by demonstrating that Austen shares many characteristics commonly associated with the male poets and that the male poets share characteristics commonly associated with Austen.

One shared issue that Austen and the male poets explore in their works is the power and the dangers or the uses and abuses of imagination. Traditionally, the male poets have been characterized as celebrants of a godlike creative imagination and Austen as the advocate of reason, common sense, and empirical reality. Marilyn Butler expresses a common reading of Austen's *Emma* when she declares that the novel is "steadily critical" of the protagonist's "intuition, imagination, [and] original insight" and that "Emma matures by submitting her imaginings to common sense, and to the evidence." Anne Mellor agrees with Butler that *Emma*'s central theme is the heroine's need to "curb her romantic imagination"; she "must cease being an 'imaginist' like Cowper before his fire in *The Task*, 'Myself creating what I saw,' and learn to perceive others more correctly." Mellor goes on to directly contrast Austen's negative reference to Cowper in *Emma* to Coleridge's positive reference to the same Cowper passage in *Frost at Midnight*, which according to Mellor celebrates "the freely associative and unifying romantic imagination." "Jane Austen," Mellor concludes, "in contrast to Coleridge, explicitly identifies the liberated imagination with the errors of perception to which Emma and others … are prone." Even Stuart Tave, in an essay that argues for many similarities between Austen and Wordsworth, distinguishes the two writers' treatment of imagination. For Wordsworth, according to Tave, the moment of highest insight comes from a combination of "the object seen and the eye that sees"; for Austen, by contrast, insight involves "a conquest over an imagination which imposes itself upon the world" and an ability to see oneself and others accurately and objectively.[4] On the contrary, I argue that Austen and the male poets are similar in both their suspicion and their celebration of various forms of imaginative activity.

## The Abuses of Imagination

To be sure, *Emma* and other Austen novels contain passages and plot elements that support the view that Austen condemns flights of imagination as epistemologically

---

*Abbey*: Growth and Maturation," *The Wordsworth Circle* 35 (2004): 65–8; "Home, Exile, and Wanderlust in Austen and the Romantic Poets," *Pacific Coast Philology* 41 (2006): 91–107; and "Jane Austen and John Keats: Negative Capability, Romance and Reality," *Keats-Shelley Journal* 55 (2006): 81–110. The last article includes some points on Austen, Keats, and the imagination also addressed in this essay.

4    Marilyn Butler, *Jane Austen and the War of Ideas* (Oxford: Clarendon Press, 1975), 273–4; Mellor, *Romanticism and Gender*, 53, 222n.21; Stuart Tave, "Jane Austen and One of Her Contemporaries," 71–2.

unreliable and morally suspect. Emma, who the narrator labels an "imaginist" (*Emma*, 335), delights in discovering romantic connections between Harriet Smith and both Mr. Elton and Frank Churchill and between Jane Fairfax and Mr. Dixon, all of which prove false, to Emma's embarrassment and to the potential harm of others and herself.[5] The sensible Mr. Knightley deplores the fact that Emma "will never submit to … a subjection of the fancy to the understanding" (37) and constantly opposes her romantic inventions with his own perceptions of reality, which prove more accurate than hers. When Emma witnesses Harriet's grief upon learning that Mr. Elton is not in fact in love with her as Emma had encouraged her to believe, the latter resolves on "being humble and discreet, and repressing imagination all the rest of her life" (142), and she later laments that "'with common sense … I am afraid I have had little to do'" (402).

In *Northanger Abbey*, the work that along with *Emma* appears most obviously to rebuke indulgence in imaginative flights, Catherine Morland is humbled when she realizes she has invented a mistaken Gothic tale about General Tilney and his late wife. Henry Tilney admonishes her by calling upon her to "Consult your own understanding, your own sense of the probable, your own observation of what is passing around you" (197). In other words, Catherine should employ her reason and empirical observation, rather than her imagination, to accurately comprehend "the probable" or reality. After Henry's reprimand, the mortified Catherine acknowledges that her suspicions about the General "had all been a voluntary, self-created delusion, each trifling circumstance receiving importance from an imagination resolved on alarm." Moreover, "the whole might be traced to the influence of" her reading of improbable Gothic novels, which accustomed her to "the alarms of romance" and obscured her perception of "the anxieties of common life" (*NA*, 199–201). Catherine has a taste of true as opposed to imaginary horror when she fears that her fantasies may have cost her Henry Tilney's regard. When General Tilney discovers that Catherine is not a wealthy heiress as he supposed and turns her out of the house, she further learns "how mournfully superior in reality and substance" the troubles of actual life are to those of romance (*NA*, 227). By dwelling in the imagination, Catherine has risked both losing what happiness is available in this life and ignoring the actual dangers that surround her.

Marianne Dashwood is similar to Catherine in that she errs by judging others and modeling her own behavior according to a script she has learned from her reading of sentimental novels and impassioned poetry, including Cowper's. Because her perception is obscured by the fog of her romantic fantasies, Marianne mistakes the unscrupulous Willoughby for a dashing hero and overlooks the solid virtues of the reliable and devoted Colonel Brandon. Marianne also nearly dies as a result of her determination to imitate a literary heroine of sensibility.

---

[5]    Austen's novels are cited from *The Novels of Jane Austen*, ed. R. W. Chapman, 3rd ed., 5 vols. (London: Oxford University Press, 1932–1934). Quotations from the novels will be documented parenthetically in the text, using the following abbreviations: *Sense and Sensibility* = *S&S*, *Northanger Abbey* = *NA*, *Mansfield Park* = *MP*.

Fanny Price is disappointed by the chapel at Sotherton, for her "imagination," fed on Walter Scott's poetry, "had prepared her for something grander than a mere, spacious, oblong room"; she expected something "awful … melancholy … [and] grand" (*MP*, 85). Like Catherine Morland, Fanny has developed romantic expectations about Gothic architecture from her reading and is let down by the plain reality.[6] Edmund Bertram, however, is more seriously misled by his imagination than Fanny is. Edmund eventually realizes that the Mary Crawford he loved had "been the creature of my own imagination" (*MP*, 458). As Fanny realized all along, Edmund was "blinded" to the "truths" about Mary that had been "before him so long in vain" (*MP*, 424). Like Marianne Dashwood, Edmund created an image of his beloved that conformed to his own desires and prevented him from perceiving her accurately.

Peter DeRose classifies *Northanger Abbey* as an "anti-romance," which he defines, quoting Samuel Johnson, as a work in which "life [is exhibited] in its true state, diversified only by accidents that daily happen in the world, and influenced by passions and qualities which are really to be found in conversing with mankind."[7] Austen's work has also been associated with Johnson's chapter on the "Dangerous Prevalence of Imagination" in *Rasselas*. In this chapter (44), Imlac, Rasselas, Princess Nekayah, and her maid Pekuah visit an astronomer who believes he controls the weather. "All power of fancy over reason is a degree of insanity," Imlac concludes after their meeting with the unfortunate astronomer, and those who spend too much time in solitude are especially prone to this affliction. Without other people and activities to engage it, the mind dwells in its own creations and eventually, Imlac warns, "fictions begin to operate as realities, false opinions fasten upon the mind, and life passes in dreams."[8] Tave compares Emma, who believes she controls the lives and especially the romantic destinies of the people of Highbury, to the deluded astronomer in *Rasselas*, and DeRose believes that Austen considers Catherine Morland's Gothic fantasies a "degree of insanity."[9]

Another tradition to which Austen's works have been linked is that of the Quixotic novel or drama, which satirizes deluded romance readers whose brains have been "turned" by their reading and who cannot distinguish fiction

---

[6]  Deresiewicz (62) mentions another instance when reality proves inferior to Fanny's imagination: the scene in which William visits and Fanny initially is disappointed in her brother's appearance because it does not match her memory or mental image of him (*MP*, 234).

[7]  Peter L. DeRose, "Imagination in *Northanger Abbey*," *University of Mississippi Studies in English* 4 (1983): 71. The quotation from Samuel Johnson comes from *Rambler*, no. 4.

[8]  Samuel Johnson, *Rasselas and Other Tales*, ed. Gwin J. Kolb (New Haven: Yale University Press, 1990), 150, 152.

[9]  Stuart Tave, *Some Words on Jane Austen* (Chicago: University of Chicago Press, 1973), 210; DeRose, 67.

from reality.[10] This genre flourished in the late eighteenth and early nineteenth centuries with works such as Charlotte Lennox's *The Female Quixote* (1752), Richard Brinsley Sheridan's *The Rivals* (1775), and Eaton Stannard Barrett's *The Heroine, or The Adventures of Cherubina* (1813), as well as Austen's juvenile burlesque *Love and Freindship* (1790). All of these works depict young women such as Catherine Morland who have lost touch with reality as a result of their overactive imaginations, fed by their reading of literary works that feature improbable plots and characters.[11]

It is a mistake, however, to conclude that Austen is part of an exclusively eighteenth-century tradition and anti-Romantic in her suspicion of the creative imagination. The male Romantic poets themselves frequently express doubts and reservations about the validity and ethical consequences of imaginative flights. It is true that, as Anne Mellor claims, Coleridge's *Frost at Midnight* eventually proves the value of the freely associating mind, even though the speaker initially disparages this as a mere "idling Spirit" that "makes a toy of Thought" (20, 23).[12] In other works, however, Coleridge's treatment of uninhibited mental activity is much more qualified. In *The Eolian Harp*, the speaker initially allows his mind to freely entertain ideas suggested by the sound of the wind harp, and his reverie culminates in a profound insight into "the one life within us and abroad" (26). At the end of the poem, however, the speaker agrees with his wife in condemning all of his previous speculations as "Dim and unhallowed" "shapings of the unregenerate mind; / Bubbles that glitter as they rise and break / On vain Philosophy's aye-babbling spring" (51, 55–7). Coleridge in this poem represents the results of imaginative indulgence as unreliable and impious.

In *The Nightingale: A Conversation Poem*, the speaker finds fault with "youths and maidens most poetical" who in keeping with literary tradition regard the

---

[10]    In Richard Brinsley Sheridan's *The Rivals*, Sir Anthony Absolute damns the circulating libraries and declares of Lydia Languish, "Z—ds! The girl's mad!—her brain's turn'd by reading!" (*The Dramatic Works of Richard Brinsley Sheridan*, ed. Cecil Price, vol. 1 [Oxford: Clarendon Press, 1973], 4.2.32).

[11]    Studies of Austen's work in relation to the burlesque or Quixotic tradition include A. Walton Litz, *Jane Austen: A Study of Her Artistic Development* (New York: Oxford University Press, 1965), 3–57 (on the juvenilia); A. B. Shepperson, *The Novel in Motley: A History of the Burlesque Novel in English* (1936; rpt. New York: Octagon Books, 1967), 130–53; Elaine M. Kauver, "Jane Austen and *The Female Quixote*," *Studies in the Novel* 2 (1970): 211–21; and Beth Lau, "Madeline at Northanger Abbey: Keats's Anti-Romances and Gothic Satire" *JEGP* 84 (1985): 30–50. Kenneth Moler allies *Emma* with satires of romance novels, especially Lennox's *The Female Quixote* and Barrett's *The Heroine* (*Jane Austen's Art of Allusion* [Lincoln: University of Nebraska Press, 1968], chap. 5, especially 156–66). Moler argues that, even though *Emma* does not refer to its heroine's reading, her romantic notions must have derived from books, so that she can be considered a deluded romance reader like Catherine Morland and Marianne Dashwood (156–7).

[12]    Coleridge's poetry is quoted from *Poetical Works*, ed. J. C. C. Mays, 3 vols in 6 parts (Princeton: Princeton University Press, 2001), pt. 1, nos. 1–2 (Reading Text).

nightingale as a "'most melancholy' Bird" (35, 13). The poem speculates that the nightingale first acquired its association with sorrow from "some night-wandering man, whose heart was pierced / With the remembrance of a grievous wrong ... (And so poor Wretch! Fill'd all things with himself / And made all gentle sounds tell back the tale / Of his own sorrow)" (16–21). Like Catherine Morland, Emma Woodhouse, or Marianne Dashwood, this figure cannot apprehend the external world accurately because he projects onto it his own subjective fancies, and subsequent young people repeat his characterization of the bird, basing their perception on what they have read in books instead of their own empirical observation of the natural world.[13]

In his 1813 lecture on *Hamlet*, Coleridge analyzes the protagonist's problems in terms that directly recall the errors of Emma Woodhouse and Catherine Morland. In *Hamlet*, says Coleridge, Shakespeare "wished to exemplify the moral necessity of a due Balance between ... the real and the imaginary World—In Hamlet this Balance does not exist—his Thoughts Images & Fancy [are] far more vivid than his Perceptions." "The effect of this overbalance of imagination," Coleridge continues, is that Hamlet's mind "is for ever occupied with the world within him, and abstracted from external things: his words give a substance to shadows: and he is dissatisfied with commonplace realities."[14]

Finally, in the late poem *Constancy to an Ideal Object* Coleridge painfully admits that the cherished image of the woman he loves is a self-created fantasy, like Marianne's image of Willoughby or Edmund Bertram's of Mary Crawford. This figure, Coleridge declares, "liv'st but in the brain" (4), and he concludes the poem by comparing it to an optical illusion seen by a woodsman on a winter morning; the false "image with a glory round its head; / The enamoured rustic worships ... Nor knows he *makes* the shadow, he pursues!" (30–32). McGann writes that this poem "passes a most devastating judgment upon Coleridge's cherished belief that the realm of ideas provides a ground for reality."[15] Coleridge certainly shares with Austen (and Samuel Johnson) a distrust of imagination and an awareness of its tendency to delude individuals and prevent them from accurately

---

[13]     Scott McEathron argues that *The Nightingale* protests the falseness of the sentimental literary tradition ("Wordsworth and Coleridge, *Lyrical Ballads*," in *A Companion to Romanticism*, ed. Duncan Wu [Oxford: Blackwell, 1998], 148). In this sense Coleridge's poem can especially be paralleled to Austen's criticism of the same tradition in *Sense and Sensibility*.

[14]     Coleridge, *Lectures 1808–1819 On Literature*, ed. R. A. Foakes, 2 vols (Princeton: Princeton University Press, 1987), 1:539, 544. The first passage is taken from Coleridge's notes for his lecture, as transcribed by Ernest Hartley Coleridge; the second passage is taken from the report of Coleridge's lecture published in the *Bristol Gazette*.

[15]     McGann, 106.

perceiving reality as they dwell in fantasies of their own creation, often influenced by misguided reading.[16]

In *Alastor*, Percy Bysshe Shelley depicts a tragically deluded Poet who ignores a flesh-and-blood "panting" young woman (139) as he vainly pursues to his death a visionary maiden, a figure according to the Preface in which he "embodies his own imaginations."[17] Like the speaker in Coleridge's *Constancy to an Ideal Object*, Marianne Dashwood, and Edmund Bertram, Shelley's Poet loves a being who is merely the projection of his own desires. In addition, like Marianne, Edmund, and Emma Woodhouse, the Poet overlooks an appropriate partner in his preoccupation with a romantic fantasy. Lucy Newlyn interprets *Alastor* as a critique of "the tendencies of Romanticism toward abstraction and sublimation" and says that the Poet errs by "refus[ing] to relinquish the safety of the imaginative realm, in order to engage with the actual."[18]

It is difficult to find in Byron's work any celebration of a godlike creative imagination. Most of Byron's remarks about his creative process and products are satirical or dismissive, as when he tells Hobhouse he has "sent [to him] an 'Oeuvre' of 'Poeshie'" or when in *Don Juan* the narrator compares poetry to "A paper kite" and offers the following, notably unexalted explanation for why he composes: "I can't help scribbling once a week … In youth I wrote, because my mind was full, / And now because I feel it growing dull" (14.8, 10) and "I ask in turn,—why do you play at cards? / Why drink? Why read?—To make some hour less dreary" (14.11).[19] In a more serious vein, in his first letter to Murray on Bowles's *Invariable Principles of Poetry*, Byron praises Pope's commitment to truth and claims that "the highest of all poetry is ethical poetry, as the highest of all earthly objects must be moral truth." "It is the fashion of the day," he continues, "to lay great stress upon what they call 'imagination' and 'invention,' the two

---

[16]    Seamus Perry explores in detail "a lingering realism" in Coleridge's thought, "tenaciously dogging the idealist success story with which romantic aesthetics is usually identified" (*Coleridge and the Uses of Division* [Oxford: Clarendon Press, 1999], 104; see chap. 3 passim). As Perry notes (104–5), Thomas McFarland also documents the competing impulses of "a hugely developed sense of inner reality" and "a hugely developed sense of outer reality" in Coleridge's writings, "with neither sense giving ground" (*Coleridge and the Pantheist Tradition* [Oxford: Clarendon Press, 1969], 111).

[17]    Preface to *Alastor*, in *Shelley's Poetry and Prose*, ed. Donald H. Reiman and Neil Fraistat, 2nd ed. (New York: Norton, 2002), 73. All of Shelley's poetry and prose are quoted from this edition.

[18]    Lucy Newlyn, Paradise Lost *and the Romantic Reader* (Oxford: Clarendon Press, 1993), 247, 249.

[19]    *Byron's Letters and Journals*, ed. Leslie A. Marchand, 12 vols (London: John Murray, 1973–1982), 6:76; Lord Byron, *The Complete Poetical Works*, ed. Jerome J. McGann, 7 vols. (Oxford: Clarendon Press, 1980–1993). Passages from these editions are hereafter documented parenthetically in the text. Quotations from *Don Juan* and *Childe Harold's Pilgrimage* are documented by canto and stanza numbers.

commonest of qualities: an Irish peasant with a little whiskey in his head will imagine and invent more than would furnish forth a modern poem."[20]

Byron declared that he himself "could describe what I had seen better than I could invent" (*Letters*, 2:122) (and Keats agrees when he tells his brother and sister-in-law that the difference between his poetry and Byron's is that "He describes what he sees—I describe what I imagine").[21] In other remarks Byron suggests that he regards direct observation as the basis for poetic authority. The Preface to the first two Cantos of *Childe Harold's Pilgrimage* announces, "The following poem was written, for the most part, amidst the scenes which it attempts to describe" (*Complete Poetical Works*, 2:3). In the letters to Murray on Bowles, Byron claims as his entitlement "to talk of naval matters, at least to poets" the fact that he had extensive experience swimming, sailing, and living by the sea, and he castigates the descriptions of nature by Hunt, Keats, and other "Cockney" poets because as Londoners they had little direct knowledge of it. "Southey, Wordsworth, and Coleridge have rambled over half Europe, and seen Nature in most of her varieties," he writes, "but what on earth—of earth, and sea, and Nature—have the others seen?"[22] As A. B. England notes, Byron's emphasis in such passages on empirical knowledge is in keeping with an Augustan rather than a Romantic world view, as is appropriate for a writer who championed Pope as his literary role model. Robert F. Gleckner similarly points out that Byron's invocation of Athena, goddess of wisdom, as his muse in Canto II of *Childe Harold's Pilgrimage* is "anti-romantic" in its focus on truth and factuality and "its implied antipathy to imagination and dream."[23]

Wordsworth in the twentieth century came to be regarded as the chief exemplar of the transcendent, visionary Romantic imagination and thus as diametrically opposed to the empirical, commonsensical Austen.[24] In a number of ways,

---

[20]     Rowland E. Prothero, ed., *The Works of Lord Byron*, vol. 12 (London: John Murray, 1901), 554; see also 559–60.

[21]     *The Letters of John Keats*, ed. Hyder E. Rollins, 2 vols (Cambridge: Harvard University Press, 1958), 2:200. Quotations from Keats's letters will hereafter be documented parenthetically in the text.

[22]     Prothero, 544, 588.

[23]     England, *Byron's* Don Juan *and Eighteenth-Century Literature: A Study of Some Rhetorical Continuities and Discontinuities* (Lewisburg, OH: Bucknell University Press, 1975), 171; Gleckner, *Byron and the Ruins of Paradise* (Baltimore: The Johns Hopkins University Press, 1967), 69–70. Byron also claims in *Don Juan* that his Muses are "pedestrian" (Dedication, 8) and that his "Muse by no means deals in fiction: / She gathers a repertory of facts" (14.13; see also 1.202).

[24]     Clayton (196n.8) surveys some of the twentieth-century critics who emphasized the visionary in Wordsworth and helped to make this a central topic in Romantic studies. Clayton argues for Austen's "opposition to Romanticism" on the basis on her "treatment of ... Romantic visionary experience" (61). Austen's relationship to the Romantic poets, however, appears differently when Romanticism is not defined chiefly in terms of the visionary.

however, Wordsworth shares Austen's distrust of an overheated imagination that divorces one from the actual world. Certainly Wordsworth, like Austen in *Northanger Abbey*, disparages the cult of the Gothic, the "frantic novels, sickly and stupid German Tragedies, and deluges of idle and extravagant stories in verse" that he feels are blunting readers' sensibilities and encouraging a "degrading thirst after outrageous stimulation."[25] Poems such as *The Idiot Boy*, *The Thorn*, *Hart-Leap Well*, *Goody Blake and Harry Gill*, and *Peter Bell* have been characterized as anti-Gothic parodies that either present characters whose imaginations have betrayed them into superstition (Harry Gill, Betty Foy in *The Idiot Boy*, and the garrulous narrator of *The Thorn*) or that seek to challenge and correct readers' desires for "extravagant stories." As Mary Jacobus writes of *The Idiot Boy*, the poem "burlesques the ballad of supernatural adventure in order to establish new priorities—the feelings and experiences which irradiate the everyday." Michael Gamer compares the misguided narrators or listeners in Wordsworth's anti-Gothic ballads, who do not maintain a proper distance from the sensational tales to which they are exposed, to Catherine Morland.[26]

A number of Wordsworth poems directly address the problems of surrendering to imagination. In *Ruth*, a simple country girl is entranced by exotic tales of the American wilderness told to her by a charming young man from that land. "Such tales as told to any Maid / By such a Youth in the green shade / Were perilous to hear," the narrator warns (40–42). The young man describes America as an idyllic world and tells Ruth that life with him there would be "bliss" (75). "Through dream and vision did she sink" (103), and she agrees to marry her suitor, after which he cruelly abandons her. "Now the pleasant dream was gone" (157) the narrator writes, as Ruth, instead of enjoying the Edenic existence the youth's tales had led her to expect, goes mad and becomes a destitute homeless woman. Like Catherine Morland and Marianne Dashwood, Ruth allows fictional, exotic stories to stimulate her imagination in a way that distorts her perception of reality, to her great harm. James Averill states that *Ruth* is "about the dangers of the imagination" or, as he expresses the point later in his discussion, alluding to Samuel Johnson's warnings

*[handwritten margin note: Austen like Wordsworth - distrust of excessive imagination.]*

---

[25]    Preface to *Lyrical Ballads*, in William Wordsworth, *Selected Poems and Prefaces*, ed. Jack Stillinger (Boston: Houghton Mifflin, 1965), 449. Unless otherwise noted, Wordsworth's poetry and prose are quoted from this edition. As Barbara Seeber notes, among the "German Tragedies" Wordsworth had in mind were the works of August von Kotzebue, whose *Lover's Vows* is featured as the dangerous, inappropriate play chosen for performance in *Mansfield Park*. Thus both Wordsworth and Austen register their objections to Kotzebue's dramas. See Barbara K. Seeber, *General Consent in Jane Austen: A Study in Dialogism* (Montreal: McGill-Queen's University Press, 2000), 61.

[26]    Mary Jacobus, *Tradition and Experiment in Wordsworth's* Lyrical Ballads *(1798)* (Oxford: Clarendon Press, 1976), 233; Michael Gamer, *Romanticism and the Gothic: Genre, Reception, and Canon Formation* (Cambridge: Cambridge University Press, 2000), 111.

*[handwritten margin note: Austen not unlike Coleridge & Wordsworth]*

about this faculty in *Rasselas*, the "dangerous pleasure of imagination."[27] In *Ruth*, Wordsworth like Austen creates a cautionary tale about the dangers, especially for young women, of allowing fantasy to detach one from reality.

Wordsworth even more radically exposes the errors of a misguided imagination in *Elegaic Stanzas, Suggested by a Picture of Peele Castle, in a Storm*. In this poem the speaker rejects his youthful perception of a benign natural world as a "fond illusion" and "Poet's dream" that served to distance him from other people; he concludes the poem by bidding "farewell [to] the heart that lives alone, / Housed in a dream, at distance from the Kind!" (29, 16, 53–4). Like Austen and like Shelley in *Alastor*, Wordsworth here regards the imagination as fundamentally illusory, a false projection of individual desire onto external reality. In addition, the imagination is dangerous in its tendency to isolate the dreamer from actual, sustaining human relationships.

Perhaps the Romantic poet who is most like Austen in his treatment of the dangers of dwelling in imaginary realms is John Keats. As James Engell notes, "Few since [Samuel] Johnson, and no one in the Romantic period with the possible exceptions of Coleridge, Byron, Goethe, and Schelling, examined the treacheries of the imagination with more honest scrutiny than Keats."[28] After an initial infatuation with romance and the imagination's ability to transport us "away from all our troubles: / So that we feel uplifted from the world" (*I stood tip-toe upon a little hill*, 138–9), Keats increasingly came to question the value of visionary flights that divorce one from reality.[29]

*On Sitting Down to Read* King Lear *Once Again*, composed in January 1818, bids farewell to "golden-tongued Romance ... Fair plumed syren, queen of far-away" and embraces instead the "bitter-sweet ... fruit" of Shakespeare's tragedy. Keats dismisses a seductively entertaining but improbable literature, such as that Catherine Morland imbibes, for literature that portrays human life realistically, with its mixture of pleasures and pains. In a 5 January 1818 letter, Keats expresses his preference for the realism of Smollet's novels over the romance of Scott's by explaining that "Scott endeavours to th[r]ow so interesting and ramantic a colouring into common and low Characters as to give them a touch of the Sublime—Smollet on the contrary pulls down and levels what with other Men would continue Romance" (*Letters*, 1:200). Keats's spelling of "ramantic" conveys his satirical attitude toward Scott's larger-than-life fiction. In a later letter Keats similarly states his preference for realistic over improbable literature when he declares, "Wonders are no wonder to me. I am more at home amongst Men and women. I would rather

---

[27]    James H. Averill, *Wordsworth and the Poetry of Human Suffering* (Ithaca: Cornell University Press, 1980), 204, 207.

[28]    James Engell, *The Creative Imagination: Enlightenment to Romanticism* (Cambridge: Harvard University Press, 1981), 292–3. It is telling that Engell apparently did not think to include Austen in his consideration of Romantic period writers.

[29]    Keats's poetry is quoted from *The Poems of John Keats*, ed. Jack Stillinger (Cambridge: Harvard University Press, 1978).

read Chaucer than Ariosto" (*Letters*, 2:234). Like Austen in *Northanger Abbey* and *Sense and Sensibility*, Keats finds fault with literary genres that distort reality and thereby distance readers from actual human life.

In *There is a joy in footing slow across a silent plain*, written during the Scottish tour of 1818, Keats voices anxieties about the consequences of prolonged abstraction from the here and now.

> Scanty the hour and few the steps beyond the bourn of care,
> Beyond the sweet and bitter world—beyond it unaware;
> Scanty the hour and few the steps, because a longer stay
> Would bar return and make a man forget his mortal way.
> O horrible! To lose the sight of well remember'd face,
> Of brother's eyes, of sister's brow, constant to every place. (29–34)

Keats fears that, like the astronomer in Johnson's *Rasselas*, he may "lose his mind" (46) and become "a madman" (25) or "half ideot" (41) if he dwells too long in his own private thoughts, and he welcomes "the gentle anchor pull" (40) of familiar faces that brings him back to sanity.

In a number of poems, Keats features a deluded romance reader in the tradition of *Northanger Abbey* and other Quixotic novels. Madeline in *The Eve of St. Agnes* is introduced as a young woman whose brain is "stuff'd … with triumphs gay / Of old romance" (40–41). She is "Hoodwink'd with faery fancy" (70) and "all amort" or oblivious to the people and activities around her as she dwells on the "old dames[']" or old wives' tale of "St. Agnes and her lambs unshorn, / And all the bliss to be before to-morrow morn" (45, 70–72). Her dreamy preoccupation with "legends old" (135) permits Porphyro to take advantage of Madeline by stealing into her bedroom and then into her bed, while she regards him as a figure in her dream rather than an actual man. Like Marianne Dashwood, Catherine Morland, and Wordsworth's Ruth, Madeline has had her imagination aroused and her perception distorted by sensational tales, with potentially tragic consequences.

The fragmentary *Eve of St. Mark*, written shortly after *The Eve of St. Agnes*, is even more explicit than the latter poem in its condemnation of the deluded female reader of romance. When Keats mentioned these two poems in a letter to his brother and sister-in-law in America, he said, "you see what fine mother Radcliff names I have" (*Letters*, 2:62), suggesting their association in his mind with the Gothic—or the Gothic satire—tradition. Bertha in *The Eve of St. Mark* is not a high-born Medieval maiden like Madeline but a modern, middle-class English girl; her name, "Bertha," contrasts with the exotic, romance-language "Madeline" and suggests that she, like Catherine Morland, is intended as an anti-heroine whose homely life is distinguished from the improbable destinies of Gothic or sentimental heroines. Throughout the poem, Bertha reads in "A curious volume, patch'd and torn, / That all day long, from earliest morn, / Had taken captive her two eyes" (25–7). The book is an ancient volume of saints' lives, filled with Medieval Catholic imagery and legends of miracles. Bertha's interest in this Medieval text, so exotic and remote from her nineteenth-century British Protestant world, is not unlike Catherine Morland's fascination with *The Mysteries of Udolpho* and ancient abbeys.

Like Catherine too who pores over the pages of *Udolpho* "lost from all worldly concerns of dressing and dinner" (*NA*, 51), Bertha is engrossed in her book, oblivious hour after hour to the town life and pleasant spring weather outside her dim room. After an entire day sitting over her book she has an "aching neck and swimming eyes" and is "dazed with saintly imageries" (55–6). A canceled line calls her a "maiden lost in dizzy maze" (*Poems*, 321). She is like Madeline in *The Eve of St. Agnes* who is "Hoodwink'd with faery fancy" (70). Keats's description of Bertha also recalls Lydia Languish and other girls in the Quixotic tradition, including Catherine Morland, whose brains have been "turn'd" by their reading.[30] Jack Stillinger argues that Bertha is similar to other "dreamers and pursuers of ritual" in Keats's poems, all of whom Keats regards as foolish for being "so wrapped up in an impossible ideal that they turn away from life itself." Stillinger characterizes *Isabella*, *The Eve of St. Agnes*, and *The Eve of St. Mark* as "anti-romances," the term Peter DeRose applies to *Northanger Abbey*. Stillinger also claims that "[Samuel] Johnson's phrase in the title of chapter 44 of *Rasselas*, 'The Dangerous Prevalence of Imagination,'"—the same chapter that DeRose and Tave ally with *Northanger Abbey* and *Emma*—"could serve as a capsule thematization of Keats's major poems from *The Eve of St. Agnes* through *Lamia*."[31]

In *Lamia*, Lycius is ambushed by the duplicitous Lamia when he is abstracted in thought, "His phantasy ... lost, where reason fades, / In the calm'd twilight of Platonic shades" (235–6). In this poem, a young man rather than a woman is made vulnerable to seduction by his abandonment of "reason" and gravitation toward otherworldly ideals. Later in the poem Lycius's former teacher, the scientific philosopher Apollonius, fights Lamia for possession of Lycius's soul in an allegory that pits reason and empiricism against the charms of imagination. Apollonius thus performs a role similar to that of the pedagogical Mr. Knightley as he (Apollonius) seeks to save his pupil from the errors he has fallen into by allowing himself to be seduced by an illusion.

Clearly Keats and the other Romantic poets share Austen's fear of the errors to which the imagination, often fed by improbable, sensational literature, could lead

---

[30]   Sheridan, *The Rivals*, 4.2.32. Keats refers to *The Rivals* frequently in his letters (1:245, 290; 2:29, 180).

[31]   Jack Stillinger, *The Hoodwinking of Madeline and Other Essays on Keats's Poems* (Urbana: University of Illinois Press, 1971), 97–8, 37, 45; DeRose, 71, 67; Tave, *Some Words*, 210; Jack Stillinger, "Keats and Coleridge," in *Coleridge, Keats, and the Imagination*, ed. J. Robert Barth and John L. Mahoney (Columbia: University of Missouri Press, 1990); rpt. in Stillinger, *Romantic Complexity: Keats, Coleridge, and Wordsworth* (Urbana: University of Illinois Press, 2006), 41. My article, "Madeline at Northanger Abbey," makes many of the points presented here on parallels between *Northanger Abbey*, *The Eve of St. Agnes*, and *The Eve of St. Mark*.

people, causing them to ignore both the legitimate dangers and the satisfactions available in this world. Evidence of a distrust of imagination, especially a visionary form, and an appreciation of empiricism, reason, the ability to distinguish truth from illusion, and the importance of maintaining a firm foothold in the actual world can be found in the works of Wordsworth, Coleridge, Byron, Shelley, and Keats. In exploring the dangers that befall those who dwell too long or travel too far in the realm of imagination, Austen is treating a central Romantic theme.[32]

## The Uses of Imagination

*Sympathy*

If the male poets, like Austen, at times distrust the imagination, Austen, along with the male poets, endorses forms of imaginative activity. One such imaginative capacity that Austen and the male poets celebrate is the ability to enter into the thoughts and feelings of others, commonly referred to as the sympathetic imagination. The idea that sympathy for others is bound up with the imagination developed throughout the eighteenth century; one of the major proponents of this concept was Adam Smith, whose *Theory of Moral Sentiments* (1759) declares in its opening pages, "Though our brother is upon the rack.... it is by the imagination only that we can form any conception of what are his sensations.... By the imagination we place ourselves in his situation ... we enter as it were into his body, and become in some measure the same person with him."[33] As James Engell notes, Smith's *Theory of Moral Sentiments* "was hugely influential" on later writers such as Hazlitt and Percy Bysshe Shelley. Engell further lists Coleridge, Wordsworth, and Keats as Romantic writers who share in the legacy of eighteenth-century theories of the sympathetic imagination.[34]

Although Austen is not included in Engell's discussion of the sympathetic imagination, her works like those of her male contemporaries reflect an engagement with this popular concept. Peter Knox-Shaw argues for the influence of Adam Smith's *Theory of Moral Sentiments* on Austen's thought and finds many parallels

---

[32]    L. J. Swingle protests that those who consider Austen un-Romantic because she "explodes illusions" ignore evidence of the same concerns in the work of the male poets ("The Poets, the Novelists, and the English Romantic Situation," *The Wordsworth Circle* 10 [1979]: 218).

[33]    Adam Smith, *The Theory of Moral Sentiments*, ed. D. D. Raphael and A. L. Macfie (Oxford: Clarendon Press, 1976), 9.

[34]    Engell, 149–50, 143. Engell traces the history of the sympathetic imagination throughout the eighteenth century in chap. 11: "The Psyche Reaches Out: Sympathy." See also the sections on sympathy in Engell's chapters on Hazlitt (198–200), Shelley (256–8), and Keats (285–8).

between that work and Austen's novels.[35] All of Austen's vindicated heroines (those who initially are unappreciated and eventually are recognized and rewarded for their virtues) possess the capacity for entering into the feelings of other people, which often distinguishes them from other, less empathic characters. Elinor Dashwood pays attention to the needs of others such as Colonel Brandon, Mrs. Jennings, and even her brother and sister-in-law while her sister Marianne remains wrapped up in her own concerns and rudely ignores those around her. Anne Elliot is the confidant of everyone at Uppercross because she is such a sympathetic listener, unlike her self-involved sister Mary. Fanny Price, despite the fact that she is judgmental about many characters, can not help entering into the sufferings of even those who mistreat her, such as Julia Bertram and her Aunt Norris.[36] It is this quality too that Austen's misguided heroines often need to cultivate. Emma's mistaken assumptions that Mr. Elton is in love with Harriet, Jane Fairfax with Mr. Dixon, Frank Churchill with herself, and Harriet with Frank Churchill, result from her inability truly to identify with others and, in Morgan's words, to "put herself in someone else's place."[37] In the scene in which Mr. Knightley eventually proposes to her, Emma initially obstructs their mutual understanding and happiness. She fears he is going to confess his love for Harriet and tells him not to speak further. When she perceives the pain she has caused him by halting his conversation, however, she overcomes her selfish concern for her own feelings and urges him to confide in her, whereupon she is rewarded by hearing him declare his love for herself. Once she begins to focus on Mr. Knightley instead of on her own preconceptions, she quickly and accurately perceives the truth of his feelings, for "While he spoke, Emma's mind was most busy, and, with all the wonderful velocity of thought, had been able—and yet without losing a word—to catch and comprehend the exact truth of the whole; to see … that Harriet was nothing; that she was every thing herself" (430). Emma does not need to learn to suppress her imagination but to use it to enter into the thoughts and feelings of others and thereby judge character and motives more accurately than she does when she inserts others into her preconceived plots.[38]

---

[35]    Peter Knox-Shaw, *Jane Austen and the Enlightenment* (Cambridge: Cambridge University Press, 2004), especially 133–50. See also Kenneth L. Moler, "The Bennet Girls and Adam Smith on Vanity and Pride," *Philological Quarterly* 46 (1967): 567–9. Although the latter article is not concerned with the issue of sympathy, it provides convincing evidence of Austen's familiarity with Smith's *Theory*.

[36]    Francis Hart notes that Fanny's "sympathetic projection is an involuntary and often painful insight into others" that "knows no limits" ("The Spaces of Privacy: Jane Austen," *Nineteenth-Century Fiction* 30 [1975]: 327–8).

[37]    Morgan, 28.

[38]    Deresiewicz says that "Given what [Emma] thinks [Mr. Knightly] is going to say" in the proposal scene "and what she has already discovered about her own feelings," her encouragement of him to confide in her "is the most self-sacrificing thing she can do" (123). Elsewhere Deresiewicz insists that "*Emma* does not condemn the imagination, it

Although Emma does err in the novel by projecting onto others her own desires, her ultimate ability to override her ego has been prepared for by many previous scenes that demonstrate her capacity for identification with others. In a work filled with characters confined by their own points of view, Emma actually emerges as one of those most capable of empathy. Her father, for example, is "never able to suppose that other people could feel differently from himself" (8) and so would starve his guests because he himself dislikes rich food. Emma, who is better able to perceive others' wishes, helps her father's visitors to "large slices of cake and full glasses of wine" (213). John Knightley, who hates being away from home, cannot comprehend Mr. Elton's delight at the prospect of being snowed in at the Weston's house over Christmas or Mr. Weston's willingness to come to a party at Hartfield after he has been away in London all day (115, 302–3). Mrs. Elton "fanc[ies] herself at" her sister's home, Maple Grove, when she visits Hartfield (272). As Tave notes, she thereby illustrates a "closed imagination" that cannot conceive of anything beyond her own narrow sphere.[39]

Emma, by contrast, frequently does enter into the feelings of others. Her care for her father illustrates her ability to understand and promote the happiness of someone wholly different from herself in temperament and needs. When she visits a poor family, the narrator comments that "Emma was very compassionate.... She understood their [the poor's] ways" and "entered into their troubles with ready sympathy" (86). Her reflections after the visit, that the sight of such genuine deprivation made her own troubles appear trifling, are juxtaposed with Harriet's insincere and clichéd response, "'Very true ... Poor creatures! one can think of nothing else'" (87). Clearly Emma is much more genuinely moved by her encounter with the poor family than Harriet is. Moreover, when Emma discovers that she has grossly erred by imagining that Mr. Elton is in love with Harriet, her first and paramount regret is not for herself but for the "evil" she has done to her friend (134).[40] Emma's eventual reformation is not so much a change of character as it is a triumph of the better qualities she has exhibited all along, especially her ability to transcend her own identity and imaginatively project herself into those of other people.

For as Morgan notes, Austen like the male Romantics believed in the imagination as a moral agent essential to our ability to sympathize with and love others.[41] As Shelley in "A Defence of Poetry" famously declared, "A man, to be greatly good, must imagine intensely and comprehensively; he must put himself in the place of another and of many others.... The great instrument of

---

only condemns its misuse by the heroine. In fact, it celebrates the imagination ... because the imagination is the faculty that enables us to rejuvenate ourselves, our world, and our relationships with other" (114).

[39]    Tave, *Some Words*, 224.

[40]    Moler notes Emma's "magnanimity" in thinking of Harriet rather than of "her own humiliation" after Mr. Elton's proposal (*Jane Austen's Art of Allusion*, 171).

[41]    Morgan, 49–50.

moral good is the imagination" (517). Both Shelley and Hazlitt, as mentioned previously, were influenced in their thinking about the sympathetic imagination by Smith's *Theory of Moral Sentiments*.[42] Hazlitt's *Essay on the Principles of Human Action* sought to refute Hobbes's claim that human beings are inherently selfish by demonstrating that, in order to calculate their interests, people must project themselves into their own futures, and this ability to identify with one's future self is the same imaginative act as that of identifying with other people. According to Hazlitt, the tendency to enter into the perspectives of others, whether other people or one's future self, is one of the most common habits of the human mind, which therefore can be considered "naturally disinterested" rather than inherently selfish (the subtitle of Hazlitt's work is "An Argument in Defence of the Natural Disinterestedness of the Human Mind").

Keats read Hazlitt's *Essay on the Principles of Human Action* and adopted Hazlitt's term "disinterestedness" for this aspect of the imagination's ability to override ego and care for other people. "Very few men have ever arrived at a complete disinterestedness of Mind," Keats writes to his brother and sister-in-law; "very few have been influenced by a pure desire of the benefit of others" (*Letters*, 2:79). Keats clearly regards disinterestedness as a moral as well as a creative attribute, since he claims it "does hold & grasp the tip top of any spiritual honours, that can be paid to any thing in this world," even beyond "works of genius," and he names Socrates and Jesus as the historical figures who best exemplify this ideal (*Letters*, 1:205; 2:80).[43] Debbie Lee cites together Keats's remarks on disinterestedness and on the selfless poetical character as expressing the same belief, which is that "the imaginative mind produced the self distanced from its own ego."[44]

---

[42]   For the influence of Smith on Hazlitt, see also Roy E. Cain, "David Hume and Adam Smith as Sources of the Concept of Sympathy in Hazlitt," *Papers on Language and Literature* 1 (1965): 133–40.

[43]   See also *Letters*, 1:293; 2:129, 279. W. J. Bate provides a useful account of the concept of disinterestedness in Keats's thinking, including its origins in Hazlitt's writings (*John Keats* [Cambridge: Harvard University Press, 1963], 201–2, 228, 237–40, 255–61, 473–6, 586–7, 597–601).

[44]   Debbie Lee, *Slavery and the Romantic Imagination* (Philadelphia: University of Pennsylvania Press, 2002), 31. Lee like Engell provides an overview of the history of the sympathetic imagination, which she also refers to as the moral, disinterested, or distanced imagination (31–5; 231n.13). Like Engell, too, Lee does not include Austen in her list of Romantic writers who draw upon this concept. One of the goals of my work on Jane Austen and the male poets is to encourage others to include Austen in more studies of Romantic thought and literary practices. See below for Keats's remarks on the selfless poetical character.

*The Shakespearean, Chameleon Writer*

The male poets, like Austen, consider the sympathetic imagination an essential component of human love and morality; they also celebrate it as a key element in the creative process. Frequently the male poets speak of the writer as a chameleon or ventriloquist who loses his own identity as he enters into those of his characters, and Shakespeare is often cited as the chief exemplar of this ability. Thus Coleridge compares Shakespeare to Proteus and contrasts Shakespeare's poetry, which "is characterless; that is, it does not reflect the individual Shakespeare" to Milton's, which expresses the author's own personality; "John Milton himself," states Coleridge, "is in every line of the *Paradise Lost*."[45] Hazlitt similarly extols the impersonality of Shakespeare's art. "He was the least of an egotist that it was possible to be," states Hazlitt. Moreover, "There was no respect of persons with him. His genius shone equally on the evil and on the good, on the wise and the foolish, the monarch and the beggar." Shakespeare, says Hazlitt, "may be said, for the time, to identify himself with the character he wishes to represent, and to pass from one to another, like the same soul successively animating different bodies. By an art like that of the ventriloquist, he throws his imagination out of himself, and makes every word appear to proceed from the mouth of the person in whose name it is given."[46]

Hazlitt's formulations helped to shape Keats's concept of the identityless poet of Negative Capability, again most effectively represented by Shakespeare (see *Letters*, 1:193–4, 223–5). Keats defined the poetical character as having "no self—it is every thing and nothing—It has no character—it enjoys light and shade; it lives in gusto, be it foul or fair, high or low, rich or poor, mean or elevated— It has as much delight in conceiving an Iago as an Imogen. What shocks the virtuous philosop[h]er, delights the camelion Poet" (*Letters*, 1:387). Shelley too characterized poets as "a very camaeleonic race," and Thomas Jefferson Hogg remarked Shelley's "disposition and habit to adopt the situation, the feelings, the colour of other persons." In Shelley, Hogg writes, "the poetic faculty of turning himself mentally into the subject of his poem, of metamorphosing himself internally into an attendant spirit, into Titania, Queen Mab herself, was conspicuous and astonishing."[47]

---

[45]    Samuel Taylor Coleridge, *Table Talk*, ed. Carl Woodring, 2 vols (Princeton: Princeton University Press, 1990), 1:125. For Coleridge's comparison of Shakespeare to Proteus see *Lectures 1808–1819 On Literature*, 1:69–70, 225 and *Biographia Literaria*, ed. James Engell and Walter Jackson Bate, 2 vols. (Princeton: Princeton University Press, 1983), 2:27–8 and 27n.2.

[46]    *The Complete Works of William Hazlitt*, ed. P. P. Howe, 21 vols (London: J. M. Dent, 1930), 5:47, 50.

[47]    *The Letters of Percy Bysshe Shelley*, ed. Frederick L. Jones, 2 vols (Oxford: Clarendon Press, 1964), 2:308. Hogg's remarks are quoted in Teddi Chichester Bonca, *Shelley's Mirrors of Love: Narcissism, Sacrifice, and Sorority* (Albany: State University of

Catherine — excessive imagination —
Henry as teacher – sympathetic imagination —

Even Wordsworth and Byron, who for Hazlitt and Keats exemplified the egoism of modern poetry, at times extol the sympathetic imagination and selfless poet. In the Preface to *Lyrical Ballads*, Wordsworth writes that the poet "bring[s] his feelings near to those of the persons whose feelings he describes, nay, for short spaces of time, perhaps ... let[s] himself slip into an entire delusion, and even confound and identify his own feelings with theirs" (453). In *Childe Harold's Pilgrimage*, Canto 3, Byron speaks of the pleasure of losing himself in his creations. Authorship is appealing, he says, for "in creating [we] live / A being more intense, that we endow / With form our fancy, gaining as we give / The life we imagine, even as I do now. / What am I? Nothing; but not so art thou, / Soul of my thought!" (3.6). Later in Canto 3 he expresses a similar pleasure in the loss of self he experiences in the natural world: "I live not in myself, but I become / Portion of that around me" (3.72). Perhaps a more central concept for Byron is expressed in Canto 16 of *Don Juan*, which celebrates "what is called mobility," or the condition of being "strongly acted on by what is nearest," a trait common among "actors, artists, and romancers" (16.97–8). In a note to the passage Byron elaborates, explaining that mobility "may be defined as an excessive susceptibility of immediate impressions" (*Complete Poetical Works*, 5:769). Critics have commented on the relevance of Byron's remarks on mobility to his own character, for his feelings and opinions shifted in accordance with his circumstances and companions. Indeed, Lady Blessington labeled Byron "a perfect chameleon" because of his changeable nature, and Susan Wolfson compares this quality in Byron to Keats's ideal of Negative Capability.[48]

Clearly the Romantic poets regarded the sympathetic imagination as essential to creativity and exalted those who possessed this capacity as the supreme poetic geniuses. The Romantic writer who best exemplifies this ideal of the selfless, Protean creator, however, is not one of the poets but the age's major novelist, Jane Austen. This point is made by nineteenth-century reviewers of Austen's work, who frequently compare her to Shakespeare in terms that recall those of Hazlitt and the male poets. Richard Whately in 1821 writes that Austen follows "the important maxim ... illustrated by Homer, and ... enforced by Aristotle, of saying as little as possible in her own person, and giving a dramatic air to the narrative, by introducing frequent conversations; which she conducts with a regard to character hardly exceeded even by Shakspeare himself. Like him, she shows as admirable

---

NewYork Press, 1999), 91. Bonca provides an extensive analysis of Shelley's impressibility, which she compares to Keats's concept of the egoless poetical character and to Byron's concept of mobility (88–95, 252–3n.51). Bonca also comments on the ways in which this quality in the male poets evokes conventionally feminine characteristics of permeable ego boundaries and susceptibility to other people and impressions.

48    Susan Wolfson, "'Their She Condition': Cross-Dressing and the Politics of Gender in *Don Juan*," *ELH* 54 (1987): 602–3; see also 589–91. Lady Blessington's remark is quoted in Wolfson, 603. On Byron's mobility see also Fischer, 76 and Bonca, cited in the previous note.

a discrimination in the characters of fools as of people of sense; a merit which is far from common."[49] Just as Hazlitt praised Shakespeare's ability to enter equally into the characters of "the wise and the foolish, the monarch and the beggar" and Keats insisted on the poet's equal "delight in conceiving an Iago as an Imogen," so Whately extols Austen's successful depictions of fools as well as "people of sense." Thomas Babbington Macaulay in 1843 had "no hesitation in placing Jane Austen" as the English writer who "approached nearest to the manner of the great master" Shakespeare in her ability to create wholly convincing, individualized characters.[50] Finally, George Henry Lewes on several occasions compared Austen to Shakespeare. In an 1847 article in *Fraser's Magazine* Lewes contrasts Austen to Sir Walter Scott, whom he calls "the Ariosto of prose romance" (recalling Keats's association of Scott and Ariosto with the romance genre). Scott is an admirable novelist, writes Lewes, "but he was not a Shakspeare: he had not that singular faculty of penetrating into the most secret recesses of the heart, and of shewing us a character in its inward and outward workings." Austen, however, did have this faculty; she is "a prose Shakspeare." In his 1859 *Blackwood's* article on "The Novels of Jane Austen," Lewes twice uses the term "dramatic ventriloquism" to characterize Austen's power, and he repeats the comparison to Shakespeare. "Instead of telling us what her characters are, and what they feel," Lewes writes, "she presents the people, and they reveal themselves. In this she has never perhaps been surpassed, not even by Shakespeare himself."[51] The male Romantic poets celebrate those works in which the author's identity is subsumed in his creations, but in their own lyric poems they often had trouble achieving this essentially dramatic effect. Jane Austen is the Romantic age's supreme exemplar of the Shakespearean, Negatively Capable writer.[52]

*Validity of Imagination*

In other respects the idea that Austen's novels denounce imagination and favor sober good sense can be qualified. Austen does not endorse a literalist approach to reality. Such an approach is exemplified by Admiral Croft in *Persuasion*, who delivers a critique of a painting he sees of a boat that could not possibly be seaworthy (169). He expresses a realistic aesthetic that values in art only what is empirically accurate. Admiral Croft, however, though kind and sensible, can

---

[49]   *Jane Austen: The Critical Heritage*, 97–8.

[50]   *Jane Austen: The Critical Heritage*, 122–3.

[51]   *Jane Austen: The Critical Heritage*, 125, 157, 162.

[52]   Clayton notes a connection between Keats's celebration of the selfless poetical character and the Shakespearean qualities of Austen's novels (74–5). Clayton insists, however, that "Although [Austen's] work clearly possesses some affinities with other works written in the period, she is not a Romantic" (60). One wonders how many affinities a writer must have with contemporaries in order to be classified among them.

hardly be held up as a spokesman for Austen's own views.[53] He cannot remember Louisa and Henrietta Musgrove's names or distinguish the two sisters from one another, and he is completely imperceptive to the emotional and psychological drama taking place in the inner lives of his brother-in-law Captain Wentworth and of the woman he is walking beside, Anne Elliot. Likewise, Catherine Morland's mother is completely devoid of imagination ("her family were plain matter-of-fact people" Catherine reflects [*NA*, 65–6]) and as a result does not suspect the truth when her daughter returns home suffering from a wounded heart. Mrs. Morland believes Catherine is pining for the luxurious lifestyle of Northanger Abbey and as a remedy seeks out the sober prose of a moralistic essay from *The Mirror* (*NA*, 241). Literalist characters in Austen are poor at judging human nature, which as we have seen requires an imaginative ability to enter into the thoughts and feelings of others.

The same point can be made in relation to Catherine herself. At the beginning of the novel, Catherine is guilty not of an overactive imagination but of excessive literalism. She perpetually mistakes Isabella Thorpe's meaning, to Isabella's annoyance, by taking her comments at face value. For example, when Isabella disingenuously tells Catherine she does not want to be followed by two young men in the Pump Room, Catherine believes her and reports "with unaffected pleasure … [that] the gentlemen had just left the Pump-room" (*NA*, 42–3), whereupon Isabella quickly goes off in pursuit of them. Catherine also is befuddled by Henry Tilney's playful comparison of dancing to a marriage; she insists that the two conditions "are so very different.—I cannot look upon them at all in the same light, nor think the same duties belong to them" (*NA*, 77). More seriously, Catherine cannot understand how Captain Tilney can flirt with Isabella when he knows she is plighted to another or how Isabella can accept Captain Tilney's attentions while she is engaged. Catherine's literal-minded approach to what other people say and do prevents her from understanding them. One can say that Catherine's reading of Gothic novels actually contributes to her growth, as those works initiate her into the darker side of human nature and train her to interpret people, appearances, and events instead of merely accepting these at face value.[54] Similarly, the Gothic story Catherine invents about General Tilney and his wife can be considered a reflection of her mental progress, as it indicates a more sophisticated mode of assessing other people and interpreting her own and others' experiences than she has exhibited previously.

One can go even further and claim, as many critics have, that although *Northanger Abbey* on one level debunks Catherine's Gothic fantasy, in many other respects it appears to validate her invention. Catherine's tale of a cruel

---

[53]    Morgan (12–15) makes a similar point.

[54]    Maria Jerinic, in somewhat different terms, argues that Catherine's reading of Gothic novels is beneficial rather than detrimental to her ("In Defense of the Gothic: Rereading *Northanger Abbey*," in *Jane Austen and the Discourses of Feminism*, ed. Devoney Looser [New York: St. Martin's Press, 1995], 140–41).

General Tilney who oppresses and imprisons his wife is ultimately not far from the truth of the Tilneys' marriage or of many marriages in the patriarchal culture of the time. In seeking to understand the family she wishes to join and to anticipate her own destiny, Catherine constructs a narrative that accurately depicts female powerlessness and masculine tyranny within the family. In other respects Catherine's actual experience in the novel ends up conforming to Gothic conventions, for she does turn out to be a heroine in distress who is persecuted by a villainous father-figure when General Tilney evicts her from his house, and she and Henry are also cruelly separated and forbidden to marry by his father. One can say that *Northanger Abbey*, especially when read with attention to the subtext, does celebrate Catherine's flight of imagination, which constructs an accurate tale of the imbalance of power between men and women in her culture.[55]

As with *Northanger Abbey*, one can also find evidence in *Emma* that qualifies the novel's apparent condemnation of its heroine's wayward imagination. For one thing, Emma is never completely cured of her tendency to arrange matches. Even after her supposed final recantation of her impulse "to arrange everybody's destiny" (413), we find her contemplating a union between Mrs. Taylor's infant daughter and either of her two nephews (461). Moreover, for all her blunders Emma meets with very little serious punishment. As Claudia Johnson notes, Mr. Knightley never even learns about the majority of her fantasies and their potentially damaging consequences (he does not know that Mr. Elton proposed to Emma or that Harriet fell in love with himself, nor is he aware that Emma imagined Frank and Harriet as well as Jane Fairfax and Mr. Dixon as romantic couples), and he actually loves her for her "brilliancy," which makes her more interesting than her sweet but conventional sister (*Emma*, 433).[56] When Mr. Knightley rebukes Emma during the Box Hill outing, it is for her narcissism and cruelty to Miss Bates, which can be considered a failure of imagination or ability to enter into the feelings of another on Emma's part. Lionel Trilling claims that readers feel kindly toward Emma because "many of her wrong judgments and actions are directed to a very engaging end," which is that "life be vivid and shapely." This impulse, Trilling

---

[55]    Critics who argue that *Northanger Abbey* actually does validate Catherine's Gothic fantasy include George Levine, "Translating the Monstrous: *Northanger Abbey*," *Nineteenth-Century Fiction* 30 (1975): 335–50; Sandra M. Gilbert and Susan Gubar, *The Madwoman in the Attic: The Woman Writer and the Nineteenth-Century Literary Imagination* (New Haven: Yale University Press, 1979), 135–45; Judith Wilt, *Ghosts of the Gothic: Austen, Eliot, and Lawrence* (Princeton: Princeton University Press, 1980), 121–51; Claudia L. Johnson, *Jane Austen: Women, Politics, and the Novel* (Chicago: University of Chicago Press, 1988), 34–41; Paul Morrison, "Enclosed in Openness: *Northanger Abbey* and the Domestic Carceral," *Texas Studies in Literature and Language* 33 (1991): 1–23; Jacqueline Howard, *Reading Gothic Fiction: A Bakhtinian Approach* (Oxford: Clarendon Press, 1994), 145–82; Seeber, 116–26; and Galperin, 85–6, 149–51.

[56]    Johnson, 140–42.

concludes, "is, in its essence, a poet's demand."[57] In other words, according to Trilling, Emma's chief appeal lies in her imaginative approach to life.

In addition, as in *Northanger Abbey*, the outcome of the novel actually conforms in many ways to the heroine's romantic fancies. If Harriet does not marry a man as socially distinguished as Mr. Elton or Frank Churchill, she still improves her status by marrying Robert Martin, who loves her so devotedly that he (like Mr. Darcy, that other ardent and highly eligible suitor) proposes to her a second time after she has initially refused him. In addition, the marriages of Miss Taylor and Mr. Weston (which Emma helped to foster) and of Jane Fairfax and Frank Churchill conform to the plot that Emma devised for Harriet: that of a disadvantaged young woman who marries a man of superior wealth and social status. Moler contrasts *Emma* to other works in the female Quixote tradition that oppose the romantic heroine's fantasy world with a dull, often harsh world of sober reality. Unlike the writers of these works, Moler argues, Austen refuses to set up an "antithesis between romance and reality, between the worlds of imagination and reason." Reality in *Emma*, "while it does not always conform to the standards of romance, nevertheless includes … an imaginatively satisfying element of romance," which serves as "a partial vindication of Emma's romantic imagination."[58]

*Conflicts and Ambivalence*

Certainly a tension exists in the idea of Austen castigating Emma for inventing stories of other people's love affairs, for that is exactly what Austen herself does. The irony of Austen condemning the exercise of imagination in *Northanger Abbey* and *Emma* is similar to that of Coleridge declaring the loss of his imagination in accomplished poems such as *Dejection* and *To William Wordsworth*. The performances themselves call into question the supposed messages of these works. One conclusion is that Austen has mixed feelings about the imagination she herself indulges, now approving it and now suspecting it of ethical and epistemological errors. She may also have felt obligated by social pressures to condemn female creativity, although details in her novels betray covert sympathy for it. Gilbert and Gubar speak of "Austen's self-division—her fascination with the imagination and her anxiety that it is unfeminine."[59]

If Austen conveys conflicted messages about the imagination, however, the same is true of many of the male poets. As mentioned previously, many of Coleridge's works express ambivalence about the creative mind, now extolling and now undermining its effects. Moreover, just as Austen may have feared transgressing codes of female decorum by overtly championing creativity in young women,

---

[57]   Lionel Trilling, "Emma," *Encounter* 8.6 (1957); rpt. in *Jane Austen: Critical Assessments*, ed. Ian Littlewood, vol. 4: *Mansfield Park*; *Emma*; *Persuasion*; *Sanditon* (Mountfield, East Sussex: Helm Information, 1998), 221.

[58]   Moler, *Jane Austen's Art of Allusion*, 182.

[59]   Gilbert and Gubar, 161.

so Coleridge feared being regarded as un-Christian if he boldly claimed godlike powers for the inspired poet. *The Eolian Harp* specifically invokes Christian precepts of humility and original sin in its recantation of statements earlier in the poem celebrating the human mind's ability to attain sublime truths. David Perkins claims that the figure of Sara in *The Eolian Harp* performs a role similar to that of the man from Porlock in the Preface to *Kubla Khan*, as well as the "friend" at the end of chapter 13 of *Biographia Literaria* who advises Coleridge not to publish his disquisition on the imagination: all represent "ordinary human beings" who put an end to Coleridge's meditations when they threaten to become transgressive by depicting "poetry and the poet as rivaling the creative power of God and/or of the demonic."[60] Both Coleridge and Austen may have qualified or disguised their support for a creative imagination out of deference to belief systems dominant at the time that counseled humility and submission to higher authority.

Similarly, one can compare Byron's refusal to take himself seriously as a poet in remarks such as those quoted above to Jane Austen's self-deprecating representation of herself as a writer, as when she contrasts her nephew's "strong, manly, spirited [literary] Sketches, full of Variety & Glow" to the "little bit (two Inches wide) of Ivory on which I work with so fine a Brush, as produces little effect after much labour," and her insistence to James Stanier Clarke that "I think I may boast myself to be, with all possible Vanity, the most unlearned, & uninformed Female who ever dared to be an Authoress."[61] Robert Gleckner protests the tendency of readers to take at face value Byron's indifference to his poetry as expressed in his letters and journals, which Gleckner attributes to the private man's "eagerness … to dissociate himself from poetry as a serious occupation" in keeping with aristocratic convention.[62] Both Austen and Byron may have been inhibited by their society's beliefs about proper behavior for ladies and gentlemen from publicly acknowledging the seriousness with which they regarded their art.

Keats's oeuvre also reflects conflicts in thinking about the visionary imagination. Although it is possible to interpret his career as a process of steadily questioning and rejecting an imagination that transports one away from the actual world, upon closer examination of his poems a more complex picture emerges.[63]

---

[60]    David Perkins, "The Imaginative Vision of *Kubla Khan*: On Coleridge's Introductory Note," in *Coleridge, Keats, and the Imagination: Romanticism and Adam's Dream*, ed. J. Robert Barth, S. J., and John L. Mahoney (Columbia: University of Missouri Press, 1990), 106.

[61]    *Jane Austen's Letters*, ed. Deidre Le Faye, 3rd ed. (Oxford: Oxford University Press, 1995), 323, 306.

[62]    Gleckner, xv–xvi.

[63]    Stillinger has most directly and consistently interpreted Keats's career as a steady rejection of the visionary imagination and embrace of a commonsensical and realistic world view. See especially the essays collected in *The Hoodwinking of Madeline and Other Essays on Keats's Poems*. Critics who qualify Stillinger's scheme and argue for a more ambivalent attitude on Keats's part toward the imagination and romance include Stuart

The very fact that virtually all of his major poems feature as their central conflict the pull of an imaginary realm versus the claims of the real indicates that the debate remained powerful and ongoing for Keats. Certain poems are especially ambivalent in their treatment of imagination. *The Eve of St. Agnes*, as discussed previously, exposes the foolishness of Madeline's absorption in romantic myths that promise her a vision of her future husband. In another sense, however, it can be said that Madeline's trust in the visionary imagination is vindicated. She desires a dream of the man she will marry, and not only does she dream of him but she wakes to find him actually beside her (see especially stanza 35). Earl Wasserman argues that the poem expresses Keats's belief in a transcendent imagination and connects it to the 22 November 1817 letter in which Keats declares his faith in "the authenticity of the Imagination," which "may be compared to Adam's dream—he awoke and found it truth."[64] Just as *Northanger Abbey* and *Emma* may be read as both condemning and validating the heroines' Gothic or romantic inventions, so *The Eve of St. Agnes* has been interpreted as both ridiculing and validating Madeline's trust in romantic visions.

In the late poem *Lamia*, the dangerous lure of fantasy is represented by the snake-woman Lamia, who is exposed and destroyed by the rational philosopher Apollonius. Instead of depicting this triumph of empirical truth over illusion as an unqualified good, however, the poem conveys profound ambivalence about this outcome, characterizing Apollonius as cold and harsh and Lamia as a sympathetic victim when she "withers" under the "potency" of the philosopher's unrelenting gaze (2.290). The narrator interrupts his story to deliver a critique of "cold philosophy" or rational, empirical thinking, which by offering a scientific explanation of the rainbow and other natural phenomena has emptied the world of "charms" and "mysteries" (2.229–38). Apollonius is even described as having "lashless eyelids stretch[ing] / Around his demon eyes!" (2.288–9), suggesting that he is actually the evil, serpentine being rather than Lamia. The result of Apollonius's assault on Lamia is that not only does she vanish but Lycius dies, suggesting the latter's inability to survive without the pleasure afforded by his mysterious, beautiful lady. Just as *Emma* for many readers is the animating force of Highbury whose lively mind we do not wish to see completely tamed by the rational Mr. Knightley, so Lamia emerges as a sympathetic figure and vital force, qualifying the poem's ostensible rejection of the imaginary realm she represents.

---

Sperry, "Romance as Wish-Fulfillment: *The Eve of St. Agnes*," in *Keats the Poet* (Princeton: Princeton University Press, 1973), 198–220; Robert Kern, "Keats and the Problem of Romance," *Philological Quarterly* 58 (1979): 171–91; Patricia A. Parker, *Inescapable Romance: Studies in the Poetics of a Mode* (Princeton: Princeton University Press, 1979), chap. 4 (see especially 159–67); Susan J. Wolfson, *The Questioning Presence: Wordsworth, Keats, and the Interrogative Mode in Romantic Poetry* (Ithaca: Cornell University Press, 1986), chap. 12.

64    *Letters*, 1:184–5. Earl Wasserman, *The Finer Tone: Keats' Major Poems* (Baltimore: The Johns Hopkins University Press, 1953), 101–3.

Wordsworth too expresses ambivalence about the imagination. He frequently celebrates its godlike creativity, as when he writes in *The Prelude* that "Of genius, power, / Creation and divinity itself / I have been speaking, for my theme has been / What passed within me" ([1850] 3.173–6) and that minds which "from their native selves can send abroad ... transformation" are "truly from the Deity, / For they are powers" (13.93–4, 106–7).[65] In many other poems, however, as we have seen, Wordsworth expresses fears and doubts about the reliability and morality of this same faculty. Similarly, Shelley's *Alastor* has been read as an ambivalent work that portrays the Poet's quest for the veiled maid as both admirable and as tragically misguided, and the maid herself as both a figment of the Poet's imagination and as an authentic being. As Michael O'Neill notes, Shelley's text "allows us, non-logically perhaps, to entertain two conflicting notions [about the veiled maid] at the same time."[66] If Jane Austen's novels convey tensions in their treatment of the imagination, expressing both distrust and faith in this faculty, the same is true of the poems of many of her male contemporaries.

*Celebration of the Creative Imagination*

It is true that Austen wrote no literary manifestos such as Wordsworth's Preface to *Lyrical Ballads*, Coleridge's *Biographia Literaria*, or Shelley's "Defense of Poetry," which contain passages boldly extolling the godlike (or legislator-like) power of the artist. Can anyone really doubt, however, that Austen gloried in her own creativity? Twice in her letters she refers to her novels as her darling children. On 25 April 1811, while *Sense and Sensibility* was going through the press, she wrote, "I am never too busy to think of S&S. I can no more forget it, than a mother can forget her sucking child." When she received her first published copy of *Pride and Prejudice* she told her sister Cassandra, "I have got my own darling Child from London" (*Letters*, 182, 201). She also continued to imagine her characters' lives after the novels in which they appear had been published. In May 1813, when she attended an exhibition of paintings in London, she amused herself with searching for portraits that reminded her of Jane and Elizabeth Bennet (*Letters*, 212), and according to family tradition, she would if asked explain subsequent events in her characters' lives, such as that "Miss Steele never succeeded in catching the Doctor; that Kitty Bennet was satisfactorily married to a clergyman near Pemberley, while

---

[65]    *The Prelude* is quoted from *The Prelude, 1799, 1805, 1850*, ed. Jonathan Wordsworth, M. H. Abrams, and Stephen Gill (New York: Norton, 1970). Unless otherwise noted, the 1805 text is cited.

[66]    Michael O'Neill, *The Human Mind's Imaginings: Conflict and Achievement in Shelley's Poetry* (Oxford: Clarendon Press, 1989), 19. Lucy Newlyn explores Shelley's conflicted treatment of both the morality and the dangers of imagination in *Alastor* and other poems (244–50). Of *Alastor* she concludes that, "If this is a difficult poem to place, that is because it allows the coexistence of two kinds of discourse, which contradict each other" (249).

Mary obtained nothing higher than one of her uncle Philips' clerks."[67] Clearly Austen took great pride and enjoyment in the creatures of her own invention, and they continued to live with her alongside her flesh-and-blood relatives and friends after the novels were concluded. Austen's delight in her characters parallels many of the male poets' enthusiastic celebrations of imaginative power, such as Wordsworth's assertion that, as a young man,

> So often among multitudes of men.
> Unknown, unthought of, yet I was most rich,
> I had a world about me—'twas my own,
> I made it. (*Prelude*, 3.140–43)

The way in which Austen's fictional characters took on independent lives for her even beyond the pages of her novels also recalls Keats's claim that "The Imagination may be compared to Adam's dream—he awoke and found it truth" (*Letters*, 1:185).

## Conclusion

It is a mistake to regard Austen as anti-Romantic in her treatment of imagination. The male poets share Austen's distrust of imaginative flights, fearing that these may dissolve one's grasp of the actual, and they often express the fear that by dwelling in visionary creations of one's own brain the individual may isolate him or herself from meaningful human relationships. Moreover, Austen like the male poets celebrates many forms of imaginative activity. They all value the sympathetic imagination, the ability to identify with the thoughts and feelings of others, as essential to love and to the creative process, and Austen stands as the Romantic period's supreme exemplar of the chameleon-like, egoless author, extolled by the male poets. The apparent criticism of imaginative flights in novels such as *Northanger Abbey* and *Emma* breaks down in many ways upon close examination. Many critics have even found evidence of the novels' covert sympathy for their heroines' bold inventions, a sympathy Austen may have downplayed in a time that looked askance on female authority and ambition. Austen's work in many ways expresses conflicts in its treatment of imagination, now condemning and now endorsing its use and effects, but the male poets also reflect significant conflicts in their attitudes toward the imagination. Finally, Austen's own comments about her work convey a joy in her creative enterprise similar to those of the male poets. Austen should be included in discussions of the Romantic imagination; her works explore the uses and abuses of imagination just as the works of the male poets do.

---

[67] William Austen-Leigh and Richard Arthur Austen-Leigh, rev. Deirdre Le Faye, *Jane Austen: A Family Record* (London: British Library, 1989), 216.

## Works Cited

Auerbach, Nina. "Jane Austen and Romantic Imprisonment." In *Jane Austen in a Social Context*. Ed. David Monaghan. Totowa, NJ: Barnes and Noble, 1981. 9–27.

—. "Jane Austen's Dangerous Charm: Feeling as One Ought About Fanny Price." In *Jane Austen: New Perspectives*. Ed. Janet Todd. New York: Holmes and Meier, 1983. 208–23.

—. "O Brave New World: Evolution and Revolution in *Persuasion*." *ELH* 39 (1972): 112–28.

Austen, Jane. *Jane Austen's Letters*. Ed. Deidre Le Faye. 3rd ed. Oxford: Oxford University Press, 1995.

—. *The Novels of Jane Austen*. Ed. R. W. Chapman. 5 vols. 3rd ed. London: Oxford University Press, 1932–4.

Austen-Leigh, William, and Richard Arthur Austen-Leigh. Rev. Deirdre Le Faye. *Jane Austen: A Family Record*. London: British Library, 1989.

Averill, James. *Wordsworth and the Poetry of Human Suffering*. Ithaca: Cornell University Press, 1980.

Bate, Walter Jackson. *John Keats*. Cambridge: Harvard University Press, 1963.

Bonca, Teddi Chichester. *Shelley's Mirrors of Love: Narcissism, Sacrifice, and Sorority*. Albany: State University of New York Press, 1999.

Brownstein, Rachel M. "Romanticism, a Romance: Jane Austen and Lord Byron, 1813–1815." *Persuasions* 16 (1994): 175–84.

Butler, Marilyn. *Jane Austen and the War of Ideas*. Oxford: Clarendon Press, 1975.

Byron, Lord, George Gordon. *Byron's Letters and Journals*. Ed. Leslie A. Marchand. 12 vols. London: John Murray, 1973–1982.

—. *The Complete Poetical Works*. Ed. Jerome J. McGann. 7 vols. Oxford: Clarendon Press, 1980–1993.

Cain, Roy E. "David Hume and Adam Smith as Sources of the Concept of Sympathy in Hazlitt." *Papers on Language and Literature* 1 (1965): 133–40.

Clayton, Jay. *Romantic Vision and the Novel*. Cambridge: Cambridge University Press, 1987.

Coleridge, Samuel Taylor. *Biographia Literaria*. Ed. James Engell and W. Jackson Bate. 2 vols. Princeton: Princeton University Press, 1983.

—. *Lectures 1808–1819 On Literature*. Ed. R. A. Foakes. 2 vols. Princeton: Princeton University Press, 1987.

—. *Poetical Works*. Ed. J. C. C. Mays. 3 vols. in 6 parts. Princeton: Princeton University Press, 2001.

—. *Table Talk*. Ed. Carl Woodring. 2 vols. Princeton: Princeton University Press, 1990.

Dabundo, Laura. "A Marriage of True Minds: Communities of Faith in Wordsworth and Austen." *The Wordsworth Circle* 35 (2004): 69–72.

DeRose, Peter L. "Imagination in *Northanger Abbey*." *University of Mississippi Studies in English* 4 (1983): 62–76.

Deresiewicz, William. *Jane Austen and the Romantic Poets*. New York: Columbia University Press, 2004.

Engell, James. *The Creative Imagination: Enlightenment to Romanticism.* Cambridge: Harvard University Press, 1981.

England, A. B. *Byron's* Don Juan *and Eighteenth–Century Literature: A Study of Some Rhetorical Continuities and Discontinuities*. Lewisburg, OH: Bucknell University Press, 1975.

Fischer, Doucet Devin. "Byron and Austen: Romance and Reality." *The Byron Journal* 21 (1993): 71–9.

Galperin, William. *The Historical Austen*. Philadelphia: University of Pennsylvania Press, 2003.

Gamer, Michael. *Romanticism and the Gothic: Genre, Reception, and Canon Formation*. Cambridge: Cambridge University Press, 2000.

Gilbert, Sandra M., and Susan Gubar. *The Madwoman in the Attic: The Woman Writer and the Nineteenth–Century Literary Imagination*. New Haven: Yale University Press, 1979.

Gleckner, Robert F. *Byron and the Ruins of Paradise*. Baltimore: The Johns Hopkins University Press, 1967.

Greene, Donald. "The Myth of Limitation." In *Jane Austen Today*. Ed. Joel Weinscheimer. Athens: University of Georgia Press, 1975. 142–75.

Hart, Francis R. "The Spaces of Privacy: Jane Austen." *Nineteenth–Century Fiction* 30 (1975): 305–33.

Hazlitt, William. *The Complete Works of William Hazlitt*. Ed. P. P. Howe. 21 vols. London: J. M. Dent, 1930.

Hofkosh, Sonia. *Sexual Politics and the Romantic Author*. Cambridge: Cambridge University Press, 1998.

Howard, Jacqueline. *Reading Gothic Fiction: A Bakhtinian Approach*. Oxford: Clarendon Press, 1994.

Jacobus, Mary. *Tradition and Experiment in Wordsworth's* Lyrical Ballads *(1798)*. Oxford: Clarendon Press, 1976.

*Jane Austen: The Critical Heritage*. Ed. B. C. Southam. London: Routledge, 1968.

Jerinic, Maria. "In Defense of the Gothic: Rereading *Northanger Abbey*." In *Jane Austen and the Discourses of Feminism*. Ed. Devoney Looser. New York: St. Martin's Press, 1995. 137–49.

Johnson, Claudia L. *Jane Austen: Women, Politics, and the Novel*. Chicago: University of Chicago Press, 1988.

Johnson, Samuel. *Rasselas and Other Tales*. Ed Gwin J. Kolb. New Haven: Yale University Press, 1990.

Kauver, Elaine M. "Jane Austen and *The Female Quixote*." *Studies in the Novel* 2 (1970): 211–21.

Keats, John. *The Letters of John Keats*. Ed. Hyder E. Rollins. 2nd ed. 2 vols. Cambridge: Harvard University Press, 1965.

—. *The Poems of John Keats*. Ed. Jack Stillinger. Cambridge: Harvard University Press, 1978.

Kern, Robert. "Keats and the Problem of Romance." *Philological Quarterly* 58 (1979): 171–91.

Knox–Shaw, Peter. *Jane Austen and the Enlightenment*. Cambridge: Cambridge University Press, 2004.

—. "*Persuasion*, Byron, and the Turkish Tale." *Review of English Studies* 44 (1993): 47–69.

Lau, Beth. "Home, Exile, and Wanderlust in Austen and the Romantic Poets." *Pacific Coast Philology* 41 (2006): 91–107.

—. "Jane Austen. *Pride and Prejudice*." In *A Companion to Romanticism*. Ed. Duncan Wu. Oxford: Blackwell, 1998. 219–26.

—. "Jane Austen and John Keats: Negative Capability, Romance and Reality." *Keats-Shelley Journal* 55 (2006): 81–110.

—. "Madeline at Northanger Abbey: Keats's Anti–Romances and Gothic Satire." *Journal of English and Germanic Philology* 84 (1985): 30–50.

—. "Placing Jane Austen in the Romantic Period: Self and Solitude in the Works of Austen and the Male Romantic Poets." *European Romantic Review* 15 (2004): 255–67.

—. "*Sense and Sensibility* and *Tintern Abbey*: Growth and Maturation." *The Wordsworth Circle* 35 (2004): 65–8.

Lee, Debbie. *Slavery and the Romantic Imagination*. Philadelphia: University of Pennsylvania Press, 2002.

Levine, George. "Translating the Monstrous: *Northanger Abbey*." *Nineteenth–Century Fiction* 30 (1975): 335–50.

Litz, A. Walton. *Jane Austen: A Study of Her Artistic Development*. New York: Oxford University Press, 1965.

McEathron, Scott. "Wordsworth and Coleridge, *Lyrical Ballads*." In *A Companion to Romanticism*. Ed. Duncan Wu. Oxford: Blackwell, 1998. 144–56.

McFarland, Thomas. *Coleridge and the Pantheist Tradition*. Oxford: Clarendon Press, 1969.

McGann, Jerome J. *The Romantic Ideology: A Critical Investigation*. Chicago: University of Chicago Press, 1983.

Mellor, Anne K. *Romanticism and Gender*. New York: Routledge, 1993.

—. "Why Women Didn't Like Romanticism: The Views of Jane Austen and Mary Shelley." In *The Romantics and Us: Essays on Literature and Culture*. Ed. Gene W. Ruoff. New Brunswick: Rutgers University Press, 1990. 274–87.

Moler, Kenneth. "The Bennet Girls and Adam Smith on Vanity and Pride." *Philological Quarterly* 46 (1967): 567–9.

—. *Jane Austen's Art of Allusion*. Lincoln: University of Nebraska Press, 1968.

Morgan, Susan. *In the Meantime: Character and Perception in Jane Austen's Novels*. Chicago: University of Chicago Press, 1980.

Morrison, Paul. "Enclosed in Openness: *Northanger Abbey* and the Domestic Carceral." *Texas Studies in Literature and Language* 33 (1991): 1–23.

Newlyn, Lucy. Paradise Lost *and the Romantic Reader*. Oxford: Clarendon Press, 1993.

*The Norton Anthology of English Literature*. Ed. M. H. Abrams, et al. 7th ed. Vol. 2. New York: Norton, 2000.

*The Norton Anthology of English Literature*. Ed. Stephen Greenblatt, et al. 8th ed. Vol. D. New York: Norton, 2006.

O'Neill, Michael. *The Human Mind's Imaginings: Conflict and Achievement in Shelley's Poetry*. Oxford: Clarendon Press, 1989.

Parker, Patricia A. *Inescapable Romance: Studies in the Poetics of a Mode*. Princeton: Princeton University Press, 1979.

Perkins, David. "The Imaginative Vision of *Kubla Khan*: On Coleridge's Introductory Note." In *Coleridge, Keats, and the Imagination: Romanticism and Adam's Dream*. Ed. J. Robert Barth, S. J., and John L. Mahoney. Columbia: University of Missouri Press, 1990. 97–108.

Perry, Seamus. *Coleridge and the Uses of Division*. Oxford: Clarendon Press, 1999.

Prothero, Rowland E., ed. *The Works of Lord Byron*. Vol. 12. London: John Murray, 1901.

Ruoff, Gene W. "The Sense of a Beginning: *Mansfield Park*." *The Wordsworth Circle* 10 (1979): 174–86.

Seeber, Barbara K. *General Consent in Jane Austen: A Study in Dialogism*. Montreal: McGill–Queen's University Press, 2000.

Shelley, Percy Bysshe. *The Letters of Percy Bysshe Shelley*. Ed. Frederick L. Jones. 2 vols. Oxford: Clarendon Press, 1964.

—. *Shelley's Poetry and Prose*. Ed. Donald H. Reiman and Neil Fraistat. 2nd ed. New York: Norton, 2002.

Shepperson, A. B. *The Novel in Motley: A History of the Burlesque Novel in English*. 1936; rpt. New York: Octagon Books, 1967.

Sheridan, Richard Brinsley. *The Rivals*. In *The Dramatic Works of Richard Brinsley Sheridan*. Ed. Cecil Price. Vol. 1. Oxford: Clarendon Press, 1973.

Siskin, Clifford. *The Historicity of Romantic Discourse*. New York: Oxford University Press, 1998.

Smith, Adam. *The Theory of Moral Sentiments*. Ed. D. D. Raphael and A. L. Macfie. Oxford: Clarendon Press, 1976.

Sperry, Stuart. *Keats the Poet*. Princeton: Princeton University Press, 1973.

Stillinger, Jack. *The Hoodwinking of Madeline and Other Essays on Keats's Poems*. Urbana: University of Illinois Press, 1971.

—. "Keats and Coleridge." In *Coleridge, Keats, and the Imagination: Romanticism and Adam's Dream*. Ed. J. Robert Barth and John L. Mahoney. Columbia: University of Missouri Press, 1990. 7–28. Rpt. in Jack Stillinger. *Romantic Complexity: Keats, Coleridge, and Wordsworth*. Urbana: University of Illinois Press, 2006. 41–61.

Swingle, L. J. "The Poets, the Novelists, and the English Romantic Situation." *The Wordsworth Circle* 10 (1979): 218–28.

Tave, Stuart. "Jane Austen and One of Her Contemporaries." In *Jane Austen: Bicentenary Essays*. Ed. John Halperin. Cambridge: Cambridge University Press, 1975. 61–74.

—. *Some Words on Jane Austen*. Chicago: University of Chicago Press, 1973.

Trilling, Lionel. "Emma." *Encounter* 8.6 (1957): 49–59. Rpt. in *Jane Austen: Critical Assessments*. Ed. Ian Littlewood. Vol. 4: *Mansfield Park; Emma; Persuasion; Sanditon*. The Banks, Mountfield, East Sussex: Helm Information, 1998. 213–27.

Tuite, Clara. *Romantic Austen: Sexual Politics and the Literary Canon*. Cambridge: Cambridge University Press, 2002.

Wasserman, Earl. *The Finer Tone: Keats' Major Poems*. Baltimore: The Johns Hopkins University Press, 1953.

Wilt, Judith. *Ghosts of the Gothic: Austen, Eliot, and Lawrence*. Princeton: Princeton University Press, 1980.

Wolfson, Susan J. "'Their She Condition': Cross–Dressing and the Politics of Gender in *Don Juan*." *ELH* 54 (1987): 585–617.

—. *The Questioning Presence: Wordsworth, Keats, and the Interrogative Mode in Romantic Poetry*. Ithaca: Cornell University Pres, 1986.

Wordsworth, William. *The Prelude, 1799, 1805, 1850*. Ed. Jonathan Wordsworth, M. H. Abrams, and Stephen Gill. New York: Norton, 1979.

—. *Selected Poems and Prefaces*. Ed. Jack Stillinger. Boston: Houghton Mifflin, 1965.

# Chapter 9
# "Beautiful but Ideal": Intertextual Relations between Letitia Elizabeth Landon and Percy Bysshe Shelley

Michael O'Neill

"With what enthusiasm do some set up Wordsworth for an idol, and others Shelley! But this taste is quite another feeling to that which creates; and the little now written possesses beauty not originality." A little later, sustaining the note of lament for belatedness, Landon asks in the same essay, "On the Ancient and Modern Influence of Poetry" (1832), her fascinating parallel to aspects of Shelley's *A Defence of Poetry* (unpublished in her lifetime): "who could for a moment have hesitated as to whether a poem was marked with the actual and benevolent philosophy of Wordsworth, or the beautiful but ideal theory of Shelley?"[1] The essay's implications are various. Landon clearly defines her age as one that has lost the "originality" of the heyday of Romantic poetry. But she hints at the advantages as well as the disadvantages of belatedness: able to hold in balance the relative merits of Wordsworth's "actual and benevolent philosophy" and Shelley's "beautiful but ideal theory," Landon implies that the poetry of her predecessors opens itself to her own responsive appropriations. At the same time, her ways of suggesting the impoverishment of the present indicate a profoundly intertextual imagination, one saturated in the dominant tropes of the Romantic poets.

My emphasis in this discussion is on Landon's intricate relationship with Shelley, a poet to whom she responds in a fluid and complex manner. If she sympathizes, she qualifies, yet if she withholds total assent from his vision, she does not disavow its hold over her imagination. In *Life and Literary Remains of L.E.L.* (1841), Laman Blanchard included this judgment by Landon of Shelley from undated correspondence:

> Of all poets SHELLEY is the most poetical:
> "Love was born with him, so intense,
> It was his very being, not a sense."—

---

[1] Quoted from F. J. Sypher, ed., *Critical Writings by Letitia Elizabeth Landon* (Delmar: Scholars' Facsimiles and Reprints, 1996), 64; hereafter referred to parenthetically as "Sypher" in the main body of the text.

The defect of his imagination was a want of being sufficiently balanced with the real; everything appeared to him through an exaggerated medium. He reasoned with his feelings; now feelings are the worst possible reasoners—they excite, and they mislead. He saw evil and sorrow, and believed too easily in redress: he was too young to make allowance—that first step in true philosophy—and fancied that to defy a system was to destroy it. It was a boy's error, who believes he is judging when he is only learning. Shelley's versification has a melody peculiarly his own. It can only be described by similitudes. It suggests the notes of some old favourite song—the sound of falling waters, or the murmurs of the wind among the branches. There is a nameless fascination in some sweet human voices, and there is the same in many of the shorter poems of Shelley (Sypher, 175).

The judgment pivots and poises itself round the key Landon term, "learning." Once she has completed her measured and critically unremarkable rebuke of Shelley's "want of being sufficiently balanced with the real,"[2] Landon is able to give expression to her sense of the "nameless fascination" exercised by Shelley, a fascination which, one senses, is bound up with her implicit admiration for his complete commitment to his "poetical" vision. Illustrating such commitment, Landon cites, close to the start of her passage, a distinctly Shelleyan couplet. Possibly written by Landon herself, it out-Shelleys Shelley, a poet for whom, on this account, "Love" was an "intensity" that consumed his "being."[3] By rhyming yet allowing for a gap between "intense" and "sense," Landon recalls a tangled effect in *The Triumph of Life*, the moment when the "Shape all light" (352) appears "confusing sense" (341), and the "sun's image"— ambivalent in the poem—burns "radiantly intense" (345).[4] Here, intensity and confused sense-perception link

---

[2]     Compare William Hazlitt's more acerbically phrased comment about Shelley: "Spurning the world of realities, he rushed into the world of nonentities and contingencies, like air into a *vacuum*" (review of Shelley's *Posthumous Poems* [1824] in *The Edinburgh Review*, July 1824; quoted from *The Young Romantics and Critical Opinion, 1807–1824*, comp. Theodore Redpath [London: Harrap, 1973], 390).

[3]     Landon may also have been remembering the account of "music so delicate, soft, and intense, / It was felt like an odour within the sense" in Shelley's *The Sensitive Plant*, a poem in which the Sensitive Plant seems a double of Shelley (certainly as Landon presents him), especially in the line, "It loves, even like Love, its deep heart is full" (Part First, 27–8, 76).

[4]     Shelley is quoted from Cyrus Redding with A. Galignani and W. Galignani, eds., *The Poetical Works of Coleridge, Shelley and Keats 1829*, intro. Jonathan Wordsworth (Otley and Washington D.C.: Woodstock, 2002). The Galignanis' edition is one possible source of Landon's knowledge of Shelley's poetry. Moreover, it includes poems which Landon may have read in earlier publications. Along with poems published in Shelley's lifetime, the Galignanis' edition incorporates poems published in Mary Shelley's edition of Shelley's *Posthumous Poems* (1824). Landon would also have had access to Shelley's poetry in the various pirated editions of his work published in the 1820s and 1830s, including *The Works of Percy Bysshe Shelley, with His Life*, 2 vols. (London: Ascham, 1834). In addition, she would have encountered poems placed by Mary Shelley and others such as Thomas

hands in a vertiginous dance. Landon's quoted or composed couplet may only fleetingly glance in the direction of such an effect, one that is almost self-ironizing in its latent mistrust of the "intense" and "sense." But her lines rekindle awareness of the way in which Shelley's poetic dealings with "Love" are, more usually, both "intense" and alert to the resources of human apprehension that make intensity possible: resources that include "sense," where that term means "the capacity for sensation," but involve the entire "being." So in Shelley's essay, "On Love," which Landon will have known since a version of it was made available by Mary Shelley for *The Keepsake*, 1829, he writes of the human impulse to "refer all sensations" to "a soul within our soul," and depicts "Love" as the desire "to awaken in all things that are, a community with what we experience within ourselves."[5]

An invocation in *The Hall of the Statues*—"God of the West Wind, awake!" (58)—argues, in context, in favor of Landon's awareness of Shelley's *Ode to the West Wind*: the context being one in which praise is expressed for those who "have head and heart on fire / With unquenchable desire / Of those higher hopes which spring / Heavenward on an eager wing" (44–7).[6] If the "fire" / "desire" rhyme is Byronic as well as Shelleyan, the "spring" / "wing" rhyme also recalls the second stanza of Shelley's *To a Skylark*:

> Higher still and higher
>    From the earth thou springest
> Like a cloud of fire;
>    The blue deep thou wingest,
> And singing still dost soar, and soaring ever singest. (6–10)

Landon's recollection of the Shelleyan rhyme, her valorization of "fire" as an image of aspiration, and her use of "higher" all indicate the impact on her of the poetic desires depicted in *To a Skylark*, a poem whose speaker seeks to create "hymns" "Till

---

Medwin in various annuals and periodicals; thus, *To Edward Williams* ("The serpent is shut out from paradise") was published in *Fraser's Magazine* in 1832. For essential information about the transmission of Shelley's texts, see Charles H. Taylor, Jr., *The Early Collected Editions of Shelley's Poems: A Study in the History and Transmission of the Printed Text* (New Haven: Yale University Press, 1958). For convenience, line numbers are provided from *Shelley's Poetry and Prose*, ed. Donald H. Reiman and Neil Fraistat, 2nd ed. (New York: Norton, 2002), or are taken from *Shelley: Poetical Works*, ed. Thomas Hutchinson, new ed. G. M. Matthews (London: Oxford University Press, 1970).

[5]   "On Love. By Percy Bysshe Shelley," in *The Keepsake for 1829*, ed. Frederic Mansel Reynolds (London: Hurst, Chance, 1829), 48, 47. Landon's poem *Verses*, beginning "Lady, thy face is very beautiful," appears on p. 121 of this volume. A version of "On Love," differing from the 1829 text, appears in Thomas Medwin, *The Shelley Papers* (London: Whittaker, Treacher, 1833), 21–4.

[6]   Unless indicated otherwise, Landon's poetry is quoted from *Letitia Elizabeth Landon: Selected Writings*, ed. Jerome J. McGann and Daniel Riess (Peterborough, ONT: Broadview, 1997), hereafter *SW*.

the world is wrought / To sympathy with hopes and fears it heeded not" (39–40). Those lines seem, in turn, to be in "sympathy" with and to underpin Landon's subsequent praise in *The Hall of Statues* for "Those wide aims which seek to bind / Man the closer with his kind — / By earth's most unearthly ties, / Praise, hopes and sympathies" (48–51). To be sure, her responsiveness to Shelley in *The Hall of Statues* has a guardedness in the midst of enthusiasm; and there is a spectatorial quality to the writing: "Thankful should we be to those / Who disdain a dull repose" (42–3). Yet the responsiveness, however guarded, is evident, as is marked by a further echo of Shelley in "dull repose." The phrase reminds us that in *Adonais* Shelley exhibits the disdain for "repose" of which Landon approves. In his elegy, he faces up to and faces down the grim possibility that consciousness is doomed to extinction, that "th'intense atom glows / A moment, then is quench'd in a most cold repose" (179–80). *The Hall of Statues* concludes in doubt and uncertainty, "All the shapes I gazed upon, / Like the dream that raised them, gone" (168–9), allowing Landon the freedom to present her imaginings both as merely the products of a "'dream" and as possessing the truthfulness peculiar to poetic inspiration. She thus sustains her independence as a poet, preventing her admiration for ardent idealists such as Shelley from dominating the poem. But the hold over her imagination of Shelley's practice and example is apparent.

In "On the Ancient and Modern Influence of Poetry," published a year after *The Hall of Statues*, Landon's prose seems imbued with Shelleyan tropes. We lack, she says, any "voice that startles us into wonder, and hurries us forth to see whose trumpet is awakening the land" (Sypher, 64). Such a voice is Shelleyan, a voice akin to that imagined at the end of *Ode to the West Wind* when the speaker implores or commands the wind to "Be through my lips to unawaken'd earth / The trumpet of a prophecy!" (68–9). Landon takes the desire for the poetic deed. Shelley engages in anguished wrestling with the wind that momentarily subdues it to his will as a poet, until the wind, rather than he, is the trumpet rather than the trumpeter. By the time of Landon's tacit allusion, the trumpet is or ought to be the possession of a dominant poetic voice, and it is "awakening the land" which remains obstinately "unawaken'd" in the original Ode. Landon suggests the possibility of poetry going through cycles, drawing on the hopeful aspects of Shelley's final question in the Ode, as well as glancingly referring to the opening of Shakespeare's *Richard III*: "Perhaps poetry too may have its atmosphere; and a long cold winter may be needed for its glad and glorious summer" (Sypher, 64). In terms that are uncannily like those used by Shelley in *A Defence of Poetry*, Landon castigates the present. Of it, she writes: "Selfishness is its principle, indifference its affection, and ridicule its commonplace. We allow no appeals save to our reason, or to our fear of laughter" (Sypher, 64). Landon here offers a parallel to Shelley's attack on the "principle of Self" at work in the present, and to his dislike of so-called "Comedy" in "the reign of Charles II" when "malignity, sarcasm and contempt, succeed to sympathetic merriment; we hardly laugh, but we smile."[7]

---

[7]    *Shelley's Poetry and Prose,* ed. Reiman and Fraistat, 520, 521–2.

The parallel indicates that we may be wise to take issue with the view that Landon, at her poetic best, is most finely understood as an undermining critic of Romantic illusion, a view eloquently expressed by Jerome McGann, who says of her poetry that "An imagination like hers has few illusions about illusory worlds, and least of all about that supreme Land of Cockayne, the romantic imagination."[8] Landon as the pitiless unmasker of Romantic poetry is an attractive proposition, but her sympathy with the Romantic project—itself hardly ever undivided in aim—shows in her poetry and criticism. In "On the Character of Mrs. Hemans's Writings," she subscribes to an expressivist, confessional poetics, saying of poetry that "Its haunted words will be to us even as our own. Solitude and sorrow reveal to us its secrets, even as they first revealed themselves to those 'Who learnt in suffering what they taught in song'" (Sypher, 67). After that allusion to Shelley's *Julian and Maddalo*, in which Maddalo remarks of "wretched men" (544) that, "cradled into poetry by wrong" (545), "They learn in suffering what they teach in song" (546), Landon continues: "I believe that no poet ever made his readers feel unless he had himself felt" (Sypher, 67). Landon's allusion to *Julian and Maddalo* works in multiple ways. It reminds us, as McGann and Riess observe (*SW*, 279), that her subject Felicia Hemans had used the line as an epigraph to her poem *The Diver*; thus Landon constructs a link connecting her with Hemans and both female poets with Shelley. Hemans's diver is a figure for the poet who pays a "price of bitter tears" for "the lonely power" won by diving "Down to the gulfs of the soul."[9] The wisdom afforded by the poem's metaphoric equivalences consists in comfortless but intense revelation: the poet is one "that has been to the pearl's dark shrine" and is addressed as "O wrestler with the sea!" Such a posture of heroic wrestling in Hemans's poem is Byronic as much as Shelleyan, and Landon's allusion to *Julian and Maddalo* points up the availability for her of Byronic as well as Shelleyan influence, since the line, as mentioned, is spoken by Maddalo, Shelley's representation of Byron. The glancing but rich intertextual nature of Landon's writing comes through in her play with the close of *Mont Blanc*, where Shelley asks of the mountain: "And what wert thou, and earth, and stars, and sea, / If to the human mind's imaginings / Silence and solitude were vacancy?" (142–4). Landon's emphasis is less on "Silence and solitude" than on "Solitude and sorrow," but her fascination with "silence" and "the human mind's imaginings" is prominent in one of her finest poems, *Lines of Life*, a poem which displays her covert yet strong responsiveness to Shelley.

That responsiveness, it should be acknowledged, entwines round Landon's reading of Byron. Like Scott, Byron stimulates Landon's narrative inventions; he also quickens her sense of the poet's life as fated, as involving deep feeling, and as inextricable from social dissimulation; Shelley is the poet on whose Utopian

---

[8]     Jerome J. McGann, *The Poetics of Sensibility: A Revolution in Literary Style* (Oxford: Clarendon Press, 1996), 149.

[9]     Hemans is quoted from *The Poetical Works of Mrs. Hemans, with Prefatory Memoir, Notes, Etc.*, The "Albion" Edition (London and New York: Warne, 1897).

imaginings she draws when envisaging possibilities of transcendence.[10] In *Lines of Life,* Landon begins rather as Shelley opens his *To Constantia, Singing,* in the version she would have known, with physiological evidence of emotion. Shelley concludes the first stanza in his ecstatic rendition of the experience of listening to the song of "Constantia" (Claire Clairmont) with a couplet that at once confesses feeling and suggests further revelations kept in check: "Even while I write, my burning cheeks are wet — / Alas, that the torn heart can bleed, but not forget!" (8–9).[11] That alexandrine moves beyond the present-tense of composition explored in "Even while I write" to a generalized sense of emotion's explosive impact. "Forgetfulness," so dearly prized by Byron in *Childe Harold's Pilgrimage,* 3.4.35, is not easily possessed by Shelley's speaker.[12] The burden of Shelley's lyric, in the version available to Landon, is a miniature drama centred on loss of self through rhapsodic identification with another, until, finally, the self imagines itself suspended by song in a net of otherness: "I have no life, Constantia, now, but thee, / Whilst, like the world-surrounding air, thy song / Flows on, and fills all things with melody" (32–4). Landon, the role of the improvisatrice always uppermost in her thoughts, performs many variations on the theme of self surrendered and rewon through poetic song.

In *Lines of Life,* we find the speaker of Shelley's *To Constantia, Singing* transported to a cold climate. "Well, read my cheek, and watch my eye" (1), she begins, echoing and half-mocking the conversational ingenuousness of Coleridge's opening to *This Lime-Tree Bower My Prison.* The invitation to "read my cheek, and watch my eye" is issued by one whose eyes are not wet with tears and whose cheeks are not "burning." "Too strictly school'd are they," she continues, "One secret of my soul to show, / One hidden thought betray" (2–4). Landon employs her near sing-song stanzaic form, with its equable eight-six balance of syllables, to communicate dissonant, unlyrical sentiments. The poetry is curious in its impact. Intimately it speaks of the poet's refusal to countenance intimacy. The failure to rhyme the stanza's first and third lines adds to a sense of repudiation. Yet Landon's relation to Shelley—the poet who in *The Triumph of Life* alludes to "thoughts which must remain untold" (21)—is not merely one of ironic dissent from emotive outcry. Much in Shelley, in fact, concerns itself with the repression of feeling. Examples

---

[10]     For a reading of Felicia Hemans's response to Byron, a response which may have influenced Landon's, see Susan J. Wolfson, "Hemans and the Romance of Byron," in *Felicia Hemans: Reimagining Poetry in the Nineteenth Century,* ed. Nanora Sweet and Julie Melnyk (Basingstoke: Palgrave, 2001), 155–80.

[11]     The poem's text and especially its stanzaic order, as Landon would have known it, differ greatly from the best contemporary texts, which are based on the poem's original publication in *The Oxford University and City Herald,* 31 January 1818. Mary Shelley based her text in *Posthumous Poems* on a draft text. Line numbers are supplied from the text in *Shelley: Poetical Works,* ed. Thomas Hutchinson, new ed. G. M. Matthews, which derives from Mary Shelley's text.

[12]     Here and elsewhere, Byron's poetry is quoted from *Byron: Oxford Authors,* ed. Jerome J. McGann (Oxford: Oxford University Press, 1986).

include the close of *Julian and Maddalo* ("she told me how / All happen'd—but the cold world shall not know" [616–17]) and the opening of *Lines Written among the Euganean Hills* where plangent trochees meet in a triplet rhyme to ask: "What, if there no friends will greet; / What, if there no heart will meet / His with love's impatient beat" (27–9). Landon occupies a lyric space that makes her the centre of a drama, the first act of which is to state that her life has not permitted her any chance to display authentic emotion. Landon's is a song of experience, yet positives gleam through the wreckage of social conformity and submission, as is signalled by the first line and a half of the poem's epigraph (presumably composed by Landon herself): "Orphan in my first years, I early learnt / To make my heart suffice itself, and seek / Support and sympathy in its own depths." Landon touches here on a motif resonantly developed by Wordsworth in *The Prelude* (unpublished until 1850), in which Wordsworth speaks of "The self-sufficing power of solitude" (*1805*, 2.78), [13] while the impulse to seek out and trust in the heart's "own depths" implies a limit to the speaker's cynicism. Indeed, accounting for the pathos of *Lines of Life* is a strong sense that the speaker has not wholly quelled her longing for emotional fulfilment.

What is offered is protest as much as analysis. "I never knew the time my heart / Look'd freely from my brow" (5–6) Landon writes in stanza 2, half-voicing belief in what her lines deny: a "time my heart / Look'd freely from my brow." Indeed, the poem might be spoken by one of the inhabitants of Shelley's fallen world in *Prometheus Unbound*, whose mode of speech is one that we know as it is negated through the millennial transformation depicted by the Spirit of the Hour at the end of Act 3. "I live among the cold, the false," asserts Landon in her third stanza, "And I must seem like them; / And such I am, for I am false / As those I must condemn" (9–12). In Shelley's altered world, "None talk'd that common, false, cold, hollow talk / Which makes the heart deny the *yes* it breathes, / Yet question that unmeant hypocrisy / With such a self-mistrust as has no name"(3.4.149–52). "Such a self-mistrust" is given a name and a local habitation in *Lines of Life*. "False" is a complex word in Shelley's poetry; it denotes both a state of being at odds with the truth and a condition of near-helpless complicity. Julian and Maddalo sympathetically diagnose the Maniac as having, for the sake of someone by whom he has been crossed in love, "fix'd a blot / Of falsehood in his mind, which flourish'd not / But in the light of all-beholding truth" (529–31). In the just-quoted lines from *Prometheus Unbound*, "false" joins hands with "cold," "common," and "hollow" to establish itself as a potent parallel to Landon's nervy, contemptuous nod towards drawing-room insincerities and treacheries. Landon rhymes "false" with itself in the usually unrhymed first and third lines of the stanza to convey the depth of her inescapable entrapment.

In her first ten stanzas, and intermittently thereafter, Landon uses a device—repetition of the first-person pronoun—which conveys a sense, not of agency, but of

---

[13]   Text used is William Wordsworth, *The Prelude: The Four Texts (1798, 1799, 1805, 1850)*, ed. Jonathan Wordsworth (London: Penguin, 1995).

clear-sighted awareness of being caught in the coils of an unfeeling, cynical social world. There may even be a suggestion of poetic as well as social dependence at the close of stanza 4: "I borrow others' likeness, till / Almost I lose my own" (15–16). Looking ahead to T. S. Eliot's posturing speaker in *Portrait of a Lady*, and backwards to Byron's attacks on social dissimulation in *Childe Harold's Pilgrimage*, Landon "borrows" a technique which she would have met in Shelley's *Hymn of Apollo* and *Hymn of Pan*, first published in *Posthumous Poems* (the poems are now usually referred to as *Song of Apollo* and *Song of Pan*). In *Hymn of Apollo* Apollo's self-centred rhetoric is glorious more than vain-glorious. "I am the eye with which the Universe / Beholds itself, and knows it is divine" (31–2); these lines, the start of the last stanza, have an eloquence that is proof against the would-be cynical interpreter. At the same time we might recall, as Earl R. Wasserman points out, that the *Hymn of Apollo* is countered by the *Hymn of Pan*. In the latter poem Pan sings, not of an "entirely self-contained subjectivity" as does Apollo, but of "lived experience."[14] So, in the last stanza of *Hymn of Pan*, Pan turns to the personal "sorrow" of which his sweet "pipings" (36) finally tell: "And then I changed my pipings, — / Singing how down the vale of Menalus / I pursued a maiden and clasp'd a reed: / Gods and men, we are all deluded thus!" (29–32). Metrical variations work expressively here, reinforcing the cry of distress in that last line. The Shelleyan poems, then, offer an object lesson in two ways of using the first-person pronoun: one that represents the self as all-sufficient and all-powerful, the other that represents the self as open to pain and suffering, but achieving an awareness of fellow-feeling ("*we* are all deluded thus"; emphasis added).

   If Landon studied Shelley's differing uses of the first-person pronoun in his two *Hymns*, she might have derived lessons which bear on her practice in a poem which takes as its subject the question of self-presentation. *Lines of Life* is aware that the idea of the self as unwoundable and in control is a social sham, even as it senses that the self is the source, too, of imaginative authority, and it verges on the discovery that the hurts inflicted by "lived experience" open the door to sympathy with others. Certainly Landon's recourse to a rhetorical use of first-person pronouns is part of her poem's subterranean drama, its deep conviction that "L. E. L."—idol and plaything of post-Romantic literary consumerism—has that within her which equals the significance claimed for himself by Shelley's Apollo, as well as the capacity for pain and sympathy shown by Shelley's Pan.[15] That composite conviction begins to surface in stanza 7. After the ironic "learn to feel their way" (20) of stanza 6, the suggestion of incompletely successful repression in stanza 7 is matter for hope, however minimalist:

---

[14]    "The Poetry of Skepticism"; rpt. of section from *Shelley: A Critical Reading* (Baltimore: The Johns Hopkins University Press, 1971); in *Shelley's Poetry and Prose*, ed. Reiman and Fraistat, 573.

[15]    For "Landon's commodified life," see chap. 6 of Anne K. Mellor, *Romanticism and Gender* (New York: Routledge, 1993); the quoted phrase is on 123.

> I check my thoughts like curbed steeds
>   That struggle with the rein;
> I bid my feelings sleep, like wrecks
>   In the unfathom'd main. (21–4)

The image of shipwreck is distinctly Shelleyan, and may derive from *Time*, which opens, "Unfathomable Sea! whose waves are years, / Ocean of Time, whose waters of deep woe / Are brackish with the salt of human tears!" (1–3), and whose gloomy metaphorical waters themselves seem to react against Byron's more august address to the Ocean at the close of *Childe Harold's Pilgrimage*, Canto IV. Certainly, Landon's sleeping "feelings" do not trust what Shelley calls the "inhospitable shore" (7) bordering the "unfathom'd main" of her inner existence. Shelleyan, too, in a more uplifting sense is the use of a negative adjective ("unfathom'd") to point towards "infinite potentiality," in Timothy Webb's phrase.[16] And the image of "the curbed steeds" conjures up a Shelleyan energy—of the kind at work in the description of the "cars drawn by rainbow-winged steeds" in *Prometheus Unbound* (2.4.130)—in the act of evoking the need to check it.

Ensuing stanzas indicate the extent to which Landon has not interiorized her society's values. Landon shares Shelley's dislike of those who "Mock at all high and early truth" (27) and belongs to that line of poets, beginning with Blake and culminating in Yeats, who would "Mock mockers after that."[17] So her line "high and early truth" asserts its superiority to those who would mock it. But the miserable fact, for Landon, and lending her poem its unique timbre, is the confession of complicity, caught in the let-down of the stanza's last line: "And I too do the same" (28). There "too," more than a line-filler, concedes the speaker's herd-following conformity. Shelley, indeed, may be among the "spiritual, the kind, / The pure, but named in mirth" (33–4) of stanza 9, and certainly that stanza exhibits a Shelleyan mournfulness as it imagines the consequences of cynical "mirth": "Till all of good, ay, even hope, / Seems exiled from our earth" (35–6). Landon might be describing the quasi-Dantescan condition of the "morally dead," to borrow Shelley's phrase from his Preface to *Alastor*, even as she herself bids to be seen as "a wonder of this earth, / Where there is little of transcendent worth," as *Julian and Maddalo* has it (590–91). "Hope" is the fundamental Shelleyan virtue, closely connected, at the close of *Prometheus Unbound*, to the creative energies that might undo the ill effects of tyranny's return, Demogorgon admonishing his listeners "to hope till Hope creates / From its own wreck the thing it contemplates" (4.573–4).

Before Landon's poem follows Demogorgon's advice, it has further depths of self-abasement to plumb. Tersely Landon concludes the opening ten stanzas

---

[16]    "The Unascended Heaven: Negatives in *Prometheus Unbound*," in *Shelley Revalued: Essays from the Gregynog Conference*, ed. Kelvin Everest (Leicester: Leicester University Press, 1983); rpt. in *Shelley's Poetry and Prose*, ed. Reiman and Fraistat, 703.

[17]    W. B. Yeats, "Nineteen Hundred and Nineteen," V.16; quoted from *The Poems of W. B. Yeats: A Sourcebook*, ed. Michael O'Neill (London: Routledge, 2004).

governed by the first person with an image, that of the sword of Damocles, used strikingly by Shelley in *Prometheus Unbound*. Landon uses it to describe her fear of "withering ridicule" (37), "A sword hung by a single hair / For ever o'er the head" (39–40). Shelley employs the image to depict what is at stake in Prometheus's resistance to Jupiter's reign: "For what submission but that fatal word, / The death-seal of mankind's captivity, / Like the Sicilian's hair-suspended sword, / Which trembles o'er his crown, would he accept, / Or could I yield?" (1.396–400). Landon brings Shelley's concern with power-politics into the gendered realm of salon and ballroom, but her diagnosis of social paralysis suggests the need for change. Her attack on "a most servile faith" (41), that of conformity to social dictates, is hardly exceeded by Shelley's hostility to religious faith.

The breakthrough comes in stanza 13 where an assertive rather than a penitent "I" takes over. In this and the next three stanzas, Landon articulates a visionary apologia, the more affecting for its apparent withdrawal in stanzas 17 and 18, when "earth, and earth's debasing stain, / Again is on my soul; / And I am but a nameless part / Of a most worthless whole" (69–72). Internal rhyme reinforces the sense of a struggle taking place in the throes of composition, a practice often found in Shelley, as in Byron. But before the descent into savage mockery of a Romantic notion of life as a "whole," Landon has uttered sentiments that again draw on Shelley's example, feeling "a loftier mood / Of generous impulse, high resolve, / Steal o'er my solitude!" (50–52). She describes, too, a longing for the "light" of stars that recalls Shelley's sense, at the end of *Adonais*, of a star-like soul that "Beacons from the abode where the Eternal are" (495). Her verse moves us by watching itself "wish, so passionately wish, / A light like theirs on high" (55–6). She expresses "eagerness of hope / To benefit my kind" (57–8) and, in a very Shelleyan rhyme ("We come from the mind / Of human kind," *Prometheus Unbound*, 4.93–4, provides an example), caps this eagerness with the conviction that "immortal power / Were given to my mind" (59–60). Landon, too, is caught up in dreams of "eternal fame" (61), momentarily allying herself, as she imagines "the gloriousness of death" (63), with that "best philosophy" (213) of which Shelley writes in *Epipsychidion*, "whose taste / Makes this cold common hell, our life, a doom / As glorious as a fiery martyrdom" (213–14). Landon compares "eternal fame" to "The sun of earthly gloom" (62), a suggestive image, since if fame is a "sun" that shines out in the midst of "earthly gloom" it is part of and even derives its lustre from the very "gloom" which it seems to transcend. The writing suggests a dialectic, both compensatory and creative, between the experience of "earthly gloom" and the hoped-for attainment of "eternal fame." Shelley and Landon share a view of "our life" as a "cold common hell" that, for both, can be transfigured; for Shelley by that "best philosophy," for Landon by "eternal fame." Landon's ideal, however, is distinctly perilous, the idealizing shadow of worldly gossip and censure, and it may be an implicit recognition of this fact that brings her poem tumbling down to earth.

When it recovers, a new tone merges, one that links Landon unabashedly with Shelley and Byron as she asks the question central to poetic composition and articulates an answer at the heart of the Romantic project:

> Why write I this? because my heart
>   Towards the future springs,
> That future where it loves to soar
>   On more than eagle wings. (73–6)

"Why write I this?": the use of "this" rather than, say, "verse" defines Landon's question as being about the current poem, *Lines of Life*. And the deferral of hope to the future is a characteristic Shelleyan posture of the spirit: "my heart / Towards the future springs" might serve as an epigraph to Shelley's poetic oeuvre, close to whose heart lies a Utopian impulse. Mercury tortures Prometheus with a chilling vista of "Eternity" as a place where all we can "imagine" of time, "age on age," "Seems but a point" (*Prometheus Unbound*, 1.417–19). Landon borrows Mercury's image as a point of departure for hope:

> The present, it is but a speck
>   In that eternal time,
> In which my lost hopes find a home,
>   My spirit knows its clime. (77–80)

Arguably, Landon's succinct charting of "futurity" as the "home" for her "lost hopes" implicitly passes a judgment on itself. The very language seems half to concede that its imaginings are compensatory. At this point, Landon draws a distinction between her quotidian self, rejected as "worthless," (82) and her inspired poetic self when "song has touch'd my lips with fire," (85) a distinction which owes much to Byron's contrast in *Childe Harold's Pilgrimage*, Canto 3, stanza 6, between his ordinary self and the "Soul of my thought," and to Shelley's movement in *Ode to the West Wind* from the self that falls upon "the thorns of life" (54) to the empowered self inspired by the wind whose "lyre" (57) he proposes to be. Landon's image of herself as "a vile link / Amid life's weary chain" (89–90) adapts both Byronic and Shelleyan images to her own condition.[18] The image of the "chain" seems especially to recall the moment in *Julian and Maddalo* when the Maniac cries out against dragging "life on—which like a heavy chain / Lengthens behind with many a link of pain" (302–3). "Oh do not say in vain!" (92) is Landon's exclamation after her proud assertion that she has spoken "hallow'd words" (91), hoping to counteract the force of the Maniac's tersely enjambed "How vain / Are words!" (472–3). Evidently Landon wears her chain with a difference;

---

[18] For the suggestion of an echo of *Childe Harold's Pilgrimage*, 3.72.685 ("A link reluctant in a fleshly chain'), see *Romantic Poetry: An Annotated Anthology*, ed. Michael O'Neill and Charles Mahoney (Malden: Blackwell, 2008), 465.

but there is kinship as well as distance between the imprisonment of disappointed yet residually heroic souls in *Lines of Life* and *Julian and Maddalo*. Just as the Maniac's conviction of the futility of words does not prevent him from speaking, so the element of creative self-doubt in *Lines of Life* cannot wholly quell the poet's desire that her "charmed chords" (94) will "Wake to the morning light of fame" (95). Such, she confesses, qualifying her earlier outburst at lines 55–6, is "My first, my last, my only wish" (93). The power of the poem lies in its compactly tensed gush of hope that the poet's "words" (96) will survive, murmured and read by future readers.

After these declarations comes the final stanza:

> Let music make less terrible
>   The silence of the dead;
> I care not, so my spirit last
>   Long after life has fled. (105–8)

Landon concludes with a "terrible" affirmation, her use of "terrible" (placed resonantly at the end of the line) strong enough to vibrate with the force of Pericles's "A terrible childbed hast thou had, my dear" (3.1.56) and yet in touch with the overlappings conjured up by Shelley in *To Night*, when he speaks of the "Spirit of Night" as having "wovest dreams of joy and fear, / Which make thee terrible and dear" (5–6).[19] Landon's own music brings out how "dear" her literary dreams of "joy and fear" have been, and bravely allows "The silence of the dead," set apart in a line to itself, its "terrible" and challenging authority. The "silence" imagined here is that which will fall upon her in death, and the "music" is perhaps that of a church-service, perhaps, more generally, composed of trumpet-blasts of fame. Such "music" now, almost as though Landon were forsaking fame, the last infirmity of noble minds, seems not to matter. "I care not," she writes, all her hopes pinned now on the survival of "my spirit." The poem lays bare, affectingly, the hopes and fears that underpin Romantic assertions that spirit is indomitable, as in its different way does a poem like *Adonais*, whose positive declarations—"the pure spirit shall flow / Back to the burning fountain whence it came" (338–9)—allow us to experience them as springing from the very human compulsion to find answers to formidable questions, in this case those broached earlier in Shelley's elegy: "Whence are we, and why are we? of what scene / The actors or spectators?" (184–5). A dramatized wildness and varied emotional turbulence fit themselves to the symmetrical neatness of Landon's stanzas, embodying the conflict between adherence to social

---

[19]     A sense that such Shelleyan tonalities are in play, and are not functioning merely as ironized quotations, obliges one to qualify McGann's view of the final stanza as not offering "any hope at all" (*The Poetics of Sensibility*, 168).

norms and the wish to break free from such norms at the centre of her strangely "terrible" poem.[20]

In response to a portrait of Keats, Landon sent to a correspondent some blank verse lines which were published in *The Examiner*, 1 September 1824. In them, she writes: "thou dost hold communion with / Thoughts dark and terrible," lines which mimic their imagined "communion" by loitering at the end of the line before the strong stresses that cluster in "Thoughts dark and terrible" (Sypher, 183–4). In this poem, Landon addresses Keats in Shelleyan terms: "thou / Wert like the lovely presence of a dream," she writes, and one recalls how the Poet of *Alastor*, republished in *Posthumous Poems* in the same year as Landon's poem about Keats appeared in print, was "driven / By the bright shadow of that lovely dream" (232–3). Landon, that is, conceives of Keats rather as the Poet shapes his imaginings of the lost "veiled maid" (151); in both Landon and Shelley the "lovely" twines disquietingly with the "terrible" (Landon) or the brightly shadowy (Shelley).

Landon responds most vividly to Shelley when she hears in his work the accents of transcendental seeker and anguishing elegist. In *A History of the Lyre* she plays her own gendered variation on the theme and mode of two Shelley poems, *Julian and Maddalo* and *Alastor*. Like Shelley in *Julian and Maddalo*, Landon surrounds presentation of a figure at the edge of society—in her case not a Maniac, but an improvisatrice, Eulalie—with a narrative frame.[21] Like Julian, the narrator writes, at the opening, of remembered experience: "This face, whose rudely pencill'd sketch you hold, / Recalls to me a host of pleasant Thoughts, / And some more serious—This is EULALIE" (5–7). And he proceeds later to a taking leave—"I soon left Italy" (378)—that echoes Julian's "The following morning, urged by my affairs, / I left bright Venice" (582–3), and to a subsequent return. Whereas Julian meets Maddalo's daughter, Landon's narrator, now married and with a child, meets Eulalie again, now virtually her own statue, an emblem of a creativity

---

20    The poem is the more powerful for complicating what Richard Cronin, in a very suggestive discussion, calls "the relationship that remains central in all of Landon's poems, the relationship between herself and her reader." For Cronin this "relationship" mimics the relationship between "poet and character": "These are stories of 'woman's tears,' and tears, for Landon, dissolve the distinction between poet and character. Her characters weep, and she represents the verse that records their tears as itself a kind of weeping" (*Romantic Victorians: English Literature, 1824–1840* [Basingstoke: Palgrave, 2002], 85). Landon's sobs are distinctly suppressed in *Lines of Life*.

21    For readings of *A History of the Lyre* see, in particular, Angela Leighton, *Victorian Women Poets: Writing against the Heart* (New York: Harvester Wheatsheaf, 1992), who argues that the poem benefits artistically from "a scepticism precisely against feeling" (68), and Angela Esterhammer, who explores "what happens when the writing poet self-consciously re-casts her own experience as that of an *improvvisatrice*" ("The Improvisatrice's Fame: Landon, Staël, and Female Performers in Italy," in *British and European Romanticisms: Selected Papers from the Munich Conference of the German Society for English Romanticism*, ed. Christoph Bode and Sebastian Domsch [Trier: Wissenschaftlicher Verlag Trier, 2007], 233).

foiling anything approaching normal human life: "Yon statue is my emblem; see, its grasp / Is raised to Heaven, forgetful that the while / Its step has crush'd the fairest of earth's flowers / With its neglect" (442–5).

Seeking to offer a sketch "from that most passionate page, / A woman's heart," as her poem's epigraph tells us, Landon also suggests that Eulalie is, in some way, a female descendant of Shelley's Poet in *Alastor*. Shelley's Poet, after a period in which he lives "without human sympathy," "seeks in vain for a prototype of his conception" (Preface to *Alastor*) of an ideal partner. If he represents from one moralizing perspective a warning against poetic solitude, he also, more powerfully, suggests the tragic fate of a figure dedicated to his own exalted conceptions. Eulalie, too, "would be beloved" (252), but she laments her inability to achieve love; like Shelley's Poet, Eulalie's commitment to the imagination seems to exile her from the world of ordinary feelings. When, at the close, then, in lines 442–5 quoted above, she seems to turn into an art-work, her own statue, she implicitly points up the life-stifling consequences of an artistic achievement that embodies transcendent yearning: the statue's "grasp" may be "Raised to Heaven," but "Its step has crush'd the fairest of earth's flowers / With its neglect." Shelley's Poet, too, treats "an Arab maiden" (129) with "neglect," before developing an obsession with his at least partially self-created and idealized "veiled maid"; moreover, in lines that Landon may be recalling, his own approaching physical dissolution inflicts a matching decay on the natural world: "from his steps / Bright flowers departed" (536–7).

Unlike Shelley's Poet, however, Eulalie receives due fame: she is "The centre of a group, whose converse light / Made a fit element, in which her wit / Flash'd like the lightning" (99–101), where Landon may draw her imagery from Shelley's *Letter to Maria Gisborne*, in which the poet recalls feeling "the transverse lightning linger warm / Upon my cheek" (149–50). But Shelley in that poem celebrates "good will" (151); Eulalie, in the midst of company, experiences a loneliness comparable to the Poet's in *Alastor*. Both Shelley and Landon unite in their admiration of "the immortal dead" (*A History of the Lyre*, 136), yet both are troubled by the status of "feeling." Just as Shelley's Maniac mistrusts language and just as Rousseau in *The Triumph of Life* worries that his words have been the "seeds of misery" (280), and yet just as in both poems the possible alternatives to Romantic intensities (suicidal despair or cynical indifference) seem untenable, so in *A History of the Lyre* Landon stages a possible impasse faced by a poet working in what Angela Leighton calls the "tradition of sensibility," and yet finally reaffirms commitment to feeling.[22] An earlier credo provoked by praise for Leigh Hunt's criticism—"in criticism as in everything else to feel is to understand" (Sypher, 184)—still abides. Eulalie's account of the unassuagable "price" (216) paid by the inspired poet again echoes emphases in Shelley. In the fragmentary lyric *The Zucca*, Shelley's speaker uses sinuous yet halting (and uncompleted) *ottava rima* to communicate a sense that "this low sphere, / And all that it contains, contains not thee" (20–21). "Thee,"

---

22    Leighton, 68.

there, is Shelley's version of Coleridge's Ideal Object, unlocatable for the younger poet in "this low sphere" and deriving its value from its unlocatableness. The poet is left to "weep / The instability of all but weeping" (9–10). In *The Triumph of Life*, Rousseau argues with fierce disdain that "if the spark with which Heaven lit my spirit / Had been with purer sentiment supplied, / Corruption would not now thus much inherit / Of what was once Rousseau,—nor this disguise / Stain'd that which ought to have disdain'd to wear it" (201–5). The complicated syntax keeps in play Rousseau's sense of being the victim of what was best about him, "the spark with which Heaven lit my spirit," even as the last line concedes a subliminal degree of responsibility for his fall.

The lines feel like the last testament of a High Romantic posture of the spirit—and to involve an embattled defence of such a posture. Landon, too, through Eulalie's history of her poetic career, speaks of disappointment but, finally, preserves a desperate faith in poetry. Eulalie's speech articulates mingled feelings of regret and longing. Like Shelley's speaker in "The Zucca," or like Rousseau, she complains that "gleams of heaven have only made me feel / Its distance from our earth more forcibly" (218–19). Yet to "feel" is to retain a spiritual distinction that has its own worth, and forces one to qualify Leighton's reading of the poem as showing that "To be sceptical is a new truth which L. E. L. learns towards the end of her poetic career."[23] "Learns," that powerful verb in Landon's vocabulary, passes over into the prose of one of her most distinguished critics, but whether the value of *A History of the Lyre* lies in a "sceptical" lesson that it supposedly teaches is a view about which one might wish to be "sceptical."

The critical desire to rescue Landon from the tearful idiom of sensibility with which she is often associated and see her as developing a maturer, skeptical reserve about feeling is understandable, but it risks overlooking her almost Blakean refusal to settle for the apparent truths of experience: hope and desire remain in the midst of clear evidence of their inevitable failure. Indeed, in the lines singled out by Leighton as marking a step towards a soberer truth, lines in which Eulalie describes how the increasingly disillusioned young poet "has turn'd sceptic to the truth which made / His feelings poetry" (297–8), Landon comes close to describing the condition against which Shelley warns in *Prometheus Unbound*, Act 1: "Ah, sister! Desolation is a delicate thing" (772). It is by no means clear that turning "sceptic to the truth which made / His feelings poetry" composes a stepping-stone towards some recompensing if disillusioned truth; indeed, poetic death is seen as the consequence of such skepticism: "What can he do / But hang his lute on some lone tree, and die?" (303–4). Eulalie, in fact, turns from such end-stopped skepticism to reawaken awareness of what cradled her into poetry in the first place and chiefly ascribes the originating impulse to "Remembrance" (311), a sense at once Wordsworthian and Shelleyan that "we must have known some former state / More glorious than our present" (305–6). Though such knowledge and remembrance are double-edged in that they bequeath a longing that takes

---

23    Leighton, 68.

away "happiness" (321), their lure is still to be felt in the poetry, which demonstrates tugs to and from "the actual world" (314): tugs of a kind often found in Shelley.

Eulalie says that it is remembrance "that fills the actual world / With unreal likenesses of lovely shapes, / That were and are not" (314–16), lines that come close to simultaneous critique of and empathy with Shelleyan idealism. Landon calls to mind Shelley's warning admonition to "Lift not the painted veil which those who live / Call Life: though unreal shapes be pictured there, / And it but mimic all we would believe / With colours idly spread" (*Lift not the painted veil*, 1–4). Eulalie speaks of "unreal likenesses of lovely shapes," but she does not condemn the shapes as "unreal," only their "likenesses"; she is still persuaded that such shapes "were," even if they "are not." Indeed, "the actual world" uses "actual" to suggest limitation; there must, she still implies, be more in heaven and earth than seems apparent in "the actual world." Shelley identifies "Life" with "unreal shapes" and "colours idly spread." In both poets the lure of the "real," as opposed to the "actual," can still be felt, for all their sense that disappointment lies in wait for the idealizing quester. Shelley's reversed sonnet features in its octave an account of one who "sought, / For his lost heart was tender, things to love, / But found them not, alas! nor was there aught / The world contains, the which he could approve" (7–10) The attitudes are balanced between detachment (his "heart" was "lost," and there is a shade of something almost arrogantly superior in "could approve") and sympathy (his heart was "tender," the quest for "things to love" sounds genuine). Shelley displaces the process on to a doubled other. Landon, too, uses Eulalie to depict a version of herself as poet. If the first-person narrative deployed by Landon makes Eulalie sound less guarded than Shelley in his sonnet, her confessions of fault are never unqualified: "My thoughts were birds of paradise, that breathed / The airs of heaven, but died on touching home" (338–9). Rousseau's rejection of a world which failed to sustain his heaven-lit spirit again resonates in the background, and it is Landon's distinction to reawaken memories of Shelley's own divided views of idealism.

The price paid as a poet in Landon's work is heavy, and frequently recounted by her. But it is, in Eulalie's words, "*my* price" (216; emphasis added). The value of poetry is never wholly rejected by Landon, even as she can see how in her culture and career poems can be merely commodified. Landon's reflections on the poetic career and on the Shelleyan or High Romantic legacy articulate themselves with most persuasiveness in her elegy for her fellow female poet, Felicia Hemans. From its opening "No more, no more—oh, never more returning, / Will thy beloved presence gladden earth" (1–2), Landon's poem alludes to other Romantic poems. Indeed, McGann invites us to see her as producing a "self-consciously quotational writing" that, so to speak, annuls itself in the act of utterance.[24] So, here one catches echoes of Byron's "Dejection Ode" stanzas in the first canto of *Don Juan*, which play on and play up a strain of plangency: "No more—no more—Oh, never more on me / The freshness of the heart can fall like dew" (stanza 214). One hears, too, Shelley's lament in *Adonais*: "He will awake no more, oh, never more!" (64). As

---

24    *The Poetics of Sensibility*, 147.

throughout her essay on Hemans, Landon is also alluding to the dead woman's poetry, especially her *No More!*, a poem which forms a lyric meditation on the "dirge-like sound" of the two words. McGann would have us respond to Landon as a pasticheur of genius who brilliantly exposes the hollowness of the poem as affect-commodity. This is more persuasive than John Constable's robust view that the opening echoes (he notes only the Byronic reference) expose Landon's threadbare lack of invention: "who but the apologist," Constable asks scornfully, "would care to distinguish the Byronism of Felicia Dorothea Hemans from that of Letitia Elizabeth Landon?"[25] The implication is that both are as bad as each other. But neither the consummate professional nor the artless amateur will quite suit as a label to define the elegist of *Felicia Hemans*. On closer inspection, the texture of the verse turns out to be less quotational than subtly aligning itself with a Romantic company of poets, all of whom win artistic recompense from experiential loss.

The very fact of beginning with multiple echoes associates Landon with poets who use words as a stay against the vanishing lamented by the content of the words. Thus, Landon invokes the visionary company of High Romantics, not as a simpering admirer nor as a gender-embattled critic, but as fellow-traveller through the same regions of initial delight in poetry's promise of supplying, Wordsworth-like, "A general bond of union" (21), then the subsequent discovery of poetry's cost—"Was not this purchased all too dearly?" (33). The power of this antistrophic turn in the poem where the original emphasis on what is "known" passes into what we "know not"—"We see the goal, but know not the endeavour" (35)—is immense. Landon's melodious, rhyming pentameters, with their alternating feminine rhymes, exist in affecting contrast to the "sorrow" that emerges in stanza 3 as inseparable from "song" (42). She plays a keenly individual variation on the Shelleyan discovery of the limits of knowledge, expressed in *To a Skylark* in the question "What thou art we know not" (31), or in *Julian and Maddalo* as Maddalo's sense that "Our thoughts and our desires" "pray" "For what? they know not" (125–7).

*Felicia Hemans* is sophisticated in its determination to tell the truth about what it is to be a female poet in Landon's culture. Landon employs dizzying double-takes: her elegy for Hemans is manifestly a poem in which the elegist dwells on her own concerns, much as the poet of *Adonais*, or his double, knows himself to be one "Who in another's fate now wept his own" (300). And what she shares with Hemans turns out to be a finally triumphant inability fully to break out of the very artistic work whose purpose is to tell us of "the long sad hours" (45) lived beyond art. The poem retains its dignity and poise, teaching in song what it has learned in suffering, which is that "song" and "sorrow" are fated always to stay apart from one another, itself a source of suffering: "We say, the song is sorrowful, but know not / What may have left that sorrow on the song" (41–2).

---

[25]     John Constable, "Romantic Women's Poetry: Is It Any Good?" *Cambridge Quarterly* 29 (2000): 142.

It is fitting that Landon uses Shelley to comprehend the nature of Hemans's (and her own) latent tragedies in two ways. She sees "The fable of Prometheus and the vulture" (55) as revealing "the poet's and the woman's heart" (56), implying the relevance of Shelley's most ambitious long poem; and she concludes by devising for Hemans an abode beyond this world that recalls Shelley's millennial imaginings in his lyrical drama. Asia is borne on by singing that is inspired by "music's most serene dominions" (*Prometheus Unbound*, 2.5.86). Landon invites Hemans to "Enter ... that serene dominion, / Where earthly cares and earthly sorrows cease" (75–6), turning Shelley's journey towards transformation into a resting-place. But even as she imagines a world beyond poetry, she finds solace and creative stimulus for her female poet in the "fascination" (Sypher, 175) still aroused in her by one of her most significant male forerunners.

## Works Cited

*Byron: Oxford Authors*. Ed. Jerome J. McGann. Oxford: Oxford University Press, 1986.

Constable, John. "Romantic Women's Poetry: Is It Any Good?" *Cambridge Quarterly* 29 (2000): 133–43.

Cronin, Richard. *Romantic Victorians: English Literature, 1824–1840*. Basingstoke: Palgrave, 2002.

Esterhammer, Angela. "The Improvisatrice's Fame: Landon, Staël, and Female Performers in Italy." In *British and European Romanticisms: Selected Papers from the Munich Conference of the German Society for English Romanticism*. Ed. Christoph Bode and Sebastian Domsch. Trier: Wissenschaftlicher Verlag Trier, 2007. 227–37.

Hazlitt, William. Review of Shelley's *Posthumous Poems* (1824). In *The Edinburgh Review*, July 1824. In *The Young Romantics and Critical Opinion, 1807–1824*. Comp. Theodore Redpath. London: Harrap, 1973. 388–96.

*The Keepsake for 1829*. Ed. Frederic Mansel Reynolds. London: Hurst, Chance, 1829.

Leighton, Angela. *Victorian Women Poets: Writing against the Heart*. New York: Harvester Wheatsheaf, 1992.

*Letitia Elizabeth Landon: Selected Writings*. Ed. Jerome McGann and Daniel Riess. Peterborough, ONT: Broadview, 1997.

McGann, Jerome J. *The Poetics of Sensibility: A Revolution in Literary Style*. Oxford: Clarendon Press, 1996.

Medwin, Thomas. *The Shelley Papers*. London: Whittaker, Treacher, 1833.

Mellor, Anne K. *Romanticism and Gender*. New York: Routledge, 1993.

*The Poems of W. B. Yeats: A Sourcebook*. Ed. Michael O'Neill. London: Routledge, 2004.

*The Poetical Works of Coleridge, Shelley and Keats 1829*. Ed. Cyrus Redding with A. Galignani and W. Galignani. Chosen and intro. Jonathan Wordsworth. Otley and Washington, DC: Woodstock, 2002.

*The Poetical Works of Mrs. Hemans, with Prefatory Memoir, Notes, Etc.* The "Albion" Edition. London: Warne, 1897.

*Romantic Poetry: An Annotated Anthology.* Ed. Michael O'Neill and Charles Mahoney. Malden: Blackwell, 2008.

*Shelley's Poetry and Prose.* Ed. Donald H. Reiman and Neil Fraistat. 2nd ed. New York: Norton, 2002.

*Shelley: Poetical Works.* Ed. Thomas Hutchinson. New ed. G. M. Matthews. London: Oxford University Press, 1970.

Sypher, F. J., ed. *Critical Writings by Letitia Elizabeth Landon.* Delmar: Scholars' Facsimiles and Reprints, 1996.

Taylor, Charles H., Jr. *The Early Collected Editions of Shelley's Poems: A Study in the History and Transmission of the Printed Text.* New Haven: Yale University Press, 1958.

Wasserman, Earl R. "The Poetry of Skepticism." Rpt. of section from *Shelley: A Critical Reading.* Baltimore: The Johns Hopkins University Press, 1971. 46–56. In *Shelley's Poetry and Prose.* Ed. Reiman and Fraistat. 570–79.

Webb, Timothy. "The Unascended Heaven: Negatives in *Prometheus Unbound.*" In *Shelley Revalued: Essays from the Gregynog Conference.* Ed. Kelvin Everest. Leicester: Leicester University Press, 1983. 37–62. Rpt. in *Shelley's Poetry and Prose.* Ed. Reiman and Fraistat. 694–711.

Wolfson, Susan J. "Hemans and the Romance of Byron." In *Felicia Hemans: Reimagining Poetry in the Nineteenth Century.* Ed. Nanora Sweet and Julie Melnyk. Basingstoke: Palgrave, 2001. 155–80.

*The Works of Percy Bysshe Shelley, with His Life.* 2 vols. London: Ascham, 1834.

## Chapter 10
# Romantic and Victorian Conversations: Elizabeth Barrett and Robert Browning in Dialogue with Byron and Shelley

Jane Stabler

In this essay I want to reconsider conversations about Lord Byron and Percy Shelley in the courtship and early married poetic partnership of Elizabeth Barrett and Robert Browning.[1] I want to look beyond the local effects of literary allusion at the ways in which Byron's and Shelley's concerns about the poet's humanity are reconfigured and re-played by the Romantic Victorians who followed them into exile in Italy. I am interested in the possibility that poets might deal with influence collectively: how influence might work through fellowship, rather than competition and anxiety. Work by Beth Lau, Lucy Newlyn and Jane Spencer has helpfully complicated monolithic notions of reception, but what William D. Brewer called the "Shelley-Byron conversation" still tends to be studied in relation to their influence on individuals.[2]

Relationships among these poets question the idea of separate gender spheres in at least two ways: Elizabeth Barrett and Robert Browning clearly identify themselves with the same poetic aspects of Byron and Shelley; related to this, Barrett and Browning see their own roles as poets in society in terms that challenge the feminization of poetry in the nineteenth century and strenuously uphold its relevance to humanity at large. As a young woman, Elizabeth Barrett carved out a masculine identity for herself as a reader of poetry, and she went on to make more political poetic interventions than her husband. The references to Byron and Shelley by Barrett and Browning show that poetic identities are not consistently gendered and also that the literary concern with posterity may establish a realm beyond binary gender divisions. Barrett felt that the office of

---

[1]   I shall refer to EBB as Barrett before her marriage and Barrett Browning after. As Mary Shelley is not mentioned in the essay, I shall refer to Percy Shelley as Shelley.

[2]   Beth Lau, *Keats's Paradise Lost* (Gainesville: University Press of Florida, 1998); Lucy Newlyn, *Reading, Writing and Romanticism: The Anxiety of Reception* (Oxford: Oxford University Press, 2000); Jane Spencer, *Literary Relations: Kinship and the Canon 1660–1830* (Oxford: Oxford University Press, 2005); William D. Brewer, *The Shelley-Byron Conversation* (Gainesville: University Press of Florida, 1994).

a poet was that of "analyzing humanity back into its elements."[3] The concept of "man" or "humanity"—so often seen as the inscription of a male culture in the Romantic period—is inflected by the Brownings with an imaginative androgyny that questions rigid gender identities.

Although this essay will argue that strict binary divisions are dissolved in the shared legacies of Byron and Shelley, "pairing" has a structural significance for Elizabeth Barrett and Robert Browning. Beyond their penchant for arranging poems in pairs in which one answers another, the discourse of opposition and complementarity also accords with the way they viewed each other as poets: "You & I seem to meet in a mild contrarious harmony. as in the 'si .. no .. si .. no' of an Italian duet" Elizabeth Barrett wrote to Browning in March 1845 (*BC*, 10:134). In May, she told him: "we stand on the black & white sides of the shield,—& there is no coming to a conclusion" (*BC*, 10:227). Their dialogues in the courtship correspondence established a mental realm of unending debate that was simultaneously erotic and genderless. At the heart of these discussions was a shared quest to connect their individual poetic identities with their souls: "to utter all myself" as Barrett urged, without forfeiting the tender, if fallible "dark edges of the sensual ground" (*The Soul's Expression*, 11, 8).[4] Given the vagaries of the poetic market place, the soul of the poet might be illuminated or traduced by published works and public reputation. The figure of Wordsworth illustrates the instability of poetic personality and reception: Elizabeth Barrett's sonnet on Haydon's Portrait (published in *Poems*, 1844) regards Wordsworth as an archetypal genius "singing … / To the higher Heavens" (10–11). For Barrett, Wordsworth is emphatically regal and masculine: "one inclined / Before the sovran thought of his own mind," a "poet-priest / By the high altar" (6–7; 9–10). Meanwhile Browning focuses on the fickle, dandyish aspects of apostasy in *The Lost Leader* (published in *Dramatic Romances and Lyrics* in November 1845): "Just for a handful of silver he left us, / Just for a ribband to stick in his coat" (1–2).[5] However, both regarded Wordsworth as a quintessentially solitary figure. For Barrett and Browning, a temperamental inclination toward poetic isolation followed by ethical rejection of that condition converges with their evolving theories on lyric and drama and subjective or objective forms of poetry.

The presentation of Byron and Shelley as a poetic dyad was set up by Shelley himself in *Julian and Maddalo; A Conversation*—and then by Leigh Hunt in *Lord Byron and Some of His Contemporaries* (1828) in which Shelley figures as an

---

[3]     *The Brownings' Correspondence*, ed. Philip Kelley, Ronald Hudson, Scott Lewis and Edward Hagan, 16 vols. (Winfield: Wedgestone Press, 1984–2007), 10:101; hereafter abbreviated and given parenthetically in the text as *BC* with volume and page reference.

[4]     Unless otherwise noted, Barrett's poems are quoted from *The Poetical Works of Elizabeth Barrett Browning*, ed. Frederic G. Kenyon (London: Smith, Elder, 1897), hereafter abbreviated *PWEEB*.

[5]     Unless otherwise noted, Browning's poems are quoted from *The Poems of Browning*, ed. John Woolford and Daniel Karlin, 2 vols. (London: Longman, 1991).

immaterial and Byron as a very material being. Their differences were accentuated and sometimes gendered in essays and debates between the 1830s and 1880s when they were seen as mutually opposing but equally negative directions for poetry. One influential strand of criticism portrays Byron's as a masculine voice while seeing Shelley's nature as

> utterly womanish. Not merely his weak points, but his strong ones, are those of a woman. Tender and pitiful as a woman and yet, when angry, shrieking, railing, hysterical as a woman. The physical distaste for meat and fermented liquors, coupled with the hankering after physical horrors, are especially feminine.[6]

For Charles Kingsley, Shelley was responsible for a "spasmodic, vague, extravagant, effeminate school of poetry"[7] and although, for several important Victorian critics, the "decadence of modern English poetry began from Keats," it was largely Shelley who was seen to have "swayed" the taste for aestheticism that allegedly filled poetry with "Tennysonian maidens and Pre-Raphaelite damosels," sending it into a region "farther and farther from normal human experience … where white peacocks wander about in gas-lit gardens of green chrysanthemums and yellow carnations": Pre-Raphaelite poetry, argued J. F. A. Pyre, lacked "the promise of a *man*."[8]

For many Victorians, Byron epitomized the poet as man even though they lamented the way in which "his demeanor, as a man, was bad."[9] For a few, of course, Byron was so bad that his nature also tilted into the realm of the womanish. Carlyle depicted him as "a huge *sulky Dandy*";[10] Henry Taylor argued that Byron's heroes "are creatures abandoned to their passions, and essentially, therefore, weak of mind" who would "excite no sentiment … in the eyes of a reader of masculine judgment."[11] However, Byron's vaunted self-division and the satirical energy of his later career retrieved his masculinity for writers like Arnold.

The nineteenth-century critics of Barrett and Browning judge them against Byron and Shelley with an ease that suggests the poetry of the Romantic generation was still very current: Elizabeth Barrett, for example, was unkindly called "*a Christian Shelley without Shelley's art*" (*BC*, 10:390). Browning's *Sordello* reminded one reviewer of "Shelley's 'Julian and Maddalo' with a touch

---

[6]   Charles Kingsley, *Miscellanies*, 2 vols. (London: John Parker, 1859), 1:314–15.

[7]   Kingsley, 1:318.

[8]   Andrew Rutherford, ed., *Byron: The Critical Heritage*, ed. (London: Routledge & Kegan Paul, 1970), 492–3.

[9]   Rutherford, 291.

[10]   Rutherford, 291.

[11]   Preface to *Philip van Arteveldte*, 2 vols. (London: Moxon, 1834), xviii. Another comment on Byron's distance from "the composite fabric which Nature has assigned to Man" is quoted in John Woolford, *Browning the Revisionary* (New York: St Martin's, 1988), 31.

of Keats's 'Endymion,' broken up into numerous pit-falls ... but there are also other occasions when it becomes spiral, and of sustained inspiration, not unlike certain parts of the 'Prometheus Unbound' put into rhyme" (*BC*, 6:387). Drawing on the contiguous relationships identified by nineteenth-century reviewers, I want to foreground the idea of a conversation between Romantic and Victorian couples, the idea of the "unpredictable outcome" Marlon Ross describes when he nominates the competition between "fellow poets" as more intense than the struggle between fathers and sons.[12]

Ross argues that pairings that involve a woman in a dominant position are repressed in Romantic poetry, but in the case of Barrett and Browning, Barrett was seen as the stronger poet by her contemporaries and by Browning. As Laura Haigwood points out:

> In their courtship and marriage, the Brownings did not contend for that "mastery" the wife of Bath and other traditional sources of marital wisdom cite as the usual object of competition between the sexes. Instead they struggled over the privilege of admiring and serving the other. Robert Browning won that competition, his victory both symptom and cause of a poetic silence that lasted throughout most of his married life.[13]

I shall now look in more detail at the way Barrett and Browning advanced their poetic aspirations for themselves and each other by re-reading Byron and Shelley. I suggest that their conversations about their Romantic doubles complicate notions of gender in the role of the poet, particularly its bearing on the question of the poet's humanity.

Before they met, Elizabeth Barrett and Robert Browning were already under the influence of Byron and Shelley, respectively, and it is clear that they regarded them, not as precursors so much as contemporaries: "Byron, Coleridge .. how many more? .. were contemporaries of mine without my having approached them near enough to look reverently in their faces ... and young as I was," Barrett wrote in 1843, "I cannot get rid of a feeling of deep regret that, so,—it shd. have been" (*BC*, 7:319).[14] As Marjorie Stone points out in her incisive chapter on Elizabeth

---

[12]   *The Contours of Masculine Desire*: *Romanticism and the Rise of Women's Poetry* (New York: Oxford University Press, 1989), 92.

[13]   Laura E. Haigwood, "Gender-to Gender Anxiety and Influence on Robert Browning's *Men and Women*," *Browning Institute Studies* 14 (1986): 97.

[14]   See Paul A. Cundiff, *Robert Browning: A Shelley Promethean* (St. Petersburg, FL: Valkyrie Press: 1977); John Maynard, *Browning's Youth* (Cambridge: Harvard University Press, 1977); Herbert F. Tucker, Jr., *Browning's Beginnings: The Art of Disclosure* (Minneapolis: University of Minnesota Press, 1980); James Thorpe, "Elizabeth Barrett's Commentary on Shelley: Some Marginalia," *Modern Language Notes* 66.7 (1951): 455–8; Margaret M. Morlier, "The Death of Pan: Elizabeth Barrett Browning and the Romantic Ego," *Browning Institute Studies* 18 (1990): 131–55; Richard C. Keenan, "Browning and

Barrett's Romantic revisionism, Barrett's formative years "belong to the Romantic, not the Victorian period."[15] Harold Bloom's theory of poetic influence is a linear, vertical, patriarchal one, but it makes much more sense to see the Brownings' engagement with Byron and Shelley as an uneven, lateral, sibling matrix, one in which episodes of love, hate, and rivalry are not separate stages but much more enfolded. As Juliet Mitchell's psychoanalytic work has established, ambivalence is a key feature of sibling relationships that are never wholly resolved.[16]

Elizabeth Barrett was cooler about Shelley than Byron—this is, in part, because she saw Shelley as a cold poet: "high, & yet too low, elemental poet, who froze in cold glory between Heaven & earth, neither dealing with man's heart, beneath, nor aspiring to communion with the supernal Humanity, the heart of the God-Man. Therefore his poetry glitters & is cold" (*BC*, 5:60). "Coldness" is a property Barrett always associates with the non-latitudinarian or inhuman, the most telling example being Lady Byron: "There are two false wives, within the last century, standing cold upon pedestals of alabaster . one of them being called by their admiring publics, '*Innocence*'.. the other .. '*Virtue*',—Marie Louise [Napoleon's widow] & Lady Byron! Oh! I know that Lady Byron is of course 'wisest virtuosest discreetest best' .. but 'all that' just makes her odiousest to *me*" (*BC*, 7:60). Meanwhile, of Byron: "*He* was not by nature cold & heartless—but his affections were turned into bitterness" (*BC*, 2:139). For Barrett, Byron's suffering connects him with the heart. Her *Stanzas on the Death of Lord Byron* salute his "generous heart" (16); paradoxically, his intense subjectivity makes him "[stand] nearer to the crowd, because everybody understands passion" (*PWEBB*, 647). "Take out my heart," she says to her mentor Hugh Stuart Boyd in 1842, "look at it … & tell me if I do not love & admire Byron more warmly than you" (*BC*, 6:192). Throughout her early work, Barrett instinctively categorizes her major influences using a scale of humanity on which Shelley appears as a disembodied visage, "in his white ideal, / All statue-blind" (*A Vision of Poets*, 406–7).[17] In the same Romantic pantheon, Byron is simultaneously more human and more mobile:

> And poor, proud Byron, sad as grave
> And salt as life; forlornly brave,
> And quivering with the dart he drave. (*A Vision of Poets*, 412–14)

---

Shelley," *Browning Institute Studies* 1 (1973): 119–45; David Latane, "Shelley's 'Baleful Influence,'" *Studies in Browning and His Circle*, 11.2 (1983): 31–6; Loy D. Martin, "Browning: The Activation of Influence," *Victorian Newsletter* 53 (1978): 4–9.

[15]    Marjorie Stone, *Elizabeth Barrett Browning* (New York: St Martin's Press, 1995), 49.

[16]    Juliet Mitchell, *Siblings* (Cambridge: Polity, 2003).

[17]    "Blind" is the word Elizabeth Barrett uses of herself when she imagines her life before Robert Browning as one of sensory deprivation and disconnection from life. Barrett refers to Byron as "blind" in *The Book of the Poets*: "Poor Byron (true miserable genius, soul-blind great poet!)" (*PWEBB*, 647).

Barrett's triplets in *A Vision of Poets* interweave the company of poets in a dreamy pageant, and while "quivering" yields a degree of instability, "salt" suggests the earthy taste of Byron—pungent, physical, and erotic. The salacious side of Byron's writing held ambiguous appeal to Barrett: she could joke about her father's belief that it was indecorous for a young woman to read *Don Juan*, leading him to keep it as a locked book, but it is a more pious *Don Juan* that becomes the prime model for *Aurora Leigh*. Despite this corrective swerve, her formal discipleship does not precisely match the Bloomian trajectory described by Marjorie Stone, just as G. K. Chesterton found that she did not "fit" with customary assumptions about gender: "She was too strong and too weak, or (as a false sex philosophy would express it) too masculine and too feminine."[18] Chesterton's wariness about a reductive categorization based on gender is instructive, and his comments on a simultaneous mixture of masculine and feminine in Barrett's work anticipate our investigation of the significance of "humanity" in her poetry, which is a conscious correction of the "incomplete" manhood of Byron (*PWEBB*, 647).

Stone sees a steady Bloomian chronological development across Barrett's successive volumes with the *Battle of Marathon* and *An Essay on Mind* as revealing "a desire for absolute assimilation" with the Satanic School; then the 1838 volume *The Seraphim, and Other Poems*, entering into the second and third phases of Bloomian poetic incarnation: competition and the rise of individual aspiration.[19] The 1844 collection including *A Drama of Exile* and *A Vision of Poets* reveals a "revisionary swerve" in which Barrett enters the later phases of poetic realization and establishes her own "veritable presence" (Stone, 93). The intertextual dynamics of Barrett's writing are surely less orderly than Stone's account suggests. From her earliest verses, Barrett was attracted to Byron's masculine isolationism but soon channeled the force of his Promethean rebellion into earth-bound relationship rather than exile.

Barrett's poem *Leila*, written when she was sixteen, takes the name of one of Byron's silent women victims from *The Giaour*, Byron's first Turkish Tale. It is written in Spenserian stanzas, the measure of Byron's 1812 best seller, *Childe Harold's Pilgrimage*, and it borrows Byronic incident with a twist. In Barrett's poem, Leila is responsible for releasing the prisoners of her father, the Corsair, one of whom dies almost immediately while the other charges out and kills her father. The poem is full of Byronic echoes, but the daughter's plea for Christian reconciliation instead of revenge, followed by her unleashing of the force that kills her parent, complicates the narrative appeal of outlaw action with its social consequences. Barrett's Leila is a mixture of Byron's most active female principals—Haidee, in charge of her island during the father's absence and Gulnare, visiting the Corsair in his prison. Barrett realized the potential of Byron's heroines to be other than the

---

[18]   G. K. Chesterton, *The Victorian Age in Literature* (London: Oxford University Press, 1955), 110.

[19]   Stone, 56.

"yielding slaves" depicted by Hazlitt,[20] and she rewrote Byron from the beginning of her career.

Elizabeth Barrett's deployment of the page figure is a significant re-orienting of Byronic gender roles. Barrett famously admitted that, as a girl, she had wanted to be Lord Byron's page. Nearly all her critics have taken this as a submissive, hero-worshipping gesture, but the cross-dressed page holds a position of ironic authority over her master, aware of more than the lord she ostensibly serves, and Barrett considerably heightens this ironic dimension in her "Romaunt." Marjorie Stone reads the poem as a legacy of the Romantic ballad tradition, particularly influenced by Sir Walter Scott's *Marmion*. Scott's poem certainly includes a cross-dressed page, but a more likely model is Byron's *Lara*.[21] The key point of contact between the two poems is in the glowing red "blush" of the page that reveals a preternatural sensitivity. Here is Byron's page:

> Light was his form, and darkly delicate
> That brow whereon his native sun had sate
> But had not marr'd, though in his beams he grew,
> The cheek where oft the unbidden blush shone through;
> Yet not such blush as mounts when health would show
> All the heart's hue in that delighted glow;
> But 'twas a hectic tint of secret care
> That for a burning moment fevered there. (*Lara*, 528–35)[22]

This "darkly delicate form" is ambiguous in racial and gender terms and linguistically hedged with qualification ("But ... Yet ... But"). Youthful epicene beauty is tantalizingly marked with experience ("secret care"), so that the body signals its enthrallment to another. Elizabeth Barrett's page is, by contrast, a much more poised, cerebral being:

> Slowly and thankfully
>   The young page bowed his head;
> His large eyes seemed to muse a smile,
>   Until he blushed instead,
> And no lady in her bower, pardiè,
>   Could blush more sudden red. (63–8)

The meter is closer to a ballad form than to Byron's loose couplets, but there are no such revealing blushes in Scott's *Marmion*. The watchfulness of Barrett's

---

[20]  Rutherford, 270.

[21]  Mary Sanders Pollock discusses the same episode of cross dressing in *Elizabeth Barrett and Robert Browning: A Creative Partnership* (Aldershot: Ashgate, 2003), 32–4.

[22]  Lord Byron, *The Complete Poetical Works*, ed. Jerome J. McGann, 7 vols. (Oxford: Oxford University Press, 1980–1993).

page is clearly that of Byron's Kaled—"For hours on Lara he would fix his glance, / As all forgotten in that watchful trance" (545–6)—but Barrett's page is "musing" not "burning." The cool assessment that accompanies the devotion works metonymically to figure Barrett's attitude to her fellow poet.

From the beginning, Elizabeth Barrett Browning exerts a watchful and protective gaze over Byron, trying to "rescue" him from the prevailing negative critical assessments after his death, but also judging him. She refused to read Leigh Hunt's *Lord Byron and Some of His Contemporaries* when it was published because "I had understood that he said cruel things … of poor Byron" (*BC*, 5:156). She always refers to him as "poor" Byron or "poor, poor Byron," that is, someone more vulnerable than herself.[23] When Richard Hengist Horne asserted that Caroline Norton's verses about her broken marriage were less vindictive than Byron's notorious *Poems* marking his separation from Lady Byron (1816), Elizabeth Barrett gallantly defended him:

> Poor, poor Ld. Byron! Now wd. I lay the sun & moon against a tennis ball that he had more tenderness in one section of his heart, than Mrs. Norton has in all her's,—though a tenderness misunderstood & crushed, ignorantly, profanely & vilely, by false friends and a pattern wife. His blood is on our heads—on us in England! Even as Napoleon's is!- (*BC*, 8:176)

One of her early poetic fantasies is that of saving or converting the alienated Romantic egotist. This is partly a religious salvation, but it also involved a salving of masculine and feminine elements. In Barrett's early poems, the isolated male hero needs the help of a tenacious female guide. Her poems present women who stand by their men, even if that means being dragged from a horse as in *The Rhyme of the Duchess May* (1844) or turning up as a corpse on the doorstep as in *The Poet's Vow* (1838). In *The Poet's Vow*, the scroll Rosalind's dead hands present to the male poet constitutes a critical bequest, a woman's last word and a claim for equality:

> "Look on me with thine own calm look:
> I meet it calm as thou.
> No look of thine can change *this* smile,
> Or break thy sinful vow:
> I tell thee that my poor scorned heart
> Is of thine earth—thine earth, a part:
> It cannot vex thee now." (423–9)

Like "clay," "earth" is a word loaded with Byronic resonance because of its corporeal materiality. When one of Elizabeth Barrett's correspondents questioned

---

[23]   See, for example, *BC*, 2:138–9, 5: 156, 6:42, 6:127. Barrett also refers to Keats and Shelley in this way, effacing the usual gendered division between Byron and Keats.

her love of Byron because "the stream of his poetry has such an earthy flavour," he unwittingly identified exactly what appeals to her (*BC*, 8:131). Barrett, like Browning (but unlike his idealistic painter), welcomes the sweetness of water with "such specks of earth" (*Pictor Ignotus*, 72), and she resists the pull into splendid isolation even while she acknowledges the appeal of a more rarified zone. Elizabeth Barrett accused herself of having lived "only inwardly,—or with *sorrow*, for a strong emotion" (*BC*, 10:133), for all of her adult life before Robert Browning. To him, she expressed her guilt about being the cause of her brother's death, "how, 'not with my hand but heart' I was the cause" (*BC*, 11:43), using words (not glossed by Barrett's editors) from Byron's *Manfred* and revealing the extent of her identification with the lone Byronic hero.

In the early stages of their acquaintance, Robert Browning deflected Barrett's fear of premature intimacy by describing his interior world as a cold and inhospitable one with "huge layers of ice and pits of black cold water" (*BC*, 10:233). He too understood the lure of a remote, artistic existence: Barrett intuited the hidden side of his social life when she wrote, "You are Paracelsus—and I am a recluse" (*BC*, 10:133). The hero of *Paracelsus* (1835) laments the fact that he is "Not Christ nor Cain" (5.320). As this echo from *Adonais* suggests, Browning is usually seen as infatuated with Shelley the seer in the 1830s and 40s after his early flirtation with the declamatory Byron in *Incondita* (1824). While critics have limited Byron's influence on Elizabeth Barrett to her earliest volumes of poetry, what has been overlooked in Browning's case is the influence of Byron's history plays, a mode in which the isolation of the Romantic hero is subject to corrosive dramatic irony.

Browning's early involvement with the theater was overshadowed, if not eclipsed, by Byron's posthumous existence. William Macready, the famous Victorian actor manager who put Browning's first play, *Strafford*, on stage was also famous for his versions of Byron's dramas. Browning and Macready met briefly at the end of 1835, and at the beginning of 1836 Browning began to sketch out the possibility of writing a tragedy. Macready encouraged him but soon regretted that impulse. "Read over *Strafford* to the persons in the green-room," he recorded in his journal on 8 April 1837, "but did not produce the impression I had hoped—it dragged its slow length along."[24] During his time at Drury Lane and Covent Garden, Macready produced Byron's *Marino Faliero*, *Werner* and *The Two Foscari* successfully and Browning's *Blot in the Scutcheon* unsuccessfully— it ran for three nights only. In 1842 Browning sent a letter to tell the actor "how impressed I was by your admirable Faliero" (*BC*, 6:103). Nevertheless, critics have

---

[24]    J. C. Trewin, ed., *The Journal of William Charles Macready*, (London: Longmans, 1967), 94. The problem is exactly the one that Macready had earlier diagnosed with Byron's plays. See, for example, his verdict on *The Two Foscari* as "not dramatic" because of "the slow, almost imperceptible progress of the action" (Frederick Pollack, ed., *Macready's Reminiscences and selections from his Diaries and Letters* [New York: Macmillan, 1875], 316).

persistently underestimated the presence of Byron the playwright in Browning's early career.

Byron's Italian plays, in particular, dramatize the cost of political ambition on home and family life. Angiolina in *Marino Faliero* protests that she is "shut out" from her husband's world (2.1.214); Marina questions the humanity of all Venetian power brokers, including her husband; in *Werner*, Josephine contrasts the communal life of Tuscany with the politics of the north where "despots ... appear / To imitate the ice-wind of their clime, / ... And 'tis to be among these sovereigns / My husband pants!" (1.1.720–25). These dramatizations of public life as a cold, masculine sphere that inflicts huge psychic damage by excluding the feminine may explain why the last scene of Browning's *Strafford* (which is set in the Tower of London in the time of Charles I) uses children singing a Venetian boat song borrowed from Leigh Hunt to underscore the pathos of the disintegration of family life.

Byron and Shelley both explored ways in which the poetic hero, for all his intense insight, lacked a full participation in life. Victorian critics expressed similar fears about the hero as an anxiety about gender: Charles Kingsley's attack on Shelley was an attempt to counter a spreading "notion of artistic genius," which had fostered men

> affecting the pettiest absurdities in dress, in manner, in food; giving themselves credit for being unable to bear a noise, keep their temper, educate their own children, associate with their fellow men. ... The brain may be large, but the manhood, the "virtus," is small.[25]

For Kingsley, Byron passed the test of being able to associate with his fellow men: he "'had no objection to a pot of beer;' and ... might, if he had reformed, have made a gallant English gentleman." Shelley, on the other hand, "if once his intense self-opinion had deserted him, would have probably ended in Rome, as an Oratorian or a Passionist"—that is in retreat from the world, under a quasi-female vow of obedience.[26]

In response to critical doubts about the efficacy of poetry, Barrett and Browning both take the position that poetry must be connected with contemporary life: "[Y]ou tempt me with a grand vision of Prometheus," Barrett writes to Browning in March 1845, "Why should we go back to the antique moulds ... Let us all aspire rather to *Life*—& let the dead bury their dead" (*BC*, 10:135). *Aurora Leigh* champions poetry of "this live, throbbing age" (6.203). In his essay on Shelley (written 1851; published 1852), Browning argues that "it is with this world, as starting point and basis alike, that we shall always have to concern ourselves: the world is not to be learned and thrown aside, but reverted to and re-learned."[27] Their

---

[25]   Kingsley, 1:322.

[26]   Kingsley, 1:311.

[27]   *Shelley: The Man and the Poet* (Hull: J.R. Tutin, n.d [1908]), 10.

attempts to connect poetry with contemporary life involve issues of gender and genre, but also reach beyond these orders into matters of faith.

Browning's essay on Shelley discusses the poet's relationship with his age: Shelley is featured as the exemplary "subjective poet," that is, the poet who writes "not so much with reference to the many below as to the one above him... . Not what man sees, but what God sees" (8). God, according to *Paracelsus* was "the perfect poet" (2:648). Browning's famously convoluted objective and subjective categories evolved from his esteem for Barrett's ability to "speak out" while he "only [makes] men & women speak" (*BC*, 10:22).[28] She had answered that she found him "both subjective & objective in the habits of [his] mind," a range that she found "'masculine' to the height" (*BC*, 10:26). For Barrett, Byron was the ideal subjective poet whose soul emits "inspired pages" (Preface to *The Battle of Marathon*; *PWEBB*, 2), but who retained his connection with "the many below." Browning equaled Byron's ability to scale "those high faint notes of the mystics which are beyond personality .. to dramatic impersonations, gruff with nature" (*BC*, 10:79). Her admiration for Browning's grasp of a full humanity is evident in *Lady Geraldine's Courtship* (the poem that impelled Browning to write to her), where she describes her character reading "From Browning some 'Pomegranate,' which, if cut deep down the middle, / Shows a heart within blood-tinctured, of a veined humanity" (163–4). The question of which mode of poetry could best touch "humanity" informs their debates about how to combine objective and subjective modes, as Browning's essay allowed for the possibility that "these two modes of poetic faculty may ... issue ... from the same poet in successive perfect works" (*Shelley*, 11).

Eventually, the Brownings produced poems in which the subjective and objective modes of poetic faculty were conjoined: Barrett's early desire to speak "without mask" (*BC*, 10:103) was modified by Browning's brilliance with masks and her own games with identity in *Sonnets from the Portuguese*. For both poets, soul found an outlet in experimental hybrid modes that explains why, for them, the soul could be a gender neutral "it" rather than the inevitably feminine agent of poetic creation.[29] The androgynous nature of the soul blends generic and gendered divisions into composite unions, mirroring the new identity the Brownings discovered as they edited each other's writing. Barrett and Browning

---

28    Daniel Karlin makes clear that "Elizabeth Barrett is a type of what Browning, in *Shelley: The Man and the Poet,* was later to call the 'subjective poet.'" See *The Courtship of Robert Browning and Elizabeth Barrett* (Oxford: Clarendon Press, 1985), 184.

29    For the soul's (feminized) gender in the work of Byron and Shelley, see Susan Wolfson, *Borderlines: The Shiftings of Gender in British Romanticism* (Stanford: Stanford University Press, 2006), 297–300. Barrett Browning refers to her soul as feminine in *Finite and Infinite* and in *Love* (see below), but the soul is an "it" in *An Essay on Mind, The Soul's Travelling, A Drama of Exile, Rhapsody on Life's Progress, Casa Guidi Windows* and *Aurora Leigh.*

found another model of fusion in the hybrid mental theater employed by an earlier Romantic generation.

In May 1836 Macready, Walter Savage Landor, and Browning dined with William Wordsworth. They were discussing Talfourd's latest tragedy *Ion* and what it was that makes a successful drama. Macready recorded:

> Wordsworth seemed pleased when I pointed out the passage in *Ion,* of a "devious fancy", etc., as having been suggested by the lines *he* had once quoted from a MS tragedy of his; he smiled and said. "Yes, I noticed them," and then he went on:
>       "Action is transitory—a step—a blow,
>       The motion of a muscle—this way or that—
>       'Tis done; and in the after vacancy
>       We wonder at ourselves like men betrayed."[30]

Browning would have heard the lines as confirmation of his own dramatic principle: in the Preface to *Strafford* he wrote that the play is one of "Action in Character rather than Character in Action" (the principle that went on to guide his dramatic monologues). It is exactly what Wordsworth has advertised as the principle of *Lyrical Ballads*: "the feeling therein developed gives importance to the action and situation and not the action and situation to the feeling."[31]

Six years later, and three years before her first meeting with Robert Browning, Elizabeth Barrett returned the newly published *Borderers* to her friend Mr. Kenyon with the observation, "The Tragedy will be considered probably 'naught' as a whole, but of considerable entity of beauty in detached parts. … There are … very noble passages which are not dramatic—for instance that noblest of the noble which the poet employed before—long ago—as a motto—& which seemed then to belong to the great 'didactic poem' in the treasure-house .... 'Action is transitory .. a step, a blow.' Altogether we surely ought to be grateful for it .. call it tragedy .. poem—discrepancy .. what you please" (*BC*, 5:311).

The gendering of Wordsworth's tragedy is indeterminate: Browning hears Wordsworth reciting the part of a male tragic hero, and Barrett recognizes the text of an epigraph from *The White Doe of Rylstone* (1815), in which the capacity to suffer is transferred to the Lady Emily. In *The Book of the Poets* (1863), Barrett argues that Wordsworth was "intensely rather than actively human; capacious to embrace within himself the whole nature of things and beings, but not going out of himself to embrace anything; a poet of one large sufficient soul, but not polypsychical like a dramatist" (649). It would be all too easy to gender the sympathetic, permeable, objective poet as feminine and the more egotistical, abstract, subjective poet as masculine, the latter concerned, as Browning's essay put it, "Not with the combination of humanity in action, but with the primal elements of humanity

---

[30]   Trewin, 70. The lines are from Wordsworth's *The Borderers*.

[31]   *Lyrical Ballads*, ed. R. L. Brett and A. R. Jones, 2nd ed. (London: Routledge, 1991), 248.

he has to do … preferring to seek them in his own soul as the nearest reflex of that absolute Mind" (*Shelley*, 8). But, as Susan Wolfson reminds us, Wordsworth "is not the sure, secure figure of logocentric performance and egocentric confidence ascribed to him in some feminist … readings of Romanticism."[32] The "egotistical sublime" is not necessarily male. Charles Kingsley saw dramatic sympathy with the world as a correct *manly* trait whereas he classed self-involution as feminine: Shelley's repulsive femininity for Kingsley was connected with his inability to write for the stage: "he never wrote a real drama; for in spite of all that has been said to the contrary, Beatrice Cenci is really none other than Percy Bysshe himself in petticoats."[33]

When Barrett discusses Wordsworth's inability to "go out of himself," she admits that despite this profound lack of broad human sympathy, individual instances in his drama "knock against the heart" (*The Book of the Poets*, 650). This allusion is not signaled, but it takes us to Miranda at the start of *The Tempest*: "O, I have suffered / With those that I saw suffer! a brave vessel … Dash'd all to pieces. O, the cry did knock? Against my very heart!" (1.2.4–9).[34] Barrett's borrowing of Shakespeare here is suggestive of gender instability in a number of ways: firstly, she uses a female character's words, as imagined by a man, and secondly, while Miranda is a beautiful portrait of female sympathy, Coleridge pointed out that her early words show her to be untroubled by awareness of different genders.

The instability of gender in episodes of poetic allusion raises the question of the extent to which poets in any age are able to imagine a world that is not polarized by gender but is "androgynous" as Coleridge felt a great mind must be. Barrett's images of "veined humanity" (*Lady Geraldine's Courtship*, 164) and "the full-veined, heaving, double-breasted Age" (*Aurora Leigh*, 5.216), hazard an elemental definition of humanity that partakes of both masculine and feminine experience. Her poetic emphasis on "life" and "heart" and "earth" all resonate with the anthropomorphic idealism of Byron and Shelley. As the Victorians worried that poetry was becoming increasingly effeminate and irrelevant to wider social and political issues, Barrett and Browning drew on the Romantic conception of the humanity of the poet to reassert the endangered proposition that the poet is a man speaking to men. They tried to enhance the masculinity of the poetic phrase through the use of irregular metrics or rugged diction while combining it with the more feminine powers of communication and feeling. Thus they attempt to realize in contemporary poetics what Shelley cast as a utopian dream in *Prometheus Unbound*, the union of masculine and feminine principles.[35]

---

[32]   "Individual in Community: Dorothy Wordsworth in Conversation with William," in *Romanticism and Feminism*, ed. Anne K. Mellor (Bloomington: Indiana University Press, 1988), 146.

[33]   Kingsley, 1:321.

[34]   All quotations from Shakespeare are taken from the Arden edition.

[35]   For a fuller discussion of androgynous merger in *Prometheus Unbound*, see Diane Long Hoeveler, *Romantic Androgyny: The Women Within* (University Park: Pennsylvania State University Press, 1990), 148–55.

Such an androgynous fusion accords with one Victorian idealized view of angels or Christ, "that union of man and woman, sweetness and strength," which was Barrett's ultimate answer to the cross-dressed rebellion of George Sand: "Thou large-brained woman and large-hearted man.... Beat purer, heart, and higher, / Till God unsex thee on the heavenly shore."[36] Christ was, of course, a figure of mingled gender potential for Romantics like Leigh Hunt before the Victorians.[37] For the devout atheist Shelley and the agnostic Calvinist Byron, Prometheus embodied the most humane poetic qualities of Christ, being both a lover of his fellows and a voluntary exile. Elizabeth Barrett's Preface to her 1833 translation of *Prometheus Bound* meditates on the contradictory aspects of Promethean heroism previously discussed by Percy Shelley in the Preface to *Prometheus Unbound*:

> Satan suffered from his ambition: Prometheus from his humanity: Satan for himself; Prometheus for mankind ... But in his hell, Satan yearned to associate [*sic*] man; while, Prometheus preferred a solitary agony: nay, he even permitted his zeal and tenderness for the peace of others, to abstract him from that agony's intenseness. (*PWEBB*, 554)

In this passage, Barrett fundamentally agrees with Percy Shelley's preference for Prometheus over Milton's Satan as an opponent of divine tyranny, and she goes further than Shelley in her sympathy for the devil. Mermin, Cooper, Falk, and Stone have all suggested that Barrett chooses Prometheus as a peculiarly feminine hero because of his passivity,[38] but it is important to recognize that Prometheus was depicted in this way, with a "suffering, and intense ... patient energy" by Byron in 1816 (*Prometheus* 6, 40) after Shelley translated Aeschylus for him.[39] Barrett and Browning may be seen to pick up a conversation between Byron and Shelley about Prometheus's sacrificial heroism on behalf of the earth, and all four writers seize on the vital intermingling of active "resistance" and passive

---

[36]    Hallam Tennyson, *A Memoir*, 2 vols. (London: Macmillan, 1899), 2:69. I am quoting from both sonnets to George Sand; the second one answers the first (1; 12–13).

[37]    See Hunt's description of Raphael's Christ in *Shelley and His Circle 1773–1822*, ed. Donald. H. Reiman, vol. 6 (Cambridge: Harvard University Press, 1973), 886–7. For Shelley's interest in a feminized Christ, see Teddi Chichester Bonca, *Shelley's Mirrors of Love: Narcissism, Sacrifice, and Sorority* (New York: State University of New York Press, 1999), 101–2, 186–90. Bonca argues that Shelley's ideal is transsexual rather than androgynous as it entails "a crossing over from one distinctly defined gender to the other" (260) instead of the fusion of genders that constitutes androgyny.

[38]    Stone, 67–72; Helen Cooper, *Elizabeth Barrett Browning, Woman and Artist* (Chapel Hill: University of North Carolina Press, 1988), 15; Dorothy Mermin, *Elizabeth Barrett Browning: The Origins of a New Writing* (Chicago: University of Chicago Press, 1989), 47–56; Alice Falk, "Elizabeth Barrett Browning and her Prometheuses: Self-Will and a Woman Poet," *Tulsa Studies in Women's Literature* 7 (1988): 69–85.

[39]    See Douglas Bush, *Mythology and the Romantic Tradition* (Cambridge: Harvard University Press, 1937), 71.

"wretchedness" (Byron, *Prometheus*, 51). Before she met Browning, as we have seen, Barrett found these qualities in Byron but not Shelley and Browning found them in Shelley, but not Byron. Their courtship correspondence involves a conversation about the Romantic poets in which the ideas of each infiltrate the other.

"[W]hat poets have been your sponsors?" Barrett asked Browning in February 1845 (*BC*, 10:53). The question initiated a highly charged re-reading of each other's favorite authors. From the start, Browning introduces a warmer version of Shelley to Barrett than the one she had created. In May 1845, he describes his recent visit to Italy and tells Barrett how it was Shelley who "told me years ago that in the mountains it was a feast 'when one should find those globes of deep red gold—which in the woods the strawberry-tree doth bear, suspended in their emerald atmosphere,' so that when my Mule walked into a sorb-tree … and I felt the fruit against my face, the little ragged bare-legged guide fairly laughed at my knowing them so well—" (*BC*, 10:200).[40] The image of the red fruit knocking against the face is a redemptive transformation of Edenic temptation that Browning later put in *The Englishman in Italy*, his most playful evocation of Romantic exile. In terms of biography, these images encouraged Barrett's plans to visit Pisa in 1845—and eventually merge with her decision to elope with Browning.

Browning was fascinated by Barrett's response to Shelley; he claims to find her description of Shelley's "'white ideal all statue-blind'" in *A Vision of Poets* "perfect" (*BC*, 11:15) but clearly tries to encourage her to reread Shelley in autumn 1845 and is dismayed when she reads Shelley's novel *St Irvyne* and thinks it displays a "flood of boarding-school idiocy" (*BC*, 11:106) (echoing Shelley's first reviewers who found it to be an effeminate production[41]). Browning begs her: "please read a chorus in the 'Prometheus Unbound' or a scene from the 'Cenci'—and join company with Shelley again!" (*BC*, 11:108). Meanwhile, Barrett was also trying to convert Browning to Byron. She sees an affinity between them from the start. "He has had very little of the 'rank popular breath,'" she writes of Browning to Miss Mitford in January 1845 (*BC*, 10:33) and then tells him directly: "You were like Lord Byron (another point of likeness!) in imitating Ossian" (*BC*, 13:296).

Browning was not ignorant of Byron, as we have seen—he quotes both *Cain* and *Sardanapalus* before meeting Barrett—but he has to adjust his terms of reference. He learns quickly how to gain her approval. In May 1845 he expresses the fear that she will think him "attitudinizing à la Byron," but by January 1846 he can refer jokingly to her initial reservations, borrowing words from *Mazeppa*: "and 'one refusal no rebuff'" (*BC*, 10:234; 11:291). In August 1846 he assures her that "Lord Byron is altogether in my affection again .. I have read on to the

---

[40]   *BC* notes that Shelley's allusion is to *Marenghi*, st. 13 (i.e., *Mazenghi*, st. 14 in the new authoritative Longman edition).

[41]   "Had not the title-page informed us that this curious 'Romance' was the production of a 'gentleman,' … we should certainly have ascribed it to some 'Miss' in her teens." See James E. Barcus, ed., *Shelley: The Critical Heritage* (London: Routledge and Kegan Paul, 1975), 51.

end [of Moore's *Letters and Journals of Lord Byron, with Notices of his Life*], and am quite sure of the great qualities which the last ten or fifteen years had partially obscured- " (*BC*, 13:280). Just before they married, Browning wrote to Barrett: "I always retained my first feeling for Byron in many respects .. I would at any time have gone to Finchley to see a curl of his hair or one of his gloves" (*BC*, 13:280). At this point in their courtship, Browning can drop casually into a letter, "By the way, Byron speaks of plucking oranges in his garden at Pisa" (*BC*, 13:287), which is part proof that he has been reading Moore's *Life* attentively and part hint at the Edenic fulfillment they would find in Italy.[42] The warmth of Barrett's Byron has now impregnated Browning's view of the poet. To Barrett, their elopement is seen as a Byronic feat: she predicts with a mixture of dread and glee that they will be seen as "mad and bad" (*BC*, 14:6). One of the first things they do once they reach Pisa is to "accomplish" a pilgrimage to Casa LaFranchi where they re-enacted Byron's letter and plucked orange leaves from his trees. This homage to poetic divinity heralds Barrett's newly acquired sense of the soul's fulfillment in life: "Red grows the cheek, and warm the hand; / The part is in the whole: / Nor hands nor cheeks keep separate, when soul is joined to soul" (*Inclusions*, 15–18).

In the new reading contexts Barrett and Browning established for each other in 1845, the Romantic solipsism of Byron and Shelley is gradually softened by an awareness of *shared* rebellion. This revision of the Romantic rebel is immediately apparent in Barrett's spring 1845 return to her *Prometheus Bound* that she first published in 1833. Like Byron, Barrett had focused on the figure of Prometheus bound and suffering for the "crime" of kindness. Her revisions to it in 1845 are prompted by the belief that her first version was "cold as the Caucasus" (*BC*, 10:102). Robert Browning was enthusiastic about the new translation and suggested that she should go on to "Restore the Prometheus [Firebearer] as Shelley did the [Unbound]" (*BC*, 10:119). Barrett did not follow this hint but together, from 1845 onwards, the Brownings explore and question the "fix" of a single moment or the belief in cataclysmic change, especially as they contemplate their own defiance of paternal edict. They are drawn to the possibility of resistance against tyranny, but wary of the illusion of individual triumph or single combat. Singularity of form is also questioned: just as she completed the *Prometheus* in May 1845, Elizabeth Barrett was contemplating a new form of mental theater: "Did you ever feel afraid of your own soul, as I have done? I think it a true wonder of our humanity—& fit subject enough for a wild lyrical drama" (*BC*, 10:204).[43]

---

[42]    He prefers, however, to cast Barrett as a Shelleyan divine messenger, predicting a Utopian exile for them with lines from Shelley's *Ode to Naples*: "So you and I will go to Salerno ... and if we 'let sail winged words, freighted with truth from the throne of God'—we may be sure—— . Ah, presumption of it! ... you shall fill the words with their freight, and I will look on and love you" (*BC,* 13:94–5).

[43]    Browning did not miss the Shelleyan possibilities inherent in both the genre "lyrical drama" and the topic. He replied that it "reminds one of that wild Drama of Calderon's which frightened Shelley just before his death" (*BC*, 10:214).

In Browning's 1849 volume it is possible to detect a subtle modification of his earlier male dramatic heroes that seems to have been influenced by his re-reading of Byron through Barrett. After dismissing Byron's "attitudinizing," Browning positively opens his work to Byronic attitudes. Both *Luria* and *A Soul's Tragedy* are saturated with memories of Byron's (rather than Shelley's) Italy, particularly the emotional connection with a particular place epitomized in *The Two Foscari* and the exploration of a man's pain when he falls from popular adulation into exile. The character Luria (a moor) is presented as a close relation of the Byronic hero from the Turkish tales:

> Born free from any ties that bind the rest
> Of common faith in Heaven or hope on Earth,
> No past with us, no Future. (1.157–9)

But his own speeches reveal him to be acutely sensitive to the moment when the crowd turns against him:

> And always comes, I say, the turning point
> When something changes in the friendly eyes
> That love and look on you .. so slight, so slight .
> And yet it tells you they are dead and gone,
> Or changed and enemies for all their words,
> And all is mockery, and a maddening show! (3.106–11)

The whole passage suggests that Browning had in mind the Byron of 1816, while the last line in particular summons up *Manfred* ("Oh God! If it be thus, and *thou* / Art not a madness and a mockery" [1.1.189–90]). In the last plays Browning wrote for the stage, his Romantic heroes follow the path that Byron's took from *Manfred* into the historical dramas, where both dramatist and protagonist experience the judgment of the crowd and the pressure of contingency and compromise. Browning arranged his 1849 volume to begin with *Paracelsus*, but the collection ends with the voices of dramatic lyrics—*Saul* (part one), *Time's Revenges,* and *The Glove*. These poems ventriloquize partial, peripheral or oblique perspectives, which borrow the ironic shrugs of Byron's letters. Revolution is replaced by unpredictable moments of encounter whose narration interrupts the passage of history and the logic of fate. The riddling nature of these dramatic moments also takes a cue from *Julian and Maddalo* and the elliptical account of the madman's story that "the cold world shall not know" (617).

Elizabeth Barrett had used *Julian and Maddalo* in the Preface to her 1844 volume, to endorse the view that "we learn in suffering what we teach in song" (*PWEBB*, xiii; see *Julian and Maddalo*, 546). In her *Blackwood's* sonnets from 1847, published in *Poems* 1850, we can hear how she has opened her "we" to the more radical, visionary Shelley preferred by Robert Browning. *Life* and *Love* are both Italian sonnets in which the octaves describe the intensely connected nature of human life. I shall quote both together for ease of reference:

### Life

Each creature holds an insular point in space;
Yet what man stirs a finger, breathes a sound,
But all the multitudinous beings round
In all the countless worlds with time and place
For their conditions, down to the central base,
Thrill, haply, in vibration and rebound,
 Life answering life across the vast profound,
In full antiphony, by a common grace?
I think this sudden joyaunce which illumes
A child's mouth sleeping, unaware may run
From some soul newly loosened from earth's tombs:
I think this passionate sigh, which half begun
I stifle back, may reach and stir the plumes
Of God's calm angel standing in the sun.

### Love

We cannot live, except thus mutually
We alternate, aware or unaware,
The reflex act of life: and when we bear
Our virtue outward most impulsively,
Most full of invocation, and to be
Most instantly compellant, certes there
We live most life, whoever breathes most air
And counts his dying years by sun and sea.
But when a soul, by choice and conscience doth
Throw out her full force on another soul,
The conscience and the concentration both
Make mere life, Love. For Life in perfect whole
And aim consummated, is Love in sooth,
As Nature's magnet-heat rounds pole with pole.

"Life answering life" is a distinctly Shelleyan form of echoing within the line. The "man" in the first sonnet becomes Barrett Browning herself as speaker in lines 12 to 13, an androgynous Shelleyan lyric "I" who can reach as far as heaven. With the "vibration" of line 6 the sonnet opens to a richly Shelleyan vocabulary of release. The image of "some soul newly loosened from earth's tombs" recalls, in particular, the emancipatory loosening of *Prometheus Unbound*. Universal reciprocity is picked up in the second sonnet with its opening gesture of reciprocity. In *Love*, the emphasis on conscience (clearly not a Shelleyan positive) is married with the much more Shelleyan uncompromising commitment to a lover that we find in *Epipsychidion* where the words "love" and "life" (as in so many Shelley poems) are interwoven. This sonnet uses the pronouns "his" and "her" interchangeably so that the "we" carries a double force of masculine and feminine to complement the doubled "Life = Love" equation of the sonnet. Shelleyan to its finger tips, the sonnet's conclusion, "Love in sooth, / As Nature's magnet-heat rounds pole with pole," dips into and draws on *Prometheus Unbound* where we find a "polar paradise, / Magnet-like, of lovers' eyes" (4.465–6).

While she learned from Browning to value Shelley, Barrett retained her allegiance to Byron. Helen Cooper assumes that Elizabeth Barrett "outgrew her adolescent fervor for Byron"; Dorothy Mermin suggests that Barrett's enthusiasm for Byron has slipped by 1838; and Marjorie Stone is convinced that Elizabeth Barrett's Romantic Hellenism "peters out,"[44] but Byron still haunts *Casa Guidi Windows* (1851), despite Barrett Browning's explicit wish to dissociate *Casa Guidi* from traditional Romantic representations of Italy. Byron is one of "the others" led on by Filicaja; he is one of the "worthier poets" who have stood in Italy: "I kiss their footsteps, yet their words gainsay" (51), she writes as she challenges sentimental images of Italy as a Sea-Cybele or Niobe of Nations—a beautiful (feminine) lost cause. But just after her formal disavowal of Byron's influence, the voice of Byron is eerily present:

> I can but muse in hope upon this shore
> Of golden Arno as it shoots away
> Through Florence' heart beneath her bridges four:
> Bent bridges, seeming to strain off like bows,
> And tremble while the arrowy undertide
> Shoots on and cleaves the marble as it goes. (52–7)

"Arrowy" is a very unusual word for "swift or darting motion." The *OED* dates it to where it appears in *Childe Harold's Pilgrimage* to describe the blue Rhone just as Byron rejects the crushing crowd,

> Is it not better, then, to be alone,
> And love earth only for its earthly sake?
> By the blue rushing of the arrowy Rhone,
> Or the pure bosom of its nursing lake. (3.71)

Barrett Browning wants to bless the feminized city but her poetic language draws her apart, and despite Mermin's insistence that in *Casa Guidi Windows* "the speaker defines herself explicitly both as a woman and as a poet,"[45] it is the voices of Byron and Shelley who become the "undertide." Barrett Browning measures her own involvement as a spectator against Romantic misappropriations of Italia,

---

[44]   Cooper, 37; Mermin, 63; Stone, 53.

[45]   Mermin, 163.

but the Arno passage revisits the epicene vision of Byron in *A Vision of Poets*, "quivering with the dart he drave." Attempting to break out of the removed and authorizing overview of the Romantic spectator in Part 1, Barrett Browning turns first to Byron and then to Shelley. As *Casa Guidi Windows* calls for communal action, she reaches for Shelley's language of peaceful revolution in *The Mask of Anarchy* ("Rise like lions after slumber / In unvanquishable number— / Shake your chains to earth like dew" [368–70]):

> Will, therefore to be strong, thou Italy!
> Will to be noble! Austrian Metternich
>     Can fix no yoke unless the neck agree;
> And thine is the like the lion's when the thick
>     Dews shudder from it …
> Roar, therefore! Shake your dew-laps dry abroad. (661–70)

The calls to assert will and strength and the roaring lion all sound thoroughly masculine, but a second voice behind these lines is, of course, Shakespeare's Theseus in *A Midsummer Night's Dream*, who is offering to take his bride hunting and hoping that she will share his enthusiasm for his dogs:

> My hounds are bred out of the Spartan kind,
> So flew'd, so sanded; and their heads are hung
> With ears that sweep away the morning dew;
> Crook-knee'd and dew-lapp'd like Thessalian bulls;
> Slow in pursuit, but match'd in mouth like bells. (4.1.118–22)

Although it is a distant echo, it is immensely significant that Barrett Browning's picture of a people coming together draws, not just on Byron's rejection of crowds and Shelley's call for peaceful collective resistance, but also on the image of a marriage in which the uncompromising masculinity of "bulls" is balanced by the harmony of "bells." Optimism about Italia in *Casa Guidi*, Part 1 (composed 1847) meets with historical rebuff in Part 2 (both parts published 1851), but Barrett Browning's response to the interval she identifies in her Preface "between aspiration and performance, between faith and disillusion, between hope and fact" is to turn to "Posterity … smiling on our knees" (2.774):

> Howe'er the uneasy world is vexed and wroth,
> Young children, lifted high on parent souls,
>     Look round them with a smile upon the mouth
> And take for music every bell that tolls. (*Casa Guidi*, 2.768–71)

The "cherub face" of her baby son allows Barrett Browning to locate hope for the future in a realm as free from adult disappointment as it is free from gender. For this reason it matters that she does not leave the poem on its penultimate note of trust in God, but allows the last three lines to re-assert infant smiles before the "Mercy-seat" (2.781–3).

Published the year before *Casa Guidi*, Browning's *Christmas Eve and Easter Day* (1850) also mingles the voices of Byron and Shelley on the way to a realm beyond gender—the "warmth and wonder and delight" of "God's mercy being infinite" (21.4–5).[46] These poems correct what both Brownings saw as the central failing of Byron and Shelley—their blindness to "Christ's liberty" and their inability to live and work with other men. Browning's narrator in *Christmas Eve* experiences a moment of Byronic repugnance at the crowd but discovers that "I, a man, with men am linked" (20.19); he chooses to return to the service in the chapel and to take his place with the rest of the grotesque congregation. In *Easter Day* the speaker ponders "How very hard it is to be / A Christian!" and relates how his skeptical self confronts a waking dream of God from whose gifts he chooses firstly the world of nature, then art, then the mind, before belatedly realizing:

> How love repaired all ill,
> Cured wrong, soothed grief, made earth amends
> With parents, brothers, children, friends! (29.8–10)

Browning's speaker is unmanned by God's interrogation ("No man now" [19.32]), and learns to be "happy that I can / Be crossed and thwarted as a man" (33.15–16). Individual identity including distinct gender is overwhelmed by God's mercy. Despite its utterly serious message—"Christ rises! Mercy every way / Is infinite, — and who can say?" (33.34–5)—the striking formal feature of both poems is Browning's choice of robust tetrameter couplets and double rhymes often verging on the comic as if the narrator of *Mazeppa* had taken over Shelleyan dream vision.

By the time of their settled married life in Italy, Barrett and Browning had reached accord over Byron and Shelley. They both wanted to temper Romantic solitude with a greater emphasis on community and human bonds, but their own ambivalent reactions to "the crushing crowd" often makes them closer to their Romantic precursors than is first apparent. Both wished that Byron and Shelley had embraced Christianity, although the androgynous Prometheus figure envisaged by Byron and Shelley in many ways anticipates the infinite patience of the Brownings' God. Above all we can see how a shared experience of Romantic fellowship challenges any simple attribution of gender to poetic voice. G. K. Chesterton is one of the earliest and most coherent exponents of the "masculinity" of Elizabeth Barrett (although he distrusts the terminology); his categorization of Browning and Barrett Browning as "eccentric" and "extreme" identifies them (in his terms) as English Romantic poets of the early nineteenth century. Their shared "eccentricity" or deviation from a central axis suggests that Romantic and Victorian and male and female traditions are, in many ways, inseparable.[47]

---

[46] All quotations from the first edition (London: Chapman and Hall, 1850).

[47] Chesterton, 103, 110, 15.

## Works Cited

Barcus, James E., ed. *Shelley: The Critical Heritage*. London: Routledge and Kegan Paul, 1975.

Bonca, Teddi Chichester. *Shelley's Mirrors of Love: Narcissism, Sacrifice, and Sorority* (New York: State University of New York Press, 1999).

Brewer, William D. *The Shelley–Byron Conversation*. Gainesville: University Press of Florida, 1994.

*The Brownings' Correspondence*. 15 vols. Ed. Philip Kelley, et al. Winfield, KS: Wedgestone Press, 1984–2005.

Browning, Elizabeth Barrett. *The Poetical Works of Elizabeth Barrett Browning*. Ed. Frederic G. Kenyon. London: Smith, Elder, 1897.

Browning, Robert. *Christmas Eve and Easter Day*. London: Chapman and Hall, 1850.

—. *The Poems of Browning*. Ed. John Woolford and Daniel Karlin. 2 vols. London: Longman, 1991.

—. *Shelley: The Man and the Poet*. Hull: J. R. Tutin, n.d. [1908].

Bush, Douglas. *Mythology and the Romantic Tradition*. Cambridge: Harvard University Press, 1937.

Byron, George Gordon. *The Complete Poetical Works*. Ed. Jerome J. McGann. 7 vols. Oxford: Oxford University Press, 1980–1993.

Chesterton, G. K. *The Victorian Age in Literature*. London: Oxford University Press, 1955.

Cooper, Helen. *Elizabeth Barrett Browning, Woman and Artist*. Chapel Hill: University of North Carolina Press, 1988.

Cundiff, Paul A. *Robert Browning: A Shelley Promethean*. St. Petersburg, FL: Valkyrie Press, 1977.

Falk, Alice. "Elizabeth Barrett Browning and her Prometheuses: Self–Will and a Woman Poet." *Tulsa Studies in Women's Literature* 7 (1988): 69–85.

Haigwood, Laura E. "Gender–to Gender Anxiety and Influence on Robert Browning's *Men and Women*." *Browning Institute Studies* 14 (1986): 97–118.

Hoeveler, Diane Long. *Romantic Androgyny: The Women Within*. University Park: Pennsylvania State University Press, 1990.

Karlin, Daniel. *The Courtship of Robert Browning and Elizabeth Barrett*. Oxford: Clarendon Press, 1985.

Keenan, Richard C. "Browning and Shelley." *Browning Institute Studies* 1 (1973): 119–45.

Kingsley, Charles. *Miscellanies*. 2 vols. London: John Parker, 1859.

Latane, David. "Shelley's 'Baleful Influence'." *Studies in Browning and His Circle* 11.2 (1983): 31–6.

Lau, Beth. *Keats's Paradise Lost*. Gainesville: University Press of Florida, 1998.

Marlon, Ross. *The Contours of Masculine Desire: Romanticism and the Rise of Women's Poetry*. New York: Oxford University Press, 1989.

Martin, Loy D. "Browning: The Activation of Influence." *Victorian Newsletter* 53 (1978): 4–9.

Maynard, John. *Browning's Youth*. Cambridge: Harvard University Press, 1977.

Mermin, Dorothy. *Elizabeth Barrett Browning: The Origins of a New Writing*. Chicago: University of Chicago Press, 1989.

Mitchell, Juliet. *Siblings*. Cambridge: Polity, 2003.

Morlier, Margaret M. "The Death of Pan: Elizabeth Barrett Browning and the Romantic Ego." *Browning Institute Studies* 18 (1990): 131–55.

Newlyn, Lucy. *Reading, Writing and Romanticism: The Anxiety of Reception*. Oxford: Oxford University Press, 2000.

Pollock, Frederick, ed. *Macready's Reminiscences and Selections from His Diaries and Letters*. New York: Macmillan, 1875.

Pollock, Mary Sanders. *Elizabeth Barrett and Robert Browning: A Creative Partnership*. Aldershot: Ashgate, 2003.

Reiman, Donald H. ed. *Shelley and His Circle 1773–1822*. Vol. 6. Cambridge: Harvard University Press, 1973.

Rutherford, Andrew, ed. *Byron: The Critical Heritage*. London: Routledge and Kegan Paul, 1970.

Spencer, Jane. *Literary Relations: Kinship and the Canon 1660–1830*. Oxford: Oxford University Press, 2005.

Stone, Marjorie. *Elizabeth Barrett Browning*. New York: St Martin's Press, 1995.

Taylor, Henry. *Philip van Artevelde*. 2 vols. London: Moxon, 1834.

Tennyson, Hallam. *A Memoir*. 2 vols. London: Macmillan, 1899.

Thorpe, James. "Elizabeth Barrett's Commentary on Shelley: Some Marginalia." *Modern Language Notes* 66.7 (1951) 455–58.

Trewin, J. C., ed. *The Journal of William Charles Macready*. London: Longmans, 1967.

Tucker, Herbert F., Jr. *Browning's Beginnings: The Art of Disclosure*. Minneapolis: University of Minnesota Press, 1980.

Wolfson, Susan J. *Borderlines: The Shiftings of Gender in British Romanticism*. Stanford: Stanford University Press, 2006.

—. "Individual in Community: Dorothy Wordsworth in Conversation with William." In *Romanticism and Feminism*. Ed. Anne K. Mellor. Bloomington: Indiana University Press, 1988. 139–66.

Woolford, John. *Browning the Revisionary*. New York: St. Martin's Press, 1988.

Wordsworth, William, and S. T. Coleridge. *Lyrical Ballads*. Ed. R. L. Brett and A. R. Jones. 2nd ed. London: Routledge, 1991.

# Index

*Adonais* (Shelley) 214, 220, 222, 226–7, 239
*Alastor* (Shelley) 79, 99, 102, 124–7, 131, 133, 136, 186, 189, 204, 219, 223, 224
*Alcaeus to Sappho* (Coleridge) 57n40
Alexander, Meena 2
Anderson, John M. 128–9
androgyny 243–4
Angelleti, Gioia 5
animal rights 8, 11, 160–74
anthropomorphism 163, 174
apostrophe 134–6
*Apotheosis, The: or, The Snow-drop* (Coleridge) 41, 44–56, 57, 60, 63, 65
Armstrong, Isobel 3, 123
Auerbach, Nina 180
*Aurora Leigh* (Browning) 236, 240, 243
Austen, Jane 12
    on animal and women's rights 8, 160, 162
    as anti-Romantic 160n5, 179, 184, 205
    and Cowper 159–61, 181
    imagination in works of 179–210
    and male Romantics 2, 3, 7, 8, 159–74, 179–205
    on rural sport 159–77
    Shakespeare compared with 197–8
    works
        *Emma* 159, 181–2, 184n11, 191, 193–4, 200–201, 203, 205
        *Love and Freindship* 184
        *Mansfield Park* 159, 165–70, 174, 183, 193
        *Northanger Abbey* 160n4, 165, 166, 167, 174, 182, 183, 188, 190, 191, 199–200, 201, 203, 205
        *Persuasion* 159, 166, 170–74, 193, 198–9
        *Pride and Prejudice* 160n4, 166, 168, 204–5
        *Sense and Sensibility* 159–60, 160n4, 166, 167, 169–70, 182–3, 190, 193, 204

Austen-Leigh, J. E. 159
autobiography
    meta-autobiography 18, 20, 22–3, 30
    in Smith's letters 23
    in Smith's *Sonnets* 27, 28, 36
    in Wordsworth's *Lyrical Ballads* 29, 36

Bakhtin, Mikhail 135
Barker, Jane 6–7
Barrett, Eaton Stannard 184
Barth, J. Robert 79
*Battle of Marathon* (Browning) 236, 241
*Beachy Head* (Smith) 19, 31, 31n48, 36
Beer, John 72, 72n4, 88n60
Behrendt, Stephen C. 1, 110n30
Bennett, Betty 3, 74n7
*Biographia Literaria* (Coleridge) 63, 77, 202, 204
Blackwood, William 100, 100n4
Blake, William 3, 9, 225
Blanchard, Laman 211–12
Blessington, Lady 197
Bloom, Harold 9, 9n17, 235, 236
*Blot in the Scutcheon* (Browning) 239
Bodenheimer, Rosemarie 166
Bonca, Teddi Chichester 4, 196n47
*Book of the Poets, The* (Browning) 242, 243
*Borderers* (Wordsworth) 242–3
Bowles, William Lisle 56n36, 186, 187
Boyd, Hugh Stuart 235
Brewer, William D. 231
*Bride of the Greek Isle, The* (Hemans) 117–18, 146
Bronfen, Elisabeth 87n58
Browning, Elizabeth Barrett 12, 232
    and Byron 2, 8, 231–51
    as Christian Shelley 233
    masculine poetic identity of 231–2, 251
    Romantic influences on 234–5
    and Shelley 2, 8, 231–51
    on thought and feeling in her husband's poetry 141n10

works
  *Aurora Leigh* 236, 240, 243
  *Battle of Marathon* 236, 241
  *The Book of the Poets* 242, 243
  *Casa Guidi Windows* 249–51
  *A Drama of Exile* 236
  *An Essay on Mind* 236
  *Inclusions* 246
  *Lady Geraldine's Courtship* 241, 243
  *Leila* 236–8
  *Life* 247–9
  *Love* 247–9
  *The Poet's Vow* 238
  *Prometheus Bound* translation 246
  *The Rhyme of the Duchess May* 238
  *The Seraphim, and Other Poems* 236
  *Sonnets from the Portuguese* 241
  *The Soul's Expression* 232
  *Stanzas on the Death of Lord
    Byron* 235
  *A Vision of Poets* 235–6, 245, 250
Browning, Robert 232
  and Byron 2, 8, 231–51
  dramatic monologues of 31n47,
    141n10
  plays of 239–40
  and Shelley 2, 8, 231–51
  works
    *Blot in the Scutcheon* 239
    *Christmas Eve and Easter Day* 251
    *The Englishman in Italy* 245
    *The Glove* 247
    *Incondita* 239
    *The Lost Leader* 232
    *Luria* 247
    *My Last Duchess* 31n47
    *Paracelsus* 239, 241, 247
    *Saul* 247
    *Shelley: The Man and the Poet* 241
    *Sordello* 233–4
    *A Soul's Tragedy* 246
    *Strafford* 239, 240, 242
    *Time's Revenges* 247
Burke, Edmund 42, 102, 106–7, 114, 119
Burns, Robert 30, 52, 53–5, 141
Butler, Marilyn 89n64, 181
Byrne, Paula 39n3
Byron, Lord 3, 9, 12
  on abuses of imagination 186–7

  ambivalence about imagination 202
  and Austen 159, 160n4, 186–7,
    197, 202
  on "bluestocking" women poets 143
  and the Brownings 2, 8, 231–51
  on Coleridge's *Christabel* 76–7, 90
  in *Frankenstein*'s origins 88–9
  and Hemans 2, 8, 123–38, 143, 144,
    145–6, 227
  history plays of 239–40
  Kingsley on 240
  and Landon 215
  Moore's biography of 143
  and Shelley as a pair 232–3
  on sympathetic imagination 197
  and Wordsworth 144
  works
    *Cain* 245
    *Childe Harold's Pilgrimage* 123,
      132, 134, 187, 197, 216, 218,
      219, 221, 236, 249
    *Don Juan* 144, 167, 168–9, 186,
      187n23, 197, 226, 236
    *The Giaour* 236
    *Lara* 237
    *Manfred* 124, 125, 126, 127,
      129–33, 136, 239, 247
    *Marino Faliero* 239, 240
    *Mazeppa* 245, 251
    *Prometheus* 244, 245
    *Sardanapalus* 245
    *To These Fox Hunters in a Long
      Frost* 168
    *The Two Foscari* 239, 247
    *Werner* 239, 240

*Cain* (Byron) 245
Carlyle, Thomas 233
*Casa Guidi Windows* (Browning) 249–51
*Cathedral Hymn* (Hemans) 147–50
*Celestina* (Smith) 27–8
*Cenci, The* (Shelley) 103, 104–15, 117,
  119, 243, 245
Chatterton, Thomas 41, 51, 52, 53, 59–63,
  67–8
Chesterton, G. K. 236, 251
*Childe Harold's Pilgrimage* (Byron) 123,
  132, 134, 187, 197, 216, 218, 219,
  221, 236, 249

Chorley, Henry 124, 130, 131, 132–3, 136, 141
*Christabel* (Coleridge) 76–7, 86, 90
*Christian Temple, The* (Hemans) 156–7
*Christmas Eve and Easter Day* (Browning) 251
Clairmont, Claire 75, 84, 216
Claridge, Laura 4, 83, 84n45
Clarke, James Stanier 202
Clayton, Jay 187n24, 198n52
Clemit, Pamela 39n3
Coleridge, Samuel Taylor 9, 12
  on abuses of imagination 184–6
  ambivalence about imagination 201–2
  and Austen 159, 160n4, 181, 184–6, 196, 201–2
  and Della Cruscans 41, 47, 48, 49, 51n, 58, 62–3, 64, 65, 66–7
  family relationships of 82
  on friendship and love 78–9, 80
  and Godwin 75
  imagery of 41, 51–2, 67–8
  insecurity as writer 89–91
  lectures on Shakespeare and Milton 75, 79, 80, 185, 196
  loneliness experienced by 81
  at *The Morning Post* 40, 41, 68
  on pity 48–9
  pseudonyms used by 45
  relationship to women writers 42–3
  and Robinson 2, 7, 39–70
  and Shelley, Mary 2, 7–8, 43, 71–93
  and Shelley, Percy Bysshe 75–7
  on sympathetic imagination 192, 196
  and Wordsworth 40, 42, 56, 63, 67
  works
    *Alcaeus to Sappho* 57n40
    *The Apotheosis: or, The Snow-drop* 41, 44–56, 57, 60, 63, 65
    *Biographia Literaria* 63, 77, 202, 204
    *Christabel* 76–7, 86, 90
    *Constancy to an Ideal Object* 185, 186
    *Dejection: An Ode* 91, 134, 201
    *Destiny of Nations* 46
    *Effusion XXXV* 50–51, 55–6, 59
    *The Eolian Harp* 50–51, 55–6, 125, 126, 184, 202

*Fears in Solitude* 91
*Fire, Famine and Slaughter* 76
*France: An Ode* 76
*The Friend* 76
*Frost at Midnight* 125, 134, 181, 184
*The Improvisatore* 80
*The Kiss* 51n30
*Kisses* 51n30
*Kubla Khan* 40, 76, 89–90, 91, 202
*Lines to an Unfortunate Woman, in the Back Seats of the Boxes at the Theatre* 45
*Lyrical Ballads* 23, 29–35, 36, 41, 49, 54, 58, 63, 66, 146, 197, 204, 242
*Monody on the Death of Chatterton* 59–63
*The Nightingale, A Conversation Poem* 63, 64, 66–7, 68, 125, 184–5
*Ode to Tranquility* 76n18
*On Observing a Blossom on the First of February, 1796* 52, 53–5, 56, 57, 61
*Osorio* 82
*Reflections on Having Left a Place of Retirement* 91
*Remorse* 75, 77
*The Rime of the Ancient Mariner* 46, 71–97, 164–5
*Sibylline Leaves* 90–91
*The Sigh* 51n30
*A Stranger Minstrel* 40
*This Lime-Tree Bower My Prison* 216
*The Three Graves* 90
*To a Young Ass, Its Mother Being Tethered Near It* 163–4
*To the Nightingale* 63, 64, 65–6
*To William Wordsworth* 91, 201
*The Vision of the Maid of Orleans, A Fragment* 46
*The Wanderings of Cain* 82
Constable, John 227
*Constancy to an Ideal Object* (Coleridge) 185, 186
*Convict, The* (Wordsworth) 45–6
Cooper, Helen 244, 249
*Corra Linn* (Wordsworth) 140
Cottle, Joseph 63

Cowley, Abraham 6–7, 9
Cowley, Hannah 49, 56
Cowper, William 12
    on animal rights 160–62, 174
    and Austen 159–61, 181
    works
        *Epitaph on an Hare* 161–2
        *Epitaphium Alterum* 162
        *The Progress of Error* 170
        *The Task* 160–61, 162, 170, 181
Crabbe, George 142, 159
Craciun, Adriana 4
Crisafulli, Lilla Maria 5–6, 10
Crisman, William 84, 92n73
Cronin, Richard 5, 223n20
Cross, Ashley 7, 11
*Cuckoo, The* (Wordsworth) 140
Curran, Stuart 103n14

Davidson, Cathy N. 6
De Man, Paul 136
De Staël, Madame 3
"Defence of Poetry, A" (Shelley) 194–5,
    204, 211, 214
*Dejection: An Ode* (Coleridge) 91, 134, 201
Della Cruscans 21, 49
    and Coleridge 41, 47, 48, 49, 51n30,
        58, 62–3, 64, 65, 66–7
    and eolian harp image 56, 57
    and Robinson 41, 43, 47, 49, 57n41,
        58, 64
Deresiewicz, William 3, 159, 160n4, 166,
    172, 180, 183n6, 193n38
DeRose, Peter 183, 191
*Destiny of Nations* (Coleridge) 46
Deuchar, Stephen 164
*Diver, The* (Hemans) 215
*Don Juan* (Byron) 144, 167, 168–9, 186,
    187n23, 197, 226, 236
*Drama of Exile, A* (Browning) 236
dramatic monologues
    of Browning 141n10
    key elements of 21–2
    of Smith 17, 18, 24, 26, 36
    of Wordsworth 17, 18, 20–21, 30, 32,
        34, 36
Dyck, Sarah 88, 88n60

*Ecclesiastical Sonnets* (Wordsworth) 140,
    142n12, 147–50, 156

*Effigies, The* (Hemans) 149
*Effusion XXXV* (Coleridge) 50–51, 55–6, 59
egotistical sublime 17, 18, 20, 22, 35
*Elegiac Sonnets* (Smith) 19, 22, 23–9, 35
*Elegiac Stanzas, Suggested by a Picture
    of Peele Castle, in a Storm*
    (Wordsworth) 189
Ellison, Julie 43, 49
*Emma* (Austen) 159, 181–2, 184n11, 191,
    193–4, 200–201, 203, 205
*Endymion* (Keats) 234
Engell, James 189, 192, 195n44
England, A. B. 187
*England and Spain; or, Valour and
    Patriotism* (Hemans) 101–2
*Englishman in Italy, The* (Browning) 245
*Eolian Harp, The* (Coleridge) 50–51, 55–6,
    125, 126, 184, 202
eolian harp image 41, 42, 48, 49, 50–51,
    52, 55–6, 63, 65, 67
*Epipsychidion* (Shelley) 220, 249
*Epitaph on an Hare* (Cowper) 161–2
*Epitaphium Alterum* (Cowper) 162
Erdman, David 41, 46
Erskine, Lord 162
*Essay on Mind, An* (Browning) 236
Esterhammer, Angela 223n21
*Eve of St. Agnes, The* (Keats) 190, 191, 203
*Eve of St. Mark* (Keats) 190–91
*Excursion, The* (Wordsworth) 9, 151, 154
*Extempore Effusion Upon the Death of
    James Hogg* (Wordsworth) 139,
    141–2

Fairer, David 60n47
Fay, Elizabeth 20, 21, 21n18, 26, 26n35
*Fears in Solitude* (Coleridge) 91
*Felicia Hemans* (Landon) 226–7
Fenwick note (Wordsworth) 34
Ferber, Michael 44n14, 57n40
Ferguson, Frances 20, 34
*Fire, Famine and Slaughter* (Coleridge) 76
flower image 41, 42, 44, 51, 52–3, 67
Foakes, R. A. 85
Forbes, Deborah 20, 32, 33n52, 36
*Forest Sanctuary, The* (Hemans) 128
*France: An Ode* (Coleridge) 76
*Frankenstein* (Shelley) 107, 71–97, 131
Fricker, Sara 62n51

*Friend, The* (Coleridge) 76
*Frost at Midnight* (Coleridge) 125, 134, 181, 184
Fulford, Tim 4, 42, 42n10, 43

Galperin, William 3, 20, 31, 33n52, 180
genius 39, 41, 42, 51, 54, 60, 62, 240
*Giaour, The* (Byron) 236
Gifford, William 44, 53, 58
Gilbert, Sandra M. 9n17, 74n8, 83, 201
Gilfillan, George 99–100
Gill, Stephen 33, 144, 157
Gilligan, Carol 78
Gleckner, Robert F. 187, 202
*Glove, The* (Browning) 247
Godwin, William 3, 39n3, 73, 75, 83
Godwin, William, Junior 83
Goodwin, Sarah Webster 73, 74, 84n45, 87
Gothic novels 182, 188, 199, 203
Greene, Donald 179n1
Grey, J. David 174
Gubar, Susan 9n17, 74n8, 83, 201
Guilhamet, Leon 19, 20, 29n42

Haigwood, Laura 234
Hall, Jean 81n36, 84
*Hall of Statues, The* (Landon) 213–14
Hamilton, William 152
*Hamlet* (Shakespeare) 185
Harding, Anthony 79, 125
Hart, Francis 193n36
*Hart-Leap Well* (Wordsworth) 164, 165, 168, 169, 172, 188
Harty, E. R. 22n22
Hatcher, Jessamyn 6
Hazlitt, William 192, 195, 196, 197, 198, 212n2, 237
Hemans, Felicia 8, 12, 99, 128, 136
    and Byron 2, 8, 123–38, 143, 144, 145–6, 227
    and Shelley 2, 8, 99–122, 123–38
    and Wordsworth 2, 7, 8, 136, 139–58
    works
        *The Bride of the Greek Isle* 117–18, 146
        *Cathedral Hymn* 147–50
        *The Christian Temple* 156–7
        *The Diver* 215
        *The Effigies* 149

*England and Spain; or, Valour and Patriotism* 101–2
*The Forest Sanctuary* 128
*The Image in Lava* 149
*The Indian City* 118–20, 146
*Modern Greece* 116–17, 142
*No More!* 227
*Poems* 100–101
*A Poet's Dying Hymn* 151
*Prayer of the Lonely Student* 151–6
*Records of Woman* 104, 117–20, 140, 143, 145, 146, 155
*The Restoration of the Works of Art to Italy* 142
*The Ruined Castle* 100
*Scenes and Hymns of Life* 145–56
*The Spartan Mother and Her Son* 100
*A Spirit's Return* 123–38
*The Suliote Mother* 116, 117
*Tales, and Historic Scenes, in Verse* 99, 103, 115–16
*To My Younger Brother on His Entering the Army* 101
*To Patriotism* 100–101
*To Wordsworth* 140
*The Widow of Crescentius* 102–3, 115
*The Wife of Asdrubal* 115, 116
*Wood Walk and Hymn* 150–51
Hickey, Alison 3
Hill-Miller, Katherine C. 87, 87n57
*History of the Lyre, A* (Landon) 223–6
Hoeveler, Diane 82n41
Hogg, Thomas Jefferson 196
Holmes, Richard 91
Homans, Margaret 2
Hopkins, Brooke 35
Horne, Richard Hengist 238
Hughes, Harriet Browne 124
Hunt, Henry 113, 114, 114n38
Hunt, Leigh 103, 109, 109n27, 113, 187, 224, 232–3, 238, 244
Hunter, J. Paul 72n4
hunting 160–74
*Hymn of Apollo* (Shelley) 218
*Hymn of Pan* (Shelley) 218
*Hymn to Intellectual Beauty* (Shelley) 126, 130, 131

*Idiot Boy, The* (Wordsworth) 188

*Image in Lava, The* (Hemans) 149
imagination 179–210
 abuses of 182–92
 ambivalence about 201–4
 celebration of creative 204–5
 sympathetic 192–8
 uses of 192–205
 validity of 198–201
*Improvisatore, The* (Coleridge) 80
*In Memoriam* (Tennyson) 32
*Inclusions* (Browning) 246
*Incondita* (Browning) 239
*Indian City, The* (Hemans) 118–20, 146
infanticide 116–17
*Ion* (Talfourd) 242
*Isabella* (Keats) 191

Jackson, H. J. 43
Jacobus, Mary 188
Janowitz, Anne 115n40
*Jasper* (Robinson) 54
Jerinic, Maria 199n54
Jewsbury, Maria Jane 5, 139
Johnson, Claudia 200
Johnson, Samuel 159, 183, 185, 188–9,
 190, 191
Joseph, M. K. 72n4
*Julian and Maddalo* (Shelley) 215, 217,
 219, 221–2, 223, 227, 233, 247

Karlin, Daniel 241n28
Keach, William 51n30
Kean, Edmund 110
Kearns, Sheila 20
Keats, John 9, 12
 on abuses of imagination 187, 189–92
 ambivalence about imagination
 202–3, 205
 and Austen 189–91, 195, 196,
 202–3, 205
 and Landon 223
 on Negative Capability 196, 197, 198
 on sympathetic imagination 192, 195,
 196–7
 on wordsworthian sublime 18, 21, 35
 works
 *Endymion* 234
 *The Eve of St. Agnes* 190, 191, 203
 *Eve of St. Mark* 190–91

*Isabella* 191
*Lamia* 191, 203
*Ode to a Nightingale* 64
*Oh Chatterton! How very sad thy
 fate!* 61n49
*On Sitting Down to Read* King
 Lear *Once Again* 189
*There is a joy in footing slow
 across a silent plain* 190
Kenyon-Jones, Christine 162, 164
Kestner, Joseph 173
Kiely, Robert 72, 79, 85n51
Kilcup, Karen 6, 10, 11
King, Kathryn R. 6–7, 9, 10n18
Kingsley, Charles 233, 240, 243
*Kiss, The* (Coleridge) 51n30
*Kisses* (Coleridge) 51n30
Knoepflmacher, U. C. 83, 89, 92
Knox-Shaw, Peter 192–3
Komisaruk, Adam 84n45
*Kubla Khan* (Coleridge) 40, 76, 89–90,
 91, 202

Labbe, Jacqueline 7, 11
*Lady Geraldine's Courtship* (Browning)
 241, 243
*Lamia* (Keats) 191, 203
Landon, Letitia 12
 and Shelley 2, 7, 8, 211–29
 works
 *Felicia Hemans* 226–7
 *The Hall of Statues* 213–14
 *A History of the Lyre* 223–6
 *Lines of Life* 215–23
 "On the Ancient and Modern
 Influence of Poetry" 211,
 214–15
 "On the Character of Mrs.
 Hemans's Writings" 215
Landor, Walter Savage 242
Landry, Donna 162n8
Langbaum, Robert 18, 19, 20–21
Langland, Elizabeth 4
*Laodamia* (Wordsworth) 133
*Lara* (Byron) 237
Lau, Beth 7–8, 11, 60, 231
Lee, Debbie 195, 195n44
Leighton, Angela 223n21, 224, 225
*Leila* (Browning) 236–8

Lennox, Charlotte 184
*Letter to Maria Gisborne* (Shelley) 224
*Letter to the Women of England*
(Robinson) 54
Levin, Susan 2
Levy, Michelle 73, 77n27, 80n35, 85
Lewes, George Henry 105, 109n28, 198
*Life* (Browning) 247–9
*Lift not the painted veil* (Shelley) 226
*Lines left upon a Seat in a Yew-Tree*
(Wordsworth) 30–31, 32, 33, 34
*Lines of Life* (Landon) 215–23
*Lines to an Unfortunate Woman, in the*
*Back Seats of the Boxes at the*
*Theatre* (Coleridge) 45
*Lines to Anna Matilda* (Merry) 56
*Lines Written among the Euganean Hills*
(Shelley) 217
*Lines written in early spring*
(Wordsworth) 32
Linkin, Harriet Kramer 1
Lipking, Lawrence 85, 87n58, 92
Lokke, Kari 4, 4n9
Longinus 128
*Lost Leader, The* (Browning) 232
*Love* (Browning) 247–9
*Love and Freindship* (Austen) 184
Lovejoy, A. O. 1
Luria, Gina 74
*Luria* (Browning) 247
Luther, Susan 42, 42n10, 46, 66
*Lyrical Ballads* (Coleridge and
Wordsworth) 23, 29–35, 36, 41, 49,
54, 58, 63, 66, 146, 197, 204, 242
*Lyrical Tales* (Robinson) 36, 54

Macaulay, Thomas Babbington 198
McEathron, Scott 185n13
McGann, Jerome 47, 49, 51, 51n30, 56,
57n39, 58, 63, 65, 111, 179, 185,
215, 222n, 226, 227
Macready, William 239, 242
*Mad Mother, The* (Wordsworth) 75
Magnuson, Paul 57n37, 61, 62
*Manfred* (Byron) 124, 125, 126, 127,
129–33, 136, 239, 247
*Mansfield Park* (Austen) 159, 165–70, 174,
183, 193
*Marino Faliero* (Byron) 239, 240

*Mask of Anarchy, The* (Shelley) 103–4,
114–15, 117, 250
Mays, J. C. C. 60n47, 66n59
*Mazeppa* (Byron) 245, 251
Medwin, Thomas 100
Mellor, Anne K. 2, 43, 86n55, 92n76, 173,
179, 181, 184
Melnyk, Julie 7, 8, 9, 11
*Memoirs* (Robinson) 39, 68
Mermin, Dorothy 244, 249
Merry, Robert 49, 56
Messenger, Ann 6
meta-autobiography 18, 20, 22–3, 30
Milton, John 65, 66, 75, 79, 106, 112, 129,
132, 141, 196, 244
Minot, Leslie Ann 73n6, 77n26, 86n53,
90n68
Minot, Walter S. 73n6, 77n26, 86n53,
90n68
Mitchell, Juliet 235
*Modern Greece* (Hemans) 116–17, 142
Moler, Kenneth 184n11, 194n40
Monckton-Milnes, Richard 76n22
*Monody on the Death of Chatterton*
(Coleridge) 59–63
*Monody to the Memory of Chatterton*
(Robinson) 59–63
*Mont Blanc* (Shelley) 215
Moore, Thomas 143, 246
Morgan, Susan 3, 180, 193, 194
Mortensen, Peter 164n16
*My Last Duchess* (Browning) 51n47

*Narrow Glen, The* (Wordsworth) 140
*Natural Daughter, The* (Robinson) 54
Newlyn, Lucy 186, 204n66, 231
*Nightingale, A Conversation Poem, The*
(Coleridge) 63, 64, 66–7, 68, 125,
184–5
nightingale image 41, 42, 51, 52, 63–8
*No More!* (Hemans) 227
*Northanger Abbey* (Austen) 160n4, 165,
166, 167, 174, 182, 183, 188, 190,
191, 199–200, 201, 203, 205
*Nutting* (Wordsworth) 30, 31, 34–5, 150

*Ode: Intimations of Immortality*
(Wordsworth) 151–3, 156
*Ode to a Nightingale* (Keats) 64

*Ode to Della Crusca* (Robinson) 49, 56, 57n41

*Ode to Duty* (Wordsworth) 156

*Ode to Genius* (Robinson) 57n41

*Ode to Naples* (Shelley) 246n42

*Ode to the Harp of Louisa* (Robinson) 57n41

*Ode to the Muse* (Robinson) 57n41

*Ode to the Nightingale* (Robinson) 64–7

*Ode to the Snow-drop* (Robinson) 41, 44–5, 47–8, 52, 53–5, 61

*Ode to the West Wind* (Shelley) 118, 124, 126, 132, 213, 214, 221

*Ode to Tranquility* (Coleridge) 76n18

Oerlemans, Onno 163, 164–5

*Oh Chatterton! How very sad thy fate!* (Keats) 61n49

"On Love" (Shelley) 79, 213

*On Observing a Blossom on the First of February, 1796* (Coleridge) 52, 53–5, 56, 57, 61

*On Sitting Down to Read* King Lear *Once Again* (Keats) 189

"On the Ancient and Modern Influence of Poetry" (Landon) 211, 214–15

"On the Character of Mrs. Hemans's Writings" (Landon) 215

*On the Medusa of Leonardo da Vinci, in the Florentine Gallery* (Shelley) 112, 115

O'Neill, Eliza 110

O'Neill, Michael 7, 8, 9, 11, 12, 204

Onorato, Richard J. 32

*Osorio* (Coleridge) 82

Palmer, Sally B. 174

*Paracelsus* (Browning) 239, 241, 247

parricide 105–10

Parrish, Stephen Maxfield 18

Pascoe, Judith 17, 20, 22n21, 23–4, 26n35, 34, 49

Patton, Lewis 52n31

Paulson, Ronald 106

performativity 20, 24, 26, 35

Perkins, David 19, 34, 162, 163n14, 164, 165, 169

Perry, Seamus 186n16

*Persuasion* (Austen) 159, 166, 170–74, 193, 198–9

Peterloo Massacre 103, 113, 119

Pietropoli, Cecilia 5–6, 10

*Poems* (Hemans) 100–101

*Poems* (Wordsworth) 9

poetry; *see also* women writers
  authenticity as goal of 19
  and contemporary life 240–41
  drama of self-representation in 21–2
  eolian harp associated with 55–6, 67
  flowers' association with 44
  masculinist theories of 58
  performativity of 26
  poet as chameleon 196
  poet as role 17–18
  poet as seer 144
  poet as tormented genius 39
  prominence in Romantic period 12
  public neglect of poets 54, 60–61
  referential aberration of 28
  Romantic poets as misunderstood geniuses 41, 42, 51, 54, 60, 62
  Smith's construction of Poet 24, 26, 35–6
  Wordsworth's construction of Poet 31, 34, 35–6

*Poet's Dying Hymn, A* (Hemans) 151

Polidori, John 76

Polwhele, Richard 44, 53

Poovey, Mary 74n8, 86n55, 87, 89, 91

Pope, Alexander 186

*Prayer of the Lonely Student* (Hemans) 151–6

*Prelude, The* (Wordsworth) 35, 36, 217

*Pride and Prejudice* (Austen) 160n4, 166, 168, 204–5

*Progress of Error, The* (Cowper) 170

*Prometheus* (Byron) 244, 245

*Prometheus Bound* (Aeschylus) 244, 246

*Prometheus Unbound* (Shelley) 217, 219, 220, 221, 225, 228, 243–5, 248, 249

Pyre, J. F. A. 233

Quintilian 135

Quixotic literature 183–4, 190, 201

*Rasselas* (Johnson) 183, 189, 190, 191

*Records of Woman* (Hemans) 104, 117–20, 140, 143, 145, 146, 155

*Reflections on Having Left a Place of Retirement* (Coleridge) 91

Reiman, Donald 76
*Remorse* (Coleridge) 75, 77
*Restoration of the Works of Art to Italy,
    The* (Hemans) 142
*Rhyme of the Duchess May, The*
    (Browning) 238
Richardson, Alan 8, 9, 11
*Rime of the Ancient Mariner, The*
    (Coleridge) 46, 71–97, 164–5
Ritson, Joseph 162
Robinson, Charles 76
Robinson, Daniel 24, 27
Robinson, Henry Crabb 80
Robinson, Mary
    affair with Prince of Wales 39, 41, 54
    and Coleridge 2, 7, 39–70
    and Della Cruscans 41, 43, 47, 49,
        57n41, 58, 64
    imagery of 41, 51–2, 67–8
    poetic authority of 12, 43–4
    as poetry editor of *The Morning Post*
        40, 41, 46, 68
    pseudonyms used by 45, 62
    and Wordsworth 40, 43
    works
        *Jasper* 54
        *Letter to the Women of England* 54
        *Lyrical Tales* 36, 54
        *Memoirs* 39, 68
        *Monody to the Memory of
            Chatterton* 59–63
        *The Natural Daughter* 54
        *Ode to Della Crusca* 49, 56, 57n41
        *Ode to Genius* 57n41
        *Ode to the Harp of Louisa* 57n41
        *Ode to the Muse* 57n41
        *Ode to the Nightingale* 64–7
        *Ode to the Snow-drop* 41, 44–5,
            47–8, 52, 53–5, 61
        *Sappho and Phaon* 49, 54, 57–9,
            63, 64
        *Second Ode to the Nightingale*
            64n56
        *To the Muse of Poetry* 57n41
        *To the Poet Coleridge* 40
        *Walsingham* 44–5, 46, 61
Robinson, Maria Elizabeth 54
Rogers, Samuel 140
Romanticism
    alienation in 126
    apostrophe in 134
    authenticity as goal of 19
    common points of engagement among
        men and women writers 2–12
    feminine style rejected by 50
    *Frankenstein* seen as reaction to
        masculine 74, 74n8
    gender complementary model of 1–2,
        3, 5
    on imagination 181–205
    masculine versus feminine 92–3, 126, 179
    and misunderstood genius 41, 42, 51,
        54, 60, 62
    and nightingale image 64
    poet as seer for 144
    on rural sports 160, 164
    Wordsworthian paradigm of 144–5
Ross, Marlon 1, 2–3, 234
Rowley, Thomas, poems (Chatterton) 60, 62
Rowton, Frederic 10
*Ruined Castle, The* (Hemans) 100
rural sport 159–77
*Ruth* (Wordsworth) 188–9

Saglia, Diego 6
*St Irvyne* (Shelley) 245
Sand, George 244
*Sappho and Phaon* (Robinson) 49, 54,
    57–9, 63, 64
*Sardanapalus* (Byron) 245
*Saul* (Browning) 247
*Scenes and Hymns of Life* (Hemans)
    145–56
Scott, Sir Walter 142, 159, 160, 160n4,
    183, 189, 198, 215, 237
Scrivener, Michael 110n30, 114n38
*Second Ode to the Nightingale* (Robinson)
    64n56
Seeber, Barbara K. 8, 11, 188
*Sense and Sensibility* (Austen) 159–60,
    160n4, 166, 167, 169–70, 182–3,
    190, 193, 204
*Sensitive Plant, The* (Shelley) 212n3
*Seraphim, and Other Poems, The*
    (Browning) 236
Shakespeare, William 185, 189, 196,
    197–8, 214, 243, 250
Shelley, Mary 12, 80, 108

and *The Cenci* 104n16, 107n24, 111
and Coleridge 2, 7–8, 43, 71–93
family relationships of 82–4
father William Godwin's influence on
   3, 73, 83
*Frankenstein* 107, 71–97, 131
husband Percy's influence on 3, 72, 73
insecurity as writer 89, 91
loneliness experienced by 81
mother Mary Wollstonecraft's
   influence on 73–4
Shelley, Percy Bysshe 9, 12
   on abuses of imagination 186
   ambivalence about imagination 204
   on animal rights 162, 168, 174
   and Austen 186, 194–5, 196–204
   and the Brownings 2, 8, 231–51
   and Byron as a pair 232–3
   and Coleridge 75–7
   in *Frankenstein*'s origins 88–9
   and Hemans 2, 8, 99–122, 123–38
   influence on wife Mary 3, 72, 73
   Kingsley on 240
   and Landon 2, 7, 8, 211–29
   on poets as chameleons 196
   on sympathetic imagination 192, 194–5
   works
      *Adonais* 214, 220, 222, 226–7, 239
      *Alastor* 79, 99, 102, 124–7, 131,
         133, 136, 186, 189, 204, 219,
         223, 224
      *The Cenci* 103, 104–15, 117, 119,
         243, 245
      "A Defence of Poetry" 194–5, 204,
         211, 214
      *Epipsychidion* 220, 249
      *Hymn of Apollo* 218
      *Hymn of Pan* 218
      *Hymn to Intellectual Beauty* 126,
         130, 131
      *Julian and Maddalo* 215, 217, 219,
         221–2, 223, 227, 233, 247
      *Letter to Maria Gisborne* 224
      *Lift not the painted veil* 226
      *Lines Written among the Euganean
         Hills* 217
      *The Mask of Anarchy* 103–4,
         114–15, 117, 250
      *Mont Blanc* 215

*Ode to Naples* 246n42
*Ode to the West Wind* 118, 124,
   126, 132, 213, 214, 221
"On Love" 79, 213
*On the Medusa of Leonardo da
   Vinci, in the Florentine Gallery*
   112, 115
*Prometheus Unbound* 217, 219,
   220, 221, 225, 228, 243–5,
   248, 249
*St Irvyne* 245
*The Sensitive Plant* 212n3
*Time* 219
*To a Skylark* 213–14, 227
*To Constantia, Singing* 216
*To Night* 222
*The Zucca* 224–5
*Shelley: The Man and the Poet*
   (Browning) 241
Sheridan, Richard Brinsley 184
*Sibylline Leaves* (Coleridge) 90–91
*Sigh, The* (Coleridge) 51n30
Simpson, Richard 179n1
sincerity, Wordsworthian 18–19
Sinfield, Alan 22
Siskin, Clifford 180
Sisman, Adam 39n3
Slinn, E. Warwick 26, 26n35, 28, 35–6
Smith, Adam 192–3, 195
Smith, Charlotte 12, 22, 28
   and dramatic monologue 17, 18 24,
      26, 36
   letters 23, 23n24
   meta-autobiography in works of 18,
      22–3
   novels 24, 27
   poetic identity of 23–4
   sincerity and authenticity of 18–19, 20,
      21, 22, 36
   unhappiness of 23, 24
   and Wordsworth 2, 7, 17–38
   works
      *Beachy Head* 19, 31, 31n48, 36
      *Celestina* 27–8
      *Elegiac Sonnets* 19, 22, 23–9, 35
Smollet, Tobias 189
snowdrop poems (Coleridge and Robinson)
   41, 44–55
*Song for the Feast of Brougham Castle*

(Wordsworth) 140

*Sonnets from the Portuguese*
(Browning) 241

*Sordello* (Browning) 233–4

*Soul's Expression, The* (Browning) 232

*Soul's Tragedy, A* (Browning) 246

Southey, Robert 54, 62n51, 187

*Spartan Mother and Her Son, The*
(Hemans) 100

Spencer, Jane 231

*Spirit's Return, A* (Hemans) 123–38

Stabler, Jane 8, 9, 10n17, 11

*Stanzas on the Death of Lord Byron*
(Browning) 235

Stelzig, Eugene 81n40

Stillinger, Jack 88, 91n69, 92n75, 191,
202n63

Stone, Marjorie 3, 234–5, 236, 237, 244, 249

*Strafford* (Browning) 239, 240, 242

*Stranger Minstrel, A* (Coleridge) 40

Stuart, Daniel 45

*Suliote Mother, The* (Hemans) 116, 117

Sulloway, Alison G. 169n26

Sunstein, Emily 72, 75

Swingle, L. J. 92n75, 192n32

sympathy 192–7


*Tales, and Historic Scenes, in Verse*
(Hemans) 99, 103, 115–16

Talfourd, Thomas Noon 242

*Task, The* (Cowper) 160–61, 162, 170, 181

Tave, Stuart 181

Tayler, Irene 74

Taylor, Anya 4, 43

Taylor, Henry 233

Tennyson, Alfred, Lord
*In Memoriam* 32

Thelwall, John 25n33, 62–3

*There is a joy in footing slow across a
silent plain* (Keats) 190

*This Lime-Tree Bower My Prison*
(Coleridge) 216

Thompson, Judith 3

Thomson, James 56n37

*Thorn, The* (Wordsworth) 18, 188

*Three Graves, The* (Coleridge) 90

Thrupp, Frederick 164

*Time* (Shelley) 219

*Time's Revenges* (Browning) 247

*Tintern Abbey* (Wordsworth) 20, 30, 31–5,
125, 134, 151, 152, 155–6

*To a Mountain Daisy. On Turning One
Down, with the Plough, in April----
----1786* (Burns) 52, 53–5

*To a Skylark* (Shelley) 213–14, 227

*To a Young Ass, Its Mother Being Tethered
Near It* (Coleridge) 163–4

*To Constantia, Singing* (Shelley) 216

*To My Younger Brother on His Entering
the Army* (Hemans) 101

*To Night* (Shelley) 222

*To Patriotism* (Hemans) 100–101

*To the Muse of Poetry* (Robinson) 57n41

*To the Nightingale* (Coleridge) 63, 64,
65–6

*To the Poet Coleridge* (Robinson) 40

*To These Fox Hunters in a Long Frost*
(Byron) 168

*To William Wordsworth* (Coleridge) 91, 201

*To Wordsworth* (Hemans) 140

Trickett, Rachel 162n10

Trilling, Lionel 19, 200–201

*Triumph of Life* (Shelley) 212, 216, 224, 225

Tuite, Clara 3, 180

*Two Foscari, The* (Byron) 239, 247


Veeder, William 72n4, 79n30, 84

*Vision of Poets, A* (Browning) 235–6,
245, 250

*Vision of the Maid of Orleans, A Fragment,
The* (Coleridge) 46


Waldoff, Leon 77n27, 82n41, 87, 91

Wallace, Anne D. 3

*Walsingham* (Robinson) 44–5, 46, 61

*Wanderings of Cain, The* (Coleridge) 82

Webb, Timothy 219

*Werner* (Byron) 239, 240

Werther sonnets 27

Whately, Richard 197–8

*Widow of Crescentius, The* (Hemans)
102–3, 115

*Wife of Asdrubal, The* (Hemans) 115, 116

*Wild Wreath, The* (Maria Elizabeth
Robinson) 54

Wilkes, Joanne 3

Williamson, Michael 125n8

Wolfson, Susan J. 5, 8, 9, 11, 143, 146, 243

Wollstonecraft, Mary 43, 73, 82
women; *see also* women writers
    animal rights and those of 160, 162,
        169–70, 174
    creativity in young 201–2
    Hemans's *Records of Woman* 117–20
women writers
    Byron on "bluestocking" women
        poets 143
    and Coleridge 42–3
    common points of engagement among
        men writers and 2–12
    in gender complementary model of
        Romanticism 1–2, 3, 5, 123–4
    the Other seen as subject for 17
    place in canon for 10
    works that focus on 4–7
*Wood Walk and Hymn* (Hemans) 150–51
Wordsworth, Dorothy 67
Wordsworth, William 9, 12, 18, 22, 31
    on abuses of imagination 187–9
    ambivalence about imagination 204
    and Austen 159, 160n4, 181, 187–9,
        197, 204, 205
    and Browning, Elizabeth Barrett 232,
        242–3
    and Browning, Robert 242
    and Byron 144
    on Chatterton 62
    and Coleridge 40, 42, 56, 63, 67
    and dramatic monologue 17, 18,
        20–21, 30, 32, 34, 36
    Fenwick note 34
    and Hemans 2, 7, 8, 136, 139–58
    and Landon 211
    meta-autobiography in works of 18,
        22–3, 30
    on passivity of the Ancient Mariner 86
    and Robinson 40, 43
    Romantic paradigm of 144–5
    sincerity and authenticity of 18–21, 36
    and Smith 2, 7, 17–38
    on sympathetic imagination 192, 197

    works
        *The Borderers* 242–3
        *The Convict* 45–6
        *Corra Linn* 140
        *The Cuckoo* 140
        *Ecclesiastical Sonnets* 140,
            142n12, 147–50, 156
        *Elegiac Stanzas, Suggested by a
            Picture of Peele Castle, in a
            Storm* 189
        *The Excursion* 9, 151, 154
        *Extempore Effusion Upon the
            Death of James Hogg* 139,
            141–2
        *Hart-Leap Well* 164, 165, 168, 169,
            172, 188
        *The Idiot Boy* 188
        *Laodamia* 133
        *Lines left upon a Seat in a Yew-
            Tree* 30–31, 32, 33, 34
        *Lines written in early spring* 32
        *Lyrical Ballads* 23, 29–35, 36, 41,
            49, 54, 58, 63, 66, 146, 197,
            204, 242
        *The Mad Mother* 75
        *The Narrow Glen* 140
        *Nutting* 30, 31, 34–5, 150
        *Ode: Intimations of Immortality*
            151–3, 156
        *Ode to Duty* 156
        *Poems* 9
        *The Prelude* 35, 36, 217
        *Ruth* 188–9
        *Song for the Feast of Brougham
            Castle* 140
        *The Thorn* 18, 188
        *Tintern Abbey* 20, 30, 31–5, 125,
            134, 151, 152, 155–6
        *Yarrow Visited* 140

*Yarrow Visited* (Wordsworth) 140

*Zucca, The* (Shelley) 224–5